JAMES MADISON

The
FOUNDING FATHER

JAMES MADISON
The
FOUNDING FATHER

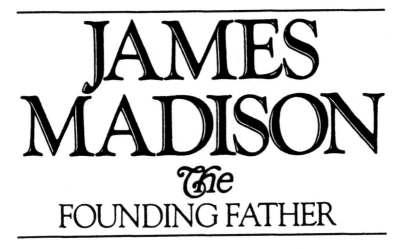

ROBERT ALLEN RUTLAND

University of Missouri Press
COLUMBIA AND LONDON

Copyright © 1987 by Macmillan Publishing Company
First University of Missouri Press paperback printing 1997
University of Missouri Press, Columbia, Missouri 65201
Printed and bound in the United States of America
All rights reserved
5   4   3   2   01   00

Library of Congress Cataloging-in-Publication Data

Rutland, Robert Allen, 1922–
    James Madison : the founding father / Robert Allen Rutland.
      p.   cm.
    Originally published: New York : Macmillan ; London : Collier
Macmillan, © 1987.
    Includes bibliographical references and index.
    ISBN 0-8262-1141-0 (alk. paper)
    1. Madison, James, 1751–1836.   2. Presidents—United
States—Biography.   3. United States—Politics and government—
1789–1809.   I. Title.
E342.R88   1997
973.5'1'092—dc21
  [B]
                                               97-20591
                                                CIP

♾ ™ This paper meets the requirements of the
American National Standard for Permanence of Paper
for Printed Library Materials, Z39.48, 1984.

To
James Morton Smith
Best of scholars, best of friends

CONTENTS

PREFACE

As an undergraduate at the University of Oklahoma I picked up the bad habit of skipping prefaces when reading books. Fortunately, a wise professor of English sternly warned our class in Elizabethan literature that a serious reader *cannot* skip prefaces; and I have remained in his debt. A preface can be a quick review of a book, the kind Dumas Malone placed in his *Jefferson in His Times*; or a preface can explain what the author's intentions were when he wrote the first draft of the book in hand. (I had to rewrite a little biography of George Mason six times, and the only sensible thing to do was to allow Mr. Malone to write an introduction to the book and be done with it.)

In this book my goals were to write a book that would appeal to the reader who does not want to face Irving Brant's six-volume biography and who has no easy access to the recent works by Ralph Ketcham and Harold S. Schultz. All are excellent, all are out of print, and only Schultz's is brief enough for the general reader. I also wanted to remind our generation that Madison was a man of character, an American who was committed to the ancient idea of "virtue" in a public man. He placed his country ahead of his own personal requirements and throughout his life eschewed any chance to make a dime from information, gained through public business, that he might have turned to profit. He shared this sense of "disinterestedness' (the opposite of the excesses of Crédit Mobilier or Teapot Dome) with his peers. Madison as well as Jefferson and Monroe died either land-rich or dollar-poor, or both. Given their code of conduct and the economics of the day, the situation could not have been otherwise.

Another purpose of writing the book was to make some corrections in our public conception of this Founding Father. Madison was short and he was shy, and his closest friend was tall Thomas Jefferson. Madison was best in small groups; both he and Jefferson disliked crowds. This shyness has translated into the myth that Dolley Madison was a marvelous hostess who overcompensated for her "withered little apple-john." And in Henry Adams's history of the Jefferson and Madison administrations, this false picture was carried forward to make it appear that Madison was a weak-kneed president who bumbled around Washington until the British burned it. Readers will come to know that Madison was totally dedicated to the idea of a republican presidency, and that meant he worked with Congress in a fashion that is incomprehensible today. If Madison was lucky in that the War of 1812 ended in a standoff, followed by the glorious victory at New Orleans, let us acknowledge that he deserved a break.

Finally, I wanted to make clear the feelings of a Virginia planter toward the institution of slavery. Madison hated slavery, but he was trapped by a system that he found he could not change. He worried far more about Union, at a time when the cement of Union was still in the curing stage. He loved the Union more than he abhorred slavery. It was as plain as that.

A multivolumed biography of Madison, critical of his mistakes and analytical of his successes, may appear late in this century. Meanwhile, this book may help readers know of Madison's frustrations and his dreams, his victories and his defeats, the stuff of life we all experience to some degree. Madison was a leading actor among the *dramatis personae* assembled in Philadelphia in 1787 to give this nation its higher purposes of liberty and self-government. Then, in Congress, as secretary of state, and as president he labored to make the lamp of freedom shine in the United States as a beacon for all mankind. If readers have a heightened appreciation of Madison's role, this book has served its purpose.

ACKNOWLEDGMENTS

My grateful thanks to Jeanne Kerr Sisson and Donna Godwin for their help in keeping the manuscript moving along; to the libraries at the University of Virginia and the University of Tulsa for staff assistance; and to Elly Dickason of Macmillan Publishing Company for her careful editorial overview and sharp blue pencil. My debt to the late Dumas Malone is enormous, for we talked many hours about the Jefferson–Madison relationship, and any insights in that regard are probably his, not mine.

CHAPTER 1

A HEADQUARTERS ON MANHATTAN

Right and left, the streets on Manhattan led to the waterfront. On horseback or afoot, a citizen eventually wandered down to the wharves where a variety of snows, brigantines, barks, flatboats, and an occasional frigate strained on their moorings as the tide rose and fell. It was thus on an autumn morning—October 27, 1787—with a tinge of chill in the air as housewives picked at the vegetables and fish piled in carts on Front Street. On Queen Street workmen unloaded lumber amid the sound of sawing and hammering. Along the wharves merchants scanned billboards announcing the wares to be auctioned before noon. Seagulls glided overhead on the incoming ocean breeze, screeching as they surveyed the scene for discarded fish heads and other trash dumped in gutters or thrown off piers.

At the London Coffeehouse conversations took place amid steaming cups of tea, coffee, chocolate, or hot water flavored with black West Indian rum. If James Madison wandered as far as the coffeehouse that day he must have dodged the fishmongers and the draymen without giving them much thought. Surely a stop at John McLean's print shop was on Madison's itinerary, for the day's business began with a quick perusal of the New York *Independent Journal*. To reach McLean's busy establishment Madison walked down Maiden Lane to Crown, turned left at the Fly Market and strolled to 231 Queen Street. Madison could not tarry at the printer's but stayed long enough to pick up his paper and probably exchange a few greetings with other subscribers. The newspaper's columns were filled with an essay signed by "Publius," which Madison was eager to see in print. The author was Alexander Hamilton, but that was the printer's secret, shared with Madison and John Jay.

Chances are good that Madison soon was chatting with Hamilton, either at McLean's or at his rooms, for the young New York lawyer lived at 57 Wall Street. Not a towering figure of a man (neither was the five-foot, six-inch Madison), Hamilton had sparkling, alert eyes. The idea for a series of essays designed to bring New York into the pro-ratification column for the proposed constitution was his. Hamilton was a good arm-twister when he used his charm. So Madison agreed to help, as did Hamilton's friends, Jay and William Duer. Gouverneur Morris, the peg-legged gentleman who had written the final touches into the proposed Constitution six weeks earlier at Philadelphia, also was asked to contribute. At any rate, the arrangements were made secretly, to give the essays the appearance of objectivity as though the real author was a public-spirited citizen who ground axes for no one.

Hamilton, convinced that public opinion might force the stubborn New York political machine headed by Governor George Clinton to backtrack, found the printers cooperative. John McLean's best customers were the lawyers and merchants who regarded Clinton as a provincial character jealous of any attempt to weaken the state government he controlled. Clinton's strength was upstate New York, and around the Manhattan Battery he had more critics than friends. John Lansing and Robert Yates, Clinton's political allies, had walked out of the Philadelphia convention in a huff. They wanted no part of the new plan of government that would diminish the power of Clinton and his coterie; but Hamilton, placed on the New York delegation to please Manhattan's merchant community, had a different idea. Quietly he pursued the notion that newspapers could exert enough pressure to weaken Clinton's resistance to the new plan. And Hamilton knew the local scene well enough to realize that only one newspaper printer was sympathetic to Clinton's policies. Besides the Independent Journal, Hamilton found the printers of the New-York Packet and the Daily Advertiser willing to give him space. The plan was to submit four essays each week, to appear until the state ratifying convention met next June. Accordingly, Hamilton chose the pen-name "Publius," buttonholed his friends for aid, and even (if tradition is to be credited) wrote his first essay on board a sloop bound from Albany to New York.

The original scheme had its drawbacks. Madison soon learned that despite Hamilton's assurances, the brunt of the work would fall on his pen and Hamilton's. Duer's essays proved a disappointment, Morris begged off completely, and illness forced Jay to quit after writing four articles.

Thus the burden of writing what came to be known as *The Federalist Papers* fell to nonlawyer Madison and his aggressive, restless associate. At a time when both discretion and custom favored the use of a pseudonym carrying overtones of public virtue, Hamilton chose "Publius"— the Latin equivalent of a Christian name loaded with the connotation of disinterestedness. The essays had as their immediate target "the People of the State of New York." Both Madison and Hamilton saw New York as the critical battleground for ratification, and they promised to keep printers busy until the issue was settled. Their commitment involved journalistic deadlines, Madison recalled, so "it frequently happened that whilst the printer was putting into type the parts of a number, the following parts were under the pen, & to be furnished in time for the press." If newspapers elsewhere chose to reprint the essays, so much the better; but without New York among the ratifying states, the constitution had little chance of succeeding. The secret authors received not a copper penny for all their trouble, either at the time or later. Ratification without a second convention became their only goal, and their common agreement on that matter was almost the last instance of their unanimity.

At the outset "Publius" promised a series of papers designed to show how the proposed constitution conformed to the "true principles of republican government" and how it would promote the advantages of "UNION, a point, no doubt, deeply engraved on the hearts of the great body of the people in every State." All of the ninety-eight or ninety-nine newspapers then printed in the new republic had printed the entire constitution since it was made public after the September 17 signing. Any citizen who had read a newspaper during the past month could not escape the subject. Washington's powerful covering letter for the constitution, usually reprinted with the Constitution, was taken as an endorsement from the nation's first citizen. In such circumstances, as "Publius" said, one would think the new plan would overwhelm any opposition. "But the fact is that we already hear it whispered in the private circles of those who oppose the new Constitution, that the thirteen states are of too great extent for any general system, and that we must of necessity resort to separate confederacies of distinct portions of the whole."

Madison could turn the words over in his mind because the threat Hamilton recognized was real, and somewhat depressing. "It has been frequently remarked that it seems to have been reserved to the people of this country, by their conduct and example, to decide the important question, whether societies of men are really capable or not of establishing good government from reflection and choice, or whether they are forever destined to depend for their political constitutions on accident and force." Here was Hamilton at his brilliant best. He and Madison had talked about the constitution since Madison reached New York to resume his place on the Virginia delegation in the Continental Congress. In Philadelphia, Hamilton spoke his mind and left no doubt where he stood after his mid-June speech that took up most of the day. The British constitution "was the best in the world." The Virginia Plan, mainly Madison's work, had been the framework which delegates debated for days on end, but the republic it outlined had no real merit in Hamilton's eyes. People were too frightened by one word: king. Very well, he would vouch for an elected monarch, who would serve for life, supported by an upper house akin to the House of Lords and a lower one modeled along the lines of Britain's Parliament. Add a high court, reduce the powers of the several states by appointing their governors and forbidding their legislatures to pass laws in conflict with the national constitution. That, Hamilton said, was too rich a government for the American people, but this was what was needed. Then he took off for New York, leaving the convention delegates shaking their heads. At least the man was candid.

Almost four months had passed since Hamilton made his reckless speech. Ultimately he returned to Philadelphia and stayed to the end while the other New York delegates kept their distance. Hamilton was not an easy man for Madison to know. Hamilton was a lawyer and Madison was not; Madison was still single while Hamilton was married to Elizabeth Schuyler, daughter of the great New York landowner Philip Schuyler. Their only common ground seemed to be their shared belief that the jeopardized new nation was close to collapse. As to why the Union was worth preserving, they could debate that point later. What mattered at the moment—what made these two bright young men listen intently to each other—was the survival of the United States of America.

❦

The high drama Madison helped create at Philadelphia was the outcome of a career he had stumbled into, not a course carefully laid out after he graduated from Princeton (class of 1771). From his first days at the Virginia Convention of 1776, Madison seemed to make people notice his cleverness in debate despite a voice so soft one had to strain to hear him. Disdaining a life spent with either the Bible or Blackstone, Madison filled the traditional Virginia planter's role when he rode to Williamsburg in May 1776, as the largest royal colony was preparing to kick over the royal traces. From that spring day forward, all of Madison's instincts and training forced him into leadership roles in the state legislature, Virginia council of state, and at the Continental Congress. More than any man alive, Madison was the involved manipulator who conceived and brought about the convention in Philadelphia.

How would it all end? This thought must have crossed Madison's mind during those solitary hours on the stagecoach ride from Philadelphia to New York—a time to think about all the intensity of debate and committee wheedling during the past four months. Of one thing Madison was certain. Another meeting like the Philadelphia convention could not be assembled. Washington's name had been the magnet that attracted the most level-headed men in the country—most of them experienced in public affairs since the days of 1776 and still willing to risk everything for the cause of American liberty. Thank God, Washington had agreed to serve; and all the promises to spare him from the tedium of presiding over the business had been kept by quickly electing him president. Then the real business was handled by the delegates acting as a Committee of the Whole, with rotating chairmen. Washington came every day and said nothing until the last moment. Washington's host in Philadelphia, Robert Morris, was another silent type. Indeed, during that whole time Morris never opened his mouth once. So there they were, fifty-five men from twelve states (Rhode Island refused to sanction the meeting), converged on the largest city in the Union to do what had to be done to keep the young republic from falling apart. They all agreed that the Articles of Confederation must be scrapped. The empty federal treasury, the quibbling among a dozen states over everything from land titles to customs duties, and the fright engendered by the farmers' tax revolt in western Massachusetts had brought on a sense of urgency.

A year earlier, when the pitiful Berkshire farmers had routed a sheriff and threatened a tax-gatherer, the alarm had spread southward. Washington heard of Daniel Shays and then told Madison: "Without some alteration in our political creed, the superstructure we have been seven years raising at the expence of so much blood and treasure, must fall. We are fast verging to anarchy and confusion!"[1] That signal was all Madison needed to push ahead with his plan for a national convention to follow on the heels of the aborted meeting at Annapolis. Working behind the scenes Madison saw to it that a bill was passed by the Virginia legislature and sent to all the states, urging them to converge on Philadelphia in May.

Once the word was out that Washington would serve on the Virginia delegation, as Madison well knew, the leading men in other states would somehow find a way to come to Philadelphia themselves. And so it turned out, as some of the best lawyers in the New England states jostled for the privilege of attending. The chance to serve in the same room with Washington enticed lawyers Rufus King, Roger Sherman, and William Samuel Johnson into the Yankee delegation, alongside James Wilson, George Read, Gunning Bedford, John Dickinson, Hamilton, William Livingston, and William Paterson from the mid-Atlantic states. Thirty-nine of the fifty-five delegates were members of the bar, a fact that might amaze us, considering the simplicity of their final draft. Madison was no lawyer and neither was fellow Virginian George Mason, but the other southern delegations were loaded with legal talent. Luther Martin from Maryland was long-winded but knew his way around juries. Governor Edmund Randolph was a leader of the Virginia bar, and few attorneys were a match for the two Pinckneys or John Rutledge from South Carolina.

Madison had thought about a lawyer's life at one time and then abandoned the study after agonizing over the maze of words in Coke's *Commentary on Littleton*, the eighteenth-century obstacle course for every American yearning for a lawyer's shingle. He struggled with Coke and other legal treatises available in the library at Montpelier and at Edmund Randolph's through the winter of 1784–85, but by summer confessed that for all his reading he was "far from being determined ever to make a professional use of it."[2] With a quick mind and ready grasp of how bills could be drafted in plain English, Madison found his lack of a formal lawyer's license no handicap when he served again in the state legislature. By the time Daniel Shays drew a bead on a misbegotten sheriff, Madison had long since abandoned any plans for a lawyer's life.

Native intelligence and a basic knowledge of how a legislative body functioned (learned at sessions in Philadelphia and Richmond) gave Madison an assurance that he was on the right track. One of the lessons Madison learned from his experience in the Continental Congress was that the United States was not yet a union but only a loose-knit confederation filled with extremely strong-willed members. Those from New England were ready to do battle over codfish markets, while the South Carolinians bristled when anyone criticized slavery as an inhuman institution. When a haughty Spanish emissary talked about trading American rights to use the Mississippi River as an international highway for a codfish market in Europe, Madison had seen how readily the northern delegates were inclined to swap one interest for another. The Kentucky settlers, most of them native Virginians, had smarted when told that the Yankees were eager to give up the Mississippi in exchange for a fish market. Madison needed no urging to stamp the whole issue as spurious. He forgave the American negotiator John Jay for his impetuousness but would not budge an inch on the basic issue. This was a Union. New England did not give the Union solidity by trying to spin off the Kentuckians' claims to a fair market for their whiskey, tobacco, corn, hemp, or whatever they could float down to New Orleans for hard Spanish dollars.

That exploration in international diplomacy left its mark on Madison. He did not want to think the New England delegates were selfish, but he had to be impressed with the tendency of the Massachusetts delegates to sacrifice the interests of other sections while safeguarding their special rights in diplomatic bargaining.

Then there was the matter of western land claims. Although the status of Vermont was still up in the air, and Connecticut lawyers talked about their claims to a western reserve, most of the claims to western lands were vested in the southern states. Virginia, after all, had been chartered by the crown as a "sea to sea" colony. In the midst of the war, with the treasury woefully empty and jealous claims abounding, Virginia had come forward as magnanimously as possible and offered to surrender all western claims to the new United States, provided some soldiers' claims were allowed. To the Virginians this splendid gesture deserved the applause of other states, but Maryland delegates dragged their feet until a sly word from a French emissary moved the reluctant Maryland delegates to push for a final ratification of the Articles of Confederation. Thus not until 1781 had the wartime government been sanctioned—and the Articles of Confederation finally become legal—at almost the moment when most public men realized the individual states were the seats of power anyway.

Madison not only realized all these elements in the new republic; he understood them. He had developed an extraordinary sense of how the government worked, and after most sundowns he delved into ancient histories, questioning what had gone wrong with the Articles of Confederation. Madison found most of his historical evidence of human error in Diderot's *Encyclopédie* and Fortunato Felice's thirteen-volume *Code de l'Humanité*, contemporary works much esteemed by the literati of the day.

His own experience was a better guidepost than books, however, for he had seen enough bickering over taxes and local prejudices to last a lifetime. As a Virginia delegate in Congress, Madison knew the jealousy directed toward his home state. Virginia was the largest in terms of territory, population, and wealth. When Madison left the Congress in November 1783 the war with England was over, liberty and independence were no longer great issues, and local animosities over such problems as high taxes and Indian raids often took priority.

America's postwar months were not the halcyon days envisioned at Valley Forge or Morristown. One difficulty led to another. Virginia had tried to meet some of its requisitions and pay off the wartime costs, but Massachusetts had scarcely bothered, New Hampshire pleaded poverty, and Rhode Island—well, Rhode Island went its own way by reveling in all the French *louis d'or* spent there in the 1780s and then looking the other way when later talk dealt with national responsibilities.

Madison spent little time worrying about Rhode Island. What concerned him was the tendency of delegates from Massachusetts and New York to vote as though the Union were a flimsy paper arrangement that served nobody well. The emotions aroused by the Boston Port bill and the fall of Charleston were a distant memory, but Madison could remember his own feelings in 1775 when other young men hastened to enlist in units of the Virginia Line. "He was restrained from entering into the military service," Madison later recalled, "by the unsettled state of his health and the discourageing feebleness of his constitution." A brief attempt at soldiering ended when Madison found that being a minuteman required more stamina than he possessed. For the next sixty years, hardly a month passed when Madison did not complain of high fevers, diarrhea, or seizures similar to those suffered by epileptics.

Denied a place on the firing line by his bodily ills, Madison abandoned hope of a military role in the Revolution but settled on making a contribution as a public servant in the state councils. Only twenty-five when he went to the Virginia Convention of 1776 in Williamsburg, he had left his mark there by helping to revise some of the key phrases in George Mason's Declaration of Rights, and he had impressed his older colleagues with a mature judgment, a speaking voice noted not for resonance but for conviction, and an ability to dig into the heart of a problem without a lot of small talk. Patrick Henry was the orator, and nobody could touch him when it came to making a point by metaphors and grand flourishes. Madison was the original thinker and powerful penman, and when the business involved home work, logic, and good judgment, the delegate from Orange County was usually on the right side.

As a delegate in Congress serving the usual three-year term (Virginia law set his pay at eight dollars per day, plus "fifteen pence per mile going, and the same returning"), Congressman Madison had impressed fellow delegates with the erudition that mixed well with the common sense he picked up talking to neighbors in the Virginia piedmont. In the Continental Congress Madison also learned the value of his northern education. His attendance at the College of New Jersey, where a few other Virginia planters sent their sons, introduced Madison to men he would work with for the rest of his public life: William Bradford, Philip Freneau, Hugh Brackenridge, Gunning Bedford, Jr., Aaron Burr, and Henry "Lighthorse Harry" Lee. Unlike most young Virginian gentlemen he had avoided the College of William and Mary, where a boisterous student body was said to be given to strong drink and card-playing. Moreover, Madison was warned the climate at Williamsburg "was unhealthy for persons going from a mountainous region." No doubt Madison was nudged in the direction of Princeton by the Reverend Thomas Martin, a graduate of the same school. Martin had packed his smallclothes and a few books and vowed to carry the blessings of Presbyterianism to Anglican Virginia as a young gentleman's tutor. In time, he took his bed and board at the home of James Madison, Sr., in Orange County, Virginia, which was no hotbed of Anglicanism (or anything else), and began drilling young

Madison on Latin verbs and French pronunciations. An earlier school-master instilled in the frail, teenaged Madison a love of books—now Thomas Martin opened the door to the wonderful world of ancient languages and all the treasures stored in Hebrew, Greek, and, of course, Latin.

With the college at Williamsburg ruled out—the low ground was also said to be a fearful place with noisome vapors that could affect Madison's unhealthy frame—the decision to head toward Princeton must have posed more than a few problems. The 300-mile journey with dangerous ferry crossings on the Rappahannock, Potomac, and Susquehanna rivers drew no comment from the young Virginian. What did excite him was the opportunity of it all. He quickly proved that his educational background with private tutors was more than adequate for the competition awaiting in Nassau Hall. Indeed, Madison so impressed the inquisitive Dr. Witherspoon and his handful of faculty that they advanced him to second-year status. Surely he would have been bored and unchallenged with the young men his own age; as a rising junior he found time to join the Whig Society with classmates Bradford, Brackenridge, and Freneau in attacks on the rival Cliosophians.

Heady days, those, when the nastiness of the Stamp Act riots had all but disappeared and the Princeton scholars drank hot tea, saved hard rolls for a midnight supper, and wondered as all collegians wonder what would become of them after graduation. "If a collegiac-life is a state of bondage, like the good old Chinesian I am in Love with my chains," Madison's best friend at Princeton wrote. " 'Tis the common fault of Youth to entertain extravagant hopes of Bliss in their future life. Tis this that makes us quit College without regret & rush with rapture on the stage of action."[3] Madison himself rushed, too. He finished his four-year curriculum in thirty months, but at a high price. How he avoided a physical breakdown he never knew, for as Madison later recalled, this cram course in the classics was made possible by "an indiscreet experiment of the minimum of sleep & the maximum of application. . . . The former was reduced for some weeks to less than five hours in the twenty four."[4]

Years later, the good President Witherspoon made his star pupil sound a bit prissy. Madison, he told a friend, never did or said "an improper thing" while at Princeton. Of course, Witherspoon had forgotten the snippy doggerel Madison wrote as a member of the Whig Society that spoke of "a wanton ruddy dame," chamber pots, and rival McOrkle's "bum . . . which now becomes a battering ram." All in good fun, and quickly forgotten by the serious-minded Madison as he lingered on at Princeton for a few months, uncertain of his next move when most of his classmates were thinking of taking holy orders or less-than-holy orders from lawyers who would teach them the mysteries of Coke on Littleton.

As the eldest son, Madison realized that the management of the family plantation at Montpelier would be his some day. But his spry little father gave no hint of ill health or need for an assistant, so Madison barricaded himself in the family library back in Orange County and tried to read Coke with some discernment if not pleasure. But he could find no taste for the jumble of Latin and custom.

If he had no stomach for the law, the idea of turning into a clergyman was even more repugnant to Madison. Early in 1774, Madison was offended by overzealous Anglicans living in his own St. Thomas's parish when they hounded the Baptists who wanted to preach on Sundays without harassment. Vindictive vestrymen swore out warrants that caused harmless Baptist preachers to serve time in the jail at Orange Court House, infuriating Madison. To a college chum, who was bound for a black suit and turned collar, Madison vented his rage. "That diabolical Hell conceived principle of persecution rages among some and to their eternal Infamy the Clergy can furnish their Quota of Imps for such business," Madison huffed. "This vexes me the most of any thing whatever."[5]

Frustrated by his isolation and lack of good books Madison surely felt depressed during his postgraduate days around Montpelier. The place abounded with slaves, but he had seen what life was like in the North where black men were few and most of them free tradesmen. Beyond the embarrassment of being a slaveholder himself he worried excessively about his health. The self-imposed regimen at Princeton left Madison convinced that he was sickly by nature, and from his twentieth year forward his health was never far from his consciousness. More often than not his physical condition was poor, and one looks in vain through thousands of scraps of paper for a single expression of good health and vigor. In fact, Madison was somewhat like his mother, who was *always* unwell but lived to celebrate her ninety-seventh birthday.

Then came the Revolution. With Madison *père* as one of the leading men of the county, it was easy to place the young Princeton graduate in the right circles. Not that Madison needed to parade his learning, but in Virginia the few who possessed a bachelor's degree were set apart from the run-of-the-mill gentry. Plantation tutor Philip Fithian had looked around in Virginia society a few years earlier and concluded that a Princeton degree carried a price tag: £10,000. "And you might come, & go, & converse, & keep company, according to this value; and you would be despised & slighted if you rate yourself a farthing cheaper."[6] Perhaps Fithian (Princeton, '72) overstated the class consciousness of Virginians on the eve of the Revolution, but not by much.

So young Madison was welcomed to the Orange County Committee of Safety, traveled the dusty roads to Williamsburg, and there managed to change the Virginia Declaration of Rights on a cardinal point. There Madison made his first precocious move on the stage of history. The opportunity came when George Mason whipped out his committee draft of a declaration with the advanced view that religion needed special treatment and wrote "that all men should enjoy the fullest toleration in the exercise of religion, according to the dictates of conscience, unpunished and unrestrainted by the magistrate." Madison rose to suggest an alteration of the article that would have stopped the state-supported Anglican clergy in their tracks. His substitute changed Mason's "toleration" to the broader "full and free exercise" of religion and went on: "therefore that no man or class of men ought, on account of religion to be invested with peculiar emoluments or privileges; nor subjected to any penalties or disabilities. . . ." In theory at least, Madison's change would have cut off salaries for Anglicans and allowed Baptists to preach without restraint—but this went a bit too far for old-fashioned Anglicans. The convention accepted the expanded idea of freely exercising religion, but was not ready to deal the already reeling Anglican ministry a death blow.[7] The compromise seemed to please nearly everybody, and in sorting things out Madison got to know Mason better. The friendship thus struck during a discussion of religious freedom endured and welded the convictions of these men who, along with Jefferson, gave the American Revolution its ideological appeal to men everywhere.

The Williamsburg encounter with the leading men and foremost minds in Virginia gave Madison a taste for politics that would never desert him. But he learned that his constituents could desert him. He grew overconfident, and when he went home to stand for the newly created House of Delegates, he found that he knew more of books than of men. Forced to run against an older man who knew how important a keg of fermented applejack might be on election day, Madison took the higher ground. He insisted that elections in a free society needed no embellishment with the traditional grog. Convinced that virtue was enough, Madison learned that there was a penalty to be paid by those who refused to resort to "the corrupting influence of spiritous liquors." The higher ground cost Madison his job. The voters took his high principles for parsimony and turned him out.

The defeat hurt Madison deeply. He reacted like a puppy cuffed for chewing up an old shoe. In his memoirs Madison simply recalled that he had been an unsuccessful candidate because of his moral principles. He stood as an unflinching Republican with an empty cup while his opponent plied the voters with ardent spirits. "The consequence was that the election went against him; his abstinence being represented as the effect of pride or parsimoney." In all likelihood, Madison made certain that in all his other election campaigns a full barrel of mellow cider was available for the thirsty electorate. He never lost another election over the next forty years.

∽∾

Memories of the days at Princeton, the heartaches of those wearying congressional sessions, and the frustrations he had known in the Virginia legislature were all fused into Madison's character as he rode the ferry across to Manhattan in September 1787. Awaiting Madison at his boarding house was mail from France, where Jefferson now served as the American minister amid disturbing scenes of hunger and despair. (Hunger was the only problem Madison had not seen created by weaknesses in the Confederation.) In long letters to Jefferson, with whom he had served since the Revolutionary days first as a privy councillor and then as a Congressman, Madison told of the malaise affecting their young nation. When they parted in 1784, Madison trusted his friend to send books from the Parisian stalls, and in turn he resurrected and guided Jefferson's long-delayed bill "establishing religious freedom" to passage through the Virginia legislature. After Madison wrote a supportive petition ("Memorial & Remonstrance") in 1785, he was able to swamp Patrick Henry's countermoves a year later. Early on, the Jefferson–Madison friendship involved both a love of books and a shared contempt for Henry. Told by Madison of Henry's niggardly provincialism, Jefferson wrote (in their private code) that while Henry lived there was little hope for reforms in Virginia. "What we have to do I think is devoutly to pray for his death," Jefferson advised.

Jefferson's letters to Madison during those years show that Paris, the center of Western culture, was the American minister's oyster. He told Madison of the court foolishness and intrigue, but his Virginia friend probably was more eager to hear about the state of literature. With Jefferson as his agent, Madison relished the flow of books coming by trans-Atlantic freight. In letters taking six to eight weeks to reach their destination they traded information about weather, mammals, and mortal men. They shared a common interest in natural history. "What is the price of Buffon's birds coloured?" Madison asked. He turned aside from dissecting a marmot to tell Jefferson that the American mole he had examined had only thirty-three teeth, while Buffon described a European species with forty-four. "It is perhaps questionable whether any of the dormant animals if any such be really common to Europe & America can have migrated from one to the other," the amateur scientist told his friend in Paris.[8]

Events rushed forward. Madison kept Jefferson informed of what was going on in America and uncrated the books that Jefferson sent. All the while, both men were aware that the financial underpinnings of both Louis XVI and the United States of America seemed to be verging on the disastrous. Hence, Madison made his pleas in Virginia for a Con-tinental taxing power to save Congress from an imminent bankruptcy, and Jefferson saw Louis XVI's finance minister try in vain to prop up the extravagances of the French court.

The American crisis of 1787 came a bit ahead of the French one. Madison's correspondence with Jefferson allowed him the leisure for self-examination as he described the home scene to his absent friend. The books Jefferson purchased had strained his budget, but Madison needed them for practical purposes as well as for his scientific excursions. As a preliminary to the Philadelphia convention he had written the treatise on ancient confederations; and when the convention was only weeks away he once again took to his books to write a memorandum on "Vices of the Political system of the U. States." Mainly an indictment of the state legislatures he detested, Madison showed the breadth of his mind as he cited repeated instances of ignored Continental requisitions which imperiled the nation's credit. The local lawmakers displayed no sense of national interest when parochial concerns hung in the balance, and they overlegislated to the point that they created a "multiplicity of laws . . . a nu[i]sance of the most pestilent kind." In this private paper, Madison added a section on causes lying in "the people themselves," with an analysis of the self-interested segments in society, which was a precursor of his most famous *Federalist* essay:

> All civilized societies are divided into different interests and factions, as they happen to be creditors or debtors—Rich or poor—husbandmen, mer-chants, or manufacturers—members of different religious sects—followers of different political leaders—inhabitants of different districts—owners of different kinds of property &c &c. In Republican Government the major-ity[,] however composed, ultimately give the law.[9]

Madison saw that combinations of these elements became a headstrong majority capable of "unjust violations of the rights and interests of the minority, or of individuals." He perceived that a republic had to bend to the will of the majority, but where there were no checks on rapacious factions chaos would result. Thus the challenge to republican government: "to controul one part of Society from invading the rights of another, and at the same time [be] sufficiently controuled itself."

Madison needed only to look around his native Virginia to see that conditions were deteriorating and had been going downhill since the euphoric days of 1776. Amid his studies and memorandum-writing Mad-ison reported to Jefferson in Paris: "Our specie has vanished. The people are again plunged in debt to the Merchants, and those circumstances added to the fall of Tobo. in Europe & a probable combination among its chief purchasers here have reduced that article to 20/." The times were bleak: empty pocketbooks at home, low-bidding tobacco agents who bought American produce at bargain prices, and avaricious rascals in state houses pushing paper-money laws. To cap it all the outbreak of tax-burdened farmers in western Massachusetts foretold an early end to the American experiment in self-government and liberty. A natural-born worrier, Madison looked at this host of woes and decided something had to be done quickly.

The scenes of 1786 were still fresh in his mind when, as an old man, Madison recalled the precarious threads holding the Union together when the delegates gathered in Philadelphia. Looking back on the days following Shays' Rebellion, Madison recalled with clarity the atmosphere of crisis then prevailing. "Such was the aspect of things, that in the eyes of the best friends of liberty, a crisis had arrived which was to decide whether the American experiment was to be a blessing to the world, or to blast for ever the hopes which the republican cause had inspired," he noted. The forces which hoped "to give the new System all the vigour consistent with republican principles," he said, felt more pressure because some Americans opposed the calling of the Federal Convention. This disdain "was attributed to a secret dislike to popular Government, and a hope that delay would bring it more into disgrace, and pave the way for a form of Government more congenial with Monarchical or aristocratical predelictions."[10] Like Jefferson, Madison was convinced that some citizens' commitment to republicanism was only skin-deep. What they really longed for was a British-type of constitution—king and all.

❧

The last leg of the journey that carried Madison from the status of an important state figure to national leadership took place in Virginia. Madison's accomplishments in the Virginia legislature between early 1785 and the end of 1786 showed signs of great statesmanship. He kept the forces of local intolerance at bay, worked for a cooperative effort with Maryland to redress interstate problems on the Potomac, and then fashioned a call for a national meeting in Annapolis to discuss remedies for the faltering confederation. At first not much developed; even Maryland would not bother to send delegates to his Annapolis convention. But Madison talked there with a few delegates and particularly with Alexander Hamilton, who agreed that matters were moving from bad to worse. The vague plan that emerged from Annapolis took Madison back to Richmond, where a national call was endorsed by the authority of the Virginia legislature. (Congress asked each state to send delegates to Philadelphia on May 14, 1787, for a general meeting.) Then, to Madison's delight, General Washington himself accepted a place on the Virginia delegation. That settled the matter of whether good men or second-raters would attend. The purpose of the emergency meeting at Philadelphia was clearly. As one of the delegates later said: "A nation without a national government" was "an awful spectacle."

As Madison saw matters, so far so good. Providence and hard work were providing the young republic a second chance. Madison saw only one remedy—a strong national government that could pay its bills and keep the people committed to the ideals of 1776. The problem: how to create such a blessing amid the shambles of the Confederation.

No doubt Madison missed Jefferson's counsel, but he was a forceful character as he stood up in the Virginia caucus to plead for a framework that would mend the frailties of the existing Confederation. Since the Virginia delegates reached Philadelphia ahead of the pack, Madison used the interval to beg his fellow delegates for a united front in the convention. The Virginians met each day after a leisurely breakfast and listened as Madison dissected the political corpse of the Confederation, delving into causes and effects. By the weekend of May 19–20 he must have had the blueprint of a startling new plan ready. When the Federal Convention finally had a quorum and was able to proceed to serious business, there was Madison at Edmund Randolph's elbow with what became the Virginia Plan. Almost two weeks had passed, but now the delegates were able to talk unabashedly about the crisis they faced, having voted for secrecy so the newspapers would not report their deliberations. In short order, Madison urged Governor Randolph forward as their spokesman. Randolph was willing, and he was everything that Madison was not—tall, handsome, a glib speaker, and essentially a weakling.

The orderliness of Madison's mind still astonishes us. Without intending to do so, he carved a special niche for himself in American history by determining to keep a record of the convention. All the verve of those days when the fate of the Republic seemed to hang like a cobweb on the State House rafters would have been lost to history if Madison had not taken on the self-assigned task of keeping up his daily jottings and transcribing a fuller version later in his candle-lit quarters. the ordeal, he later claimed, "almost killed him; but having undertaken the task, he was determined to accomplish it." That much decided, Madison also knew that some device had to be invented to keep the convention from wasting time arguing about a revision of the Articles of Confederation. Hence the Virginia caucus, hence the Virginia Plan.

So on May 29, 1787, it fell to Randolph to bring forward, on the first real day of convention business, a framework for a totally new constitution—a plan that disarmingly suggested that the Articles of Confederation needed revision and then proposed in the next breath to abandon them forever. The Madison-Virginia Plan offered to the delegates promised a solution. The states would give up their right to vote equally— Rhode Island and Virginia would no longer be equal in the ballot tallying—but a two-house legislature would be based on population. The legislators would pick "a National Executive" who would serve one term as the chief magistrate of the nation and who would have the power to make appointments, see that the national laws were enforced, conduct the nation's business when its legislature was not in session, and (in a vague way) conduct foreign policy. The acts of state legislatures might be nullified by the national congress, and a council of revision would work with the executive to review national acts before they went into operation; and if the executive and his council thought an act from the national congress improper, they could block its implementation. However, the questioned act would become law if the legislature became insistent by passing it a second time. This was Madison's Virginia Plan—the embodiment of much research and a decade of experience in public life.

Undoubtedly Madison urged these ideas before the Virginia caucus because they appeared to remedy the chief flaws in all earlier attempts at representative government. Madison was no Demosthenes or Patrick Henry, but in small groups he was convincing and persuasive; and the Virginia Plan which he pushed through that state caucus bore his hallmark on almost every clause.[11] The first draft which Madison probably gave to Randolph was both a knockout blow to the old Articles and the framework of all future convention discussion.

The events of May 29 set the convention on a deliberate course. Madison planned his next steps and settled down in Mrs. Mary House's boardinghouse at Fifth and Market streets with a stack of foolscap at hand. He knew it was going to be a busy summer. Each day Madison took a seat close to the front of the assembly room, near the desk "of the presiding member with the other members, on my right & left hand." Using his own special kind of shorthand Madison took notes during the day, then transcribed his longer version during the waking hours after each daily adjournment. "It happened, also," Madison recalled, "that I was not absent a single day, nor more than a casual fraction of an hour in any day, so that I could not have lost a single speech, unless a very short one." Owing to the circumstances and the severity of the secrecy rule Madison was circumspect to the point that, with two exceptions, he never asked a speaker to help him later to correct his remarks or expand them.[12]

A retelling here of the drama in Philadelphia during that summer in 1787 seems unnecessary. What now seems remarkable is that Madison walked into a sort of lion's den (thirty four of the fifty five delegates were lawyers), yet he kept his head even when the convention almost broke up over the frustrating small-state–large-state battle. Madison was busy night and day—speaking by day (he arose more than 200 times), then transcribing his notes after dining on the roasts and chops from Mrs. House's kitchen. Almost fifty years later, Madison demurred when called "*the* writer of the Constitution. . . . You give me a credit to which I have no claim." As much as Madison insisted in 1834 that the Constitution "ought to be regarded as the work of many heads & many hands," he earned all the honors that would be heaped on him later.[13]

Consider Madison's involvement from mid-May 1787 onward. He was the primary force behind the Virginia Plan; he was the master behind the careful scenario that recognized the flaws of the old confederation by explicit provisions for majority rule, the direct election of the largest branch of a two-house Congress, and an enumeration of the powers vested in it. The presidency and an independent national judiciary were created. Provision was made to admit new states, and amendments to the new constitution could be proposed and adopted without "the assent of the National Legislature." The new government would have the backing of all its officers, who would "be bound by oath to support the articles of Union." Madison was instrumental in the shaping of most of these decisions; and only the details needed to be added, once the compromise over Senate representation was settled. That produced concessions Madison ruefully accepted, and he lamented the deathblow rendered to his idea of a "negative" on state laws (meant to kill, among other evils, paper-money schemes). He doggedly insisted that the people must be the ultimate source of power for the new government, and he recognized the lurking danger of a North–South split over trade, taxing programs, and chiefly the *bête noire* of slavery.

Madison's judgment matured as the debates proceeded and tempers sometimes flared. He made mistakes, however, or at least Madison miscalculated the mood of his fellow delegates on several occasions. His dream of a veto power over state legislation never had a chance, and as he fought to save the idea Madison became too enamored with the proposition to realize how unnecessary it would be. When the "supreme law of the land" clause was implanted, Madison's negative power on the states was hardly worth a second thought.

On the matter of proportional representation, which became an *idée fixe* with Madison, his commitment caused him to consider at least one preposterous solution. On June 30 Madison harped on his pet theory that it was not the size of a state but its geographical location and its laws regarding slavery that determined a state's true interests. After struggling with the problem, Madison admitted, he had devised an expedient solution: let one house in Congress *not* be apportioned by including slaves "in a ratio of 5 to 3," but in one branch let a state "be represented . . . according to the number of free inhabitants only, and in the other according the whole no. counting the slaves as free." This would give the South an advantage in one branch and allow the North to dominate the other, he explained. Lacking support, Madison abandoned his brain-child, but could not reconcile himself to the small-state compromise eventually accepted by the Convention in mid-July. Overworked and under pressure, Madison was depressed by the outcome of the voting on July 16 (when the compromise between small and large states was resolved, giving the former equality in the Senate); but now it was clear that some kind of constitution was going to be prepared and sent to the states for ratification. And after July 16, Madison worked for a stronger, offsetting presidency.

Clinton Rossiter, reviewing Madison's role at the Federal Convention, has said that Madison's performance "was a combination of learning, experience, purpose, and imagination that not even Adams or Jefferson could have equalled." Irving Brant, whose careful narrative of Madison's work at the convention is the best source on his day-to-day involvement (next to Madison's own notes), believed that Madison's intellectual grasp was manifest, particularly as the presidential office grew during the debates. In setting forth principles "in the actual construction of the government," Brant gave Madison high marks; only in terms of compromise did Brant find Madison on the weak side. Most students of the Federal Convention tend to rate James Wilson as more of a force for making the Constitution democratic, and Roger Sherman was Madison's superior in seeing politics as "the art of the possible." Harold S. Schultz has observed that Madison's disclaimer as *the* author of the Constitution "was good history not false modesty."[14]

Contemporaries rated Madison highly. William Pierce, a Georgia delegate, left his impression of all the delegates, and in Pierce's notes Madison sounds almost too good to be true:

> Mr. Maddison is a character who has long been in public life; and what is very remarkable every Person seems to acknowledge his greatness. He blends together the profound politician, with the Scholar. In the management of every great question he evidently took the lead in the Convention, and tho' he cannot be called an Orator, he is a most agreable, eloquent, and convincing Speaker. From a spirit of industry and application which he possesses in a most eminent degree, he always comes forward the best informed Man of any point in debate. The affairs of the United States, he perhaps, has the most correct knowledge of, of any Man in the Union. He has been twice a Member of Congress, and was always thought one of the ablest Members that ever sat in that Council. Mr. Maddison is about 37 years of age, a Gentleman of great Modesty—with a remarkable sweet temper. He is easy and unreserved among his acquaintance, and has a most agreable style of conversation.[15]

These qualities landed Madison a place on the all-important Committee of Style, which placed certain finishing touches on the constitution. With that "remarkable sweet temper" it is still a mystery as to why he failed to keep Virginians Randolph and Mason from kicking up a fuss in the last days of business over a bill of rights (Madison opposed it) and some local peeves. Possibly Madison underrated Mason, but he knew Randolph very well indeed. At any rate, Madison was on the right side in all the final skirmishes. He went to bed tired but happy on September 17, 1787.

Madison emerged from the convention, for all his modesty, as a famous public man. His reputation, despite the secrecy rule, spread by word of mouth. Monsieur Otto, the French diplomat based in New York, wrote his superiors in Paris that Madison was "Instruit, sage, modéré, docile, studieux; peut être plus profond que M. Hamilton, mais moins brillant." Madison would have smiled at that judgment. Otto also spoke of Madison's modesty and concluded: "C'est un homme qu'il faut étudier longtemps pour s'en former une idée juste."[16]

Less than two weeks before the convention finished its business Madison had written Jefferson that the constitution about to emerge "will neither effectually answer its national object nor prevent the local mischiefs which every where excite disgusts agst the state governments."[17] Madison promised to explain his apprehensions in "a future letter," but by the time he reached New York and saw the array of talent forming to block the constitution Madison had changed his mind. Nothing hardens a man's resolve like telling him that he is making a big mistake. In Madison's case, after he took his seat in the Continental Congress and fell in with the Virginia delegation, he quickly learned that the constitution had not dazzled all the delegates and was particularly criticized by Richard Henry Lee. Within a few days Madison rapidly changed from a lukewarm supporter to become the boldest advocate for the proposed constitution.

Madison dropped all reserve when he sent a printed copy of the new constitution to Jefferson. In a long, revealing letter to his friend in Paris, Madison told of "the sincere and unanimous wish of the Convention to cherish and preserve the Union of the States." A year earlier there had been back-room whisperings about a scheme to split the Union into northern and southern confederacies but in Philadelphia, Madison explained, "No proposition was made, no suggestion thrown out, in favor of a partition of the Empire into two or more Confederacies." Instead the delegates had sought to build a republic based on the fact of thirteen states and "embraced the alternative of a Government which instead of operating, on the States, should operate without their intervention on individuals composing them: and hence the change in the principle [of federalism] and proportion of representation." Then Madison explained what the convention tried to accomplish by establishing a presidency, a bicameral legislature, and a supreme court. He told of some of the infighting, "the clashing pretensions of the large and small States," and the difficulties posed by "the natural diversity of human opinions on all new and complicated subjects." Considering all the tensions, Madison wrote, "it is impossible to consider the degree of concord which ultimately prevailed as less than a miracle."[18]

Miracle or not, Madison was still displeased that his plan to have a "constitutional negative on the laws of the States" had been dropped. "The mutability of the laws of the States is found to be a serious evil," he ventured, and then proceeded to tell Jefferson what he later told the world in his *Federalist* #10. Looking for "the true principles of Republican Government," Madison saw that civilized society was a mass of citizens of diverse interests and stations who (in a free government) pursued gain and acquired property. "There will be rich and poor; creditors and debtors; a landed interest, a monied interest, a mercantile interest, a manufacturing interest." There would be divisions and factions since "the bulk of mankind . . . are neither Statesmen or Philosophers." A majority united by a common interest would arise, and the challenge facing a republic based on majority rule was to maintain a government where

> no common interest or passion will be likely to unite a majority of the whole number in an unjust pursuit. In a large Society, the people are broken into so many interests and parties, that a common sentiment is less likely to be felt, and the requisite concert less likely to be formed, by a majority of the whole. . . . Divide et impera, the reprobated axiom of tyranny, is under certain qualifications, the only policy, by which a republic can be administered on just principles.[19]

There in a nutshell was Madison's conception of how the new government was going to survive. Every thinking citizen had read Montesquieu's warning that republics could not survive in a larger country. Not so, Madison insisted. The size of the new nation, with nearly four million people and growing by the hour, would in fact ensure the new republic's success. "In the extended Republic of the United States, The General Government would hold a pretty even balance between the parties of particular states, and be at the same time sufficiently restrained by its dependence on the community, from betraying its general interests."

Jefferson could have said this with more flair—he always was able to catch the right phrase while Madison never used three words if he could find five. But this conception had matured in Madison's mind as a kind of rationale for the government of checks and balances created at the Philadelphia convention. If Congress passed a foolish or wicked law, the president could veto it, or the supreme court could rule it invalid. The likelihood of a unifying wrongheadedness in all three branches was not great; and as each branch had separate powers assigned to it and it alone, there were further safeguards built into the system.

In a sense, Madison's ponderous letter was a flight of the fancy that had been building up in his mind for weeks and months. Time and time again, Madison recurred to its economic and regional themes. In sharing with Jefferson his innermost thoughts, Madison tried to make a good case for a bad cause as he claimed that the negative power would allow the central government to act as a "disinterested & dispassionate umpire in disputes between different passions & interests in the State." But Jefferson had heard the argument before, and Madison's claims occasioned one of the few instances of a genuine disagreement between the two friends. Jefferson thought Madison was overreacting in his efforts to curb the states' powers. What Madison proposed, Jefferson said, was like mending "a small hole by covering the whole garment." In this case, as in the matter of a bill of rights, Jefferson was sorry to see Madison so determined to concentrate powers in a national government.

Jefferson received Madison's long apologia in late December and lost no time in replying. Much of the proposed constitution he liked, and he was "captivated by the compromise of the opposite claims of the great & little states" that had upset Madison so markedly. Turning to what he did not like, Jefferson headed his list with "the omission of a bill of rights providing clearly & without the aid of sophisms" for a long train of civil liberties. Lecturing his friend, Jefferson went on: "Let me add that a bill of rights is what the people are entitled to against every government on earth, general or particular, & what no just government should refuse or rest on inference."[20] By the time Jefferson's admonishing letter had traveled from Paris to Orange County, Madison was ready to surrender to the bill-of-rights assailants. Once again, Madison learned that political battles need not be completely won, or totally lost.

Nor could Madison learn his political lessons leisurely. When he read Jefferson's reply, Madison was already in the thick of the struggle to ratify the Constitution. Almost overnight, the pace and scope of politics in the new republic had changed from provincial to national. In a way that nobody planned and few understood, Madison became the key figure running a national campaign headquarters out of his room on Maiden Lane. The exhilaration of battle soon replaced all the worries about digestion and "bilious fevers."

CHAPTER TWO

A VOLUNTEER CAMPAIGN MANAGER

One of the pitfalls facing modern man is his sense of superiority regarding communications. A few buttons pushed will link offices in Paris and Chicago; a satellite bounces an image from a royal wedding in London to Los Angeles in a fraction of a second. We reflect on these technological miracles as proof of an enormously efficient civilization. Yet we are baffled by diplomatic procedures that require agonizing weeks for a proper seating arrangement before any discussion can occur; and proposals for a twentieth-century constitutional convention seem chimerical. The business of picking delegates, that first step, is too formidable a stumbling block. And, perhaps more important, there is no modern equivalent of James Madison to take charge.

Every great movement requires a leader, it seems, and in 1787 Madison shouldered much of the burden for implementing the work of the Philadelphia convention. At the most, a year would be required. He also came to realize that the movement to ratify the constitution needed a self-appointed leader who could take charge and coordinate the process.

While still in Philadelphia, tidying up his affairs, and before heading for the Continental Congress session at New York, Madison had been warned that he had no time for "leisurely movements." Another Virginia delegate, Edward Carrington, urged Madison to hasten to Manhattan. "One of our Colleagues Mr. R. H. Lee is forming propositions for essential alterations in the Constitution," Carrington warned, "which will, in effect, be to oppose it."[1] Lee had seen George Mason's objections to the new plan and was ready to pick up his friend's battle cry. "There is no

Declaration of Rights," Mason thundered, and the alarm bell he barely tinkled at the Philadelphia convention was shoved forward as a rallying point for those critics of the constitution who shared Mason's thought that the whole plan had serious flaws.

So Madison hurried to New York and listened with his usual earnestness as Lee moved to throw a roadblock in the path of the constitution by sending it to state legislatures without an endorsement or call for action, implying that hasty action was unnecessary. Only Lee, William Grayson, and a few on the New York delegation favored this plan, clearing the way for a resolution that sent the constitution to the states by absolving the Philadelphia gathering of exceeding its proper duties. Congress took note that the convention had prepared a constitution that "appears to be intended as an entire system in itself, and not as any part of, or alteration in the Articles of Confederation," and while the device went beyond the powers "constitutionally confined" to Congress, the assembled state delegations unanimously favored sending the new document to the states "with all convenient dispatch." The last sentence might have been Madison's own brainchild. Everything was out in the open now. The state conventions would do the rest.

Meanwhile, Richard Henry Lee was in a huff. "It was with us, as with you," Lee snapped in his report to Mason, "this or nothing; & this urged with the most extreme intemperance. The greatness of the powers given, & the multitude of Places to be created, produces a coalition of Monarchy men, Military Men, Aristocrats, and Drones whose noise, impudence & zeal exceeds all belief—Whilst the Commercial plunder of the South stimulates the rapacious Trader."[2] Lee told how he had tried to amend the constitution before it was sent to the states, but again he had been howled down. In despair, Lee had tried to slip into a package being sent to the state governors a general statement calling for a bill of rights, eliminating the office of vice-president, and enlarging membership in the house of representatives.

Lee's maneuvering caused Madison and other supporters of the constitution some anxiety, but they beat back the suggestion for the side-by-side amendments and worded a resolution sending the constitution on the road to ratification with "very moderate terms" of approval. The key was "unanimity"—a majority of the state delegations voting to dispatch the constitution to the states.[3] Edward Carrington, one of the three Virginians who voted to move things along as quickly as possible, understood that "the people do not scrutinize terms. The unanimity of Congress in recommending a measure," he reported, "naturally implies approbation."[4] Determined to have the last word, Lee insisted that the action by Congress smacked of skulduggery. "It is certain that no Approbation was given," he told Mason, while admitting the constitution had "a great many excellent Regulations." The proper way to proceed,

Lee counseled, was to send it back to Congress "with amendments Reasonable and Assent to it withheld until such amendments are admitted."

One month after Lee's attack on the constitution, Madison took stock of what had happened in the interval. In the newspapers Lee and his friends were being called Antifederalists, but the label was loosely applied. Did those who opposed the constitution want to throw the convention's work aside, or merely amend it, as Lee suggested? In New York, Governor George Clinton's distaste for any change in the status quo was evident. Unlike some of the other states, New York was prosperous and nobody could say that her farmers and merchants had been hurt under the Confederation. Madison needed only to look down Front Street to see that business was good. In the taverns and boardinghouses men talked more of prices than of politics. Building lots in town, farms on upper Manhattan, and shares in outbound ship cargoes were the grist for most daytime conversations in the vicinity of Coffeehouse Slip. Bills of exchange on reliable London firms were at a premium, but few buyers were interested in the weak market for the depreciated Continental securities that could be picked up for a third of their nominal value. Military scrip redeemable in public land, interest certificates for the state debts incurred during the Revolution, and other financial papers bearing signatures of Patrick Henry or Benjamin Franklin or John Hancock caused a glut on the market. A gold guinea bearing George III's countenance commanded far more respect than a wheelbarrow loaded with Continental scrip.

Nobody knew the value of a gold coin more than Madison. A Virginia planter rarely saw hard money in the old days, before the Revolution, when tobacco warehouse receipts and bills of exchange made it possible to pay bills once or twice a year, feed a large family and sixty slaves, and buy the books and madeira and mahogany furniture that separated these velvet-coated gentlemen from the hardscrabble farmers who were their neighbors. Since the flood of paper money from the printing presses had finally receded, Madison paid his bill at the Maiden Lane boardinghouse with whatever came his way. For eighteen days his room and board came to £7.4.0, plus £3 for a slave's upkeep and £2.4.4 for "wine and porter." Hundreds of pounds of broadleaf tobacco would have to be coaxed from the reddish soil in Orange County to help supplement Madison's pay as a congressman. Life on Manhattan, it seems, has always seemed extravagant to citizens from the hinterland.

The fretting about bill-paying was only one of Madison's worries that fall. His habitual dark short-clothes draped a body never fully fit, so that Madison was often in his sickbed with a mild case of diarrhea, or afflicted with the piles that made horseback riding painful on all but the best of days. Beyond problems of wealth and health, there was also the matter of friendship. Madison had many acquaintances, but few friends. On the Virginia delegation, only Carrington seemed to enjoy

Madison's confidence; and indeed Carrington might well have been the friend of Hamilton's who had suggested that Madison would be useful in preparing the essays signed by "Publius." Somehow, Hamilton had drawn agreement from both Madison and John Jay that they would help write the newspaper essays intended to soften opposition to the proposed constitution in New York.

Madison disliked writing for the newspapers, but this was an emergency. Everything possible had been done to send the constitution to the state legislatures with gestures bespeaking confidence and urgency. Washington's covering letter from the convention, once Gouverneur Morris took charge of writing it, turned into a ringing endorsement. Morris understood the mood of the country as well as any man, and he knew that unsettled conditions in New England and particularly in Boston had sounded a note of gloom during the Shays uprising that persisted. Notes were protested, debts piled higher, and farm prices stayed low as flour, tobacco, wheat, and corn were denied their natural market in the British West Indies by a crown edict. The market for public securities became a joke.

Madison absorbed the anxieties of Philadelphia and New York lawyers and businessmen and well knew the unstable conditions in Virginia markets. The thought that the young nation was headed for bankruptcy must have haunted Madison, for that gloomy prospect was the alternative to ratification. If failure came, it would be a mockery of the wartime sacrifices. Even worse, what a fate this would be for the grand experiment in self-government after the bloodstained snow at Valley Forge, the stinking prison ships in New York harbor, and the humiliation after the fall of Charleston. The ultimate humiliation would be a confession that after winning on the battlefield the Americans were totally inept at running their own affairs and needed to crawl back under the protecting folds of the Union Jack. Doubtless Madison knew there had been talk of this in Boston, New York, and Philadelphia; and only a short time before the Philadelphia convention there had been strong hints in conservative circles that what the country needed to save it from falling into a financial morass was a strong man on horseback—even a king. In a sense, Washington was Madison's ace-in-the-hole. Washington despised the talk of an American monarchy as much as he did.

The best way to kill such talk was to ratify the constitution, as quickly as possible. Madison saw that despite the prestige of Washington's endorsement and the blessed cloak of secrecy that had prevailed at the convention, there was still a great risk to ratification if a mixed reception came from the state legislatures. "Nothing can exceed the anxiety for the event of the meeting here," Madison had observed during the last moments of the convention. "My own idea is that the public mind will now or in a very little time receive anything that promises stability to the public Councils & security to private rights, and that no regard ought to be had to local prejudices or temporary considerations. If the present moment is lost, it is hard to say what may be our fate."[5]

Madison realized that the printed version of the constitution would have an impact, in part because the last statement above Washington's signature had an air of finality and unanimity. "Done in the Convention by the Unanimous Consent of the States present," it read, thus discounting the recalcitrance of Mason, Randolph, and Elbridge Gerry, who had balked and finally talked themselves into a corner reserved for nonsigners. Then Congress had sent the constitution forward—also with the appearance of unanimity. Every newspaper in the land printed the constitution—the greatest blanket coverage of an event in American journalistic history. "The circumstance of unanimity must be favorable every where," Madison told Washington.[6]

Madison's stature had grown in Washington's eyes that past summer. The general had corresponded with the younger Virginian over the years and respected his advice, but Madison's performance in Philadelphia impressed Washington most favorably. When Madison renewed their correspondence with his first report on how Congress had treated the constitution, Washington shot back his reply. "This apparent unanimity will have its effect," he wrote Madison. "Not every one has opportunities to peep behind the curtain; and as the multitude often judge from externals, the appearance of unanimity in that body, on this occas[io]n, will be of great importance."[7]

Madison realized that Washington's name had been used about as much as the general would permit. He also sensed that the momentum created by the newspaper reprinting of the entire constitution had been bumped along by the covering letter from Congress. Madison further perceived that there were some question marks underlying the critical essays beginning to appear in the New-York Journal and Philadelphia Independent Gazetteer. Old George Mason had hit the mark with his pamphlet's ringing first sentence: "There is no Declaration of Rights." Opponents everywhere picked up that cry, complaining too that the constitution's backers were hustling the ratification conventions forward at an indecent pace. When the Pennsylvania Federalists scheduled their state convention for November 20, Antifederalists reacted against their haste. "They dread a thorough Knowledge & public Discussion of the Subject, & wish to hurry it down, during the short & raging Fever of Approbation," Mason wrote Gerry.[8]

Madison worked at less than a fever pitch, but he found little time for rest either. With his franking privilege offering free postage and the main North–South post roads converging in New York, Madison found that his room was becoming an informal message center for friends of the constitution. In his earlier political experience the atmosphere was, technically, partyless. Both in Congress and in the Virginia legislature delegates voted by interest blocs but cautiously avoided labels, except for a pejorative "tory" hurled at an unfortunate opponent. Now, however, the newspapers passed out labels quickly and freely to make supporters of the constitution Federalists and those opposed to ratification Anti-federalists. Madison was not enthralled by the device, and since party labels smacked of British precedent he was, on principle, opposed to party alignments; but in this case the newly christened Federalist party was where Madison found himself. Indeed, he became its de facto leader as the ratification campaign moved forward.

At the outset, Madison considered the city of New York safely Federalist, while Clinton and his country party would be "strongly opposed" to the constitution. "As far as Boston & Connecticut have been heard from, the first impression seems to be auspicious," Madison observed. "I am waiting with anxiety for the echo from Virginia but with very faint hopes of its corresponding with my wishes."[9]

At the heart of the distinction between friends and opponents of the constitution was a basic difference of opinion on the role of a national government. Madison and his group believed that America's salvation lay with an "energetick government" empowered to collect taxes, regulate commerce, and pay off the public debt. If some local control had to be surrendered to the federal government, so be it. To the opposition, and nowhere more so than in Madison's home state, resistance to a strong central government was a natural outgrowth of their Revolutionary experience. Besides this philosophical undertow there was the figure of Patrick Henry—a power to be dealt with in the Old Dominion ever since the Stamp Act days. Madison had deftly outwitted Henry in 1785, when the older man's back was turned, by ushering Jefferson's bill on religious freedom through the General Assembly. Henry never liked to be outsmarted, and in the spring of 1787 he broke off any connection with Madison's reform movement by announcing he would not serve at the Philadelphia convention. Later, he excused his conduct by saying that he "smelt a rat." Once the convention finished its work, Henry was far from overawed by Washington's endorsement. The constitution-rodent, as Henry explained, betrayed an "awful squinting toward monarchy" and in time the vortex of political power would rest in northern hands. Meanwhile, the federal government could interfere with slavery and compel Virginia to pay its prewar debts to British merchants. In short, Henry declared political war on Madison and hoped he could send his Orange County colleague into oblivion once this constitution had been rejected.

In the waning hours of the Philadelphia convention Madison had helped beat back the trump card Edmund Randolph tried to play: a call for another general convention which would consider amendments submitted by all the states.[10] When he returned to Virginia, Randolph fell under Henry's influence for a while, proving Jefferson right when he called Randolph "the poorest Chameleon I ever saw having no colour of his own, & reflecting that nearest him."[11] Henry badgered the legislature into scheduling a ratifying convention for the following June (no hurry here) and providing expenses for delegates if a second general convention was called. Randolph told Madison that this strategy was fortunate, "for I am thoroughly persuaded, that if it had been propounded by the legislature to the people, as we propounded it, the constitution would have been rejected and the spirit of union extinguished."[12] In other words, Randolph thought Henry was going to have his way, not only in Virginia but in the nation.

Personally, Madison still stood high with his erstwhile colleagues in the Virginia legislature. They reelected him to the Continental Congress, 126 to 14; and they also voted to send him to the following session (that is, for 1788–89), 137 to 3. Influential people in Virginia were not ready to hurry ratification along.

When uncertain as to his reelection, Madison paid a brief visit to Philadelphia and there took soundings on ratification. He saw and perhaps compared notes with Gouverneur Morris, who was a political realist and something of an optimist. The Pennsylvanian thought most of New England would support ratification, partly because "their Preachers are advocates." New York was evenly divided, but New Jersey was "near unanimity in her favorable opinion." In his home state Morris was optimistic, although he confessed a fear of "the cold and sour temper of the back counties."[13] Morris thought Washington's shadow lengthened over the whole process, and he was more than glad to spread the rumor that Washington would most certainly be the first president.

Back in Manhattan for another Congress, Madison turned his attention to the essays s he had promised Hamilton for the local newspapers. In something less than a week he wrote and polished his first contribution as "Publius," turned it over to the printers, then awaited a reaction. How his contemporaries greeted the essay which is known to history as *The Federalist* #10 is uncertain, for the readers tended to lump the series together and hail or condemn it according to their political bias. The identity of the author, or authors, was not a well-kept secret within the inner circle of Federalists. Elsewhere, the French diplomat Louis Guillaume Otto viewed the writing as "trop savant et trop long pour les ignorans"—too tedious for the masses; and Antifederalist writers tried to belittle "Publius" as longwinded and pompous. Jefferson, aloof in Paris but interested in everything Madison did, in time received a bound copy of *The Federalist* and was told the authors were Jay, Hamilton, and Madison. "I read it with care, pleasure and improvement, and was satisfied there was nothing in it by one of those hands, and not a great deal by a second. It does the highest honor to the third, as being in my opinion, the best commentary on the principles of government which ever was written," Jefferson wrote. Madison sent the first essays, including his #10, to Washington on November 30 after an earlier statement of complicity. "I will not conceal *from you* that I am likely to have such *a degree* of connection with the publication here, as to afford a restraint of delicacy from interesting myself directly in the republication elsewhere," he told Washington. The general took the hint and shuttled the papers on to Richmond, where they soon began appearing in the *Virginia Independent Chronicle*. But Washington's private endorsement was not to be public, for he refused to tell the intermediary who the authors were, adding, "nor would I have it known that they are sent by *me* to *you* for promulgation."[14]

For his part, Madison viewed the "Publius" papers as part of a heated political campaign. (During his lifetime Madison rarely looked back at the work as a major accomplishment, but he was careful to tell those who asked which essays had been from his pen, and which came from Hamilton's.) Had their friendship continued, no doubt the case would have been different. In the circumstances, Madison was content to pour all of his experience and research into the joint venture, which probably had little effect on the ratification campaign but which has been regarded as a remarkable statement of republican theory. Many years later Madison recalled:

> The papers were first meant for the important and doubtful state of New York and signed a "Citizen of New York"—afterwards meant for all the States under "Publius." In the early stage the papers were shown by the writers to each other before going to the press. This was inconvenient four nos. being required for a week and committing [the authors to such excessive demands] that was dropped.[15]

Madison's first contribution became his masterpiece. All of the twenty-nine manuscripts Madison wrote for the series have been lost, so there is no telling how many times he drafted *The Federalist* #10 or any other essay. He had used the language of #10 before, and at the Philadelphia convention Hamilton himself had spoken of "separate interests [that] will arise. There will be debtors & Creditors &c."[16] Thus the essay was an amalgam of ideas then current among the men who read David Hume, Adam Smith, and other writers of the so-called Scottish Enlightenment. Madison gave an American twist to his distillation, as historian Douglass Adair later discerned. Perhaps Madison took Hume too literally—"the same causes always produce the same effects"—but he was trying to disprove Montesquieu's axiom that a republican government could not operate effectively in a large geographic area. Hence the reverse judgment in *The Federalist* #10, that of all systems of government for an "extended republic" a republican form was best. Factions had caused the downfall of past republics, small and large, and Madison defended the Constitution as a means of declawing factions while preserving order.

Madison also placed his finger on the problem of rich and poor that society has never solved satisfactorily. "The most common and durable source of factions has been the various and unequal distribution of property." The effect of Madison's words reached a new plateau a century later, when Karl Marx started a whole school of thought trying to deal with the same problem. Here we need only say that scholars and politicians are still groping for the last word on *The Federalist* #10 ("a more compactly logical, almost mathematical piece of theory than anything ever written by an American," Robert Dahl adjudged).[17]

Madison had more time to work on his essays as Congress dragged along without a quorum from late November until the middle of February 1788. Besides writing twenty-eight more essays, Madison continued in his informal role as campaign coordinator for the ratification and kept his eye on the critical situation in Virginia. If Randolph continued to play the role of a political Hamlet and Mason joined forces with Henry, the Constitution was in jeopardy in Virginia. And since Virginia was the largest state (stretching from the Atlantic to the Ohio River) and the most populous one (747,600 souls in 1790) an American republic without the Old Dominion was unthinkable. Madison was in a unique position to observe the efforts New York Antifederalists were making to coordinate their efforts with those of the Virginia Antifederalists. An Antifederal alliance of that nature could wreck the Constitution.

After the early ratifications in Delaware, Pennsylvania, and New Jersey the Federalists found an active, disturbing opposition in Massachusetts. "Our prospects are gloomy," Rufus King told Madison, "but hope is not entirely extinguished." Heavily weighted with lawyers, the Bay State convention became a kind of unequal chess game. The educated attorneys outmaneuvered until they finally outvoted the poorly led farmers. Even so, the Massachusetts ratification battle would have been delayed (if not lost) had popular John Hancock not allowed himself to be manipulated. A series of proposed amendments that would be recommended for action *after* ratification was introduced as the governor's handiwork and passed the convention. Samuel Adams walked into some parliamentary blunders and had difficulty extricating himself, to the high amusement of Federalists who passed the word that the delegates' pay would be in jeopardy if the vote went against the Constitution. With the recommended amendments tacked on, the Massachusetts convention ratified on February 6, 1788. "The majority although small is extremely respectable," Madison heard, "and the minority are in good Temper."[18]

Such a close call gave Madison pause. Then there was more scary news from New Hampshire, where the convention was supposed to be firmly controlled by Federalists. The records are difficult to untangle, even now, but it seems clear that the delegates first rejected the Constitution, then rescinded their action and voted for an adjournment until June 18—just when the Virginia convention would be in full swing.

Madison was counting. The magic number was NINE. Until the ninth state had ratified the Constitution he could not relax. With listless Rhode Island politicians prepared to do nothing, the battleground shifted to Virginia. Madison decided he should return to Virginia and campaign enough to assure himself a place in the June convention. "The Convention of New Hampshire," he wrote Washington, "has afforded a very disagreeable subject of communication. It has not rejected the Constitution; but it has failed to adopt it."[19] This first setback would "probably be construed in Virga. as making co[n]temporary arrangements with her" possible. In other words, the Antifederalists might be overcoming their initial disarray and have some counterproposals that could delay or derail the ratification altogether. Then from Randolph in Richmond Madison heard what seemed to be a caustic comment from a Federalist. The governor spoke of the Massachusetts ratification with a sneer. Calling the Boston action "a paltry snare," Randolph deemed some of the recommended amendments "admissible, [while] others pointed against the Negro states, and others [were] milk & water."[20] Madison must have pondered the arrogance of some Virginians, and particularly Henry's strutting in a Richmond barnyard as though the other states would not dare offend the statehouse crowd he dominated. "Mr. Henry," Madison learned, "is determined to amend & leave the fate of the measure to depend on all the other States conforming to the Will of Virginia."[21]

Shortly after New Year's Day 1788 Madison had other things on his mind than Patrick Henry's ego or the Boston convention. Hamilton seems to have told Madison that for several months he would have to keep the letters from "Publius" flowing steadily to the printer. On January 11, The Federalist #37 appeared, and for the next seven weeks Madison managed to write twenty-four essays, producing an average of three per week. Madison began #37 by pleading for an unbiased examination of the Constitution. With a backhanded slap at the Antifederalists Madison wrote:

> As our situation is universally admitted to be peculiarly critical, and to require indispensably, that something should be done for our relief, the predetermined patron of what has been actually done, may have taken his bias from the weight of these considerations, as well as from the considerations of a sinister nature. The predetermined adversary on the other hand, can have been governed by no venial motive whatever. The intentions of the first may be upright, as they may on the contrary be culpable. The views of the last cannot be upright, and must be culpable.[22]

Having disposed of wrongheaded Antifederalists, Madison proceeded with a series of integrated essays that gave a philosophical undertone of extraordinary breadth to *The Federalist*. In his earlier essays Madison drew on his historical knowledge of failed governments; in *The Federalist* #37–58 (plus 62 and his final 63), Madison spoke of the republican dream: self-government by a responsible legislature elected by and responsible to the whole citizenry. In the masterful #39 he defined a republic as "a government which derives all its powers directly or indirectly from the great body of the people" and delineated the difference between a federal and a national government. The process of ratification, by conventions elected by the people, made the constitution "a federal and not a national act. . . . Each state in ratifying the constitution, is considered as a sovereign body independent of all others, and only to be bound by its own voluntary act."[23]

If the ardor of essay-writing and corresponding with friends strained Madison, his work did not show it. His style seemed more animated, his prose came more easily, and his logic gained momentum as he dashed off these essays to meet deadlines at the three friendly New York printing offices. We can only guess at the work habits Madison kept, but there was little time for proofreading or revision when the type was hand-set for five or six columns, particularly between Friday, January 11, and Saturday, January 19, when five numbers appeared in eight days. And some of this writing was the best of Madison's life.

> Cool and candid people will at once reflect, that the purest of human blessings must have a portion of alloy in them; that the choice must always be made, if not of the lesser evil, at least of the GREATER, not the PERFECT good; and that in every political institution, a power to advance the public happiness involves a discretion which may be misapplied and abused [#41].

> The federal and state governments are in fact but different agents and trustees of the people, instituted with different powers, and designated for different purposes [#46].

> A reverence for the laws, would be sufficiently inculcated by the voice of enlightened reason. But a nation of philosophers is as little to be expected as the philosophical race of kings wished for by Plato [#46].

> If men were angels, no government would be necessary. If angels were to govern men, neither external nor internal controls on government would be necessary. In framing a government which is to be administered by men over men, the great difficulty lies in this: You must first enable the government to control the governed; and in the next place, oblige it to control itself [#51].

The feverish activity seems to have been a tonic for Madison. No complaints of fevers or fluxes were heard as he pushed himself physically as he had when a student at Princeton or during his frantic note-taking of the preceding summer. With the completion of #63 on March 1, 1788, Madison began packing his bags for a trip to Montpelier.

Ordinarily Madison depended on his neighbors to see that he was elected without the bother of coming home, but warning letters told of rising opposition in Orange County. He knew some unusual exertion was necessary if he was to be accredited to the June convention in Richmond. "Your Friends are very solicitous for your appointment in the convention to meet in June next," a fellow Federalist wrote. "I trust were it not practicable for you to attend your election will be secured, but your being present would not admit a doubt."[24] Despite misgivings, Madison knew duty compelled him to make the torturous coach trip to Virginia over frozen ruts, with a few hazardous ferry crossings to be dreaded. Once the physical discomfort ended there would be human problems. "I foresee that the undertaking will involve me in very laborious and irksome discussions; that public opposition to several very respectable characters whose esteem and friendship I greatly prize may unintentionally endanger the subsisting connection," he told Washington. His mind was made up, particularly since he was "informed that my presence at the election in the County [may] be indispensable."[25] So the ink was hardly dry on the printing of Madison's last "Publius" letter when, during the first week in March 1788, he boarded a coach bound for the ferry to New Jersey. Mount Vernon was his first destination.

Six states had ratified the Constitution when Madison's coach was met by Washington a few weeks later. The roads in some places had been quagmires, snow was on the ground in Virginia, and Madison needed a warm bed and well-cooked food before the final ordeal over seventy-five miles of mud would end at Montpelier. Madison tarried at Mount Vernon for two days, and when he looked across the Potomac to see the Maryland shore he must have wondered how certain the Federalists were of a coming victory—Maryland's convention was scheduled to assemble in late April. Madison had talked to James McHenry in Annapolis a few days earlier and was handed a note which George Mason had given "to one of the Maryland deputation for their consideration." This list of eleven proposed alterations in the Constitution, Madison was told, would make that instrument "unexceptionable."[26] Was Mason hinting that Maryland should take the bait from Virginia Antifederalists and make the changes (including one to limit presidential tenure to one term) as a condition for ratification? If Maryland ratified without such strings attached, and South Carolina followed suit in May, this would mean Virginia might become the vital ninth state that would assure the Constitution a fair trial.

At the Fredericksburg post office Madison picked up a letter from an Orange County friend urging him to hurry home. One of Madison's opponents was roaming the county, attacking the Constitution "in such

Horred carrecters that the weker clas of people are much predegessed agains it by which meens he has many which as yet, appears grately in favour of him."[27] Speed was needed, for the election was on March 24 and Madison's carriage did not wheel into the Montpelier driveway until sometime on the twenty-third. Madison was tired, of course, but glad to embrace his ailing mother and shake the hand of his spry father. At once he learned that the "County [was] filled with the most absurd and groundless prejudices against the foederal Constitution." His dander up, Madison forced himself to do what he had never done before: make a campaign speech. "I was therefore obliged at the election which succeeded the day of my arrival to mount for the first time in my life, the rostrum before a large body of people, and to launch into a harangue of some length in the open air and on a very windy day," he reported to a friend.

Whether Madison's speech was supplemented with hard cider is not certain. What is factual is the result: Madison 202, James Gordon, Jr., 187, and the Antifederalists James Barbour, 54, and Charles Porter, 34. Madison had whipped them badly, enough to feel encouraged although results came in slowly. He continued to fret over Henry's influence in southside Virginia, "the great district . . . which is said to be most tainted with antifederalism."[28] News trickled in that Mason had won in Stafford County after Fairfax County wanted none of his Antifederalism; Henry was easily chosen, along with Governor Randolph, John Marshall, James Monroe, and some lesser characters.

As he ticked off the names of friends and opponents, Madison decided that the delegates coming to Richmond from the Kentucky district (the three westernmost counties of Virginia) might hold the balance. So he wrote to his friend and fellow congressman, Kentuckian John Brown, and said it might be a good idea to spread word "in that quarter [of] my opinion that the constitutional impediments to improper measures relating to the Mississ[i]ppi will be greater as well as the pretexts for them be less under the new than the existing system." Madison was also worried about "the Counties on the western side of the Alleghany" where slavery had a weak hold and row-crop farmers often resented much of the lawmaking done in Richmond. Still mulling the election returns, Madison read that in Rhode Island the legislature had sent the Constitution directly to the towns for votes by citizens without any convention. Madison suspected the results would probably go against the Constitution, leaving "a determination there to involve all things in Confusion."[29] Reading between the lines, one can see that Madison meant that the necessary ninth state would not yet be in the constitutional fold when the delegates converged on Richmond in June. Then he heard some bad news about Kentucky. John Brown informed him the Constitution "has few or no Supporters in that Country."[30] Bad as this sounded, Madison was experienced enough to know how dark it can be before the light breaks through.

And, indeed, the Richmond convention was Philadelphia all over again. Mason and Henry played their trump card at the outset by obtaining a resolution that the Constitution would not be voted on hurriedly but debated clause by clause before the final determination. That suited Madison well enough, except that the Antifederalists and Henry in particular never abided by the rule. Instead, Henry made emotional attacks on the preamble, the slavery clause, the bugbear of contracts vis-à-vis the British debt problem, and whatever else lay at hand that his oratory could conjure into certain ruin for Virginians. Mason failed to match his performance at Philadelphia, and became somewhat confused as the days dragged by. Randolph, at first thought to be friendly to Mason and influenced by Henry, surprised everybody except Madison by coming out of his neutral shell in favor of an unconditional ratification. The attempt to coordinate a set of conditional amendments with New York Antifederalists was badly bungled, so that after three weeks of desultory debate the voting ultimately hinged on whether the Antifederalists could count enough hands to pass a resolution favoring conditional amendments. Madison attacked the idea in a powerful speech on June 24 in which he suggested that by such a tactic, after eight states had ratified (both Maryland and South Carolina had approved by late May), only enormous confusion would ensue.

> The gentlemen who within this house have thought proper to propose previous amendments, have brought no less than forty amendments—a bill of rights which contains twenty amendments, and twenty other alterations, some of which are improper and inadmissible. Will not every state think herself equally entitled to propose as many amendments? And suppose them to be contradictory, I leave it to this convention, whether it be probable that they can agree, or agree to any thing but the plan on the table; or whether greater difficulties will not be encountered, than were experienced in the progress of the formation of this constitution.[31]

In short, all the months of preparation would go for naught, the whole reform movement would be jeopardized, and the Constitution would become a dead letter. Surely Madison must have said to himself: "If only Washington were here." But Washington was there as the unseen presence.

The Antifederalists talked on as Madison and his friends kept trying to dampen sectional appeals, hints about the abolition of slavery, and other bugaboos. Realizing that the opposition strategy was pegged on the call for a second convention, Madison had little to add to his views expressed in The Federalist #38. After pointing to the variety of objections from Antifederalists, Madison asked what might happen if the country supported their criticisms "and should accordingly proceed to form them into a second convention, with full powers, and for the express purpose of revising and remolding the work of the first." In a rare show of halfway humor, Madison said it required "some effort to view it seriously even in fiction" and hinted that the discordant objections he had cited were indicative of "the discord and ferment that would mark their own deliberations. . . . I leave it to be decided," Madison said,

> whether the Constitution now before the public would not stand as fair a chance for immortality as Lycurgus gave to that of Sparta by making its chance to depend on his own return from exile and death, if it were to be immediately adopted and were to continue in force, not until a better, but until another, should be agreed upon by this new assembly of lawgivers.

Madison never wavered from this position. When any Federalist delegate suggested some kind of compromise, Madison said there would be no deals, no conditional amendments, no second convention. For all his small frame, Madison could be tough.

The drama in Richmond reached a climax when the Antifederalists moved for a vote on amendments previous to ratification—the maneuver needed to assure a second convention. As the fateful vote was tallied, Kentuckians voted against the Constitution and for the Henry-Mason amendments, but the mountain men from beyond the Alleghenies sent a bloc into the Federalist column. Previous amendments were defeated, 88 to 80. The ratification resolution was only a formality after such a tense vote. Had Madison's masterful oratory made the difference? Reporting a post mortem on the convention to Jefferson in Paris, Monroe gave Madison credit for "the principal share in the debate for it," but the conduct and views of the absent Washington were known to every delegate. "Be assured his influence carried this government," Monroe added.

Madison was hardly overjoyed by the outcome, but he was mightily pleased that (so he thought) Virginia became the crucial ninth ratifying state. He later learned New Hampshire had acted positively a week earlier. But the joy among the Federalist circles in Richmond was contained. They had conceded some recommendatory amendments, tacking them to the ratification to appease Henry's supporters. There was no need to rub Antifederalist noses in the dirt. That moderating tone that was to give the emerging constitutional system its vitality was already evident. "There was no bonfire illumination &c." to celebrate the victory, Monroe explained to Jefferson, "and had there been I am inclin'd to believe, the opposition would have not only express'd no dissatisfaction, but have scarcely felt any at it, for they seemed to be governed by principles elevated highly above circumstances so trivial and transitory in their nature."[32]

Elated but unable to rest, Madison shook hands and played the part of a gracious winner. Some delegates gave him more credit than Monroe.

John Marshall, who knew a good speaker when he heard one, later said Madison "was the most eloquent man I ever heard." Well might Marshall have been thinking of Madison's speeches of June 24 and 25 that beat back the greatest orator in Virginia history, Patrick Henry.[33]

There was a worrisome aftermath to the final vote. The Antifederalists threatened to send out a public message to the people that could breed trouble. For his part, Henry had not been gracious at all. "Mr. H---y declared previous to the final question that altho he should submit as a quiet citizen, he should seize the first moment that offered for shaking off the yoke in a *Constitutional way*," Madison reported to Washington. "I suspect the plan will be to engage 2/3 of the Legislatures in the task of undoing the work; or to get a Congress appointed in the first instance that will commit suicide on their own Authority." In any event, Madison figured that the Antifederalists were not going to leave the situation with a gracious exit. Randolph had mentioned a second convention during the last days of the first, and if the Antis revived that notion anything could still happen.

Meanwhile, Hamilton was working his own kind of miracle in New York. When the glorious news arrived in Manhattan from the New Hampshire convention, Hamilton personally paid an express rider to carry the news straightway to Richmond. "Our only chance of success depends on you," he told Madison in a prescient comment on the day Virginia ratified. Madison sent the state treasurer his bill for twenty-four days' service at the convention and travel of seventy-five miles, totaling £14. He wound up all business in Richmond, climbed aboard a northbound carriage, and took off for Mount Vernon. The Richmond heat and humidity during the convention left Madison feeling queasy and receptive to an invitation from Washington to pause at his plantation en route to New York. "Relaxation must have become indispensably necessary for your health, and for that reason I presume to advise you to take a little respite from business and to express a wish that part of the time might be spent under this Roof on your Journey thither," Washington wrote. "Moderate exercise, and books occasionally, with the mind unbent, will be your best restoratives."[34]

Madison took Washington's hint. He arrived at Mount Vernon during a break in the heat wave, accompanied by Dr. David Stuart and Richard Henry Lee's young son, William. Washington recorded the July 5 temperature—a pleasant 79° at noon, adding, "I remained at home all day with Mr. Madison." Their conversation remained a private matter, but it must have concerned the shape of things to come and particularly the presidential chair created at Philadelphia last August. After another day spent as Washington's guest, Madison felt well enough to continue his journey. The easy atmosphere at Mount Vernon gave way to more hours of waiting at ferries and roads choked with the July dust. In addition to the ordinary inconveniences of eighteenth-century travel, Madison "had on the road several returns of a bilious lax which made my journey more tedious & less agreeable than it would otherwise have been."[35] He paused at Philadelphia to talk with friends of the Constitution, then hurried on to New York where Congress was still in session. The main business before the delegates was to arrange for the decent burial of the old confederation and implement the upstart Constitution without indecent haste.

The news looked good from Poughkeepsie, where Hamilton was sweating through the New York ratifying convention's gyrations. Governor Clinton seemed to have the situation under control despite a short-circuited letter he had written to Richmond proposing a conditional ratification. (Randolph withheld the letter until after the convention dissolved.) The Antifederalists had an overwhelming majority but never could quite get down to business. Hamilton and his friends used delaying tactics to ward off a vote, for Clinton's strategy seemed to imply New York was free to join the Union or stay aloof by ratifying conditionally. Surely Hamilton passed around Madison's view of such a plan, sent to Poughkeepsie a few days after Madison returned from Virginia. "My opinion is that a reservation of a right to withdraw if amendments be not decided on under the form of the Constitution within a certain time, is a *conditional* ratification that it does not make N. York a member of the New Union, and consequently that she could not be received on that plan," Madison observed. "The Constitution requires an adoption *in toto,* and for ever."[36]

Governor Clinton allowed the leadership to slip from his hands. The news from Virginia and pressure from Federalists created a power vacuum. The Antifederalists began a retreat that ensured a debacle for the Clinton faction, which crumbled when charged with fostering disunionism. On July 23 the rout was complete when the convention voted, 31 to 29, to ratify the Constitution "in full confidence" that desirable amendments eventually would be added to the instrument.[37] What North Carolina and Rhode Island would do, in light of New York's ratification, no longer worried Madison.

Not that Madison lacked for reasons to furrow his brow. In a conciliatory mood, the Federalists at Poughkeepsie voted for a circular letter endorsing another convention. Although the Antifederalists kept talking about the lack of a bill of rights, a confidant of Madison's in Philadelphia assured him the opposition planned to change their tactics. From outright obstructionism they were moving to grudging acceptance provided some amendments could be obtained. "Among them is *constantly* the resumption of the power of direct taxation," Tench Coxe wrote. Antifederalists opposed to a direct federal tax claimed "that no uniform mode can be devised that will be found practicable, & that, if the mode is not uniform, it will be considered as partial," Coxe added. "In other places it has been opposed because it will reduce the importance of the state governments."[38] Madison pondered Coxe's letter with pessimism. "The conspiracy agst. direct taxes is more extensive & formidable than some gentlemen suspect," Madison replied. "It is clearly seen by the enemies to the Constitution that an abolition of that power will re-establish the supremacy of the State Legislatures, the real object of all their zeal in opposing the system."

The circular letter from New York signed by Governor Clinton was, in Madison's view, far more sinister and potentially dangerous. Madison overreacted. He sent Jefferson a copy of the letter, which urged the several state legislatures to provide for another federal convention to consider amending the constitution. More talk of still another convention, Madison wrote, kept alive the hopes of discordant Antifederalists. "The great danger in the present crisis is that if another Convention should be soon assembled, it would terminate in discord, or in alterations of the federal system which would throw back *essential* powers into the State Legislatures," he told Jefferson. Why all the haste? "The delay of a few years will assuage the jealousies which have been artificially created by designing men and will at the same time point out the faults which really call for amendment. At present the public mind is neither sufficiently cool nor sufficiently informed for so delicate an operation."[39] Thinking about the situation overnight, Madison sent Washington his analysis of the harm contained in the New York circular. "It has a most pestilent tendency," he wrote Washington. "If an Early General Convention cannot be parried, it is seriously to be feared that the system which has resisted so many direct attacks may be at last successfully undermined by its enemies." Perhaps Rhode Island should not be pressed to act "till this new crisis of danger be over."[40]

If Madison had stepped back and reviewed the situation he might have relaxed. The Antifederalists' clock was ticking away and they had little to show for the lost time. Federalist newspapers made every effort to make the opposition appear to be more quarrelsome than constructive as the nation marked time awaiting the start of the new federal machinery of government. Many citizens no doubt felt as Samuel Osgood did when he told Elbridge Gerry, "I consider the first Congress as a second Convention." When Judge Edmund Pendleton wrote Madison that he favored a cooling-off period, Madison hailed this influential man's disdain of "a premature Convention." "An early Convention threatens discord and mischief," Madison replied. If called, "It will be composed of the most heterogenious characters . . . men having insidious designs agst. the Union—and can scarcely therefore terminate in harmony or the public good." Finally, Madison gave a judgment that became—in effect—the nation's judgment on the second convention. "Let the enemies of the System wait until some experience shall have taken place, and the business will be conducted with more light as well as with less heat. In the mean time the other mode of amendments may be employed to quiet the fears of many by supplying those further guards for private rights which can do no harm to the system."[41]

Madison pondered his mail by night, wrote of his alarm over this second-convention threat, and spent long hours in the halls of Congress where the debate centered on selecting a temporary national capital. Madison was not overly concerned about the first location for a capitol; instead he looked ahead to the final result of all the infighting he witnessed in Congress. Baltimore, Philadelphia, Wilmington, New York, and Lancaster, Pennsylvania, all had some support as the first meeting place for the new government. Madison preferred a site on the banks of the Potomac and based his tactics on that long-term goal. "The only chance the potowmac has is to get things in such a train that a coalition may take place between the Southern & Eastern States on the subject, and still more that the final seat may be undecided for two or three years, within which period the Western & S. Western population will enter more into the estimate," he wrote Washington.[42]

The deadlock in Congress exposed the raw sectional bias and the tenuous ties of union Madison wished to bind more closely. Henry's warnings at the Richmond convention seemed all too true as New England delegates banded together to serve the imagined interests of their constituency. Henry himself was up to no good as the October session of the Virginia General Assembly convened. Madison quickly made it clear that he thought it best that he seek a place in the new House of Representatives and avoid any clash with Henry's power over the legislators who would pick the two Virginia senators. Madison knew his home territory well enough to think he could win a House seat without a fight. "My preference I own is somewhat founded on the supposition that arrangements for the popular elections may secure me agst. any competition which wd. require on my part any step that wd. speak a solicitude which I do not feel, or have the appearance of a spirit of electioneering which I despise," he told Governor Randolph.[43] The shyness Madison felt in public had not left him at that first campaign speech in Orange County.

Henry, however, would not let Madison get off so easily. Henry's wish for a coalition that would carry forward the New York circular letter was evident. "Much talk of closing with New York in her proposal for a new convention," a friendly delegate reported to Madison. "Prima facie—I see no impropriety in it."[44] This red flag drew Madison's immediate reply. Citizens sincerely in favor of certain amendments might object to the cumbersomeness of a second convention as the only means of bringing alterations in the constitution, he explained. Nor could a convention be called "without the unanimous consent of the parties who are to be bound by it"—an almost impossible circumstance. Third,

> If a General Convention were to take place for the avowed and sole purpose of revising the Constitution, it would naturally consider itself as having a greater latitude than the Congress appointed to administer and support as well as to amend the system; it would consequently give greater agitation to the public mind; and election into it would be courted by the most violent partizans on both sides; it wd. probably consist of the most heterogeneous characters; would be the very focus of that flame which has already too much heated men of all parties. . . . Under all these circumstances it seems scarcely to be presumeable that the deliberations of the body could be conducted in harmony, or terminate in the general good.[45]

Madison said a mouthful, but still had a final thought which he hoped would be spread among friends in Richmond. A second convention would be interpreted abroad "as a dark and threatening Cloud hanging over the Constitution just established . . . and wd. therefore suspend at least the advantages this great event has promised us on that side."

Obviously, Madison was disturbed by the sugarcoating Henry placed on the second-convention pill. To have the reform movement he had conceived and nurtured fall into disarray because of Henry's jealous parochialism vexed Madison. But there was more to the new Constitution than petty politics. National bankruptcy was the alternative to the Constitution, Madison believed, and with that disaster the whole dream of an exemplary American republic would tumble into the dust. Madison was dedicating his life to avoid such a catastrophe.

> We are not sufficiently sensible of the importance of the example which this Country may give to the world; nor sufficiently attentive to the advantages we may reap from the late reform, if we avoid bring[in]g it into danger. The last loan in Holland and that alone, saved the U. S. from Bankruptcy in Europe; and that loan was obtained from a belief that the Constitution then depending wd. be certainly speedily, quietly, and finally established, & by that means put America into a permanent capacity to discharge with honor & punctuality all her engagements.

Madison threw into the letter every argument he could muster, and friends in Richmond decided it ought to be published in the newspapers. Madison demurred, so only his supporters in the legislature read it.[46] But they were the ones who counted.

If Patrick Henry listened when Madison's letter was read to him the logic of it would only have made him hunker down, determined to thwart his opponent and suspend a final judgment on the Constitution. That is precisely what Henry tried to do. "The Cloven hoof begins to appear,"

Madison's friend warned. "I want no arguments to convince me . . . intrigue and antifoederalism and artifice go hand in hand."[47] Early in November the Virginia legislators passed over Madison to elect Richard Henry Lee and William Grayson, avowed enemies of an unaltered constitution, to the Senate. The formal ballot: Lee 98, Grayson 86, Madison 77. "Mr. Henry on yr. being nominated for the senate publicly declared in the house that you were not to be trusted with *amendments* since you had declared, that not a letter of the Constitution cou'd be spared," Madison learned.[48] Moreover, Henry was slicing the congressional districts around Orange County so that Madison would have strong opposition in the election scheduled for February 1789. A well-meaning friend assured Madison that "your Election might be secured in any of the lower districts in the state"—a hint that a contest on his home ground ought to be avoided.[49]

Henry seemed all-powerful and all-vindictive. To foil any attempt to place Madison in the House from another region, the districting bill contained a provision that candidates had to reside in the area for at least a year before the voting. "I am inclined to think that the Anti's inserted this with a view to you, and that the feds have assented to it from feeling their inferiority," a Federalist delegate wrote Madison. A piddling matter came up, the selection of delegates to the waning Continental Congress, and Henry voted to keep Madison on. The art of legislating was also the art of dissembling. "I do verily believe that Mr. Henry Voted for you to Congress this time with no other Veiw but to keep you [away] from Country untill some more favor'd man, some minion of *his* or *his* party shall have had an opportunity to supplant yr. Interest," another well-wisher reported.[50]

Madison knew Henry well enough and understood Virginia politics so completely that he realized the purpose of all this intrigue. Edmund Randolph, cut off from friendship with Henry by his vote for ratification in the Richmond convention, warned Madison: "the destruction of the whole System, I take to be still the secret wish of his heart, and the real object of his pursuit." Plain enough and easy for Madison to understand as news filtered in of bills passed by the Virginia legislature. In an era when dual officeholding was normal and acceptable, a resolution passed which excluded all federal officials except those holding military posts from taking a state office. Another resolution called on the Congress to schedule a second general convention, while a third authorized a circular letter to all the states in support of the one issued by the New York convention. Federalists tried to ward off Henry's blow with a counter-proposal calling for a cooling-off period on action for a second convention, "provided Congress at their first meeting, will consider the necessary amendments and forward them to the state Legislatures for their adoption—these were negatived by 70 to 50."[51]

Perhaps that night Madison remembered Jefferson's remark, the one about praying for Henry's early death. In 1784 it probably caused Madison to smile, but not in 1788.

Henry was very much alive, however, and eager to throw Madison into a district where powerful opposition was certain. "The Anti's have levelled every effort at you," Madison heard from Richmond. "Your district is composed of the Counties of Amherst, Albemarle, Louisa, Orange Culpeper, Spotsylvania Goochland & Fluvanna—we wished to get Fauquier but the powers of the Anti's were too strong for us."[52] This would be no safe election and campaigning could not be avoided. "Your absence, My Dear Sir, is woefully felt by your Country," said one friend. "Your friends wish you however to come into this district at an early period, in order to Counteract a number of reports which may take hold upon the Minds of the people . . . that you declared in Convention that the Constitution required no alteration whatever," wrote another.[53]

How far would Henry go in his efforts to send Madison into retirement? To any length, it seemed, for Henry counted William Cabell of Amherst County a close ally, and there were rumors Cabell might oppose Madison in the congressional election. A distant cousin, the Reverend James Madison, wrote from his post as president of the College of William and Mary to say that "If a Freehold be required in the District for wch. the Representative is chosen, Lots in this Town may be had at a very low Rate."[54] Madison had no choice but to do battle on his home ground, however, and more mail came urging a return to Montpelier in the dead of winter.

Then Henry delivered what was calculated to be the knockout blow to Madison's chances. "It is as yet not ascertained who will be started against you: within a few days there has arisen some reason to suspect that Colo. Monroe will be the Man."[55] James Monroe of Fredericksburg—a friend and congressional colleague, and a protégé of Jefferson's—was Henry's choice of a challenger for the House seat in Madison's home district. Such a contest would pit the undersized scholar against the tall war hero. This was the kind of uneven race that Henry enjoyed because he nearly always won. Usually, it wasn't even close. Someone even spread a rumor that Madison was ready to give up American shipping rights on the Mississippi. Labeled a lie by Madison's friends, the story hurt.[56]

The letters from Virginia failed to frighten Madison; besides, he had other things on his mind as the nights on Manhattan turned frosty and ice formed in the sidewalk puddles. There was some good news coming in to Madison's listening post, as Congress set up the machinery for the new government to begin operating in February or March 1789 with the election of a president and the convening of the new Congress. Glad tidings came from Massachusetts, where the New York circular letter was scuttled by delaying tactics adopted by Federalists in the state legislature.

Predictably, lawmakers in Rhode Island and North Carolina responded favorably to Governor Clinton's letter, but the official word from Virginia was delayed until mid-December. Bad roads, worse weather, and an inefficient postal system seemed part of a conspiracy to keep friends of a second convention from communicating with each other. After an attempt to rally the opposition failed at a Harrisburg convention, the Pennsylvania legislature reacted to the circular letter by rejecting the implications of Antifederalist strategy. In a call for harmony, the Pennsylvania lawmakers asked that the constitution be placed in operation "undisturbed . . . by premature amendments."[57] Generally the state legislatures reacted to the second-convention call as had the Connecticut assembly, where "No Antifederalist had the hardiness to call it up for consideration, or to speak one word of its subject."[58]

Madison did not need the final word from the several state capitals to know that the second-convention plan was dead as a doornail. What had appeared to be a dangerous timebomb tossed out a few weeks earlier had fizzled, for it became evident that the new government was going into operation; and the extremists in Rhode Island and North Carolina had found no imitators and few supporters. "Was this a time to smoak a pipe, & suck the paw like a surly Bear," asked an anguished Tarheel Federalist, "when your house was on fire?"[59] Apparently not, events seemed to say.

The doldrums of the Continental Congress gave Madison an excuse to stay in New York until early December, when a quorum disappeared and would never return. As he prepared for a wintry trip back to Montpelier, Madison gave Jefferson his assessment of the political situation and threw in some gossip about the French minister. Election returns from New England southward assured a Senate well disposed toward the Constitution, and at the most Antifederalists in the House would make something less than "a very formidable minority." Even in Virginia, Madison calculated, "7 out of the 10, allotted to that State, will be opposed to the politics of the present Legislature." Friends of the new system were agreed that some amendments to the Constitution ought to be considered. "But they wish the revisal to be carried no farther than to supply additional guards for liberty, without abridging the sum of power transferred from the States to the general Government," and were unalterably opposed "to the risk of another Convention." While some Antifederalists involved in the hue and cry for a second convention were doubtless "friends to an effective Government . . . there are others, who urge a Second Convention with the insidious hope, of throwing all things into Confusion, and of subverting the fabric just established, if not the Union itself."

Not yet ready to commit himself to a firm pledge to seek amendments that would embody a bill of rights, Madison indicated that the first Congress could solve the matter by proposing "of themselves, every desireable safeguard for popular rights; and by thus separating the well meaning from the designing opponents, fix on the latter their true character, and give to the Government its due popularity and stability."

With the second-convention plan squelched and reports of safe men elected to the first Congress arriving daily, Madison overcame his distaste for travel and boarded a stage for Philadelphia by December 8. After a pause in Philadelphia Madison was southward bound again. At Alexandria he met with the erstwhile governor, "Light-Horse Harry" Lee, and they talked about a wild land speculation that the war hero was trying to exploit. Then Madison was taken to Mount Vernon amid snow and bitter cold, arriving at the dinner hour in late afternoon. A roaring fire restored some circulation to Madison's chilled hands and feet, after which the general presided at a good table where the conversation had to turn on the forthcoming congressional elections. Madison stayed at Mount Vernon for almost a week, then departed on Christmas morning when the thermometer was barely above 14°.[60] At Fredericksburg he probably found among his delayed mail the letter from Burgess Ball warning him of impending defeat in the race for Congress. The crucial vote would come in Culpeper County, Ball explained, and a henchman of Henry's "meens to exert himself in favour of your opponant, Colo. Monroe, who has declar'd himself for the District."[61]

Advice surrounded Madison as he struggled through the frozen mud, his discomfort increased by the hemorrhoid attack which struck before he left New York. Nearly all the mail had a common theme: Monroe's candidacy required Madison's immediate presence or the election was lost. Joseph Jones, Monroe's uncle and a former member of the Virginia delegation in the Continental Congress, confessed the situation was discomfitting. "I am sorry to find two persons for whom I have real friendship in opposition as candidates," Jones wrote. "M----e has I fear been prevailed on to do what I think if he succeeds will hurt his private prospects."[62] An Orange County neighbor listed the eight counties in Madison's district, adding, "the Sooner your personal appearance could be in those Countys the better."[63] In Richmond Madison's replacement in the state legislature was candid, hinting that a mere announcement of candidacy would no longer ensure a victory at the polls.

> With many this is sufficient, but with all it is not. Col: Monroe is also nominated & the most active unceasing endeavours will not be wanting among his friends to secure his election. It therefore becomes indispensably necessary that your return to Virga. should be hastened as much as possible. . . . I know that this has not been your usual practice, and am certain that it will be very irksome to you, but your friends hope that you will make some sacrifices of this sort however disagreable they may be."[64]

Madison was home in time for a Sunday dinner at Montpelier, where his father must have confirmed all the reports. The Baptists were active and looking for a candidate who could assure them that he was their friend. Were reports that Madison was hostile to amendments akin to a bill of rights—protecting the precious religious freedom obtained in 1776—true or false?

While the house servants at Montpelier kept the fireplaces glowing, Madison assessed the letters and conversations. There could be no thought of attacking Monroe—he was a friend. In such circumstances, Madison believed his campaigning must be limited to admitting that he had changed his mind and was now persuaded that amendments, particularly whatever might affect religious liberty, were in order. His brother William had talked to George Eve, a Baptist minister serving as pastor at the Blue Run church, and the preacher promised that he would spread the word Madison was ready to support constitutional changes to preserve "the rights of Conscience." "I freely own that I have never seen in the Constitution as it now stands those serious dangers which have alarmed many respectable Citizens," Madison admitted. Now the Constitution had been established by the solemn will of the people of eleven states, however, and proper amendments "may serve the double purpose of satisfying the minds of well meaning opponents, and of providing additional guards in favour of liberty."

> Under this change of circumstances, it is my sincere opinion that the Constitution ought to be revised, and that the first Congress meeting under it, ought to prepare and recommend to the States for ratification, the most satisfactory provisions for all essential rights, particularly the rights of Conscience in the fullest latitude, the freedom of the press, trials by jury, security against general warrants &c.

Madison went on to say he preferred that the amendments be proposed in Congress rather than in another general convention. Working in a constitutional way through Congress would prove to be a quicker method, and the desired amendments might even come to pass from the first session set for next March. "Lastly, it is the safest mode. The Congress, who will be appointed to execute as well as to amend the Government, will probably be careful not to destroy or endanger it."[65]

Meanwhile Washington pondered their Christmas conversations at Mount Vernon and wrote Madison a confidential letter that apparently concerned the first presidential message to the new Congress. Lost to history, this message (copied by Washington, but drafted by his secretary David Humphreys) covered some seventy-three manuscript pages and left room for a prayer. The proposed speech seems to have been too florid for Washington's taste—he pretty much ignored it—probably at Madison's urging. A busybody pedant who came across it a generation later snipped it to pieces for curiosity seekers.[66]

Although Madison's letter to the Orange County preacher furnished some proof that he had changed his tune regarding amendments, the Baptists were still not totally convinced. Madison heard that the Baptist ministers were convening in Louisa County soon, and he needed no agenda to guess at their purpose. Monroe reportedly was hurrying to reach the meeting and a friend advised Madison to imitate him. Aware of the important meeting but not willing to electioneer in the precincts of a Baptist ministerial gathering, Madison chose instead to write influential Thomas Mann Randolph in Louisa with an unequivocal pledge that, if elected, he would work in the first Congress so "that the clearest, and strongest provision [will] be made, for all those essential rights, which have been thought in danger, such as the rights of conscience, the freedom of the press, trials by jury, exemption from general warrants, &c." A copy of this letter was sent to Richmond and appeared in the *Virginia Independent Chronicle* on January 28, on the eve of the election.[67]

For the second time in his life, Madison really wanted to be elected and was not willing to let matters go by a simple announcement that he was available. Without revealing his anxiety, Madison wrote Washington, "I have pursued my pretensions much farther than I had premeditated; having not only made a great use of epistolary means; but actually visited two Counties, Culpeper & Louisa, and publicly contradicted the erroneous reports propagated agst. me."[68] Madison avoided a head-on confrontation with Monroe at Culpeper Court House but learned that an Orange County Baptist alleged that the full report of debates at the Richmond convention had been suppressed to prevent the truth about Madison's animosity to amendments from being known. Friends denied the accusation and told Madison that, barring "insidious means taken in future," his pledge to work for amendments that spring had a powerful effect. An apocryphal story that Madison sought out Elder John Leland, an influential Baptist then living in Orange County, and made a personal pledge to work for a bill of rights is part of the local mythology; it is more likely that Madison sent Leland a message in unmistakable terms and let it go at that.

Weather in those days provided a well-worn excuse for the outcome of an election. On January 31, two days before the voting, a ten-inch snowfall blanketed much of Madison's district, to be followed by bitterly cold weather that made a trek to the polling places both uncomfortable and burdensome to any citizen who had to traverse the miserable dirt roads leading to the courthouses. On election day the thermometer fell to zero at Fredericksburg and over much of the district. Perhaps the story that Madison stood around Orange Court House until his nose was frostbitten is true. Certainly it was cold enough; but the outcome had a warming effect. It was a testimonial to Madison's popularity and even more to the hardiness of his supporters. The final count showed that Monroe had carried four counties (one by a single vote) while Madison had a majority in the other four. The chief difference was that Madison won in his home county by a vote of 216 to 9 as Monroe was carrying his 189 to 115. The total vote was Madison 1,308, Monroe 972. Madison's return home, his letter writing, and the two personal appearances on courthouse steps had paid off. In spite of Patrick Henry, freezing weather, and everything but high water, James Madison was going to sit in the First Congress.

CHAPTER THREE

TO SAVE
THE
REPUBLIC

When the First Congress convened in March 1789, the country was in
high spirits. New York was the temporary capital of the Republic. Few
cities in the New World were a rival for the burgeoning village when it
came to cosmopolitan atmosphere, and in 1789 still fewer were a match
for Manhattan when it came to signs of prosperity. The harbor teemed
with the towering masts of sailing vessels, most of them flying British or
American flags, as much of the commerce formerly sent to Philadelphia
now came into the deep harbor surrounding New York. While the Pennsylvania city was losing its title as America's busiest seaport, the banking
gentlemen of Boston worried about the shift southward of the commerce
and banking they coveted. An efficient postal service made communication with Boston only a matter of three or four days from lower Manhattan; Philadelphia was less than two days away by courier; and in a
time when life was not measured by the ticking of a clock, New York
made a fair bid to become America's most attractive and accessible city.

What was on Madison's mind late in February of 1789 was the business of starting a new government from scratch. Events of the past eighteen months gave him a feeling of optimism. Even Patrick Henry's tactic
that denied Madison a seat in the federal Senate was regarded as a disguised blessing. If Madison had been picked by the Virginia legislators
as a senator he would have been expected to do their bidding, as had
been the practice when he served in the Continental Congress. But as
the elected representative from his home district, Madison saw himself
as responsible only to his neighbors and his own sense of duty. The dis-

tinction proved to be important, particularly when he was reminded of that campaign promise concerning a bill of rights. "Be assured we did every thing in our power for you," a disappointed friend in the House of Delegates wrote Madison. "You got Sixty Six Single Votes but Mr. Henrys Interest in the House at that time was too powerfull, but whatever department you are In I well know your Object is the good of your Country."[1]

Madison tried to align his priorities as he prepared to return to the Maiden Lane boarding house. The paradox was that while commerce was flourishing and every citizen had a full stomach the government was broke, no mistaking that. Hence the first thing Congress had to pass was legislation that would create federal income. Surely he was surprised by the mail, conversations, and personal pressure that ignored the nation's financial crisis to focus attention on political patronage. Madison was embarrassed by the urgency of the pleas.

> I beg leave to Recommend One Gentleman in My Real Opinion as the Most fitting Man in my Acquaintance for a Naval [customs] Officer. . . . I flatter myself my long experience in that business, would enable me to secure its duties with propriety . . . I shou'd be very happy to serve Congress abroad & thankfull for any appointment they may be pleas'd to honour me with, & from wch. a decent income may be deriv'd . . . having parted with nearly all the savings of ten years service, in the marriage and settlement of an unfortunate Sister, I found myself unable to make the necessary remittance for the support of aged parents, reduced by misfortune to a dependance on me, and oppressed with the care of an unhappy son deprived of his reason. Considerations, Sir, which, altho' they may excite your sympathy, I hope you will regard as merely intended to explain the seeming incongruity of applying for Office.[2]

On and on came the letters, pleading for Madison's aid when the loaves and fishes of office were distributed. They had piled up at the New York post office, awaiting Madison's arrival. After a brief interval at Mount Vernon, where he discussed with Washington ways of starting the new government on a fast track, Madison had tried to hurry northward. But muddy roads and balky horses provided a reminder that timetables give way to the realities of weather and human endurance. Madison dragged into New York on March 14, a full ten days late, and would wait two more weeks before the newly constituted House of Representatives finally had a quorum. What a way to begin anew!

At last enough congressmen and senators appeared to make all the business official. As Madison told Jefferson (who was witnessing the first moves in the French Revolution from a box seat in Paris): "The season of the year, the peculiar badness of the weather, and the short interval between the epoch of election and that of meeting, form a better apology for the delay than will probably occur on your side of the Atlantic."[3] Nor was Congress prepared for a whirlwind start, once the quorum was on hand. First, the speaker and clerk had to be picked; then the Electoral College votes had to be opened and Washington's election made official. Then the main order of business, as Madison saw matters, was the fiscal emergency. The empty federal treasury forced Congress to pass, without much delay, a tax bill. The joyride for American merchants and consumers was about to end. There would be taxation, but *with* representation.

No member of the newly created House of Representatives was more aware of the nation's near-bankruptcy than Madison. As a delegate to the old Congress Madison witnessed the bickering and jealousies that had thwarted all efforts to raise state quotas during the Revolution, or grant Congress a power to tax imports in the postwar years. While his own state was fairly conscientious in meeting its quotas (pay-as-you-go is an indigenous concept in Virginia), most of the states either ignored the pleas from Philadelphia or made only token payments to the Confederation treasury. After Robert Morris resigned as superintendent of finance, the failure of the Articles of Confederation to provide for the ongoing expenses of government was so glaring that honorable men of Madison's stamp fretted until they were desperate for a solution. The states, or at least some of them (such as New York, which had plenty of impost money coming in at the New York harbor collection point), proceeded about their business with no great concern over what happened to the United States' credit in Amsterdam or Paris. Meanwhile, the money foreigners had loaned to the infant republic during the war years through the purchase of various securities was an embarrassment—the interest was in arrears and the securities were heavily discounted. Various kinds of scrip, pledging interest on the obligations of Congress, circulated among speculators and bankers for less than a third of their nominal value. Only the good graces of some Dutch investors kept the American war loans from collapsing. Unless the United States could start paying its bills, there was no hope that the Union could survive. To Madison, the problem was as simple—and as complicated—as that.

For a brief time every man in the House of Representatives was a de facto volunteer. There was talk of setting their salary at five or six dollars a day, but until some revenue was raised the whole subject was moot. After the routine business had been covered, Madison showed an impatience that would be characteristic of his conduct in that historic First Congress. He wanted action. As other congressmen dawdled over their private business, took long hours for breakfasting and newspaper reading, Madison's frustration became more evident. While his colleagues appeared content to postpone serious business until Washington's inaugural, Madison served notice that he was going to be a ramrod throughout the session.

"The union, by the establishment of a more effective government [and] having recovered from the state of imbecility, that heretofore prevented a performance of its duty, ought, in its first act, to revive those principles of honor and honesty that have too long remained dormant," Madison said. "The deficiency in our treasury has been too notorious to make it necessary for me to animadvert upon that subject. Let us content ourselves with endeavouring to remedy the evil."[4] The tricky matter involved was the raising of money without being "oppressive to our constituents."

Speaking as a former colonial who had grown to manhood in the British Empire, Madison made it clear that the revenue system he yearned for would not bear any "Made in England" label. As the session wore on it became clear that Madison was no admirer of the British navigation acts, and he was determined to leave the regulation of commerce "as free as the policy of nations will admit." He conceded that in his interpretation of Adam Smith's *The Wealth of Nations* the lesson to be learned was that the cumbersome bureaucracy England created to enforce the restrictive laws did more harm than good. This was a long-range policy matter, however, and Madison was thinking of that bare American treasury as he introduced a resolution calling for the imposition of specific duties on a list of commodities ranging from rum to cocoa, with an ad valorem duty on all other imported goods. He also favored tonnage fees on American ships, higher charges on the ships coming from abroad having treaties with the United States, and still higher duties on ships and goods from countries with no commercial agreements with the new nation. The target of the last grouping was obvious, for most of the ships coming and going into American harbors flew the Union Jack, and Great Britain eschewed any pretense of making commercial concessions to its former American colony. The result was painfully obvious to Madison, for the new nation was an economic satellite of British mercantilism. Retaliation was the proper antidote. By making the proposal for "commercial discrimination" against the British Madison fired the opening shot of his long battle to force the English to concede that the United States deserved to be a major force in the expanding world market. A generation and a war later, Madison would be aware of his failure.

In 1789 Madison still hoped the British might treat their American cousins with something akin to respect. He had not yet learned the power of the pro-English forces in New England, who had settled back comfortably into their prewar habits of handling cargoes to and from Liverpool and Bristol. They read Madison's proposals and were grossly offended, and before long the New England crowd picked up support as far south as Charleston. Madison made long speeches explaining the advantages of laws that would penalize the English as long as they froze Americans out of the lucrative British West Indian market. The budding trees told the congressmen that spring was approaching, and that meant English merchantmen were already headed for American ports, their holds jammed with textiles, hardware, glass, paint, dinnerware, and other manufactured items they would land duty-free in some ports, or lightly taxed in others, with not one penny earmarked for the federal coffers. To neglect this obvious source of revenue when the government was impoverished seemed so irresponsible that Madison kept hammering on the issue, despite the yawns of other House members who preferred an unhurried taxing plan. Not a few congressmen would concede only that tariff barriers should go up to protect infant American industries. "The prospect of our harvest from the spring importations is daily vanishing," Madison protested, "and if the [House] committee delay levying and collecting an impost, until a system of protecting duties shall be perfected, there will be no importations of any consequence, on which the law is to operate, because, by that time all the spring vessels will have arrived."[5]

When remarks by other congressmen made it clear that the House was not going to be goaded, Madison was forced to check his impatience. All right, he said, if we cannot move quickly, at least let us not move in the wrong direction by adopting a tax on imports that would favor the manufacturing part (the North) and hurt farmers everywhere.

> It would be of no advantage to the shoemaker to make his own clothes to save the expence of the taylor's bill, nor of the taylor to make his own shoes to save the expence of procuring them from the shoemaker. It would be better policy to suffer each of them to employ his talents in his own way.

In the same manner, Madison continued, it would be better to encourage city-dwellers to do what they were best fitted to do, and let farmers till their fields without the disadvantage of paying more for goods they imported. "The less this exchange is cramped by government, the greater are the proportions of benefit to each. The same argument holds good between nation and nation, and between parts of the same nation."

Madison was, of course, far ahead of his time. He was not so much a disciple of Adam Smith in espousing the cause of free trade as he perceived that it was in the best interest of a rising America to have free access to world markets when barrels of corn, wheat, pork, tobacco, and rice were piling up on American wharves in prodigious quantities. With land cheap, Madison reasoned, "we may be said to have a monopoly in agriculture. The possession of the soil and lowness of its price, give us as much a monopoly in this case, as any nation or other parts of the world have . . . with this advantage to us, that it cannot be shared nor injured by rivalship." Madison acknowledged there were advantages to be gained by protective tariffs, and to throw American ports open when other countries restricted access to theirs would be an invitation to dump goods on our shores. The point, Madison concluded, was that tax revenues were needed urgently; and since the situation was so critical, the law-makers needed to enact an impost law "and some [duties] may protect our domestic manufacturer, tho' the latter subject ought not to be too confusedly blended with the former."[6]

Every congressman who heard Madison talk was impressed. The breadth of his knowledge, his willingness to compromise, and his focus on the need for immediate action marked him as a leader during that First Congress. In effect, he became floor leader for the bill establishing a revenue system by his strong position and his determination to keep the House moving steadily toward passage of the required legislation.

Madison had done his homework, and it showed. The precedent he established made him a natural leader in the House where the com-mittee system, which is now the operative force in Congress, was un-known. The animosities that formed a year or two later had not yet taken shape, either, so that New Englanders in Congress overlooked Madison's soft Virginia accent to concentrate on the substance and style of his speeches. Fisher Ames, who grew to dislike Madison intensely later, con-fessed in 1789 that the Virginian "possessed a sound judgment." Madison "perceives truth with great clearness, and can trace it through the mazes of debate, without losing it."

> As a reasoner, he is remarkably perspicuous and methodical. He is a studious man, devoted to public business, and a thorough master of almost every public question that can arise, or he will spare no pains to become so, if he happens to be in want of information. What a man understands clearly, and has viewed in every different point of light, he will explain to the admiration of others, who have not though of it at all, or but little, and who will pay in praise for the pains he saves them.[7]

No wonder Madison met the expectations of colleagues who had heard of his performance at Philadelphia in 1787. The cadre of leadership in America was still so small that reputations spread rapidly. When, a year later, Benjamin Rush asked Jefferson what he thought of Madison, the tall Virginian had a ready answer that probably took Rush aback. James Madison, Jefferson said, was simply "the greatest man in the world."[8]

Nobody was more acutely aware of Madison's standing among sen-ators and congressmen than Washington. Whether he was glad Madison had talked him into going to Philadelphia two summers earlier is not recorded. What is certain, however, is Washington's dependence on Madison for advice as the new government and its president moved cau-tiously, as though the Republic itself were no more permanent than a brilliant sunrise. A chief executive was something new on the American scene, and neither Washington nor Congress knew quite how to handle the delicate relationships and precedents created by each day's business; but both the president and Congress tended to look to England for precedents. Even the most inveterate Anglophobe had to admit that the British had a deft way of handling ceremonial decorum; and there was obvious comfort in being able to say, "we can do as they do in England."

When the House of Representatives prepared to congratulate the president upon his inauguration, Madison was made chairman of the committee charged with sending a felicitous message to the chief executive. Madison realized Washington had to take a stance somewhere to the right of a king but still not make himself one of the multitude; so in his draft message to Washington the younger Virginian hailed the new president for enjoying "the highest, because [it is] the truest honor, [that] of being the first Magistrate, by the unanimous choice, of the freest people on the face of the Earth."[9] There was more, but in Madison's s view all that was important had been said.

Washington accepted the House's good wishes and turned to Madison to write, in effect, a reply to himself. Excessively conscious of the way each action or slight movement was setting a future precedent, Washington relied on Madison to keep things in perspective. "As the first of every thing, *in our situation* will serve to establish a Precedent, it is devoutly wished on my part, that these precedents may be fixed on true principles," the president wrote. Would Madison write the proper kind of reply? Of course he would, in a 101-word model of republican simplicity. "I feel that my past endeavors in the service of my Country are far overpaid by its goodness: and I fear much that my future ones may not fulfill your kind Anticipation," he had Washington replying. "All that I can promise is, that they will be invariably directed by an honest and an ardent zeal."[10] The tone and style suited Washington so well that he and Madison continued their discreet shuffling of papers.

During that first tentative year in New York Madison was often called upon by Washington to help the president keep from becoming a man-on-horseback. Washington's presence at the helm of state was like a tonic to the nation, however. In spite of the laziness in Congress and a variety of minor worries the country perked up. While the skeptics kept wondering when the young nation was going to collapse, the more perceptive business men were starting to buy the depreciated Continental and state loan securities at their rock-bottom prices. Aside from the French loans and the wildcat scrip issued by the old Continental Congress, the Revolution had been paid for by a variety of securities issued to civilians for food or services, and to soldiers for their wartime exertions. Some of this paper eventually fell into foreign hands, but the largest share of the public debt (some $40 million) was constantly shifting from speculator to banker to speculator where a $10,000 certificate bought for $2,800 in hard cash seemed almost foolhardy. Some of the paper, particularly the "loan office certificates," appeared to be the best risk since the states were pledged to make eventual redemption with interest. The "final settlement certificates" issued to soldiers were at the other end of the scale. Most of the army veterans sold their holdings for a pittance, and with the market glutted these securities appeared in 1785 to be virtually worthless. Then the Federal Convention had acted, and the new Constitution said that the debts of the old Confederation were to be the debts of the new government. Hardly anybody professed to know exactly what that meant, except for a few bankers and their associates who began a slow, steady accumulation of all the paper they could buy at about twenty cents on the dollar.

Whether Madison realized what was happening in the open marketplace and in the coffee houses, where these pieces of paper freely changed hands, is no mystery. His salary now fixed by law was six dollars a day, which left Madison no surplus funds for a speculative binge. But he was too perceptive, and he moved in circles where these things were well understood, not to have noticed the increased tempo of speculation.

Meanwhile, the bill imposing a tariff on imported goods was tortuously drafted in a committee, debated at length in the House, and finally passed. Then the Senate had its hands full trying to adjust differences among the twenty-two lawmakers. In time a conference committee was called together to resolve differences in the two legislative versions. Finally, on the Fourth of July 1789, the first tariff bill was signed into law, making the nation's thirteenth birthday memorable. The teen-aged Republic was finally going to have something in its treasury besides a fistful of paper promises.

As at Philadelphia in 1787, Madison was forced to settle for something far less than what he yearned for; various committees emasculated his first wishes on tariffs and tonnage duties. By the time the Senate acted on the impost bill, the bonanza from levies on the spring imports had disappeared. Admittedly the establishment of a customs service, particularly an honest customs service, is no easy task, but few congressmen shared Madison's sense of urgency; and when he insisted that some higher duties ought to be imposed on British goods as a retaliation against English discrimination his supporters dwindled to a handful. The old wartime cry of no taxation without representation seemed inverted into a general distaste for all taxes, so that bargains had to be struck before the last version emerged from the conference committee. The din from New England over a proposed six-cents-a-gallon tax on West Indian molasses (the chief ingredient in Yankee-distilled rum) caused so much unhappiness that Madison stood on notice of the lengths to which Northerners would go to protect a favored industry.

At times Madison must have wondered if there was another man in the House who was not out to serve local interests while ignoring the national welfare. Jefferson was still in Paris, but itching for permission to come home on leave, and while he awaited official approval for an ocean voyage Madison kept him informed of happenings in the First Congress. The Senate had stymied his hope for some kind of a higher tax on British shipping, he said, and some senators even said "that if G.B. possessed almost the whole of our trade, it proceeded from causes which proved that she could carry it on for us on better terms than the other Nations of Europe—that we were too dependent on her trade to risk her displeasure by irritating measures which might induce her to put us on a worse footing than at present." On and on the apologists for England droned (Madison reported) until even Richard Henry Lee, one of the Virginia senators, voted to let British ships enter American ports by paying the lowest possible fees.[11]

Madison found all this scratching of English backs both mystifying and mortifying. He began the debates by asserting that America would "soon be in a condition, we now are in a condition, to wage commercial warfare with that nation." Overstating matters, Madison then insisted that American produce "is more necessary to the rest of the world than that of other countries is to America." Tough talk, Madison believed, was to be followed by tougher sanctions. He could not convince enough members of the House, however.

Madison lost his fight for a tariff discrimination against England, but it was one of the few in which he suffered from a short count in 1789. He introduced the motion that led to the legislation creating the State, Treasury, and War departments; he resorted to delaying tactics to keep the site for the permanent national capital in limbo (until the Southerners enamored of a Potomac River location could muster more power); and he defended the concept of an independent and well-paid federal judiciary when some of his parsimonious colleagues began to quibble about judges' salaries and jurisdictions. These achievements aside, Madison's greatest accomplishment during that first session of Congress was his introduction of a bill of rights in fulfillment of his campaign pledge to the folks back home.

Whether Madison first made his pledge to work for a bill of rights with a dead seriousness of purpose, or only to win votes, is beside the point. Once he told his Baptist friends in Orange County that he was going to introduce legislation to gain a federal bill of rights and stick it right into the middle of the Constitution he took the matter seriously. He started a scrapbook in which he pasted newspaper clippings from every nook and cranny of the country where proposed amendments were discussed. Madison collected his clippings from all the state conventions that had ratified the Constitution with an appended set of recommended amendments. Starting with the nine proposed amendments from the Massachusetts convention in February 1788, the list had grown as the ratifying bodies up and down the coast made further suggestions. The gist of these propositions ranged from the ever-present proposal for freedom of the press to thirty-two specific propositions from the New York ratifying convention that included a two-year limitation on the presidency.[12]

Before Madison whittled his list down to manageable size, to essential amendments with universal appeal, a diversionary skirmish gave him a warning that the champions of civil liberties a few years earlier now had more important things on their minds. When the Senate and House started talking about a proper title for the president, Madison was aghast at some of the suggestions. Vice-President Adams favored a regal-sounding title and was seconded by Richard Henry Lee. Madison told Jefferson of the ludicrous debate. "The projected title was—His Highness the President of the United States and Protector of Their Liberties," Madison reported with a grimace. "Had the project succeeded it would have subjected the president to a severe dilemma and given a deep wound to our infant government."[13] Before the foolishness proceeded too far, Madison helped squelch the Adams-inspired title. "I am not afraid of titles because I fear the danger of any power they could confer, but I am against them because they are not very reconcilable with the nature of our government, or the genius of the people." When Madison was appointed head of the House committee sent to confer with its Senate counterpart, a strong signal went to the upper chamber, and the final form—"the President of the United States"—rang with Republican simplicity. Madison was relieved.

During each day's debate Madison took notes and busied himself with preparing legislation that would place the bill of rights proposal on the House calendar. He had hoped to bring up the matter on May 25, but a postponement was agreed upon so that the revenue bill could move with dispatch. The exact form the amendments ought to take was still not clear to Madison—he wavered between changes in the original Constitution and setting the amendments apart to stand by themselves. "On Monday sevennight it will certainly come forward," he promised Jefferson (whose support for such a proposition was well known). "A bill of rights, incorporated perhaps into the Constitution will be proposed, with a few other alterations most called for by the opponents of the Government and least objectionable to its friends," Madison added.[14] Here was testimony from the horse's mouth—if the Antifederalists had been less insistent during the ratification fight Madison would not have been obligated to keep pace with the people's desires.

Madison had learned at Philadelphia that he could not always have his way. Though he had suffered when the small states forced an equality in the Senate, Madison had learned the value of compromise. In 1788 he saw what was required to achieve ratification and was now prepared to keep his campaign promise, despite strong hints from a coterie that insisted the House had far more important business than making good on an electioneering pledge. William Jackson of Georgia took a nautical tack. "Our constitution, sir, is like a vessel just launched, and lying at the wharf. . . . Let us, gentlemen, fit our vessel, set up her masts, and expand her sails, and be guided by the experiment in our alterations."[15] Roger Sherman had "strong objections to being interrupted in completing the more important business" before the House "because I am well satisfied it will alarm the fears of twenty of our constituents where it will please one." William L. Smith of South Carolina told Madison "he had done his duty: he had supported his motion with ability and candor, and if he did not succeed, he was not to blame." In short, a considerable number of Madison's colleagues thought that the Virginian had done what he had promised to do, filled his campaign promised, and now it was time to let the matter drop.

None of the congressmen who had served with Madison in the old Continental Congress harbored such notions, for time and again Madison had displayed a tenacity that evoked both their anger and their admiration. John Vining of Delaware had moved into the old Congress in 1784 when Madison took his leave, and had not yet taken Madison's measure. "The wheels of the national machine cannot turn, until the impost and collection bill are perfected," Vining said, "these are the desiderata which the public mind is anxiously expecting. . . . For my part, I do not see the expediency of proposing amendments . . . the most likely way to quiet the perturbation of the public mind, will be to pass salutary laws."[16]

Despite such discouragement and the implied criticism of his motives, Madison realized that for many congressmen there would never be a satisfactory time to introduce a bill of rights. In the ratifying conventions the same apathy had prevailed as Federalists then denigrated the idea and now cited the overwhelming ratification votes in their own state conventions as evidence that the people were not excited about the lack of a bill of rights. To them Madison said, in effect, "Sorry, but further delay is hardly better than a broken pledge." He asked the House to help him keep a promise and at the same time prove that Federalists were trustworthy.

Whether Madison was bothered by the short memories of some of his colleagues is not recorded, but what is clear is that in his speech delivered on June 8 Madison threw out some reminders. A justification for moving forward on a bill of rights, Madison pointed out, was the impact of the effort: "To prove fed[eralis]ts. friends of liberty."[17] In a sense, this brief statement encapsulated the whole of Madison's argument.

If the Federalists could not show that they were as committed to liberty as the Antifederalists, then they were not going to have power for long, or know how to deal with it while they held it. When Madison began speaking and other congressmen appeared impatient, Madison said he believed the bill of rights matter could not be postponed any further. Further delays might "occasion suspicions, which, though not well founded, may tend to inflame or prejudice the public mind, against our decisions: they may think we are not sincere in our desire to incorporate such amendments in the constitution as will secure those rights, which they consider as not sufficiently guarded." If some good citizens thought a bill of rights necessary, "it is certainly proper to consider the subject, in order to quiet that anxiety which prevails in the public mind. . . . I hold it to be my duty to unfold my ideas, and explain myself to the house in some form or other without delay."[18]

Never one to browbeat the opposition, Madison explained that he only wanted to move things along. As other speakers hinted that Madison was becoming an obstructionist, Madison denied their implications. "I am sorry to be accessory to the loss of a single moment of time by the house," he said, and he then moved that a select committee be chosen to make a report on a proposed bill of rights. If only the House would devote a single day to debate on the subject, Madison said, it would have "a salutary influence" because the fact would be reported in the newspapers. Further, this would prove the friendly disposition of those who had been Federalists in 1788 by showing "that they were as sincerely devoted to liberty and a republican government" as those who charged them with wishing the adoption of this constitution in order to lay the foundation of an aristocracy or despotism.

Madison then covered the history of ratification and reminded his fellow representatives that two states still had not ratified the Constitution. By approving amendments that would embody a bill of rights, Madison suggested, recalcitrants in North Carolina and Rhode Island could not hold out much longer. Respectable citizens had objected to the Constitution because of the dangers they perceived in the newly created presidency, or because the Senate had judicial powers in some cases; still, Madison said, the best argument for acting now was "that the great mass of the people" who opposed the Constitution "disliked it because it did not contain effectual provision against encroachment on particular rights . . . nor ought we to consider them safe, while a great number of our fellow citizens think these securities necessary."

Then Madison unveiled his proposals, nine in number and the skeleton for what became the twelve amendments that would emerge from the several committees and House-Senate conferences. Indeed, Madison's proposals included all the safeguards he had gleaned from his catalog of the ratifying conventions' proposals, plus a change in determining the size of congressional districts, a restriction on the salaries congressmen could vote themselves, and several abstract ideas on republicanism (lifted almost verbatim from the Virginia Declaration of Rights). There was also a suggestion that a new Article VIII be inserted in the original Constitution explicitly stating that each of the three branches of government was limited, and could not exercise a power reserved in the Constitution for another branch. No doubt Madison thought, at the time, that all these changes could be incorporated into the Constitution without difficulty, and probably considered as part of the original document, since the experimental government was barely moving anyway. This would have been the easy way, but as Madison soon learned, Congress consisted of two houses. Neither branch of Congress seemed to prefer easy solutions or quick ones.

Nowadays it is difficult to think of a speaker holding his audience's attention for several hours, but in Madison's time a speech consuming the better part of a four or five-hour workday was not a great rarity. Madison's speech of June 8, 1789, took the better part of a day; even so, one suspects few of his colleagues left the Congress Hall for more than a brief interlude. Already there was public recognition that Madison was a leading member of the House, with his speeches reported in the *Gazette of the United States* and then reprinted up and down the Atlantic coast with increasing frequency. Alongside Washington, Franklin, and Jefferson, he was becoming one of the authentic public figures whose views were not only sought out but known to carry influence with thinking citizens who had learned to respect his judgment during the summer of 1787, if not earlier. Thus when Madison said that many of his suggested amendments amounted to "what may be called a bill of rights," a sigh of relief swept through the ranks of lukewarm Federalists who had shared doubts with Antifederalists concerning such matters as freedom of religion or the right of petition.

> The people of many states, have thought it necessary to raise barriers against power in all forms and departments of government, and I am inclined to believe, if once bills of rights are established in all the states as well as the federal constitution, we shall find that altho' some of them are rather unimportant, yet, upon the whole, they will have a salutary tendency.

When wiseacres had pointed out that bills of rights simply amounted to "parchment barriers," Madison had been listening. Now Madison told the House there was a power in a bill of rights beyond the regular scope of laws. "It may be thought all paper barriers against the power of the community, are too weak to be worthy of attention," he said. "I am sensible they are not so strong as to satisfy gentlemen of every description . . . yet, as they have a tendency to impress some degree of respect of them, to establish the public opinion in their favor, and rouse the attention of the whole community, it may be one mean[s] to controul the majority from those acts to which they might be otherwise inclined."[19] He had seen the overbearing Anglicans in action before the Revolution, when they were a majority, and not a pretty one, when it came to pushing the Baptists around Orange County. Madison talked in abstract terms, but he and his audience knew the specific situations he could cite to back his argument.

Madison's critics had already pointed out that many states had a bill of rights, and since the states were the agencies operating directly on people's lives, a federal list of civil rights was, to these naysayers, unnecessary. However, Madison observed, not all states had such protective covers, and "there are others provided with very defective ones, and there are [still] others whose bills of rights are not only defective, but absolutely improper; instead of securing some [rights] in the full extent which republican principles would require, they limit them too much to agree with the common ideas of liberty." Madison realized that states played a major role in protecting a citizen's rights, and that was the reason for his insertion of a proposed amendment: "No state shall violate the equal rights of conscience, or the freedom of the press, or the trial by jury in criminal cases."[20] Clearly the men listening to Madison realized that the bill of rights he was offering was more a beacon light than a set of ordinances—the states would provide the real testing ground for a citizen's personal rights.

Beaconlight or not, Madison also perceived a bill of rights as an instrument that the courts could use to hold republican principles aloft. Freely admitting that some state governments had violated their own bills of rights in the name of expediency, Madison pointed out that lapses by some states did not destroy their efficacy. "If they are incorporated into the constitution, independent tribunals of justice will consider themselves in a peculiar manner the guardians of those rights; they will be an impenetrable barrier against every assumption of power in the legislative or executive [branch]; they will be naturally led to resist every encroachment upon rights expressly stipulated for in the constitution by a declaration of rights."[21]

The hour was late when Madison finished, so the House adjourned and the congressmen betook themselves to their boarding houses and dining halls for refreshment. Madison had set them to thinking, however; no longer was there any question of whether the campaign promise was to be an unredeemed pledge. Madison's amendments were, a Massachusetts colleague admitted, "the fruit of much labor and research"; and a friend in Philadelphia praised the introduction of the subject as a kind of masterstroke that neither Federalists nor their adversaries could fault. "In short the most ardent & irritable among our friends are well pleased with them," he observed, and perhaps the most salutary effect was "that the proposed amendments will greatly tend to promote harmony among the late contending parties and a general confidence in the patriotism of Congress."[22]

As Madison might have foreseen, praise from within his own state delegation was neither universal nor deafening. Senator William Grayson reported to Patrick Henry in a surly mood. Madison's amendments, Grayson wrote, failed to strike at the chief weaknesses in the Constitution and were simply a ploy intended "to break the spirit of the Antifederalist party by divisions. . . . In this system however of *divide & impera*, they are opposed by a very heavy column, from the little States, who being in possession of rights they had no pretensions to in justice, are afraid of touching a subject which may bring into investigation or controversy their fortunate situation."[23] From Williamsburg, Madison heard that his proposals had the support of Federalists there, while in Richmond they were hailed "as an anodyne to the discontented." The only amendments the malcontents really sought, Edmund Randolph assured him, were not "a soporific draught to the restless" but stronger measures. "Nothing, nay not even the abolishment of direct taxation would satisfy those, who are most clamorous."[24]

If Madison seemed self-assured as he figured out a way to guide the bill of rights proposals through a select committee, he confessed to his father that he sometimes had to rein in his enthusiasm. "The business goes on still very slowly," he confessed to his father. "We are in a wilderness without a single footstep to guide us. It is consequently necessary to explore the way with great labor and caution. Those who may follow will have an easier task."[25] The knowledge that he was blazing a legislative trail may have given Madison that extra impetus he needed, for in addition to his congressional chores and long hours at the writing desk Madison decided he needed to revise the notes he had taken at the Federal Convention. The official journal had been placed in Washington's hands for safekeeping. Now Madison sought Washington's permission to check his notes against the official record of proposals and votes so that he could harmonize his unofficial account with that kept by the official secretary, Major William Jackson. Washington consented. As it turned out, Madison was as accurate as Jackson in keeping the tabulations but, unfortunately, Madison sometimes trusted Jackson's sloppy account more than his own. When nothing better occupied his time, Madison worked through the journal and at a later time made changes in the interests of accuracy. Then he turned the journal back to Washington; but he began to realize that his notes were not only a better account of what went on than the official version but also a valuable piece of property in their own right. For the time he shared his secret only with Washington and Jefferson.

Besides his daily House business, Madison performed a dozen little chores from his New York base. Friends and family in Virginia expected him to settle bills of exchange, order seeds, sell tobacco and wheat, send newspapers, and be on the lookout for bargains as he threaded his way along the wharves where the world's wares were on display. If he attended Washington's weekly levees, the visits were short and lacking in ceremony. The president's tendency to indulge in these small parties broke the tedium of early summer heat, and when the pretty wife of Senator William Bingham was around the gentlemen present (including Washington, who knew a lovely dimple when he spotted one) seemed to sparkle. But Madison had little taste for sweet cakes and if he dipped snuff in large pinches we are left with no record of such an indulgence. His main delight was in reading his mail, and particularly so when a letter from Jefferson was in the stack. Jefferson was still in Paris, but anxious to return to America, and he delighted in the intimate reports sent from New York by Madison.

Madison's account of John Adams's role in the business of selecting a proper title for the president had been particularly amusing. Jefferson's comment on the senatorial reaction to the various suggestions must have brought a smile to Madison as he read: "The president's title as proposed by the Senate was the most superlatively ridiculous thing I ever heard of," Jefferson wrote. Vice-President Adams's role in the foolishness, he added, reminded him that Benjamin Franklin had characterized Adams as "always an honest man often a great one but sometimes absolutely mad."[26]

Earnest republicans sniggered at Adams's inflated sense of dignity, but there was meatier stuff for the gossip mills. Some of the rumors involved Madison's motives in pushing for a heavier tax on British goods, and thus they may have been invented to tarnish Madison's growing reputation. According to one rumor, Madison had favored higher duties on British imports to curry favor with the French, who reveled in anything that might harm English competitiveness in trade. Senator William Maclay, the suspicious Pennsylvanian who kept a revealing diary, wondered if Madison was "guilty of another charge—viz., his urging the doctrine of taking away the right of removals of officers from the Senate in order to pay his court to the President, whom, I am told, he already affects to govern."[27] For his part, Madison had no reason to apologize for his anti-British tariff plans; and insofar as the president had a right to remove his appointees to office, Madison saw no flaw in that position even though it touched off sharp debate and drew howls of protest from senators with a different viewpoint. In general, people like Senator Maclay did not know what to make of Madison. Toward the end of the session the testy Pennsylvanian decided that Madison and House clerk John Beckley simply dominated the Virginia delegation, and let it go at that.

Then as now, Sunday mornings on Manhattan were calm. At his

boardinghouse, Madison probably fortified himself with a good breakfast before he started a full day of letter writing and reading. If the weather allowed he might have ridden in the woods beyond Murray Hill. On these excursions Madison may have noted a slight change in the scenery— before the war he saw little difference between the countryside north and south; but little more than a decade later he observed that the northern farms looked a bit more prosperous, the fences in better repair, and the cattle somewhat sleeker. Stubbornly he refused to concede that the northern climate was better than they knew at home. What made the difference? Could it be slavery? The thought must have crossed his mind as his horse clopped his way back to Maiden Lane. There were several churches nearby, but Madison avoided them and turned instead to his full supply of quills and inkpots to occupy the remainder of his Sabbath.

Romance was out of the question. Seven years earlier, Madison had been smitten with the charms of a fifteen-year-old New York lass, Kitty Floyd, the winsome daughter of a fellow delegate to the Continental Congress. In short order smiles and furtive glances had led to an informal arrangement that seemed destined for more serious planning. Madison was then thirty-one, and something of a catch; but Kitty Floyd had a mind of her own and found the charms of another teenager (who was studying medicine in Philadelphia) more to her liking. The romance was brief and, for Madison, painful. Kitty Floyd broke off their relationship, such as it was, with "a profession of indifference" that wounded Madison more than he cared to admit. Learning of the misadventure, as Jefferson termed it, Madison's dear friend reminded him that "should it be final . . . the world still presents the same and many other resources of happiness."[28] That closed the chapter on Miss Floyd and, for a long time, it was assumed that Madison spent most of his Sundays at the writing desk because he was turning into a confirmed bachelor. After all, he was approaching forty.

Not that the temporary capital lacked for young men from Virginia who did what young congressmen were supposed to do. William Branch Giles, who soon became an apostle at Madison's republican table, took his seat in the House and outdid himself at one of President Washington's dinner parties. "Canvas-back ducks, ham and chickens, old Madeira, the glories of the Ancient Dominion, all fine, were his constant theme," a fellow guest reported. "Boasted of personal prowess . . . wine or cherry bounce from twelve o'clock to night every day. He seemed to practice on this principle, too, as often as the bottle passed him."[29] Giles was everything Madison was not—boastful, talkative, inclined to drink too much, and easily led into betraying his craving for power. Madison, on the other hand, was excessively shy in public. The Kitty Floyd business had left its scars. So he avoided the social encounters when possible, fortified himself with pen and paper rather than wine, and spent hours relaying news from New York to his family, to his friends, and to Jefferson in particular.

There was some good news, too, for Jefferson had decided to return to America. His request for a leave of absence had been granted, and while Madison concentrated on the legislative business piled on his desk he was consoled by the thought that his old friend was coming home to Monticello. As the House quarreled about the site of a permanent capital Madison must have wished that Jefferson would hurry home to give him some practical advice. Devious deals were being hatched in the corridors of the Congress, as the haughty New Yorkers bargained for some kind of arrangement that would place the capital close to the Hudson. The only river suitable for the capital had to be the Potomac, Madison reasoned, and nothing would ruin the new republic more quickly than some kind of shady trading of votes that would fix the national capital close to the moneychangers in Philadelphia or New York.

Thus while Jefferson was turning over in his mind the apt phrase, "the earth belongs to the living," Madison was sparring with the Yankees and their New York allies who ridiculed the notion of a capital on the banks of the Potomac. Among other flaws in the proposed southern site, the Massachusetts delegates avowed, there was the distinct unhealthiness of the place in summertime. Manhattan or some territory adjacent to the Susquehanna was said to be far healthier. Not so, said Madison.

> If we regard their comparative situation, westwardly, the spot on the Potowmack is almost as much farther to the west, as it is distant from the proposed spot on the Susquehanna; and he well knew that generally speaking, as we retire towards the western and upper country, we are generally removed from the causes of those diseases to which southern situations are exposed.

As for a capital on Manhattan, Madison said, "there is a difference of [no] more than a degree and five or six minutes between the latitude of New-York and the place proposed on the Powtomack."[30] Most of the northern delegates were not impressed.

All the sectional jealousies Madison had witnessed in the old Continental Congress and at the Federal Convention were aroused by the capital site debate. Meanwhile, the House hammered on his proposed bill of rights until it began to take a new shape. The idea of incorporating the provisions into the original Constitution was dropped as the committee settled on seventeen articles of amendment that included all of Madison's favorites (including the ban on state interference with personal rights, which was the fourteenth proposal). Sent to the Senate for prompt action, the committee report was ridiculed by Senator Pierce Butler as mere "milk-and-water amendments," and Ralph Izard, the other senator from South Carolina, moved to postpone them until the next session, which would have killed the whole thing. Not until September 2 did the Senate begin talking about the House version, and by whittling here and there the Senate managed to reduce the amendments to twelve. Madison, serving on the conference committee chosen to iron out differences, saw his pet article (making states as responsible as the federal government in protecting a citizen's rights) fall to the cutting room floor. Imbued with a sense of mission and determined that something resembling a bill of rights survive, Madison swallowed hard. He took the final twelve amendments as a better solution that the alternative: bringing the whole matter up again next year, then fighting over the old ground. The twelve amendments that came out of the committee included all of the basic articles Madison had submitted in June plus two dealing with apportionment of legislators and pay for congressmen. The last two had nothing to do with personal freedom, of course, and they eventually fell by the wayside in the amending process. For the time, Madison was simply relieved that on September 25, 1789, a proposition was ready for joint approval and the president's blessing. Not everything he wanted was in the bill-of-rights package Congress finally approved, but Madison understood how far his colleagues could be pushed. Besides, he had kept his promise.

In the last flurry of bills and postponements before Congress adjourned for the harvest Madison worked with the other Virginians to solidify their position on a permanent national capital. This was the one issue on which even Senators Lee and Grayson found themselves in Madison's company, and they had much better connections in the key state of Pennsylvania. While there was some talk in both houses about alternative sites at Germantown or on the Susquehanna, the real choice lay between New York and a location somewhere in the tidal basin of the Potomac. The New England delegates apparently reneged on a deal to vote for a Delaware River location, angering a host of Pennsylvanians in the process. While Madison was still badgering votes for his bill of rights the Pennsylvanians caucused to discuss a compromise with the Virginians. Representative Thomas Scott told Senator Maclay "if any agreement was made it must be with the Virginians," and "Virginia's terms seem to be, 'Give us the permanent resident, and we will give Philadelphia the temporary resident' for a decade."[31]

Sectional differences between the North and the South, as Madison admitted in 1787, were a political fact of life that a public man had to face. Madison acknowledged the problem at the Federal Convention. Then he warned: "The great danger to our general government is the great southern and northern interests of the continent, opposed to each other. Look to the votes in congress, and most of them stand divided by the geography of the country, not according to the size of the states."[32] A few days later, he told the delegates that "the great division of interest in the U. States . . . lay between the Northern and Southern [states]."[33] The tug of war now going on in Congress confirmed Madison's diagnosis. He had been calling a spade a spade, and a black spade at that, for the northern delegates seemed to think that their lack of the taint of slavery somehow left them in a morally superior position.

At this stage in his life, Madison was unwilling to become an apologist for slavery. In fact, what appears to have started as a boarding-house conversation on the subject led Madison to make his first stab at the problem, a memorandum setting forth in positive terms the establishment of a black settlement in Africa based on the eventual abolition of slavery in America "by degrees both [of] the humanity & policy."[34] Madison's undigested ideas at that time centered on an African sanctuary:

> [I]t may be remarked as one motive to the benevolent experiment that if such an asylum was provided, it might prove a great encouragement to manumission in the southern parts of the U.S. and even afford the best hope yet presented of putting an end to the slavery in which not less than 600,000 unhappy negroes are now involved.[35]

Earlier in this first session of Congress, Madison alluded to the sensitive issue when, during a debate on the import duties on slaves, he flatly said "that by expressing a national disapprobation of this trade, we may destroy it, and save ourselves from reproaches, and our posterity [from] the imbecility ever attendant on a country filled with slaves."[36]

When Madison seemed about to denounce slavery as a cancer in the nation's body politic requiring drastic surgery, he was called up short by fellow Southerners. Raised eyebrows in the South Carolina and Georgia delegations, as well as among his Virginia colleagues, forced Madison to tread softly. Like most of his southern friends who detested slavery in the abstract but enjoyed the fruits of slave labor in their own backyards, Madison was reluctant to do battle on the slavery issue. Besides, that 1808 ban on slave trade, written into the Constitution, promised a healthy change within two decades. If a citizen wanted to believe that the slavery problem would melt away in another decade or so, all they had to do was point to the Constitution and its shimmering "1808 clause" that implied all kinds of restrictions on the abominable human traffic. It remained a secret whether Madison believed that the clause represented some kind of indelible pledge or simply was one way of avoiding a frightening problem.

Beyond doubt, however, was Madison's joy upon learning that his friend Jefferson was headed for home, and might even be in Virginia at the same time as Madison. In mid-October Madison began packing his linen and his books for the trip homeward, buoyed by the Senate's confirmation of the nomination by Washington of Jefferson as the first secretary of state. State department business suffered little from several months of inaction, for the young republic's problems were mostly internal.

Jefferson learned of his appointment on his arrival home. He was not at all eager for the key cabinet post, so some arm-twisting was needed (for one thing, Madison was unaware of Jefferson's flirtation with pretty Maria Cosway). "It is of infinite importance that you should not disappoint the public wish on this subject," Madison argued. "Let me particularly intreat you not to yield hastily to objections. The President is anxious for your acceptance of the trust." Madison stressed the sectional interests involved. "The Southern and Western Country have it particularly at heart. To every other part of the Union, it will be sincerely acceptable."[37] Madison wanted Jefferson to waive all his objections because he needed a trusted ally in the new administration. He sensed a growing division in Congress where some men were showing more interest in their personal fortunes than in the future of the republic. He headed for Virginia, with the air full of uncertainties.

CHAPTER FOUR

BACK HOME IN THE PIEDMONT

By the time Madison reached Orange County the first frosts had struck, making the piedmont alive with the red-gold maple and oak leaves. There was no word at Montpelier of Jefferson's pending arrival. Reunited with his family, Madison heard an account of how parents, sisters, brothers, and cousins had fared despite the usual bodily complaints. For the young ladies he carried a bundle of bonnets, ribbons, and laces customarily bestowed on the women folks after a trip to Philadelphia or New York.

Dozens of Orange County residents had moved west in recent years, and word from Kentucky was passing from hearth to hearth as the first bite of winter settled on the shingled rooftops. From George Nicholas, a leading Virginia expatriate in Kentucky, Madison soon learned that a movement to seek statehood for Virginia's transmontane counties was afoot. Meanwhile, Spain played cat-and-mouse with these erstwhile Virginians by paying high prices for tobacco at one moment and threatening to close the Mississippi to all American commerce in the next. Madison listened intently to the grievances over Indian problems, too, for the Kentuckians tended to believe the Easterners were indifferent to their frontier jitters. Let the older states, Nicholas warned, "take such steps as will convince the Indians that the Americans are one people, that they shall never attack any of them with impunity, and that in future their real wants will be supplied in time of peace: this is all we ask."[1] Madison made a mental note of Nicholas's plea and checked the mails to see if anything had come up from Monticello.

While awaiting Jefferson's return, Madison mended a few political fences. As the state legislature convened in Richmond he signaled the forthcoming battle over a national capital site. He dropped a heavy hint to Henry Lee, the legendary "Light-horse Harry" who was serving in the House of Delegates, suggesting that a Susquehanna locale might be "the least of the evils from which a choice must be made."[2] "I have resisted every idea of compromise, and shall continue to do so," Madison promised. Lee took the bait and drafted a bill ceding to the United States a ten-square-mile area, the gift to be contingent upon a choice of a Potomac capital site.[3] Neither Lee nor Madison foresaw the desperate struggle taking shape, so they thought in terms of conventional political swapping that was akin to a horse-trade on market day. Senator William Grayson wrote Madison after talking with the Pennsylvanians while en route to Virginia. Most of them thought "the Potomack a marvelous proper place," Grayson reported. "Our great danger is in stirring the subject, & fright[e]ning the Yankees into measures (which if left to themselves) they abhor."[4]

When Madison reached home he admitted to great fatigue and he was still queasy from the "bilious fever" which had detained him in Philadelphia and kept him in bed for some days. Before heading home a letter had arrived from Hamilton, asking Madison to "send me your thoughts on such objects as may have occurred to you for an addition to our revenue, and also as to any modifications of the public debt which could be made consistent with good faith [in] the interest of the Public and of its Creditors?"[5] Madison had carried the letter to Virginia and carefully worded his reply to the secretary of the treasury. Speaking frankly in his private letter, Madison told Hamilton that a tax on whiskey and a land levy offered the most revenue for the least trouble; then as an afterthought he tacked on the suggestion that "A stamp tax on the proceedings of federal courts" might help bolster the bare treasury coffers. The expression "stamp tax" had so many negative connotations Madison hastened to add that he did not mean "a General Stamp tax, because with some it would be obnoxious to prejudices not yet worne out" and a variety of local circumstances "would make it a fresh topic for clamor."[6]

Although he recognized that "the public debt is a subject on which I ought perhaps to be silent," Madison offered Hamilton some advice. He hoped some means could be found to place the public securities now in foreign hands on a "most satisfactory footing," that is, "turned into a debt bearing a reduced interest." The loan certificates and other public indebtedness (indents, impressment script, and military notes held by Americans) posed more difficulty. "It might be a soothing circumstance to those least favorably disposed, if by some operation the debt could be lessened by purchases made on public account; and particularly if any impression could be made on it by means of the Western lands," Madison counseled.

Madison still was dreaming of a fairly easy solution to the debt problem—all those millions of acres in the public domain might somehow be sold to settlers with the income used to cut down that mountain of public securities. This was a pipe dream Madison shared with many public men who hoped the millions of acres ceded to the national government by the states during the Revolution might turn into a treasure trove in two ways: provide cheap land for restless folks who loved the lure of the wilderness, and extract from settlers a dollar or so an acre for a comfortably sized farm. Madison admitted his vision of a western land bonanza might be overrated, but at least a trickle of money from land sales was better than nothing.

Then Madison struck at the notion that a national debt ought to be considered a fixed, permanent part of the nation's financial structure. This was a British idea which Madison considered as a blight, not something to be nurtured as Hamilton seemed to believe. He told Hamilton that provisions should be made to place "the debt in a manifest course of extinguishment." Madison said he knew respectable men who were "in favor of prolonging if not perpetuating it" (he probably had Hamilton in that class); but an essential part of Madison's republicanism was his commitment to pay-as-you-go government. Taxes collected to pay interest on the public debt, in Madison's view, were peculiarly disliked by Americans. Another reason for Madison's antipathy was that United States bonds would "slide into the hands of foreigners" once it was clear that the interest was to be paid regularly. Hamilton and Madison both knew that the recent loans from Dutch bankers reinforced this point, but the Virginian did not mention any country by name. "As they [foreigners] have more money than Americans, and less productive ways of laying it out, they can and will pretty generally buy out the Americans."[7]

Although Hamilton's immediate reaction to Madison's assessment of the debt situation is not known, he could not have been overjoyed. The treasury secretary was almost Madison's direct opposite in many ways. Hamilton loved the ladies—all the ladies—while Madison was so shy he seemed doomed to bachelorhood. Hamilton took the company of Manhattan bankers and fellow lawyers in stride or converted them into admirers, while Madison kept to his quarters and attended only enough social affairs to avoid the nametag of a recluse. Here on the vital matter of coping with a multimillion dollar national debt, Hamilton's effort to imitate the Bank of England's debt management was 180 degrees away from Madison's disdain for British institutions. At heart, Hamilton was the city man-of-business; Madison was the planter's son with a farmer's fear of debt. On matters of political theory, both men took a more jaundiced view of their fellow men than a Tom Paine or a Jefferson, but that did not give them a bond of permanent friendship. Although their polite nods and occasional evening suppers continued for a while, it was no secret that the two erstwhile collaborators on the Publius papers found their friendship growing more and more strained.

Meanwhile, Jefferson was back in America. He soon learned that while he was on the high seas Washington's nomination for secretary of state had rushed through the Senate process in a single day. Landing at Norfolk on November 23, 1789, Jefferson had found he was something of a celebrity. Social duties, family business, and an attitude toward the pace of life which we can now neither understand nor imitate detained Jefferson for weeks. He finally brought his family back to Monticello, after a five-year absence, on the day before Christmas Eve. This was welcome news for Madison, who was under pressure to return to New York for the next session of Congress, but he welcomed the delay and soon was on the road toward Monticello. The warmth of the greetings and the firm grasp of Jefferson's handshake must have come amidst a scene of pleasant pandemonium.

Once the conversational level became calm, Madison talked with Jefferson about Washington's proffered cabinet post. At first, Jefferson's reaction was to turn the job down. Then Madison explained what had been going on in the new government and stressed the importance of able men in office during their critical juncture in the life of the Republic. "His difficulties seemed to result cheifly from what I take to be an erroneous view of the kind and quantity of business annexed to that which constituted the foreign department," Madison explained to Washington a few days later.[8] Congress had added some responsibilities to the office (the Patent Office, and overseeing territorial matters), it was true, but Madison thought "the domestic part will be very trifling." Then Madison told Washington what he wanted to hear. "After all," Madison added, "if the whole business can be executed by any one man, Mr. Jefferson must be equal to it." Thus the matter seemed settled; and by the time Madison finished explaining to Jefferson that the main business was foreign affairs, "which has of itself no terrors to him," the matter was settled.

People who lived their lives one day at a time were inclined to take Madison at face value. The first Congress had been more productive than anyone accustomed to the sluggish old Continental crowd could have imagined. The tariff bill had passed, a judiciary act created a national court system, and efforts to shape a bill of rights led to the twelve-amendment package sent to the states. Madison failed to prod Congress into some kind of retaliation against the British for their discriminatory trade regulations, but his accomplishments were impressive. Yet to people like Hamilton, who lived not one day at time but whose mind jumped ahead of nearly everybody's, there was something about Madison that was disturbing. Hamilton could not figure Madison out. They had been friendly and mutually respectful when preparing for the Federal Convention, and their cooperation had had solid results during the ratification struggle. Hamilton could not pin down his hunch that Madison was becoming perverse, but one element of Madison's makeup that could not be understood by a man like Hamilton was the Virginian's hostile attitude toward the British. Indeed, was Madison an Anglophobe?

Newspaper accounts of the House debates fed Hamilton's suspicions. Since the debates in the House (unlike those in the Senate) were made public through the newspapers, foreigners working in New York had easy access to what was said in that branch of Congress each day. George Beckwith, the unofficial British minister in New York, read the newspapers and was struck by Madison's stance. In a confidential conversation with Hamilton, Beckwith told the cabinet officer he was "much surprised to find amongst the gentlemen, who were so decidely hostile to us in their public conduct, the name of a man, from whose Character for good sense, and other qualifications, I should have been led to Expect a very different conduct."[9] Oh, said Hamilton,

> You mean Mr. Maddison from Virginia. I confess I was likewise rather surprized at it, as well as that the only opposition to General Washington was from thence. The truth is, that although this gentleman is a clever man, he is very little Acquainted with the world. That he is Uncorrupted and incorruptible I have not a doubt; he has the same End in view that I have, and so have those gentlemen, who Act with him, but their mode of attaining it is very different.

Hamilton was so eager to get on well with Beckwith that he overstated the case. What Hamilton meant by saying that Madison was "the only opposition to General Washington" defies interpretation. Except on the matter of pretentious titles Madison had been the chief abettor of the president's position on removal of appointees from office, on cabinet responsibility, and a Potomac site for the capital. On the other hand, Madison's resentment of British commercial regulations separated him from the men who would become leaders in the emerging Federalist party. With men of Hamilton's stripe, it took only one wrong vote to upset an old friendship. Two wrong votes, and the alienation was complete.

When Madison reached New York in January 1790 the main business facing Congress pertained to the ever-present national debt, selection of a permanent capital site, and passage of a naturalization bill. As the congressmen assembled, their anxiety was not focused on the national debt but on the choosing of a capital. Senator Maclay noticed the prevailing mood when he attended a dinner party and found most of the table conversation slanted in one direction. "I thought uncommon pains were taken to draw from me some information as to the part I would act respecting the Federal residence," Maclay noted in his diary. As the business of vote-swapping was still in its infancy, a prudent congressman proceeded cautiously as he tried to learn where the safety nets were placed. Madison missed the earliest maneuvering, for he had only reached Georgetown, Maryland, when hit by a vicious attack of dysentery. After some days in bed, he resumed the journey much the worse for lost weight; on top of his "complaint in my bowells" the suffering man felt "a slight attack of the piles." Wretched roads and indifferent inns made matters worse. When Madison finally took his seat on January 20 the House was proceeding sluggishly without much guidance. Now the chief steersman was back, and fortunately, Madison told his father, "No business of consequence has yet been done."[10]

Hamilton had been busy, however. His report on public credit was offered to Congress when Madison lay in a sick-bed. In some ways the report was a doctor's remedy for the nation's ills but too drastic for a republican who could not stomach the thought of a permanent national debt. A masterful state paper filling 165 printed pages, Hamilton's plan revealed the scope of the secretary's mind as he gathered all the loose threads of information and announced that the amorphous national debt (including the arrears in interest) actually came to $54,124,464.[11] Hamilton calculated that nearly $12 million rested in foreign vaults, the remaining $42 million were part of the "domestic debt," and interest was accumulating at the rate of nearly $2 million annually. If the states' indebtedness were added, Hamilton reported, the grand total came to about $70 million.

These were painful facts, but for the first time the country and its leaders knew what they faced. Hamilton had not simply told the truth and then stood back. He offered a plan that promised to bring some order out of the present chaos. Hamilton proposed to create a funded debt that would stabilize the nation's credit rating through the issuance of gilt-edged government securities paying interest as high as 6 percent. Hamilton's plan was thorough, but it was not a new approach. As Madison and most well-informed citizens realized, Hamilton borrowed the plan from the British, who had issued government bonds earlier in the century in consolidating their national debt. These "consols" worked an economic miracle in England, and Hamilton knew it. What had worked in England could also work in America; what Parliament had done, Congress could now do. Thus ran Hamilton's logic.

There was no gainsaying the brilliance of Hamilton's report. What bothered Madison, as soon as he had read it, was the secretary's assumption that the speculative, floating securities and the old notes (held by speculators, soldiers, farmers who had sold supplies to the army, and veterans' widows) would all have equal treatment. According to Hamilton, the debt from whatever source would be converted at par value despite their going price in the open market. In short, the plan might give speculators windfall profits by allowing them to buy up all the securities they could lay their hands on at depreciated prices.

Hamilton's report turned out to be no bombshell on Wall Street, where the trading in public paper had already begun in a modest way at coffeehouses, lawyer's offices, and places where bills of exchange were bought and sold. During the dark days in 1785, some of the certificates had changed hands for less than four shillings to the pound, but late in 1789 a rise began so that when news of Hamilton's plan was printed in newspapers the securities sold for "between 8/ and 10/ in the pound," as Madison wrote Jefferson (who was taking his time in reporting for cabinet duty).[12] Madison's fear of speculation was confirmed by other events. "Emissaries are still exploring the interior & distant parts of the Union in order to take advantage of the ignorance of holders," Madison added. Sharp swings in the prices, however, seemed to indicate "doubts were entertained concerning the plan in all its parts."

At the time, Madison had no inkling of the bitter struggle ahead. He was too much a planter, too naive in matters of finance, to think ill of Hamilton's motives. Madison owned no public securities, therefore he was a "disinterested" public man. The thought that he might buy the depreciated securities himself surely never crossed Madison's mind, and it was not Hamilton's personal honesty that bothered him. Nor could he foresee the destruction of his friendship with Hamilton over the outcome of the issue. All he could think of was the injustice of a redemption plan that short-changed the unsophisticated citizen.

Not a few of Hamilton's cronies looked upon his plan for funding the debt as akin to manna from heaven. The risks were high enough to keep the lid on moderate prices in the trading bourses of Boston, Philadelphia, and New York—but low enough to entice imprudent men into reckless commitments. A chief concern was whether Congress would swallow Hamilton's recommendation that no discrimination be recognized between recent purchasers and original owners. "There can be no doubt," Hamilton recommended, "that the rights of assignees and original holders, must be considered as equal."[13] If Hamilton's views prevailed, both the old continental debt and the debts contracted by the thirteen states would be merged into one grand national debt. If the price-tag of about $70 million seemed staggering—and Hamilton was prepared for a public outcry—he had a stifling answer: "It was the price of liberty."

Skirmish lines formed in the Congress. The first hurdle for Hamilton's program was public acceptance of the idea that the old war debt had to be converted at par value, new dollar for old dollar. If that plan failed there would be no point in pushing for a general funding of both national and state certificates. Although Hamilton insisted that "an assumption of the debts of the particular states of the union . . . will be a measure of sound policy and substantial justice," it was almost a certainty that Madison and other congressmen from states that had strained their resources since 1783 to reduce their state debt would react negatively. In Madison's view, if Virginia had gone some distance in reducing its debt while South Carolina had done virtually nothing, the bargain was too lopsided. If a congressman of Madison's stature approached Hamilton's plan with skepticism, passage of laws for implementing it appeared remote.

These subtleties were not lost on the buyers of both state and continental securities, as newspapers up and down the seaboard carried details of Hamilton's plan. Citizens with excess cash in the large cities were particularly active. Senator Maclay noted in his diary that Hamilton was "moving heaven and earth in favor of his system," and then went to hear Madison's opening remarks as the House began to consider the secretary's proposals.[14] At the outset Madison conceded that the debt was contracted by the United States to finance the Revolution and could not be dismissed. (Indeed, to men of Madison's generation that debt had taken on all the aspects of a personal burden, in which one's honor was somehow inextricably involved.) "The only point on which we can deliberate is, to whom the payment is really due?" Madison said. With notes in hand, Madison ticked off the "creditors of the union," who fell into four categories:

> First. Original creditors, who have never alienated their securities.
> Second. Original creditors, who have alienated.
> Third. Present holders of alienated securities.
> Fourth. Intermediate holders, through whose hands securities have circulated.

The first group was due their full share as "every honest citizen cannot but be their advocate."[15] But the last class deserved far less, for they "will lead us into a labyrinth, for which it is impossible to find a clue." The only real question was an equitable settlement involving the original creditors and "the present holders of the assignments." Who would get 100 cents on the dollar, the soldier first issued the certificate or a Boston banker who bought the signed-over security for a third of its face value?

A few congressmen knew that they were seeing Madison make a rare about-face. For in 1783, in his own report to the old congress on public credit, Madison had reviewed the various classes of creditors and then concluded: "To discriminate the merits of these several descriptions of creditors would be a task equally unnecessary & invidious." What caused Madison's change of heart? Hamilton, who had served with Madison at that 1783 session, eventually recorded his shock at the Virginian's change of heart. Madison's own explanation was brief: "Until indeed the subject came close into view & the sacrifice of the soldiers was brought home to reflection, he had not sufficiently scanned and felt the magnitude of the evil."[16] Perhaps Madison had second thoughts because in 1783 the debt certificates had been far more broadly held. In the intervening years securities worth millions of dollars had gravitated into the hands of speculators; moreover, they were mostly moneyed men who lived above the Mason-Dixon line.

Almost as he spoke, speculators started forcing prices for the depreciated certificates upward. It was notorious, Senator Maclay observed, that their plan was "to raise the certificates to par; [and] thus the speculators, who now have them nearly all engrossed, will clear above three hundred per cent."[17] Maclay thought Hamilton's idea was "to lay as much on the people as they can bear," but Madison's plan to discriminate between original and present holders "yields no relief as to the burden" and only "affords some alleviation as to the design the tax will be laid for." Either way, the Pennsylvanian reasoned, posterity was the ultimate loser.

The same thought crossed Madison's mind. "Having never been a proselyte to the doctrine, that public debts are public benefits," Madison said, "I consider them, on the contrary, as evils which ought to be removed as fast as honor and justice will permit."[18] If only those millions of acres of western lands could be utilized! Madison apparently clung to the hope that those vast tracts over the Appalachian mountains might somehow provide a means of avoiding the alternative of taxes laid on the next generation and the specter of a permanent national debt. Jefferson was en route to New York. Surely he would have some useful ideas, for he had recently written Madison a letter proclaiming "the earth belongs to the living." What larger millstone could be devised than the burdening of the American taxpayers with a multimillion dollar public debt?

Hamilton avoided a public attack on Madison's preference for a complex redemption plan, but his friends barely bothered to conceal their amazement. "If Mr Maddison's principles should be adopted," an associate wrote Hamilton, "what a field it would open for the intervention of Chancery powers [that is, the courts] throughout the Union."[19] Perhaps Hamilton did not worry too much about Madison's opposition to across-the-board funding because the Virginian's plan attracted so much criticism it seemed doomed the day Madison brought it forward. Several years later, when Hamilton was brimming with resentment at Madison's opposition, Hamilton recalled their exchange of letters when he had sought the Virginian's advice on the debt. "In his answer there is not a lisp of this new system," Hamilton said. "While the change of opinion avowed on the point of discrimination diminished my respect for the force of Mr. Madison's mind and the soundness of his judgment . . . yet my previous impressions of the fairness of Mr. Madison's character and my reliance on his good will towards me disposed me to believe that his suggestions were sincere."[20] In truth, the partnership that had produced *The Federalist* was crumbling faster than either man realized.

Supporters of Hamilton's plan introduced a funding bill that upon enactment would start various redemption plans for a restructured national debt. The debates created high political drama unlike anything New York had seen in decades. Verbal brickbats in the newspapers heightened the sense of conflict. Jefferson was still in Virginia, so Madison bore the brunt of the tactical planning and alignment of votes that might block Hamilton's plan. His chances seemed so slender that the debates took on a David-and-Goliath aspect. In Manhattan drawing rooms the conversation glowed with reports of debating points won or lost, until the ladies began to resent their exclusion from the galleries. Gallant Fisher Ames promised Senator Langdon's wife that he would see that she had a pass the next time he spoke; and Abigail Adams forced the issue by heading a contingent of well-connected ladies who found the hour-long speeches and two-hour replies far more exciting than a Broadway stroll.[21]

The more critics attacked Madison, the more he fought back. Four days before the House rejected his plan favoring the original holders, Madison was asked if any historical precedent existed for such a scheme. Yes, Madison said, during the reign of Queen Anne in England—1713 to be exact—debentures issued during a financial crisis depreciated until Parliament intervened to indemnify the original creditors.[22] Madison must have realized he was gaining no converts, and he undoubtedly heard rumors that express riders swarmed out of the large cities in search of hapless holders of public securities who had no idea what was taking place in Congress. Did Madison recall George Mason's warning in the summer of 1788, when they argued the meaning of the "obligation of contracts" clause in the Constitution, and Mason predicted that the depreciated paper would be redeemed at its par value "to give advantage to a few particular states in the union, and a number of rapacious speculators"?[23] Mason was not the kind of man who would let him forget it.

For a week Madison singlehandedly kept the opposition in suspense. Then on February 22, Madison's alternative plan was rejected, 36 to 13. "The proposition for compromizing the matter between original sufferers & the Stockjobbers," Madison wrote his father, "was rejected by a considerable majority, less perhaps from a denial of the justice of the measure, than a supposition of its impracticality."[24] With the congressional tide running in his direction, Hamilton asked his friends to add another $18 million to the national debt with one quick stroke in an assumption bill. The proposal was to sweep up all the old wartime state debts at their face value and reissue federal securities in their place. "The Secretary's

gladiators," as Senator Maclay called them, smelled the scent of victory
after the rejection of Madison's proposal.

The only good news reaching Madison came from Monticello, where
Jefferson had arranged for the marriage of his eldest daughter and started
packing for the trip to New York. Madison desperately needed an ally
of Jefferson's stature, for passage of the assumption bill would give an
alarming direction to the future course of the Republic. The young nation
had no fixed political parties, and with horror the leaders viewed Whigs
and Tories in England as the epitome of everything America must avoid
in politics. Yet Hamilton's financial genius was providing the grounds
for a bill of divorcement that would lead to the creation of distinctive
American parties with divergent views on finance, credit, taxation, and
foreign policy.

The republican tenets dear to farmers and planters exalted low taxes
collected by a caretaker national government, with a disappearing national
debt. This loose-jointed philosophy of government would be jeopardized
if Hamilton's funding and assumption plans gained the force of law. In
1786 Madison and Hamilton had agreed that it was the reckless state
governments that were causing the republic's ills. Now it was Hamilton's
program that was carrying the nation too far in the other direction. To
Madison, Hamilton's threat to republican principles was as grave as any
the Republic had faced.

Madison's opponents tended to regard him as a Southerner first and
an American second. This was natural enough, for Madison was the
leading member of Congress from Virginia and nothing could go forward
if Virginians dragged their feet. But in 1787 Madison had been such an
outspoken advocate of a strong national government that his actions in
1790 puzzled many of his colleagues. As Madison saw matters, however,
he was working for the common good while the men gathered around
Hamilton were either working for themselves or for local interests. Undoubtedly some of his House colleagues had bought quantities of the
depreciated securities, and there was nothing illegal about that, although
those who carried on the speculations did not advertise their dealings.[25]
Madison waded into the battle over assumption armed with his personal
integrity as his chief weapon, for nobody accused him of owing a single
depreciated certificate or of having bought any since the speculative fever
took hold. With nothing to gain personally from assumption, Madison
figured he had everything to lose unless Hamilton's plan was rejected.

The leading advocates of the assumption bill decided to move carefully. Out of doors, there were mutterings of protest from impatient congressmen who wanted the whole funding-assumption package delivered
to the president for signature. Madison realized the genius in Hamilton's
plan, conceding that if a fair way to enact it "can be accomplished, it
will do more honor to the revolution in our government than almost

any other measure." In a tone both conciliatory and careful, Madison touched on the sore point concerning those states that had tried to pay off their wartime debts and those that had done nothing. To draw the line more finely, Madison proposed a change that would give states that had worked to liquidate some of their debts credit for their efforts, calculating such credit on "the best evidence . . . that the nature of the case will permit."[26] In other words, Virginians ought not suffer for their conscientious attention to the wartime debt, and there was no need for going over the papers with a fine-tooth comb. As the debate heated up, it became clear that Madison had more support on his assumption position than in the losing fight over funding. The likelihood of a close vote began to frighten Hamilton's friends, but Madison was not too confident of his supporters, either.

What was clear to Madison was that no piece of legislation introduced since launching the new government had excited such strong feelings. His mail told him this, as he perused a letter from his old friend, Dr. Benjamin Rush. The injustice of redemption at par angered the Philadelphian, who said Hamilton's plan would discredit the American Revolution by proving that it had been fought by the "*many* for the benefit of the *few.*" Rush recalled that a French *savant*, "speaking of the name of America [as] being derived from Americus instead of Columbus, says 'it was a presage that America was to be the theater of future Acts of injustice.' " "The rejection of your motion in Congress," Rush said, tended to prove "the truth of that Observation."[27]

Madison's strategy was to keep Hamilton and his crowd guessing. Some congressmen said the amount owed to states that had tried to reduce their debt was unknown and would be for years. Yet those same critics clamored to redeem the certificates held by individuals. Were not states that had tried to treat their creditors honestly due the same treatment? Madison asked.[28] If the speculators were going to have another opportunity for windfall profits, Madison seemed to say, the few states that had worried about their wartime debts ought not be penalized in the bad bargain.

Madison's tactics kept the Federalists off guard. Fisher Ames was still an admirer of Madison's, although he grew restless as the reins of leadership passed from the Virginian's hands. Madison's presence in the House, Ames told a friend, "hangs heavy on us."

> If he is a friend, he is more troublesome than a declared foe. He is so much a Virginian; so afraid that the mob will cry out, *crucify him*; sees Patrick Henry's shade at his bedside every night; fears so much the eastern [New England] confederacy, and perhaps thinks it unpleasant to come in as an auxiliary to support another's plan; that he had kept himself wrapt up in mystery, and states new objections every day.[29]

Nothing moved forward until March 8, when Hamilton offered his ideas on how to provide the money needed to pay for the assumption of state debts. In essence, the state debts would be treated like the continental loans and all the outstanding paper would be refunded with new government bonds bearing coupons paying 4 to 6 percent interest, with payments deferred until April 1792. Except for the Massachusetts and South Carolina delegations, where they made no excuses for their poor repayment record, there was a distinct leaning toward Madison's position.

The distance between Madison and Hamilton widened when the Virginian criticized the secretary's plan as too complicated. Instead of the scheme Hamilton proposed, Madison said, there ought to be "a simple, unembarrassed system." When Ames defended Hamilton's elaborate program by comparing it to the British precedent, Madison said that America did not need British examples to guide her out of the postwar financial thicket. "He wished to simplify the debt as much as possible," and Madison added that "he wished also to shorten the duration of the debt as much as possible."[30] Madison may have perceived that his power was slipping, but he still knew how to talk as though he had the votes to shape the final bill.

One reason for Madison's confidence was that the House vote favoring assumption had been on a resolution, not on any legislation. This early vote was a mere straw in the wind, for nothing was settled (or could be) until a bill was introduced to implement Hamilton's program and a majority was convinced that the ways and means of paying for it were at hand. Primed to upset the Federalist timetable, Madison was not bluffing, for with the newly arrived representatives from North Carolina he appeared to have gained allies.

These developments caused Hamilton's friends to furrow their brows. Moreover, Madison privately continued to vent his doubts about the justice of the whole plan. That the United States could and would pay its debts was beyond doubt, but Hamilton's manner of paying them seemed to provoke a general suspicion "that there must be something wrong, radically & morally & politically wrong, in a system which transfers the reward from those who paid the most valuable of all considerations, to those who scarcely paid any consideration at all." Madison confessed to an old friend his perception "that in many instances, in more than could be prudently left to private litigation, the purchases have been viciated by fraud," with the net result creating "a miraculous shower of gold from Heaven" for the speculators.[31]

By late March Madison was convinced that the tide was moving against any effort to push the assumption measure through Congress. The signs Madison picked up reinforced his determination to halt the plan unless credit was allowed to the states for past payments. He was reassured by a correspondent, who wrote him that unless his proposal gained acceptance, "Virga. would be a great sufferer, having paid off 8 or 900,000£ of her debt."[32]

The drama took a new turn when one of the newly arrived North Carolina congressmen made a motion to postpone consideration of Hamilton's whole report. This threw the New England delegation into turmoil. Earlier, Senator Maclay chortled as the plan's supporters appeared to be making progress, with "the crew of Hamilton's galley" assembled and "all hands piped to quarters."[33] By a close vote (27–24) the House decided to take up the report, but before the day ended there was a motion to recommit the assumption resolution and it passed, 29 to 27. Madison must have voted with the 29, although no record of ayes and nays was kept. Members of the Pennsylvania delegation began to look upon themselves as the power brokers in what appeared to be an outright sectional struggle. The assumption bill in-fighting, so one onlooker reported, had "created a Southern and Eastern party that rages with some degree of virulence. The Amiable and Great Maddison [is] at the head of the former and the leader of the latter fights under cover, if any they have."[34]

Madison let others do the talking and counted heads. When the pro-Hamilton forces brought the assumption resolution forward for a vote on April 12 they were turned back, 31 to 29. Now the speculators began to sweat. Senator Maclay thought he saw Representative Sedgwick, Hamilton's loyalest-of-the-loyal, unable to hold back tears. "Clymer's color, always pale, now verged to a deadly white," while Fisher Ames "sat torpid, as if his faculties had been benumbed."[35] Madison was pleased, but guarded in his optimism. " 'Tis impossible to foretell the final destiny of the measure," he told Henry Lee. "Mass. & S. Carolina with their allies of Connecticut & N. York are too zealous to be arrested in their pursuit, unless by the force of an adverse majority." To another Virginian Madison confided: "We hoped that this vote would have been mortal to the project. It seems however that it is not yet to be abandoned."[36]

Hamilton's lieutenants in the House decided to keep the whole program in suspense until the assumption business was finally settled. Meanwhile, Jefferson reached New York at last, and took up his duties as secretary of state with a desk piled so high with work he had no time to watch the House debates. No doubt he learned of the tension from an eye witness, perhaps over a friendly glass of madeira, one of the few luxuries Madison surrendered to after the day's verbal skirmishes ended. To their mutual friend, Monroe, who was trying to make a living practicing law in Virginia, Madison reported that the New England congressmen "talk a strange language on the subject" of the national debt. Some of the Yankee representatives vowed "a determination to oppose all provision for the Public debt which does not include this, and intimate danger to the Union from a refusal to assume."[37] When debate on the matter resumed in earnest on April 20 Madison observed "that the proper order of proceeding was to provide for the debts of the United States, on the idea that the state debts would not be assumed."[38] Plain talk, which could only irritate Hamilton's friends.

Madison fired his heaviest artillery on April 22. Reckless threats of disunion if assumption failed, Madison said, were dreadful if true. But what was more to be dreaded was any precipitous action, based on a close vote where one or two changes of heart made all the difference. If the people everywhere could be polled, Madison continued, "I believe we should find four fifths of the citizens of the United States against the assumption."[39] Then Madison dwelt on the fundamental issue that was causing the realignment of political allegiances in Congress: should the public debt be regarded as a blessing or a curse? Madison knew where he stood. "If the public debt is a public evil, an assumption of the state debts will enormously increase, and, perhaps, perpetuate [that evil]."

The haggling continued, with little charity shown by the Hamilton supporters. A bold group now formed a political party, the Federalists, in everything but name. To a man, they looked to Hamilton for a program that would imitate England with everything but a king—a bank, a funding scheme, and a means of protecting home industries through legislation. In Madison's view, there was no telling what else might be up Hamilton's sleeve! The suggestion that the immense public domain should be sold, with the proceeds committed to paying off the public debt, was scoffed at by George Clymer. He said the idea that the western territories would stay in the Union was in itself "entirely romantic." Sensitive to rumblings from Kentucky and disturbed by what he regarded as irresponsible loose talk, Madison answered that Clymer's remarks "should have no sort of weight in the house."[40] Then the House voted to send Hamilton's report, minus the assumption portion, to a drafting committee. This meant that some days would pass before a bill to implement Hamilton's plan could be considered.

As it happened, Madison needed an interval, for as he left the House chambers on that day when assumption seemed pigeonholed he was not feeling well; by nightfall he was extremely ill, and for the next week Madison suffered so from an influenza attack that colleagues expressed doubts concerning his recovery. "Mr. Madison this morning was said to be dangerous," a fellow congressman noted. Nothing important happened while Madison fought to regain his strength, however, and after a miserable week in bed Madison reported to his father that he was "pretty well over it." With recovery came hopes that the business in Congress would languish enough to allow Madison "two or three holidays for the sake of exercise & recreation."[41]

Meanwhile, Jefferson held the seals of office as secretary of state. Daily conversations with Madison must have been part of his routine, but then the migraine headaches that afflicted Jefferson struck in early

May. The pain, Madison reported, "has been very severe."[42] Slowly, Jefferson recovered, but soon Washington took to his bed with a carbuncle that was so painful Madison described the president as "dangerously and almost desperately ill."[43] Only after three worrisome weeks were the three Virginians back in form, or at least well enough to exercise their horses along the pathways leading to upper Manhattan. The House committee moved more slowly than the horses, but on June 2 the funding bill was ready and glided through the House on a voice vote. Madison probably voted for it, since the bill for locating the capital was coming up and there was no point in alienating other congressmen whose help might be needed. First came a vote on the temporary location of the capital in Philadelphia, which passed handily. Whatever chances the Potomac site had were not clear when news circulated that Rhode Island had finally ratified the Constitution and sent two senators to New York by fast stages. "As R.I. is again in the Union," Madison calculated, "& will probably [be represented in] the Senate in a day or two, the Potowmac has the less to hope & the more to fear from this quarter."[44]

From his State Department desk Jefferson recognized the hiatus in the House as both the permanent location of the capital and the assumption business seemed to bring out the worst in some congressmen. Peculiar things began to happen. The Senate rejected the House resolution calling for a move to Philadelphia, and then the House voted to relocate in Baltimore instead of the city of brotherly love. Surely Jefferson was no idle spectator as the tension around his friend mounted, but the evidence of their joint reaction is scant. Long conversations must have been a daily occurrence, supplemented by notes carried between their offices or quarters by servants. Neither man was sharply critical of Hamilton at this point, probably because Hamilton stood aloof from the stock-market speculation and apparently was not tempted to make a personal fortune out of the policies he proposed. Madison was puzzled by the erratic behavior of the House in settling first on one city, then capriciously picking another, as a temporary capital. He reassured his father that these votes were only so much skirmishing. Unhappily, it looked more and more likely "that the final event will not square with the pretensions of the Potowmac, tho' in the chances to which this question is liable, it may possibly turn out otherwise."[45] Yet within less than a month Congress had moved with unaccustomed swiftness to hand Southerners their cherished site on the Potomac and an inconspicuous Madison had soft-pedaled his opposition to the assumption bill. There was only one explanation: a political bargain had been struck.

Even now, details of the so-called Compromise of 1790 are sketchy. The gist of the business was that Hamilton and Jefferson had a chance meeting on a Manhattan sidewalk. Hamilton (as Jefferson recalled) was looking "sombre, haggard, and dejected beyond description." As the two cabinet members chatted while strolling toward Washington's office, Hamilton talked of the dreadful consequences if the assumption bill failed—as it seemed likely. The New England delegates were poised to stalk out of Congress and probably straight out of the Union. Impressed by Hamilton's mental state and predictions, Jefferson arranged for a dinner meeting with Madison on the following day. The menu for their historic dinner party is lost, but before the candles were snuffed on the dining table that next evening, Jefferson had agreed to use his powers of persuasion on several congressmen from districts along the Potomac so that they might abandon their hostility toward assumption. Hamilton was to see that enough northern congressmen would switch their votes to make the Potomac site a certainty. Madison had opposed assumption so strenuously that he could not abandon the field with a dramatic turnabout, but he could discreetly maintain a grave air and not turn another finger to stop passage of the assumption bill.[46] Thus on July 9 the House beat back three efforts to place the capital on the Delaware River, on the Susquehanna River, or at Baltimore—and then voted 32 to 29 for the Potomac location. Hamilton was delighted, and for the time being so were Jefferson and Madison. For their part, they believed they had made concessions to save the Union.

With hindsight both Virginians rued that day's voting, but when the alternatives are considered, perhaps it is fair to say that the three men struck a bargain that set the new nation on a course from which it has hardly veered since 1790. By July 26 two Virginia votes (not Madison's) had switched, and the assumption amendment passed. Whatever the original goals of the Revolution, the workings in Congress that summer prepared the young republic for its plunge into the industrial revolution, setting the tone for an experiment in investment capitalism with the blessings of the government. Moreover, the precedent was set for using the instruments of government to protect investments. The outcome of the experiment in the following decade caused Madison to become somewhat embittered, and he adopted the role of a strict constructionist of the Constitution as a defense against further political errors. He came to believe that the funding and assumption bills were political blunders of the first order; but he never admitted that the alternative was too dreadful to contemplate. Wedded to a concept of political economy that envisioned the United States as a republic of, by, and for the farming population (then over 90 percent of the population), Madison found it impossible to readjust his thinking when a new era arrived, swinging the country away from policies favoring farmers and protecting commerce and industry instead. Part of Madison's disappointment stemmed from the fact that Virginia had little in the way of commerce or manufacturing; so Madison realized that in going along with the funding and assumption plans he had been party to Hamilton's scheme.

After the vote, Madison wasted no time in assessing the pluses and minuses. Assumption was now a fact, and so was the Potomac capital site. It was more in character for Madison to treat the half-victory as a matter-of-fact affair; and after all the bitter wrangling he simply reported on the eve of passage for the assumption bill that "in its present form . . . [it] will very little affect the interest of Virginia either way." So far, so good, as Jefferson told a friend, for Virginia was scheduled to receive an allotment of $3.5 million and pay that same amount "to cover her remaining domestic debt. Being therefore to recieve exactly what she is to pay, she will neither lose nor gain by the measure."[47] Within a fortnight the bill was law, bearing Washington's signature.

The remaining business of Congress took a few more weeks. Everybody was in a better mood. Madison made no special effort to hurry back to Virginia, even though the election in his district was scheduled for September 6. In company with Jefferson, Madison began a leisurely trip toward Montpelier about the end of August; and he was still in a stagecoach when his neighbors rode to the Orange, Albemarle, Culpeper, and other courthouses in the district to tell the sheriff their choice for congressman. The final tally went unrecorded but Edmund Pendleton, who had witnessed the voting at Charlottesville, succinctly reported: "Col. Madison was elected, there were only a few votes against him."[48]

Avoiding that election day was not a calculated risk on Madison's part. Since he loathed any pretense at campaigning, he was willing to have friends drop the necessary hints and let it go at that. A few well-placed letters to friends in the district's eight counties were the sum of Madison's campaign exertions. Moreover, Madison's known predilections against a few cider barrels might have embarrassed his supporters; but with the candidate absent, there was no harm in rewarding loyalty with a friendly glass or two.

With nothing to worry about in his district, Madison rode toward Mount Vernon at a deliberate pace. His conversations with Jefferson must have centered on the outcome of Jefferson's dinner party. Possibly, with the southern location of the capital so much on their minds, the importance of Hamilton's coup escaped them. The sophistries of banking, finance, and public securities really did not interest them; land prices, commodities, crop conditions, and weather mattered a great deal. The troubles of 1781–1786, which the Virginians saw as a political crisis, were viewed by Hamilton and his friends as a financial disaster. While Madison sought a political solution, Hamilton looked beyond the turbulent scenes at the Philadelphia convention to the time when the new government could restore credit, end the stagnation threatening the commercial community, and make the discredited American dollar worth 100 cents in specie.

Hamilton's willingness to take the financial structure of England as his model would eventually exacerbate his differences with Madison, who was convinced that Great Britain represented everything corrupt and unworthy of imitation. Yet both Hamilton and Madison agreed that the Union was worth preserving. On that common ground they met, knowing there were men in Congress who did not share their sense of urgency. To the likes of Fisher Ames and Theodore Sedgwick the Union was an abstraction, but the hard-dollar financial security guaranteed by the funding-assumption-capital compromise was real. The Union was preserved, the New England men had their gilt-edged securities, and the Virginians had their capital. Not until some years later would the Virginians talk of how they had been drawn into a lop-sided bargain. At the time, Madison knew what he was doing. He was trying to save the Union.

Madison, Jefferson, and Washington talked long and earnestly about the location of the capital site. By law, the president was empowered to make the final selection of the territory that would become a ten-square-mile federal district. Between the clinking of wine glasses and talk about the president's favorite topics (horseflesh, hounds, and diversified farming, in that order) they managed to cover the subject of the capital thoroughly. The temporary capital was to grace Philadelphia for a decade, but the consolation there was that the Pennsylvania metropolis was three days closer than New York and somewhat more civilized. Much could happen in ten years, so as far as the Southerners were concerned the sooner the Potomac site could be surveyed, the better for all concerned. After their Mount Vernon visit, Madison and Jefferson moved a few miles south for a stopover with George Mason. Usually gruff and given to strong views on most subjects, Mason was (according to Madison) not himself. The master of Gunston Hall approached "the subject of the federal seat . . . with a shyness not usual to him."[49] But when he loosened up, Mason recommended the area around Georgetown as the proper locale for the new capital—the Potomac was deep enough for ocean-going vessels and the village had a head start because of its active mercantile trade and commodious dwellings. "When led to mention the Eastern Branch [of the Potomac] he spoke of it as an admirable position, superior in all respects to Alexandria," Madison told Washington. As it turned out, Washington was inclined to follow Mason's advice on the matter. Before long, surveying crews appeared to drive stakes on the knolls above the willow-lined river banks, marking outlines for future avenues; and not far behind were the land speculators, already counting their paper profits. Madison resisted any temptation to invest in lands around the capital site, leaving the main speculations to such heavy plungers as Robert Morris, James Wilson, and John Nicholson. A small piece of land in upstate New York, bought in a joint venture with Monroe, proved more than enough of a gamble for his taste. He studiously avoided any attempt to profit from the Potomac selection, with Washington's own example of integrity making an easy trail to follow. None of the Virginians who were officially involved in the preliminary selection of lands had a nickel invested in the project.

At Montpelier, Madison found his father was no longer spry. Management of the plantation was proving to be a burdensome chore for the old man, as a ride around the fences and through the fields in early November proved. As the eldest son, Madison realized that the responsibility for keeping Montpelier prosperous would fall his way; and he seems to have longed for a switch from the cares of office to the problems of a planter. He had more perspective on the worries of the world from the porch at Montpelier.

As the first fires of the season crackled in the Montpelier fireplaces, Madison checked on the barns, smokehouses, plows, harnesses, timber lands, and slave quarters. Then he wrote out instructions for the overseers, black and white, with orders to keep the meadows thick with grass as long as the weather permitted, resowing "the places too thin, and attend to weeding the whole as soon as it becomes necessary." Corn and potatoes were the slaves' staple diet, so as much land as could be spared was to be planted for the blacks' rations. The chief overseer was also admonished "to treat the Negroes with all the humanity & kindness consistent with their necessary subordination and work."[50] A loom was needed when the carpenter could find the time for its construction, along with "2 good Wheelbarrows." "If there be leisure from more urgent things, 4 or five thousands shingles" were also needed.

Madison enjoyed the role of a gentleman farmer. He never complained that decisions were left to him, when his brothers nearby might have consulted with their father and moved ahead. The rides around Montpelier provided exercise in an atmosphere where pungent barnyard odors made Philadelphia drawing rooms seem a world away. In time, Madison came to realize that Montpelier was more akin to a small village than a farming operation. Pleasant as it was to visit with relatives and ramble over the hill country, another session of Congress was beckoning, which meant Madison would soon be on the road again. His final words to the overseers made it clear that if they had any doubts about the work plans, they were "to apply to my father in all cases where application would be made to myself if present." Good help was always hard to find.

Then it was time to pack the trunks and saddlebags again, and take orders from the ladies that would involve ribbon clerks or a millinery establishment. Sister Fanny wanted a piano ever so desperately, and

Squire Madison was more inclined to indulge her fancy than her tone-deaf brother.

Madison rode to Fredericksburg, took a stage there headed northward, and turned his mind from family business to affairs of state. When the roads were not muddy the trip to Philadelphia was almost pleasant. The trick was to avoid inns and roadside taverns known to harbor bedbugs and find resting places for man and horse where the food was tolerable and the hay cheap. Madison spent exactly a week on the road, reaching Philadelphia on the same day the president came into town.

Before Congress went into session Madison tried to attend to the family shopping list. Sugar was too expensive, he found, but coffee bean prices were so low Madison was inclined to await a further drop in their market.

The weather in Philadelphia was so pleasant the residents congratulated each other on the healthiness of the season, for there was no dread of that pestilential yellow fever that could sweep through the city in late summer and early autumn before the first hard frost. Even so, there were parts of the city where the combination of houseflies and feculent vapors almost made a person gag. Dr. William Thornton, who once boarded with Madison in Philadelphia, recalled that a "Temple of Cloacina" near their quarters emitted an odor "so offensive that the very Cloaths of the Individuals who visited it were tainted."[51] For all its fame as a modern city with paving, street lights, and passable drinking water Philadelphia still produced its fair share of noxious sights and smells. By the time Congress was ready to convene, brisk breezes helped dissipate the foul odors and smoke from hundreds of chimneys, so that the conversations at President Washington's levees veered away from the commonplace. For his part, Washington avoided the nuisances of the city by publishing his resolve to hold an open house weekly but return no visits "& accept no invitations to entertainment."[52]

Gossip, of course, knew no season. Madison's vote on the federal capital furnished the diplomatic corps, small as it was, with a tidbit. "Mr. Madisson has been so strongly in favor of Philadelphia," the Comte de Moustier noted, "only because he is to marry a woman who holds an annuity there."[53] As usual, the Frenchman had it all wrong, but perhaps the gossipmongers liked to pick on Madison because there was such a small prospect that he would surrender his bachelorhood. Some months earlier, Miss Mary Coxe hinted to her brother that Madison had jilted the young widow Trist.

Poor Mrs. T. I pity her for having known, & after having known, for losing such a Lover. Patriotism has certainly in this case, absorbed the lesser passion—and if this is to be the effect of it, our Sex I think are deeply interested in checking the generous principle. What a pity it is that the human breast is not large enough for both! But if *he* cannot find room for them, I am sure they will gain admittance no where else.[54]

If amused by the ladies of Philadelphia who speculated on his tenure as a bachelor, Madison left no record of his mirth. Such rumors inevitably surrounded a public man in a society where early marriages were normal, and they had dogged Madison since that unhappy affair with Kitty Floyd. Once, when he tarried in Philadelphia longer than his friends thought justified, Henry Lee had teased Madison with the speculation created by his apparent fascination with city life. "You continued a long time in Philada.," Lee wrote. "This unexpected movement gives eye to various suggestions all tending to prove that you are in full gallop to the blessed yoke."[55] Madison dodged an entangling alliance but continued to find Philadelphia—odors and all—a more pleasant city than New York. The American Philosophical Society library was expanding, the Indian Queen tavern served some of the best food he had ever tasted, and there were far more bookstores to browse in when time allowed than on Manhattan. The Philadelphia harbor was beginning to silt up, but the sea lanes from its wharves to Virginia were well-established and provided frequent, safe passage for men or mail to a port close to Montpelier.

Not that Madison had a great deal of time for books and shopping. Washington turned more and more to Madison for the kinds of drafts or advice the younger man had furnished in the halcyon days of 1789, but after February 1790 an ever-so-slight coolness crept into their relationship as Hamilton's ideas gained ground with the president. Thereafter, the president was hospitable at Mount Vernon but in the capital he was less demanding, and sought Madison's assistance less frequently when drafting messages. Increasingly, Washington called on Madison for advice only when a constitutional interpretation was needed.

Since there was no public record of what took place at the Federal Convention, there was a good deal of speculation about what had been debated before the Constitution was signed, and the precise meaning of certain phrases. Among Virginians there was only one expert witness needed. For example, Judge Edmund Pendleton was bothered by the constitutional implications involving the nagging British debt issue. Were the old prewar debts to Englishmen collectable under the Constitution, taking precedent over state statutes? Yes, Madison said, the "supreme law of the land" meant Virginians owed those debts since the 1783 peace treaty left them "in full force." Thorny as that issue was, layman Madison could act like a lawyer since he had been at the Federal Convention every day it sat. Hamilton lacked such credentials, but he was about to spring a constitutional question on Congress and he hoped Madison would be reasonable.

Indeed, Hamilton's letters to Madison still had a friendly tone as the last session of the First Congress got under way, perhaps because Madison's help was needed to fit the last peg of his financial system in place. For Hamilton there was no resting until the national government chartered a bank that would be the agent for implementing his credit system. When Hamilton broached the idea late in 1790 Madison was reserved in his first comments on the proposed Bank of the United States. To a friend in Virginia he commented with restraint. "I augur that you will not be in love with some of its features."[56] Talking with Jefferson, Madison surely let fly with his resentment of Hamilton's tactics, for the great schism that rocked Washington's cabinet was about to occur. The secretary of the treasury had triumphed with his funding and assumption bills. A parcel of wealthy men was created almost overnight, and to Madison and his friend their riches represented a kind of parasitic growth. As they reviewed events of the past summer, Madison and Jefferson came to believe that Hamilton and his friends in Congress had higher priorities than the preservation of republican government. They began to suspect they had struck a poor bargain.

If the swap on the funding and assumption bills appeared to have backfired, a real horse trade was not going well, either. Madison sold Jefferson a horse for £25, but the creature had hardly been saddled when he took sick and died. Both men were embarrassed—Jefferson listened to Madison's suggestion that a mutual friend should decide a fair settlement—but Jefferson insisted in paying for the dead horse.

> It being impossible to entertain a doubt that the horse I bought of you was fairly sold, & fairly bought, that his disorder was of the instant, & might have happened years after as well as when it did, so as to exonerate you as is justly established, from all responsibility, I should as soon think of filching the sum from your pocket, as of permitting the loss to be yours. I therefore send you a check on the bank for 95.26 Dollars.[57]

Typically, Jefferson erred on the side of his friend, sending about twelve dollars more than their agreed price. Two Virginians who could sell a sick horse and pay for a dead one without an angry word thus maintained a friendship of historic dimensions.

Madison and Jefferson needed to share their thoughts as the hard-driving Hamilton grew anxious to test his power. Once again, Hamilton looked to England for an example, this time finding the Bank of England his model. The proposed bank, in Hamilton's plan, would be chartered by Congress for twenty years and have 80 percent of its stock in public hands. Twenty of the twenty-five directorships would be held by private citizens. In effect, the Bank of the United States would be the fiscal agent for the federal government, holding its funds on deposit, collecting its taxes, and servicing the public debt. Through its central office and several branches the bank also could regulate banking practices generally, particularly in the area of paper money issued by lesser banks.

To his planter's natural suspicion of banks in general Madison added his growing anxiety over Hamilton's motives. What was the man up to, anyway? The Constitution was full of specified powers for Congress, and not one of them covered banks or banking. In unison with Jefferson, Madison concluded that it was time to nip Hamilton's grab for power (Hamilton argued that the bank was covered by the constitutional "necessary and proper" clause) by rejecting the bank bill. If this meant the end of their friendship, the break was Hamilton's fault, not his own. In this mood, Madison came on the House floor ready to swing with all his might. Hamilton feared this reaction, but he was probably not prepared for the way Madison lined up his southern colleagues against the bank bill.

Although he was so short that he sometimes had difficulty being either seen or heard, Madison knew how to hold the attention of his colleagues. When they saw a sheaf of notes clutched in his hand, heard Madison clear his throat and pick a time when the whole day lay ahead, then there was nothing to do but edge a bit closer so that Madison's thin voice could be heard. With mounds of facts at his fingertips, Madison traced the history of banking from the fifteenth-century Italian cities down to 1694, when the Bank of England raised its starting capital in ten days. Madison spoke of the advantages banks offered, along with their drawbacks, and of various charters granted, and interest rate fluctuations. No doubt banks facilitated commercial transactions, Madison conceded, by cutting down on the practice of usury while making customs payments convenient. They also helped governments by lending them money "when deficiencies or delays happen in the revenue." Balanced against these positive features, banks diminished the circulation of specie by substituting paper money for hard, exposed the public to the evils of "a run on the bank" in calamitous times, and the subscription process for bank stock (as Hamilton proposed) would be full of inequities.

Beyond these objections, Madison said, there was the matter of constitutionality. Here was the expert witness testifying, as the House well knew. Madison said that in the Federal Convention the power to grant charters had been proposed and rejected. He went over the whole issue of constitutionality, pointed to the several powers delegated to Congress, and found nothing that permitted the legislative branch to create a bank. Madison said the remark someone had made, that Congress could charter a bank under the "general welfare" clause, was a "novel doctrine" worth examining; and then he proceeded to stretch the implication, by suggesting that Congress might "establish religious teachers in every parish, and pay them out of the Treasury of the United States" if such a liberal interpretation were warranted. Or what about the "necessary and proper" clause? Again, the argument would hold no water, Madison said, since the clause "is in fact merely declaratory of what would have resulted by unavoidable implication . . . and as it were, technical means of executing those [delegated] powers."[58]

Coming to the nub of his argument, Madison said the "essential characteristic of the government, as composed of limited and enumerated powers, would be destroyed." The Constitution was full of safeguards written to limit the powers of government, and had been handed to the people on those terms. Passage of the bank bill now would mean that the adoption of the Constitution "was brought about by one set of arguments, and that it is now administered under the influence of another set; and this reproach will have the keener sting, because it is appliable to so many individuals concerned in both the adoption and the administration." In truth, Madison said, the bank bill was condemned "by the silence of the constitution."

Other congressmen who served at the Federal Convention would not let Madison's interpretation go unchallenged. They converged on Madison with suggestions that their memories were as good as his. Tough-minded Roger Sherman bore down.

> You will admit that Congress have power to provide by law for raising, depositing & applying money for the purposes enumerated in the Constitution, & generally of regulating the Finances. That they have power . . . as they may judge necessary & proper to effect these purposes. The only qustion that remains is—Is the Bank a proper measure for effecting these purposes?[59]

Madison was unconvinced. Sherman's support of the bill probably was a clue to the way the New England delegates were headed. Every vote, as in the funding battle, would be needed to stop Hamilton.

Day after day the debate dragged on, with Madison on the defensive as it became apparent to him that the Hamilton crowd intended to create more loaves and fishes for distribution to the right people in Boston, New York, Philadelphia, and Charleston. Farmers would buy no stock in the new bank, they could not afford it; but Madison could look around the House and almost name those who would be among the first stock purchasers if the bank bill passed. Almost to a man, they were northern congressmen and their banker friends.

Madison fought his rear-guard action, but his power in the House slipped away as the clock ticked. Meanwhile, the Senate rammed its version of the bank bill through, as everybody expected. The fight, if there was to be one, would come in the House. But the battle was not even close. Madison held the southern members in line, but on the final tally the bank bill won, 39 to 20. Thirty-six of the aye votes came from Northerners, nineteen of the nays were counted among Southerners. Now was the time to test the president's veto power as they had talked of it in Philadelphia. Madison accordingly turned to the planter-president from Virginia as a means of thwarting Hamilton's Anglicized banking bill.

Washington still esteemed Madison, despite whatever remarks Hamilton must have made about the Virginian's backsliding ways since the ratification struggle. Morever, the Virginia delegation's resistance to the bank bill gave Washington pause. Eager to do the right thing, Washington turned to Madison as an authority on the Constitution, and asked him to write a veto message, in case it might be needed. In preparing the draft for Washington, Madison took two roads, leaving the president free to choose the proper one as he set forth the unconstitutionality of the bank in one set of reasons, and prepared a rejection based on "the merits alone" in the other. Besides the "delegated powers" argument, Madison suggested that the president might reject the bill on its inherent unfairness, an argument he had used in the debates, for the legislation failed "to dispense . . . [the bank's] benefits to individuals with as impartial a hand as the public interest will permit."[60] Jefferson took the same line of reasoning in urging the president to reject the bill, while Hamilton insisted that the Constitution was meaningless if every specific power had to be spelled out—the "necessary and proper" clause meant exactly what it said—and surely the Congress could create institutions to carry out its will.

Washington, vexed by doubts, turned the arguments of Madison and Jefferson aside after holding "several free conversations" with both men. On February 25, 1791, Washington signed the bill. Almost at that moment, the smoldering resentment against Hamilton's program burst into flames. All the initial harmony in Washington's cabinet disappeared, with Jefferson setting his course on resignation. Madison realized that any reconciliation with the Hamilton crowd was impossible. Probably without realizing what might happen, Madison began creating a political party based on a dread of what Hamilton's ultimate purposes might be. To Madison, Hamilton had emerged as the triumphant foe of republicanism in the national government. Every good citizen must be aroused to the danger, otherwise the "monocrats" whose admiration for everything English—from fashions to finances—was manifest would drag the Republic down and make the Constitution a façade for their government of unlimited power. Washington was a bulwark against their monarchical pretensions, but once the great man was gone, who could say what their next step might be? Much as he hated the notion of "factions" in politics, Madison realized what he had to do. He would fight Hamilton, unfurl the banner of republicanism everywhere, and with Jefferson at his side, labor to dismantle the unconstitutional machinery shaped by the opposition. Working together, Madison and Jefferson would drive the moneychangers from the temple of republicanism.

CHAPTER FIVE

INVENTING
A
PARTY SYSTEM

"If I could not go to heaven but with a party, I would not go there at all."

Thomas Jefferson, 1789

"The [Federal] convention must have enjoyed, in a very singular degree, an exemption from the pestilential influence of party animosities—the diseases most incident to deliberative bodies and most apt to contaminate their proceedings."

Madison's *Federalist #37*[1]

As an eighteenth-century liberal committed to the notion that factions have been the bane of good government since ancient times, Madison had to overcome his fear of political parties before he could build one. In his classic *Federalist #10* he warned of the baneful effect of factions. "The public good is disregarded in the conflict of rival parties," Madison wrote in 1787, with an eye cocked on the recent history of England as proof of the contention. The quotations above bear testimony to the political naiveté of the men who would eventually become the founders of the Republican-Democratic party. Neither man realized that as the new order was rising in America, so the political rules applicable in Robert Walpole's England were somewhere between old-fashioned and useless. * If Hamilton's policies were to be stopped, there was only one way to bring the wily secretary of the treasury to a halt: the ballot box.

Madison feared the majority when it was on a tear, but he was at one with Jefferson in believing that majority rule had to prevail in the new Republic. Some restrictions, such as a bill of rights, would prevent overbearing majorities from losing their democratic bearings. Another check on rampant majorities was the doctrine of strict constructionism, which Madison employed early on as a resistance measure to counter Hamilton's loose interpretation of the "necessary and proper" and "general welfare" clauses. But an emerging tenet in the political philosophy of Madison and Jefferson was that the majority of the voters provided the leverage for political change. If the people were to be trusted, the majority of those people became the moving force in a community, state, or nation. A republic was, by definition, where the majority ruled.

Madison acknowledged the newness of the American experience and gradually delineated the difference between the sordid politics of Hanoverian England and the United States. The rise of the Tory and Whig parties under the several Georges saw a train of abuses that included scandalous sinecures and preferment based on political allegiance or kinship rather than merit. Americans loved to point the finger of shame at Walpole and his successors as unwholesome examples of tainted public administration in the name of party loyalty. During his days in the Continental Congress Madison discerned something different but possibly far more dangerous—factions based on geography—where votes often followed a line of demarcation otherwise known as the Mason-Dixon line. Every key issue saw the northern delegates leaning in one direction, the southern members straining in another, at a time when slavery per se was not of great concern.

During the financial crisis of the mid-1780s sectional tensions eased as Americans faced a crisis threatening the national existence. To escape from the crisis, the Federal Convention accepted the 1808 clause on slave imports and the three-fifths clause on representation, all in the name of compromise and national solvency. With the threat of bankruptcy eased, the northern members of Congress were up to their old tricks, making snide remarks about slavery one day, and investing their money in ventures dependent upon slave labor the next. There was much more to the new politics than simply the prejudice of yesteryear, however. In the name of national interest, Madison believed, the northern congressmen subscribed to Hamilton's program because it created and fostered

*In recent years American historians have heard a great deal about the Founding Fathers' division into Country and Court factions, in the terminology of eighteenth-century English politics. Rather than lead readers astray, I suggest a perusal of articles by Lance Banning and Joyce Appleby in the *William and Mary Quarterly*, 3rd series, 43 (1986):3–34, for a lucid discussion of the issues.

commercial wealth based principally on a banking and credit system bla-
tantly imitative of the Bank of England.

Northern Anglophilism did not openly surface until the French
Revolution gathered momentum. The first reported reforms from Paris
had universal approval, but after Louis XVI tried to flee and was captured
at the Luxembourg border, the royal case began to deteriorate rapidly.
British goods, British manners, and British connections were already a
part of the northern commercial-legal network, so that when the Paris
mobs went beyond the destruction of an ancient jail to threaten the
whole of royalist society, the proper people in Boston and New York
quickly turned up their noses at the chant of Liberty, Equality, and
Fraternity. As Madison and Jefferson gloried in what was taking place
in Paris, the men around Hamilton (who preferred to be called Federalists
rather than Hamiltonians) decided they wanted nothing to do with
America's former ally.

Madison, looking through republican-tinted spectacles, saw the
events of 1789 as part of the worldwide movement started in 1776. He
welcomed French aid in spreading the doctrines and blessings of republicanism. Jefferson, who had seen at first hand the misery of the common
Frenchman under the Bourbons, applauded every step of the way as the
monarchy was dismantled. How could the man who said that the tree
of liberty required the blessed manure of a tyrant's blood be squeamish
when the French nobility ran for their lives? As the thunderclap of revolution rolled across Europe, frightening royalists from Whitehall to the
Baltic ports, Jefferson beamed his delight. On the whole, Jefferson calculated, kings were a rather worthless lot.

Madison was not far behind Jefferson in his loathing for monarchy.
As news from the reign of terror in France began to fill American newspapers, Hamilton and the Federalists spoke openly with horror of the
tri-colored excesses. As for the British, Madison came close to being an
undeclared Anglophobe. He took more seriously than his northern colleagues the indictment of George III in 1776 and had heard from Jefferson
of the contemptuous treatment American representatives received at the
Court of St. James. Since the peace of 1783, the British had done little
to show their acceptance of the terms and had done all they could to
keep the United States of America off balance. The western posts were
treated as Canadian forts, the lucrative West Indian trade was denied to
American ships and products, and when American tobacco or wheat
went to a European market it first cleared its way through a maze of
British brokers and shippers.

In the face of British political hostility, Americans fell back to their
prewar habits of buying British goods by the shipload. Madison's efforts
to force the British to concede something in the way of a tradeoff for
American ships and goods fell flat in Congress as northern congressmen

rejected Madison's proposal of "commercial discrimination" against the British until their trade barriers were lowered. A few Southerners in Congress, led by William Loughton Smith from Charleston, stuck with the northern mercantile interests when it came time for critical votes.

As Madison went on the defensive, he and Jefferson perceived that in a country where the yeoman farmer made up the vast majority of the population, a preponderance of congressmen voted for programs beneficial to a wealthy minority that held its power through speculative profits. Fortunes were built on mounds of public securities, as banking interests thrived because Hamilton's program was enacted into law, and a new set of millionaires blossomed while the farmers watched as their tobacco and wheat crops barely provided much more than subsistence. Credit, always a way of life in the South, became a chronic condition. Planters mortgaged their lands and paid interest to the Bank of the United States, while their taxes went to cover the interest on the newly issued government bonds. Like that of most Southerners, Madison's income depended on the produce of his family lands, and that income had not risen in comparison to the prosperity brought on above the Mason-Dixon line after the whole Hamilton program became law.

The fact that Washington signed the funding, assumption, and banking laws had not blinded all Southerners to the implications of the Hamiltonian system. The Virginia legislature reacted as violently as it could to the assumption measure by passing a remonstrance that branded the law as nothing more than a connivance to "prostrate agriculture at the feet of 'a large monied interest.' "[2]

Madison was too radical and too old-fashioned to be fully aware of what was going on. His father owned a small amount of the new government bonds, Madison himself owned none. Neither did Jefferson, whose idea of an investment was a new plow or a nail factory, but not a piece of paper bearing interest coupons. And then, there was the matter of the French Revolution, which had not yet become a bloodbath. Madison cautiously endorsed the reforms directed from Paris, but the imprisonment of Louis XVI upset Federalists. "However gloomy the face of things may at this time appear in France," Washington noted in September 1791, "yet we will not despair of seeing tranquility again restored." Then food riots, tumults in the French provinces and a spreading war followed. More and more, the men who had dined together in Philadelphia in 1787 found it convenient to walk on the other side of the street three years later.

Hamilton led all the rest in turning his back on Madison, but he blamed Madison for their chilled relationship. In May 1792 Hamilton wrote a confessional, of sorts, to a mutual friend in Virginia in which the secretary of the treasury said he would never have taken the job had he not been "under a full persuasion, that from a similarity of thinking, conspiring with personal good will, I should have the firm support of Mr. Madison, in the *general course* of my administration."[3] In the legislative battles over funding and assumption, Hamilton said, Madison's insistence on a full payment only to the original holders "diminished my respect for the force of Mr. Madison's mind," but he was willing to give the Virginian the benefit of the doubt until told that Madison "from a spirit of rivalship or some other cause had become personally unfriendly to me." In page after page of this revealing letter Hamilton labored the point that "Mr. Madison cooperating with Mr. Jefferson is at the head of a faction decidedly hostile to me." As Hamilton saw it, his old friend had turned on him and was motivated "in my judgment [by views] subversive of the principles of good government and dangerous to the union, peace and happiness of the Country."

Never one to pull his punches, Hamilton knew his letter to Virginia would be circulated, and he wanted his friends there to know of Madison's apostasy. For the rest of his life, Hamilton regarded his quondam associate as his inveterate enemy.

Until their final break, Madison tried to preserve the façade of a friendship with Hamilton. George Beckwith, a charming English army officer with unofficial connections in Canada, was toasted in the salons of influential New York merchants and there talked with Hamilton. When Madison tried to gain a bargaining chip with the British by suggesting some retaliatory regulations intended to force trade concessions, Hamilton quietly assured Beckwith that Congress would do nothing of the sort. Madison had to parry the thrusts of Hamilton's supporters in the House by answering the innuendoes spread by men who wished to see his reputation sullied. His father reported a rumor circulating in Georgetown that Madison was "a Partner in the Yazoo Company in a Grant for Lands, which is lookt on there as being obtained in a dishonest manner." The senior Madison's informant said that he thought the story of the congressman's involvement in a fraudulent scheme (to sell public lands for about three cents an acre) was spurious, but he wanted to hear the denial from Madison himself.[4]

Even the innocent vacation Madison and Jefferson planned for the spring of 1791 after congressional adjournment became grist for the gossip mills. Madison said the trip was meant to serve "Health recreation & curiosity," with the route laid out to take them first to Lake George and then on an eastward swing until they joined John Beckley at Portsmouth, New Hampshire. The timing coincided with the publication of Thomas Paine's pamphlet, *The Rights of Man*, which appeared in an American edition bearing Jefferson's unwitting and unauthorized endorsement. Paine's work fell into Beckley's hands. He loaned the copy to Madison, who in turn sent it on to Jefferson. Jefferson's covering letter to the printer was innocuous in itself, but to Federalists it was another red flag of rebellion and they excoriated Jefferson for associating himself with such a flaming revolutionary as Paine.[5]

This tempest-in-a-teapot affair was the chief topic of parlor conversation when Jefferson and Madison swung into their saddles and started up the Hudson River valley. As they passed through Manhattan a confidant of Hamilton's reported the Virginians had been seen in the company of Aaron Burr and Robert R. Livingston, two local politicians who detested Hamilton personally and politically. "Delenda est Carthago I suppose is the maxim adopted with respect to you," Hamilton was told. "They had better be quiet, for if they succeed they will tumble the fabric of the government in ruins to the ground."[6]

In the emerging pattern of party politics the Federalist party leaders were unashamedly in support of Hamilton's program and equally disgusted by the opposition tactics Madison used. Thus the Federalists assumed that the Virginia pair could not be taking a relaxing trip on horseback for almost a thousand miles simply to note the flora and fauna of the region. Yet Jefferson's account of the journey in his letters to Monticello and his personal journal have not a single reference to politics. Instead Jefferson commented on trout fishing, rattlesnakes, and the breathtaking beauty of Lake George. Madison's laconic account was equally free of political overtones, with most of his remarks centered on crop conditions, soils, farming practices, and trade routes.[7] Instead of seeking political cronies, the Virginia gentlemen looked for comfortable beds and edible food, having been warned in advance that near Fishkill the inn "near the new Church [has] good beds—bad dinner," and the ordinary at Rhinebeck Crossroads was "very bad." They wound through New England at a slow pace. The rendezvous with Beckley never came off because his horse went lame. So they missed a visit to Boston, and slightly disappointed, they swung south along the Connecticut River. After an easy amble down the Connecticut they took a ferry to Long Island, and there they parted company in mid-June. The hot weather caused Madison some uneasy moments when "bilious indispositions" struck, so he tarried on Long Island while Jefferson proceeded to New York and then on to Philadelphia. From the shadows of Independence Hall Jefferson reported that on the whole the trip had been good for Madison, for when they parted he looked "in better health than I have seen him" in years.[8]

In no hurry to return to Virginia during the humid summer, Madison rested in New York. He checked in at a familiar boarding house and surveyed the bustling wharves by the Coffee House, which was becoming a stockmarket bourse as men jostled on the curbs to buy and sell shares in the new Bank of the United States, government bonds, or whatever came to hand. "The Bank-Shares have risen as much in the Market here as at Philadelphia," Madison reported to Jefferson. The law gave subscribers "a moral certainty of gain . . . with scarce a physical possibility of loss. The subscriptions are consequently a mere scramble for so much public plunder which will be engrossed by those already loaded with the spoils of individuals. . . . Nothing new is talked of here. In fact stock-jobbing drowns every other subject. The Coffee House is in an eternal buzz with gamblers."[9]

The speculative fever he witnessed in New York convinced Madison that something drastically wrong was afoot. "It is said that packet boats & expresses are again sent from this place to the Southern States, to buy up the paper of all sorts which has risen in the market here." His suspicions of the Hamiltonians seemed confirmed. "These & other abuses make it a problem whether the system of the old paper under a bad Government, or of the new under a good one, be chargeable with the greater substantial injustice."[10] Reports that 23,500 of the 25,000 bank shares would be sold in northern cities confirmed all Madison's instincts. The Bank of the United States would be run by rich men who would make loans to other rich men, while the planters and farmers would be taxed to pay the interest due on government bonds held by the same rich men.

It was enough to make Madison ill. He abandoned any thought of going back to New England. "My bilious situation absolutely forbade it," he told Jefferson. There was nothing to do but convalesce until he could sit in a saddle and pull the reins in a southerly direction. "I am at present free from fever, but have sufficient evidence, in other shapes, that I must adhere to my defensive precautions."[11]

One reason Madison stayed in New York was to make an effort to remedy the journalistic situation in Philadelphia. Pro-Hamilton essays were printed day-in and day-out in the *Gazette of the United States* at the temporary capital, with only the feeblest of responses from critics of the new bank or the speculation in public securities. In their conversations Madison and Jefferson concluded that a newspaper with a national cir-culation was needed to counteract the stream of propaganda printed in the Federalist newspaper. By early August they had a reliable man of unquestioned loyalty to republican principles in mind as their choice for editor of the projected new journal. Convinced that the only way to overturn Hamilton's Anglicized program was through the ballot, the two Virginians believed that Philip Freneau (Madison's classmate at Prince-ton) could provide a newspaper that would provide republicans with a rallying point. With mounting anger Madison watched the scramble to buy public securities carrying coupons that would not become payable until 1800—the so-called "deferred debt" in Hamilton's refunding scheme. "Of all the shameful circumstances of this business," Madison reported, "it is among the greatest to see the members of the Legislature who were most active in pushing this Jobb, openly grasping its emolu-ments."[12] Was there no shame? Very little, Madison concluded, for there was not a shred of hope that the Federalists would relent until they had lined their pockets and filled their bank vaults. The only appeal left was to the people directly, who might be aroused if they knew the truth and turn out the rascally minions of the secretary of the treasury. Almost in despair, Madison agreed with Jefferson that the best way to reach the people was through a newspaper.

At first Freneau declined the offer Jefferson made of a State Department translator-clerkship that would leave time for editorial chores. After some flip-flopping, Freneau decided he could handle the light official duties (for a $250 annual salary) and hold the editorial chair. "If I can get Mr. Childs to be connected with me on a tolerable plan," Freneau wrote Madison, "I believe I shall sacrifice other consideration, and transfer myself to Philadelphia." Francis Childs, who printed the New York *Daily Advertiser*, worked out an agreement to print the fledgling newspaper with his Philadelphia connections. They believed it would serve the nation, so their choice of a name was natural: *The National Gazette*. In a matter of weeks the arrangement fell in place. Madison and Jefferson took new heart and sent out letter after letter to friends in Maryland and Virginia known to share their political views, urging them to subscribe to the newspaper that would answer Federalist mendacity with the unadorned truth.

Before heading homeward in late August 1791 Madison wrote endorsements of Freneau's project which he handed to Childs. Childs in turn broadcast Madison's message as he worked his way toward Richmond, taking subscriptions as he moved southward. The "new vehicle of information" deserved the patronage of Virginians, Madison wrote, as an accompanying prospectus explained. No doubt he offered plenty of encouragement to Freneau before departing for Georgetown. There Madison met with the newly appointed commissioners of the federal district and one of them, Daniel Carroll, promised to become a subscriber. Somewhat suspicious, Carroll said he hoped the newspaper would "be forwarded in such a manner as to be secure ag[ains]t being opened as letters."[13] There was no trusting those Federalist postmasters, who had a troublesome habit of losing newspapers critical of Washington's chief cabinet member.

After looking over the metes and bounds of the new federal district and a visit with Washington, Madison hurried to Montpelier where he expected to drum up more subscriptions for Freneau's newspaper and where he listened to the neighbors' time-honored complaints that money was scarce and farm prices too low. By mid-October he was back in Georgetown, witnessing the first and somewhat disappointing sales of lots staked out on Pennsylvania Avenue and other streets marked on Major Pierre L'Enfant's grandiose grid for a national capital. Suddenly someone realized they were all due back in Philadelphia on October 24—"on the forth Monday of October next"—instead of the last Monday as Jefferson, Madison, and Washington had all assumed. They hustled into stage coaches with less ceremony than usual, pushing through autumn downpours that turned the roads into quagmires. Madison was greeted in Philadelphia by Freneau as the editor labored for the October 31 inaugural of the *National Gazette*, which gave them the weekend for final touches before the newspaper appeared with the Monday morning daybreak.

Without intending to found a political party or start a newspaper to promote that party, Madison and Jefferson had bestirred themselves to thwart a perceived threat to the Republic. Their goal was to arrest the progress of Hamilton's system of taxing and financing to benefit special interests and bequeath to the United States a permanent public debt. They moved forward with no blueprint in hand, no carefully plotted scheme or intrigue, but there was a villain in the drama. Formal party names were a few years away, however, and the pall of the French Revolution hung over American allegiances for a time. One result was that by the winter of 1791–92 Freneau was aiming barbs at the "stock-jobbers and monarchy-jobbers" while the rival *Gazette of the United States* denounced "Gallic sycophants" who spoke with Virginia accents.

The fact of the matter was that Congress would have been a boring place for a man of Madison's talent and temperament if the party skirmishing had been eliminated. There was some concern that the promised hegira, taking the national capital to a permanent Potomac site, might never take place if the northern politicians planted their feet too firmly in Philadelphia. Early in 1791, Fisher Ames heard talk of such a plan over the polished mahogany dining tables along Chestnut Street. "It is feared that, ten years hence, Congress will be found fast anchored and immovable," Ames reported. "This apprehension has an influence on Mr. Madison, the Secretary of State, as it is supposed and perhaps on a still greater man."[14] This uneasiness explained why Madison, Jefferson, and Washington had taken such a great personal interest in the capital surveys during the past summer and fall. Now the big financiers, including Robert Morris, were shifting their credit to purchase town lots along the Potomac. Most of the bidding for the capital lots seemed to be made by Northerners who sensed that they could make a killing by cornering the real estate market before the first mortar touched a brick. In a matter of days, Morris and his partners committed themselves to thousands of dollars in speculative bids and eventually they acquired 7,234 building lots in the Maryland wilderness.[15] The heavy buying, particularly that of the Philadelphians, must have caused Madison and the other worried Virginians to relax a bit. If one of the richest men in America was buying capital real estate, the new city would not be a ghost town for long.

Madison never lacked for matters to worry about, but the business of Congress was not the cause of his sleepless nights. In the House of Representatives, the situation had become quite clear: Madison was the leader of a minority group which its detractors sometimes called "Mr. Madison's party." For all his reasoned arguments the votes were not there, so the careful debates availed little in the way of legislative accomplishment. A tipoff that Madison's reach exceeded his grasp came when the bank bill was before the House. "Mr. Madison has made a potent attack upon the bill, as unconstitutional," a fellow congressman reported. "The decision of the House, by a majority of thirty-nine against twenty, is a strong proof of the little impression that was made."[16] Opposition to Hamilton's program was drying up. Madison looked for support only from his southern friends and an occasional maverick in the Pennsylvania delegation. His pleas for a strict interpretation of the Constitution left most of his colleagues unmoved. Above the Hudson, Madison appeared to be friendless.

In the circumstances, Madison began paying more attention to the forthcoming congressional elections. Fortunately, the legislative torrent of the First Congress had provided the machinery of government, and the Constitution offered an opportunity to determine who would be in charge of that machinery by providing for biennial elections. Madison went along with the majority in voting for a tax on distilled spirits without enthusiasm, and probably did not realize what a volatile issue the excise would become in the cash-poor western counties that depended on whiskey for a meager income. But the humdrum of daily debates was evident on both sides of the House aisle. "Congress is not engaged in very interesting work," a New England congressman noted. "The first acts were the pillars of the federal edifice. Now we have only to keep the sparks from catching the shavings."[17]

Conscious of his diminished power, Madison was left with little time to brood. Shopping lists came regularly from Virginia, requiring visits to cobblers, hat-makers, and seed stores in procession. Sometimes he made a mistake, as when a brother ordered a lady's hat but mentioned the wrong style. "My brother signified to me that Miss Baynton wished a furr instead of a chip hat to be sent her," Madison explained to his father. "Unluckily the latter had been bought, packed up, & sent off in a trunk with the other articles, before his letter got to hand."[18] He also kept busy writing essays for the *National Gazette*, but their tone was so scholarly that they provided no excitement for readers itching for a fight with the Hamilton crowd. Not until a few days before Christmas did Madison come up with a newspaper article that was quotable. Writing on "Public Opinion," Madison revealed his faith in the power of newspapers in the new republic. "Public opinion sets bounds to every government, and is the real sovereign in every free one," he observed. In a country as large as the United States, "a circulation of newspaper through the entire body of the people" was a salutary means of spreading sentiments favorable to liberty.[19] Although Freneau's paper still had a limited circulation, Madison shared Jefferson's view that a newspaper critical of Federalist schemes was absolutely essential if the "monocrats" were to be thwarted. Jefferson told Madison that at a dinner party at the president's house he sat near an arch-Federalist who forced him into an argument as to "whether hereditary descent or election was most likely to bring *wise* and *honest* men into public councils."

Neither Madison nor Jefferson reacted mildly to provocations from their aristocratic-minded Federalist opponents. Old friendships were moving to a critical juncture, but the break was not yet open and avowed. The Whiskey Rebellion, the formation of the Democratic-Republican societies, and the reaction to Jay's Treaty were required to make the break complete. But Hamilton's report on manufactures, which was a darling of Federalists early in 1792, drew Madison's wrath in full. Whatever his reaction to certain of Hamilton's ideas, including the use of children in factories, Madison's overall feeling was that the use of governmental power to aid one segment of society was wrong. To Judge Pendleton in Virginia Madison wrote: "I consider it . . . as subverting the fundamental and characteristic principle of the Government, as contrary to the true & fair, as well as the received construction, and as bidding defiance to the sense in which the Constitution is known to have been proposed, advocated and adopted." Appalled by Hamilton's interpretation of the "general welfare" clause, Madison said the language was simply "copied from the old articles of Confederation, where it was always understood as nothing more than a general caption to the specified powers" of Congress. "It is a fact," Madison added, "that it was preferred in the new instrument for that very reason as less liable than any other to misconstruction." In his private letters Madison was more formidable than in his *National Gazette* essays, where his anonymity robbed Madison's strictures of the authenticity his letters to judges and fellow lawmakers carried.

More stirring than Madison's essays was the news from Georgetown that Major L'Enfant was behaving badly. Tactless and impatient, the Frenchman had ordered the house of an influential Maryland citizen pulled down because it edged a few inches into the surveyed path of a capital thoroughfare. Oblivious of the hot water he was in, L'Enfant continued to make enemies until Jefferson agreed with Washington that the major's dismissal was necessary. Madison was an interested spectator of these events but shared Jefferson's distaste for public unpleasantness. In private affairs, Madison stayed in a guarded position when possible. With some discomfort he learned from his brother in Richmond that Patrick Henry had inquired about him and suggested that the two of them should let bygones be bygones. Would Madison take the first step and write Henry a friendly letter? "I am authorised . . . to say that such an intercourse will not only be extreemly acceptable but its decline is a subject of regret to Col. Henry and his Lady," brother William wrote.[20]

Henry was one of the few men Madison detested, and he could not play the hypocrite. Instead, he chose to haggle over the word "decline." Had he once declined answering a letter from Henry, and thus broken off the relationship? He looked through his files and found that the last letter to Henry was written in 1784. Then he penned a cold note to his brother in which he was less than candid when he mentioned past dealings with Henry. Denying he had ever "indulged [in] any personal ill-will to that gentleman," Madison said he was glad to know of any friendly sentiments harbored by the old man. But the carrying on of a correspondence, or "an abrupt commencement of one, is not perhaps so proper a proof as you seem to conceive. I do not well understand, what is meant by the words of your letter—'but its decline is a subject of regret to Col. Henry and his Lady.'" Madison denied that he had broken off any such correspondence. "If any letter has been written to which it is supposed an answer was *declined* (a construction extremely improbable) it is proper to be known, that no such letter has been recd. and for that reason only, not answered."

Madison wanted no part of Patrick Henry. Henry had tried to ruin him politically in 1788. There was no reason Madison could think of, three years later, that could make him change his mind about the old demagogue.

Petulant moments aside, Madison preferred the company of loyal and trusted friends. Freneau, Jefferson, Beckley, and some of the younger Virginians serving in the House were his companions at meal times. Out of their discussions came a hardened resolve to provide some antidote to Hamilton's policies, particularly those that were making millionaires out of desk-bound, soft-handed men who knew neither rake nor plow but made their money buying and selling scraps of paper. "Too many of these stock jobbers and king-jobbers have come into the legislature," Jefferson told Lafayette, "or rather too many of our legislature have become stock jobbers and king-jobbers."[21]

During this time, when the republicans believed themselves outmaneuvered by the Hamiltonians, Madison wrote his essay on public opinion and thus provided a clue for the inner thoughts of the outnumbered Republicans. Increasingly, Madison came to see a polarized view of the Congress, where the demarcation was between honest men dedicated to preserving the republican system and those tainted with Anglophilism and avarice. If Hamilton read the "Public Opinion" essay he must have noticed that Madison was up to his old tricks of explaining how "good roads, domestic commerce, [and] a free press" would break down the barriers of an extensive republic. Here was Madison's old theme with a new twist: the United States was not too large to become a prosperous republic—it was only suffering from growing pains and an overdose of Hamilton's nostrums.

Hamilton was inclined to write Madison off as Jefferson's subordinate (a tendency followed by gullible historians ever since). The *National Gazette* attacks were stepped up, and were in Hamilton's mind inspired by Jefferson's malice. "I was never more mistaken, if he does not pronounce that it is a paper devoted to the subversion of me & the measures in which I have had an Agency," Hamilton complained.[22] The recent coolness of the *Federal Gazette* publisher also bothered Hamilton. At one time Andrew Brown had been "a zealous federalist and personally friendly to me," Hamilton wrote. "He has been employed by Mr. Jefferson as a Printer to the Government for the publication of the laws; and for some time past 'till lately the complexion of his press was equally bitter and unfriendly to me & to the Government." Surely, Hamilton reasoned, a newspaper conspiracy was brewing, with Jefferson—not Madison—behind the scheme.

Jefferson viewed matters differently. During the dead of winter Jefferson wrote nothing for Freneau while Madison kept up his essay-writing in a bland tone. In mid-February 1792 he wrote an article on the "Spirit of Governments" that compared the three forms known to mankind: a military despotism, a corrupting oligarchy, and a society ruled by the will of the people. The latter form "is the government for which philosophy has been searching, and humanity been sighing, for the most remote ages." Fortunately, "the republican governments which it is the glory of Americans to have invented" constituted such a government.[23] There was little here to upset Hamilton's supporters, even though Madison's allusion to governments "operating by corrupt influence" sounded suspiciously like the British parliamentary system.

The first spring thaws of 1792 produced an effect on more than the weather. The *National Gazette* columns grew bolder. First Freneau flexed his editorial muscle with a series of attacks on Hamilton over the nom-de-plume "Brutus." These essays were a frontal attack on Hamilton, for their target was the secretary of the treasury who had created a system "to serve the few, to encourage the undeserving speculator." The cabinet official, said "Brutus," had devised a scheme marked by "scenes of speculation calculated to aggrandize the few and the wealthy, by oppressing the great body of the people."[24] Warming to his work, "Brutus" then told of a growing army of revenue collectors, tide-waiters, and others on the federal payroll who "look up to the Secretary of the treasury as their champion and founder, and while he is originating monies by which they will exist and thrive, will with their pens, their tongues, and their votes, zealously give him all their support."

In the best of times Hamilton had precious little patience. These newspaper salvos infuriated Hamilton, for he was convinced that Madison and Jefferson were out to ruin his reputation, discredit him with Washington, and force a retreat from the funding system that would throw the country back into a morass of financial confusion. Hamilton resolved not to let these innuendoes go unnoticed, but he figured Madison was not the prime mover in these attacks. The enemy, Hamilton convinced himself, was Jefferson.

Before the month was out, Madison drew the issue as sharply as possible when Hamilton attempted to combine all the state debts still outstanding into one final assumption sweep-up. The truth was, Madison said in House debates, that states trying to pay off their old war debts were penalized by Hamilton's system through its "unequal operation." To slow down the Hamilton steamroller, Madison introduced an amendment that would have funded the remaining public debt at the lowest market price; and although the amendment barely lost (24–23) the final version of the law was as close to Madison's intentions as he could have wished. Hamilton's disgust was now complete:

> In the course of the discussion on this point, Mr. Madison dealt much in *insidious insinuations* calculated to give an impression that the public money under my particular direction had been unfaithfully applied to put undue advantages in the pockets of speculators, & to support the debt at an *artificial* price for their benefit. The whole manner of this transaction left no doubt in any ones mind that Mr. Madison was actuated by *personal* & political animosity.

For Hamilton, Madison's allegations proved the last straw. He looked back and saw every argument or difference of opinion since 1789 as a personal affront, a planned effort by Madison or Jefferson to subvert his public-spirited program that was bringing prosperity to America.

Hamilton denied that he was interested in turning the republic into a monarchy. If that were his goal, he said, "I would mount the hobby horse of popularity—I would cry out usurpation—danger to liberty &c. &c. . . . and then 'ride in the Whirlwind and direct the storm.'" On the other hand, Madison and Jefferson had friends willing to go such lengths to gain their ends. "I could lay my finger on some of them," Hamilton wrote. "That Madison does *not* mean it I also verily believe, and I rather believe the same of Jefferson; but I read him upon the whole thus—A man of profound ambition & violent passions." Hamilton claimed he had "proof of Mr. Madisons *intrigues*" that convinced him "Mr. Madisons true character is the reverse of that *simple, fair, candid one* which he has assumed." Worst of all, perhaps, was the Madison-Jefferson biases that bordered on treachery. "In respect to foreign politics, the views of the gentlemen are, in my judgment, equally unsound and dangerous. They have a womanish attachment to France and a womanish resentment against Great Britain."[25]

The Hamilton-Madison friendship of 1787–88 was now a shambles. It was a wreck, as both men admitted, because of differences that gave rise to a key issue facing American voters for the next decade: Was Hamilton a trustworthy public servant or only the willing tool of special interests? Madison shared Jefferson's view that Hamilton was no friend to the United States as the country had been conceived at its birth—a republic for all the people and particularly the farming population. While all the charges and countercharges rolled off the Philadelphia presses, the Virginians learned some unexpected news that gave a temporary check to the Hamiltonians. The high-flying speculators in public securities and western lands suddenly found themselves overextended, with William Duer, Hamilton's assistant, one of the first to take the plunge. The ensuing wave of personal failures shook the Coffee House rafters. Duer was headed for debtors' prison, to be followed by Robert Morris. "Speculating & Banking are as much execrated," Madison noted, "as they were idolized a few weeks ago." Madison thus took an I-told-you-so view of the ruined speculators, and predicted that "an earthquake though much slighter" would shake more of the venturesome financiers "within the present Month."[26]

While the news was dominated by reports of bankruptcies and ruined men, Madison proved that he was still a potent factor in Congress when constitutional issues were involved. One incident was rather trivial, concerning the design for coins, but the other struck close to the heart of republicanism. The coinage debates centered around a proposition from the Federalists to place Washington's likeness on coins; and with the president's popularity so overwhelming, the proposal seemed almost certain of passage. Then Madison unlimbered his republican batteries and questioned "the propriety of stamping the President's head on the money."[27] Implicit in Madison's criticism was the comparison between monarchies, where the reigning king's profile was stamped on every minted coin, and the notion that a president was akin to a monarch. When the smoke cleared, a design "emblematic of liberty" was substituted by the House and accepted by a surly Senate.

More fundamental was the legislation proposed to reapportion the House according to findings of the 1790 census. The Constitution provided that the number of representatives "shall not exceed one for every thirty Thousand" citizens, but the Senate took up a bill that came closer to a 1:33,000 ratio, giving Virginia nineteen congressmen. The House version was generally more favorable to the South and gave Virginia twenty-one seats. Unlike Hamilton, who saw his opposition as personally motivated, Madison had evidence of a North–South schism that influenced nearly every piece of legislation. To a friend in Virginia Madison reported dolefully: "You were right in saying 'that the Northern Cocks are true game' but have erred in adding 'that they *die* hard on the Representation bill.' Their perseverance has gained them a final victory."[28]

In a matter of days the Senate passed the bill and all that stood in the way of placing the act in the statute books was the president. Here was the last chance, and because he respected Washington's judgment, Madison almost prayed (we are not sure he did much kneeling) for a miracle. Whether brought on by prayer or respect for the judgment of Madison and Jefferson (who also beseeched Washington to veto the bill), the president exercised the veto for the first time in history. Since the bill did not threaten his overall financial plans, Hamilton lost no sleep over Washington's actions. The only source of discomfort for the Federalists was that a southern president had done what the South wanted him to do, but did it in the name of the Constitution. Madison still, on occasion, had the president's ear whenever a constitutional issue was at stake.

On personal matters, Washington also thought Madison was worth listening to, particularly when legislative pressures eased. As the session wound toward adjournment, Washington asked Madison to drop by "and spend half an hour" chatting. The conversation was about retirement—Washington's retirement—for his first four years in office were coming to an end in March 1793. Washington admitted that he had not discussed the matter with anyone—well, hardly anyone except the cabinet. Hamilton, Knox, and Jefferson importuned Washington to allow his name to go before the Electoral College (the outcome was presumably beyond doubt). Frankly, Washington said, he was pretty tired and preferred returning to Mount Vernon, there to "take his spade in his hand, and work for his bread." But what did Madison think?[29]

Madison sympathized with the president. The office was still above "the spirit of party that was taking place," and would be as long as Washington filled it. Washington was candid, and so was Madison. He revealed his fear that a faction was at work in the young nation that was "in general unfriendly to republican Govt. and probably aimed at a gradual approximation of ours to a mixt monarchy." Another four years with Washington at the helm would "give such a tone & firmness to the Government as would secure it" against such "a dangerous influence." More was said, and some obvious things were left unsaid. Madison promised to think about it and write during the summer. The president was particularly anxious to be honest with the people:

> On the one hand, a previous declaration to retire, not only carries with it the appearance of vanity & self-importance, but it may be construed into a Manoeuvre to be invited to remain. And on the other hand, to say nothing, implys consent; or, at any rate would leave the matter in doubt; and to decline afterwards might be deemed as bad, & uncandid.

No wonder Madison wanted some time to think about it. Washington was saying, in effect, that he wanted to leave the presidency but only if his obligations to the people were fully discharged. He knew that the young nation was somewhat like a colt, still wobbly on its legs, and if it came to a decision that might jeopardize the success of the American experience in self-government—well, Washington was a soldier. He knew the meaning of duty.

Aware of all these feelings, Madison waited almost a month after his meeting with Washington before he prepared an answer. Madison understood Washington's longing to retire to his plantation—Jefferson had expressed similar thoughts and the idea had crossed his own mind, too. So Madison wrote, assuming that Washington was going to retire, but ready to urge him to remain for four more years for the sake of the Republic. He then appended a draft of "a farewell address, [to be made public] before the final moment of departure." Madison said he wrote it with Washington's admonition for "plainness & modesty of language . . . in view, and which indeed are so peculiarly becoming the character and occasion." As it turned out, the occasion was further away than either man realized in the summer of 1792. When the time came to offer his valedictory, Washington still had Madison's draft and used parts of it.

Politics dominated Madison's life but he continued to play the role of an amateur scientist from time to time. Days before his departure for Virginia Madison found a note from Jefferson that demanded a quick response. Jefferson had found "a Northern hare" in a local market and was anxious to share the find with Madison, who was fond of dissecting small mammals. They were invited to Edmund Randolph's for supper, but Jefferson hinted they might delay their arrival to compare this rabbit with another species "because they must be skinned soon." Madison probably welcomed the opportunity to compare the northern hare with the more familiar eastern cotton-tail which was so troublesome in the vegetable gardens at Montpelier. He left no record of his findings, but after he reached Virginia the amateur scientist wrote Jefferson to send him a copy of a treatise "on the Disease Produced by the Bite of a Mad Dog."[30]

Before there was time to speculate on Washington's retirement intentions, Hamilton tossed a bombshell that summer to end any illusions Washington had for cabinet harmony. Starting on July 25, and running for the next four weeks, Hamilton served notice that the Federalists had declared all-out warfare on Jefferson. Signed by "T.L.," Hamilton's short letter accused Jefferson of hiring the editor of the National Gazette and paying him a government salary "to villify those to whom the voice of the people has committed the administration of our public affairs." Was not the National Gazette editor being paid from the public treasury, "T.L." wrote, "to oppose the measures of government, and, by false insinuations, to disturb the public peace?"[31]

Hamilton's timing was not capricious. The fall congressional elections were taking shape, and the thought must have crossed Hamilton's mind that if Jefferson could be discredited, those men who associated with Jefferson would share in the blame. This may explain why Hamilton took on Jefferson and almost ignored Madison's role in the founding of the *National Gazette.* Whatever Hamilton's motive, printers elsewhere gleefully took up the accusation to the point that it had to be answered. Eventually, Freneau himself denied all the charges, and Madison took pains to declare his innocence of the innuendoes in Hamilton's tirade.

Madison branded Hamilton's attack a gross perversion of the facts and said he welcomed an investigation of Jefferson's role in the business. The original idea of starting the *National Gazette* belonged to Henry Lee, Madison insisted. "That with others of Mr. Freneau's particular ac-quaintances I wish'd & advis'd him to establish a press at Philada. instead of one meditated by him in N Jersey, is also certain." The point was to advance Freneau's interest, and, said Madison:

> I entertain'd hopes that a *free* paper meant for general circulation and edited by a man of genius, of republican principles, & a friend to the Constitution, would be some antidote to the doctrines & discourses circulated in favour of Monarchy & Aristocracy.

Moreover, Madison wrote, his part in the enterprise was "a truth which I never could be tempted to conceal, or to wish to be concealed."[32] The charges that Freneau was attempting to subvert the Constitution, Madison went on, were "as impotent as they are malicious."

Jefferson left his defense in Madison's hands. Washington let it be known he would accept another term, but most of the seats in Congress were bound to be contested. Madison charged into the fray with a partisan attack on the Hamiltonians in late September 1792, in a newspaper essay titled "A candid State of Parties." Reviewing American politics from 1776 onward, Madison observed that all good men were for independence except a "disaffected class" undeserving "the name of a party." Then the Constitution caused a split in public opinion, but even those who opposed it were "certainly well affected to the union and to good government." This division ended when the Constitution became the law of the land, and gradually two factions emerged: one premised on the notion "that mankind are incapable of governing themselves . . . that government can be carried on only by the pageantry of rank, the influence of money and emoluments, and the terror of military force." On the opposite side stood men who believed in man's capacity to govern himself

> and hating hereditary power as an insult to the reason and an outrage to the rights of man, are naturally offended at every public measure that does not appeal to the understanding and general interest of the community, or that is not strictly conformable to the principles and conducive to the pres-ervation of republican government.

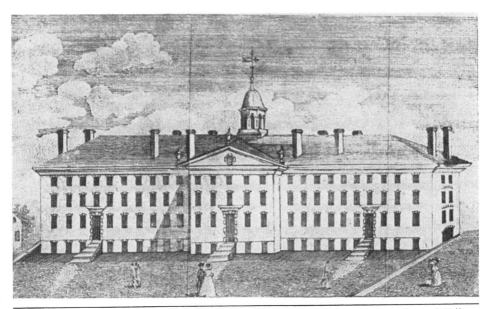

Unlike most Virginia gentry, Madison's father chose not to send his son to the College of William and Mary but instead sent him to the College of New Jersey in Princeton. There Madison took a "cram course" that brought him an early bachelor's degree in 1771 but entailed such privations that the regimen left him in "very infirm health." (Princeton University Library)

This silhouette of Madison by Joseph Sansom was made around 1781 shortly after Madison had been elected to serve in the Continental Congress. (The Historical Society of Pennsylvania)

In 1783 Madison commissioned Charles Willson Peale to paint miniatures of Kitty Floyd and himself when his romance with the young lady was in full bloom. Madison gave his likeness to Miss Floyd and he appears to have kept hers briefly. When the love affair soured, Madison apparently sent her miniature to Miss Floyd—it was too painful a reminder of their broken engagement. (The Library of Congress)

The Maryland State House was the scene of the 1786 Annapolis Convention. In its failure Madison found a cause for a national convention to revise the Articles of Confederation. (Maryland Historical Society)

When the First Federal Congress met in New York, delegates from the eleven states that had ratified the Constitution gathered here on a corner of Wall Street to conduct their business. Madison quickly pressed the House of Representatives to redeem his promise for a bill of rights, and by September 1789 proposed amendments were ready to send to the states. (Courtesy of the New-York Historical Society, New York City)

English cartoonists mocked the Americans after Washington was burned in August 1814. →
Here Madison and a cabinet member flee the flaming capital, to the great glee of two British seamen. Madison clutches his instructions from Napoleon, while an onlooker says: "The great Washington fought for Liberty, but we are fighting for shadows. . . ." (The Library of Congress)

A fellow Virginian, John Tayloe, built the Octagon House near the presidential mansion in Washington for use as a townhouse. When the British burned the White House in 1814, Tayloe made the luxurious home available to President Madison, and the First Family lived there until March 1817. (The American Institute of Architects; photo John Tennant)

Dolley Madison was the outgoing First Lady when James Wood painted her portrait in 1817, shortly before the Madisons moved out of the White House. (Virginia Historical Society)

Montpelier as it appeared when Madison returned to the Orange County estate in 1817, from a contemporary engraving. (University of Virginia Library)

Montpelier passed out of the Madison family shortly after the fourth president's death. At the turn of the century, William DuPont of Wilmington, Delaware, bought the estate and used it for fox hunting and horse breeding. A descendant bequeathed Montpelier to the National Trust in 1984, and it is now open to the public. (National Trust)

Not yet ready to call a spade a spade, Madison spoke of the "antirepublican party, as it may be called," rather than Federalists or Hamiltonians. This faction would do all within its power to prevent the majority from making its wishes known.

In the next breath, Madison talked of a party for all the people. "The Republican party, as it may be termed, conscious that the mass of the people in every part of the union, in every state, and of every occupation must at bottom be with them, both in interest and sentiment" would promote the general welfare.[33]

Which side would triumph? Events alone would answer that question, Madison wrote, but since time was on "the republican side . . . [because] the superiority of numbers is so great," every shrewd observer of human affairs could make a reasonable guess.

Hamilton's decision to make Jefferson rather than Madison his target is probably owing to the public perception of the secretary of state as a man being groomed for the presidency. The newspaper war continued, with Hamilton using an assortment of pseudonyms to make the battle seem more widespread than it really was. The result, however, was that Hamilton projected Jefferson forward as the leading opponent of his program. Madison answered the charges, wrote essays to refute Hamilton's indictments, and Jefferson stood aloof from the fray; and yet by the time the fall votes were counted, Jefferson, not Madison, was the de facto head of the new-born Republican party. Hamilton's attacks made this a certainty, but Madison wanted it that way. He was perfectly content to hoist the flag of republicanism and let the rank-and-file look to Jefferson for leadership. With Madison, it was always the end and not the means that counted.

The fall elections came and went without any major disturbances. Beckley was eager to join the New York Republicans who wanted to oust John Adams from the vice-presidency and advance George Clinton, but Madison eschewed an active role in the presidential contest. Washington won 132 electoral votes, Adams was second (and hence the vice-president-elect), and Jefferson a distant fourth with four votes. Beckley's labors paid off, however, for all of the Virginia electors gave their second ballot to Clinton. The vote was more symbolic than representative of future stakes, for Clinton was not regarded as the leader of the opposition. To reinforce Jefferson's right to that position, Madison took pains (with Monroe as a co-author) to write a public defense of Jefferson's conduct in the Freneau affair. The point was to imbed the secretary of state in the public mind as the Number One Republican in America.[34]

In his own district, Madison had nothing to fear and appears not to have spent a single hour on the campaign trail or wasted a penny in his reelection effort. The newly shaped district he represented for the

Third Congress now included Madison County, which had recently been carved out of Culpeper County and named in his honor. The Virginia elections were delayed until March 1793 by some ill-advised redistricting legislation passed in Richmond, but Madison seemed unconcerned as he was returned by his neighbors without fanfare and without opposition. He picked up a republican ally in the Senate when John Taylor was chosen by the Virginia legislature to replace Richard Henry Lee.

Meanwhile, Washington set aside Madison's manuscript announcing his departure from public life and with all returns counted by Christmas 1792 it was clear that there would be four more years with the general in charge. Madison was not displeased at that prospect, but he was ready to put more pressure on Hamilton. When not pressed by congressional business Madison wrote more essays for the *National Gazette*, convinced that the Republican philosophy needed difusion among its readers. In an article, "Who Are the Best Keepers of the People's Liberties?" Madison reminded subscribers how history taught the lesson "that the people ought to be enlightened, to be awakened, to be united, that after establishing a government they should watch over it, as well as obey it."[35] Since he was no longer the most powerful man in the House of Representatives, Madison considered himself more bound than ever to keep a Republican vigil.

Hamilton proved he could keep up with the Republicans when they pushed him for a plan to pay off the public debt. In a matter of days, Hamilton's boundless energy and genius with figures produced a "Report on the Redemption of the Public Debt" that proposed a seven-year plan for calling in government securities and redeeming them with taxes raised on horseflesh. A tax of one dollar per head was supposed to raise over $691,000 in seven years, but the scheme confused some of Madison's constituents. "The Secretaries plan of a sinking fund I have read over but do not yet comprehend," one complained, "it is intricate and so complicated it appears to me to require some time and attention to understand." And there was that old sectional bias in it too, Madison was told. "The tax on horses cannot fail to serve the purposes of easing the eastern and burthening the southern interest—there are few pleasure Horses in the eastern and middle compared to the southern states."[36]

Not all of Philadelphia was talking about Hamilton or horses or taxes. The French balloonist Jean-Pierre Blanchard came to town with plans for a grandiose exhibition. Preoccupied with politics, Madison chose to ignore the excitement Blanchard generated early in January. Washington and Jefferson found the time to attend Blanchard's much-publicized ascension from the courtyard of the Walnut Street jail, however, and Madison's silence tells something of his lifestyle (there is no record of Madison ever attending a public performance of anything). Admission tickets cost five dollars, which may have had a deterring effect on cash-poor Madison. Jefferson paid ten dollars for two tickets, took his daughter to see the yellow-and-blue contraption lift off, and helped Blanchard pay his debts later. Madison simply had more important things on his mind. Like Alexander Hamilton's devious ways.

William Branch Giles, another Virginia congressman, led a frontal attack on Hamilton's program in the House, prodded perhaps by Madison. Both men looked with suspicion on the way Hamilton was handling repayments of the French loan. Actually, Hamilton stalled on repaying the French debt to the new crowd in Paris, hoping the sans-culotte republic might collapse. A fresh attack on the secretary of the treasury in the *National Gazette*, written by an unidentified critic of Hamilton's raised Madison's ire. "The documents furnished shew that there has been at least a very blameable irregularity & secrecy in some particulars" of the French loan repayments "which at least require explanation."[37] When Giles introduced nine resolutions in the House censuring Hamilton's official conduct, the offended secretary must have thought Madison was behind the maneuver. Two days after Giles made his motion, Madison spoke in support of the implication that Hamilton had made more than a clerical error. The money appropriated to repay part of the French loan, Madison said, was diverted from its purpose without authorization from the president, which was a clear violation of the law. Where had the missing funds gone? To the Bank of the United States, where "the account of them had remained in the books of the bank without ever appearing in the books of the Treasurer," Madison charged.

The full story never came out at the time, for Hamilton's supporters branded Giles's resolutions a political smear and defeated them handily. But Jefferson calculated that Hamilton had illegally withheld $549,278 of government funds and placed the money with the Bank of the United States; and Madison would recall many years later that Hamilton had duped Washington into unwittingly signing a document authorizing this monetary juggling act.[38] The House adjourned the day after Hamilton seemed vindicated by the overwhelming rejection of the Giles resolutions, and the public turned its attention back to such matters as the spring planting weather and the progress of the French Revolution.

Madison's sympathies, of course, lay with the French as the royalty of Europe threw their resources behind massed armies bent on unraveling the French Revolution. In praise of France, Madison said, "Her conduct has been great both as a free and a martial nation. We hope it will continue so, and finally baffle all her enemies, who are in fact the enemies of human nature."[39] Indeed, Madison was speaking now as a French citizen—an honorary one, but still in good company—for he learned that on October 10, 1792, the National Assembly had conferred French citizenship upon three Americans: George Washington, Alexander Hamilton, and James Madison.[40]

Official notice of the honor must have reached Madison as the congressman was packing for his return trip to Montpelier. Jefferson had decided he would resign his cabinet post and was not returning to Virginia with Madison. Instead, Jefferson stayed north to wind up his personal affairs and have his furniture crated. Madison knew how Jefferson longed to return to Monticello and shared his friend's feeling that his usefulness in the Washington cabinet was ended. Temporarily, at least, Hamilton had the upper hand; but the fall elections had given heart to Jefferson so that he believed he was leaving at a propitious time. Under the 1790 census reapportionment, Virginia's delegation in the House grew from nine seats to nineteen, and the votes in much of the South and parts of Pennsylvania and New York were encouraging. Jefferson saw "the tide of this government as now at the fullest" and with Madison back for the Third Congress "the true principles of the Constitution" would be revived.[41] There was good news regarding the French, too. Citizen Edmond Genet had been appointed as the American minister and would arrive during the summer.

Madison had time to reflect on these developments as he relaxed at Montpelier in April 1793. The apple and cherry trees, planted so lovingly during the past decade, were in bloom, as were the wild azaleas and mountain laurel on the Blue Ridge peaks. From the upper windows of Montpelier Madison saw hillsides of dogwoods in full blossom, and the light green hues of a thousand oak and maple trees made him forget the angry scenes of February. Surrounded by the glories of a Virginia April, Madison wrote to the interior minister of the French Republic, accepting his honorary citizenship with a rhetorical flourish:

> I feel these sentiments with all the force which that reflection can inspire; and I present them with a peculiar satisfaction as a Citizen of the U. S. which have borne so signal a part towards banishing prejudices from the World & reclaiming the lost rights of Mankind.

Before leaving the subject, Madison expressed his "anxious wishes for all the prosperity & glory to the French Nation . . . and compleating the triumphs of Liberty, by a victory over the minds of all its adversaries."[42]

About the time Madison wrote to Paris an unexpected check on Franco-American amity was provided by, of all people, Washington himself. At Hamilton's urging, the president had issued a proclamation of neutrality making it official that the United States was not going to take sides with its wartime ally. The decision came after a cabinet meeting where Jefferson tried to water down Hamilton's strong stance, but the tide of public opinion in Philadelphia had turned against the French after March 15, when word swept through the city that Louis XVI had been guillotined. Although Jefferson told Madison the news had "not produced as open condemnations from the Monocrats as I expected," he may have underestimated the shock. Surely Madison had not heard the news when he wrote his letter of acceptance to Paris, and when he learned of the proclamation Madison labeled it "a most unfortunate error." But within a few weeks public opinion was taking a harder line, and hence Washington probably took the popular path when he chose to follow Hamilton's advice rather than Jefferson's. And perhaps Madison was too willing to accept Louis's fate as the price paid for liberty, for when he heard of the French monarch's execution Madison's reaction was bland. " 'If he was a Traytor, he ought to be punished as well as another man.' This has been the language of so many plain men to me," Madison wrote Jefferson, "that I am persuaded it will be found to express the universal sentiment whenever the truth shall be made known."[43] No king, dead or alive, was going to get much sympathy from James Madison.

When Madison learned that Hamilton had argued in the cabinet for a suspension of the treaty with France, this stance fitted the Virginian's view of the treasury secretary as a British sycophant. Like Jefferson, Madison never gave Hamilton the benefit of the doubt. When it came to lining up behind either England or France, Hamilton quoted the international legal authority Emerich de Vattel to prove that a treaty might be repudiated when changed circumstances made the original pact "*useless, dangerous,* or *disagreeable.*"[44] Nonsense, Madison wrote Jefferson. "The attempt to shuffle off the Treaty altogether by quibbling on Vattel is . . . contemptible for the meanness & folly of it. If a change of Govt. is an absolution from public engagements, why not from those of a domestic as well as of a foreign nature; and what then becomes of public debts &c &c"?[45] Madison thought Washington had been duped into issuing the proclamation and cringed when he read Hamilton's newspaper justification of Washington's declaration. "The Revolution in France is the primitive source of the War, in which she is engaged," Hamilton said writing as "Pacificus." "It is impossible, prejudice apart, not to perceive a delicate embarrassment between the *theory* and *fact* of our political relations to France."[46]

Madison cringed, but Jefferson was outraged. Propriety excused him from writing a blast at Hamilton's position, but Jefferson saw nothing wrong in Madison's using a quill as a sword. "For God's sake, my dear sir, take up your pen," Jefferson urged, "select the most striking heresies and cut him to pieces in the face of the public."[47] Madison demurred, aware that there was no begging off when Jefferson was insistent.

By late July Madison had taken up the task, but not without some misgivings. "I can truly say I find it the most grating one I ever experienced," he confessed to Jefferson. Even so, Madison spent hours and days writing his "Helvidius" essays to counterattack Hamilton's defense of proclaimed neutrality. Hamilton's insistence upon presidential powers which neither Madison nor Jefferson found in the Constitution was equally disturbing. At the outset Madison said the "Pacificus" essays brought "singular pleasure and applause" from "the foreigners and degenerate citizens among us, who hate our republican government, and the French revolution." Using for his pseudonym the Roman republican who suffered under Nero, Madison accused his opponent of trying to subvert the Constitution by claiming for the president broad powers really restricted to the legislative branch. The interpretation "Pacificus" gave to the Constitution smacked of the way royal prerogatives were granted in Great Britain and hence carried a flavor more fitting for "*British commentators*" than an American republican. Madison's great talent in 1787 and during the ratification struggle had been an ability to write quickly and get to the point. In the Helvidius essays he showed he had lost none of his gift. Jefferson told Madison that he was "charmed with No. V."[48]

Jefferson was happy to find anything encouraging on the horizons around Philadelphia, where he labored away in the midst of an embarrassing scene caused by the arrival of Citizen Genet. The French minister landed at Charleston, allowed the applause and good will to create delusions of grandeur, and promptly began making enemies right and left. Initially Genet made a favorable impression in Philadelphia, to the point that Jefferson reported "he offers every thing & asks nothing."[49] But the honeymoon was short-lived. Genet began imitating an imperial envoy by commissioning privateers and encouraging an American filibustering expedition against the Spanish and British outposts in America. Jefferson's patience was soon exhausted as he joined with other Republicans who had embraced Genet earlier but now demanded his recall. "He will sink the republican interest if they do not abandon him," Jefferson told Madison.[50] Madison hardly knew what to make of the plunge in Genet's popularity, for the opposition would surely capitalize on the Frenchman's blunders.

Genet's conduct threw a damper on Madison's efforts to give the appearance of spontaneity to local meetings called in central Virginia to issue pro-French resolutions as an antidote to Federalist activities. In September 1792 Madison had drafted a set of pro-French resolutions (aided by Monroe) and sent them to the right people in nearby Staunton, Culpeper, and elsewhere as proof that Virginians were not backsliding on their support for the French. Now, Genet's antics muddied the waters. "His conduct has been that of a mad man," Madison wrote to Monroe.[51] Public opinion might have turned against all of France except that the British began wholesale captures of American ships in the Caribbean— a "war on our commerce" Madison called it—and this news came as Philadelphia was struck with a devastating epidemic of yellow fever. As the dead and dying were carted off to burial grounds, Madison could be thankful that he was in Orange County. "The fever spreads faster," Jefferson wrote, "Deaths are now about 30 a day" and "All flying who can."

Hamilton was among those stricken, and Washington's servants packed the president's bags for a hurried trip to Mount Vernon.

Predictably, no Republican prayers were said for Hamilton. "His family think him out of danger, & he puts himself so by his excessive alarm," Jefferson told Madison. Only to Madison could Jefferson speak so frankly of Hamilton, knowing it would go no further, saying what was in his heart. Hamilton, he ventured, was somewhere between being a hypochondriac and an outright coward:

> He had been miserable several days before from a firm persuasion he should catch it. A man as timid as he is on water, as timid on horseback, as timid in sickness, would be a phaenomenon if the courage of which he has the reputation in military occasions were genuine. His friends, who have not seen him, suspect it is only an autumnal fever he has.[52]

Madison was more concerned about Jefferson's health than Hamilton's, so he learned with relief that his friend was safe at a summer retreat beyond the city and soon would be headed homeward. By the end of the month, Jefferson was resting in the guest room at Montpelier. For the next two weeks there was a movement of men and horses back and forth from Madison's pied-à-terre to Monticello, with good fortune bringing Monroe to Albemarle County. The trio of gentlemen farmers had much to discuss over their madeira, with no recordkeepers about to inhibit their conversation. Some of the talk must have been about Washington, who wrote Madison concerning an alternative for Philadelphia if the yellow fever persisted in the temporary capital. The question became moot as the frosts of early November ended the panic as abruptly as it started. By November 9 Jefferson was back in Philadelphia, reassuring Madison that all was well—or nearly so. The mosquitoes were gone, but the old animosities were still around, awaiting Madison's return. And more than people had perished. Freneau's newspaper had died, the victim of red ink.

CHAPTER SIX

A CHANGE
IN THE
CLIMATE

Across the republic the dreadful word from Philadelphia swept into the remotest corners, including Orange County, Virginia. The Pennsylvania metropolis, with 55,000 souls living there in May 1793, had lost over 1,200 by late September; and on October 11 the death register added another 119 names. No wonder Madison was worried.

Despite Jefferson's reassurances, Madison was in no hurry to start for the city that had turned into a collection of charnel houses. What with one illness and another, and the recent death of his brother Ambrose, Madison was more than a little concerned about his own health. Had the noxious fevers really deserted the State House environs? "Doctor Rush," a friend wrote Madison, "assured me last evening that a greater degree of health had never prevailed in this City than at present." All the houses had been fumigated, and Madison was probably comforted by reading that there was not "the smallest possible danger" if he chose to return to Philadelphia.[1]

Madison took his time covering the 210 miles. When he finally reached the familiar boardinghouse and checked with Beckley and Jefferson he found encouraging news on hand. The dreadful events of the summer and fall were forgotten. The congressional elections had given the Republicans a nine-vote margin in the House, if all the new men stayed in line. But the Congress elected in the fall of 1792, under the prevailing system, did not convene until December 1793. Republican strategy, as it unfolded, was to keep the opposition off guard. Although the Republican candidate for Speaker of the House won, all traces of discipline among the Republicans dissolved. Proof that no party line could be laid down came when the House considered the latest British action to curb American commerce—a new order in council authorizing the Royal Navy to seize any foodstuffs destined for a French port. Madison viewed this arbitrary action as contrary to international law and more proof that England was willing to strangle American agriculture if it suited her purposes. If anything, the latest British edict reinforced the strong perception that England still regarded the United States as a second-rate power but a first-rate market.

Madison reacted, possibly in hopes that the Republicans in Congress might be fed up with British arrogance. Madison took his cue from Jefferson's parting shot when he left the State Department by releasing his thick report on trade and commerce. The report could have been no surprise to Madison, but once the document was made public in mid-December, he found plenty of ammunition for his claims that England was dominating American trade at a great cost to Yankee farmers and traders.

Jefferson's report, submitted as a kind of swan song, covered the history of American dealings with European powers in considerable detail. Behind the facts lay Jefferson's implied argument that America should retaliate against British discrimination through regulations and duties. The report had all the statistics Madison needed, for it showed that British imports were seven times greater than those of French products and fourteen times larger than the Dutch, while American ships were prohibited from enjoying any advantages whatever.[2] Armed with these impressive facts, Madison once again asked the House to consider discriminatory tariffs that would hurt Great Britain in the only place that seemed to matter—the British pocket book. Madison must have hoped that the impact of Jefferson's report would be felt among congressmen from the farming areas. Implicit in his remarks, as he introduced a series of resolutions that would have placed higher duties on British goods, was Madison's conviction that somehow America was only half-independent.

Madison's opponents wasted no time in branding his proposals as needlessly risking a war with the British, who apparently would react by teaching the Yankee upstarts a lesson. A Boston newspaper suggested that Madison's real motives were to link the United States to France. "Where did Mr. Maddison . . . acquire his knowledge of commerce?" asked the Columbian Centinel. "Not surely in the interior of Virginia, where no other commerce is transacted than the buying and selling of negroes?"[3]

Long-winded Federalists pounded Madison's proposals as fraught with danger. Madison's stamina proved equal to the Federalists' as did his oratory. "Maddison Engaged our Attention for two hours and half during which time in a full House and thronged with Spectators there was such perfect Silence that you might almost have heard a Pin Fall," an admirer reported. "In Short Eloquence which baffles every thing I have ever heard and almost [defies] description."[4]

Despite the admiration of Republicans, Madison attracted little support in the full House, so that six of his seven anti-British resolutions were pigeonholed. Although stymied in the Congress, Madison's proposals were widely reprinted and helped crystallize opinion at town meetings and partisan gatherings. In New York some 2,000 eager Republicans were said to have roared their approval of Madison's plans to lay heavier duties on British goods. In Maryland artful Samuel Smith, whose connections made him a major force in Congress, bemoaned what he termed the delaying tactics of "Maddison's party." Smith denounced Madison's resolutions as "commercially wrong and politically . . . weak, [they] have taken up so much time as to retard all those other useful Bills which that party delayed the passage of, without openly opposing any but the Naval Armament."[5]

Even when the British navy began wholesale captures in the Caribbean, the Federalists reluctantly moved toward some form of retaliation. Madison's resolutions were not revived but some temporary embargoes were approved, only to be voted down in the Senate. Madison's days were filled with committee work, speech-making, and talks with the faithful Republicans whose morale needed constant reassurances of support from the mass of the people. He scarcely had time to write his family, and then only to mention tree plantings which seemed to be worrying his father. Yet amidst the hustle and bustle of congressional life, when his friends had assumed Madison was too busy to think about anything but stalled legislation, Madison did an unusual thing. He started thinking about a pretty woman.

Somewhere along the line, though we are not sure exactly when the meeting took place, Madison found time to pay a call on the lovely young widow Todd. Madison's friend from his college days in Princeton, Aaron Burr (class of '72), was the intermediary. Widow Todd was buxom, perky, and twenty-five. Burr knew everybody worth knowing, so his hand in the introduction was perfectly natural. Dolley Todd was still in her widow's weeds, having buried her husband and one child during the recent yellow fever epidemic. Madison was now forty-three, and must have thought about the kind of life he would be living at Montpelier if he went home as a retired bachelor. How long the matter had been on his mind we will never know, but once he decided to do something about his loneliness Madison moved discreetly, almost secretly, and quickly.

Jefferson knew nothing about Dolley Todd, but he finally heard disturbing reports about the smear tactics of the Federalist newspapers. Madison broke his long silence early in March 1794 to tell Jefferson how his resolutions to implement Jefferson's "Commercial Report" were moving along. The New England congressmen had prevented passage of the resolutions, thereby preventing the timid members from learning "the sense of their constituents." Although Madison would not admit that his anti-British campaign was a dead issue, he confessed that "vast exertions by the British party to mislead the people of the Eastern States" had hurt the cause. "The most artful & wicked calumnies have been propagated with all the zeal which malice and interest could invent," Madison wrote. A Boston newspaper insinuated that he had been "the counsellor & abettor of Genet in all his extravagances, and a corrupt tool of France."[6] Almost with glee Madison sent news ten days later that the New England merchants "have had a terrible *slam* in the W. Indies" where "about a hundred vessels have been seized by the British for condemnation, on the pretext of enforcing the laws of the Monarchy with regard to the Colony trade."[7]

There was some hand-wrenching and breast-beating, but in the end the northern merchants backed away from all the blustering war talk, and by the time all hopes of enacting higher tariffs on British goods disappeared Madison was sick of the whole business. Even the distraction of a letter from Montpelier (full of instructions on the purchase of a piano-forte) afforded some relief from the frustrations of life as a leader of an impotent majority. The birth-pangs of a political party, Madison discerned, were almost as bad as being with a losing minority. In his *Federalist #10* Madison had predicted that various interests might dilute their strength when brought together in a national council. Here was proof, in 1794, of what he had suggested in 1787.

Frustrated in Congress, Madison found solace elsewhere. His courtship of Dolley Todd also required some patience. For one thing, she was a Quaker and he was not—which meant that she might lose her standing in the Society of Friends if she married an outsider. Then there was Dolley's baby. Little Payne Todd was being spoiled by his mother, but his stake in the small family estate of less than £500 was a matter of concern. Quietly Madison seems to have negotiated these delicate points, and he might have been amused when old General Horatio Gates sent an invitiation for a summer visit. After Congress adjourned, Gates wrote, Madison ought to join him near Saratoga Springs for health and relaxation. "This Bethesda, they say, cures all diseases, makes the Old Young, and the Ugly Handsome! There are good Accomodations, & excellent Living, two things, Joind to the Two others, with a good Society, & fine Girls! might Tempt even Plato, when as Young as You," Gates chided.[8] Madison had a better alternative, but he kept his secret easily for there was still much activity in the House, and the city gossipmongers had more on their minds anyway. Rumors from unimpeachable sources told of a hush-hush mission to England.

Everybody knew that the British had not filled their pledge, made in 1783, to evacuate the western posts; and in American courts the settlement of old pre-Revolutionary debts limped along until the original creditors and debtors were dead or dying. The northern boundary with Canada had not been settled, either; and now the British navy was raising hell in the West Indies. Washington took counsel on all these problems and decided that some dramatic gesture was needed to bring a solution. There was talk of sending Hamilton to the Court of St. James as a special negotiator, but the Republicans would have blanched at that choice and Washington knew it. With no fanfare, Washington picked Chief Justice John Jay and dispatched him as an *envoy extraordinaire*, commissioned to break the diplomatic logjam.

Like everybody else in Philadelphia, Madison heard the rumors of Jay's mission. He was not optimistic, for Jay was more of a Federalist on some issues than Hamilton himself, and what America needed, Madison argued, was a resolute diplomat aware of the second-rate status England persisted in allotting to the United States. A friend in Virginia summed up the feelings of inferiority which England hoped to fix on Americans when he complained to Madison that the United States had not yet achieved real independence:

> No nation is really an independant one, unless their country their Laws, Government, & Manners are, taken collectively, far preferable in the View of the people to those of any other nation whatsover . . . the moment hostilities ceased, we relapsed into our old opinions & Habits concerning Britain & her productions. It is this charm of inveterate Habits founded in former Subjection & political Nothings, that every real American would wish to break & dissipate.

Madison's correspondent wanted his country to boycott British goods for a while and even pay more for inferior products. What was personal sacrifice when the national honor was at stake? "Above all we Shall begin the progress of a feat of national Character, and Not Remain independent de jure, & Colonists de facto."[9] Hearing these things from Virginia undoubtedly gave Madison confidence, for he had long believed that England considered the United States a temporary aberration on the world's political spectrum and treated America accordingly.

One incident provided slight hope that the American spine could stiffen. Reports of more ship seizures in the Caribbean so enraged the New England delegation that an embargo on commerce passed after an earlier rejection. This vote gave Madison some hope that his anti-British tariff proposals might still emerge from the session, for the New England congressmen were confronted with constituents "so clamorous under their losses in the W. Indies as to alarm their representatives."[10]

Talk was cheap, however. Luckily, Madison had Dolley Todd to think about, for he was making little progress in Congress. From Richmond Madison heard that a mass inoculation for small pox had laid half the city low, clogged the mails, and closed down most businesses. Jefferson reported rumors in central Virginia that America had declared war on England, a circumstance that allowed his neighbors "a gratification of some passions, & particularly of their antient hatred of Gr. Britain" until the report proved false.[11] With all the war talk Jefferson assumed the Federalists would be pushing hard for larger appropriations for the army and navy. "Not that the Monocrats & Papermen in Congress want war; but they want armies & debts: and tho' we may hope that the sound part of Congress is now so augmented as to ensure a majority in cases of general interest merely," Jefferson was still pessimistic. "Where members may hope either for offices or jobs for themselves or their friends, some few will be debauched, & that is sufficient to turn the decision where a majority is at most but small," he confessed.

Jefferson was not all gloom. He told Madison that he had just tasted fresh asparagus, lilacs were in blossom, and while no purple martins had yet been seen the first whip-poor-will of the season had visited Monticello the day before. This news had to be welcome, for Madison was about to propose to Dolley Todd and he wanted the weather to be perfect, the sky full of cardinals or mockingbirds, and no cares from Congress to carry along in his portmanteau. Madison's letters to his father were full of business, with no hint of marriage; yet we know that while her suitor pondered weighty matters of state, Dolley Todd was thinking hard about spending the rest of her life with James Madison.

Adjournment was still some weeks away when Madison made another effort to stiffen the congressional spine in the face of more ship seizures by the British navy. On April 18 he introduced a resolution recounting "the injuries suffered and likely to be suffered by the United States, from a violation of our neutral rights and commercial interests on the part of Great Britain," and calling for a suspension of all trade with England after a specified date.[12] The House went along, more in confusion than with dedication; however, the Senate was evenly balanced and that meant Vice-President Adams had the tie-breaking vote. Adams voted against Madison's resolution, so the temporary embargo was soon to expire and nothing lay ahead in the way of retaliation for the insufferable Royal Navy patrols. Madison kept working, however, and a bill prohibiting the importation of British products after November 1 sailed through the House, only to stall again in the Senate. Meanwhile, the rumors about a special mission to England were confirmed. Madison's only consolation was that Hamilton had not been sent.

The major piece of legislation left unfinished in Congress was Hamilton's plea for more taxes on the everyday pleasures of life, known euphemistically as the "excise bill." The bill placed a tax on chewing tobacco and some of the other little luxuries which, added together, made the proposed legislation a burden on the common man. "Tobacco excise was a burden the *most unequal*," Madison said. "It fell upon the poor, upon sailors, day-labourers, and other people of these classes, while the rich will often escape it." Like many southern lawmakers since his day, Madison felt compelled to defend the principal cash crop of his home state. "Much had been said about the taxing of luxury. The pleasures of life consisted in a series of innocent gratifications, and he felt no satisfaction in the prospect of their being squeezed."[13]

It was no use. Even a tax on carriages, which seemed patently unconstitutional to Madison, was approved by a complaisant House. As a partial admission of his failure, Madison wrote Jefferson that the talk of discipline in Republican ranks was almost a farce. "Six of the N Carolina members were in the majority" favoring Hamilton's bill, he reported.[14] A resolution from a Boston town meeting commending his stand on a general embargo may have soothed Madison's ego slightly. Efforts to lengthen the embargo failed, while the Federalists kept talking about expanding the army after Washington sent Congress a report on the woeful conditions on the frontier. Madison believed that Washington's popularity and influence were "an overmatch for all the efforts Republicanism can make." He lamented, "The party of that sentiment in the Senate is compleatly wrecked; and in the H. of Reps. in a much worse condition than at an earlier period of the Session."

So much for paper majorities, Madison thought, until suddenly the Republicans balked at a bill to increase the army to 10,000 men. Votes Madison had not counted on appeared and he was frank to say the bill "was strangled more easily in the H. of R. than I had expected."[15] Even more pleasing was the House vote on funds sought by Genet's more tractable successor, Citizen Jean Antoine Joseph Fauchet, who said France needed a million dollars rather desperately. Could the United States hurry up on its loan payments? The House said aye, but the bill went no further. Still, the Federalist dandies with their military pretensions and dreams of a huge standing army had been squelched.

Madison was having dreams, too, but none of them concerned grand uniforms or parades. When Washington hinted that he might appoint Madison the United States minister in Paris, Madison had other things on his mind. Mrs. Todd went to visit relatives in Virginia, leaving a melancholy suitor behind. Her cousin reported that the Virginian

> told me I mightd say what I pleas'd to you about him . . . he thinks so much of you in the day that he has Lost his Tongue, at Night he Dreams of you & Starts in his Sleep a Calling on you to relieve his Flame for he Burns to such an excess that he will be shortly consumed & he hopes that your Heart will be calous to every other swain but himself.

Catharine Coles spared no detail. Madison seems to have negotiated with his Venus and surrendered unconditionally.[16]

If anyone at Montpelier knew of this exciting new development in Madison's life, they kept mum. All they heard was that the congressman was coming home, with the piano-forte ready for packing along with the usual requests that made his spring return akin to a second Christmas. By late June 1794 Madison was back in Virginia, waiting for the news from nearby Hanover County. And the news came—bad news. Dolley Todd was ill, most likely from the "Spring sickness," but in no condition to make a decision on Madison's proposal. By this time, Madison was visiting back and forth with Jefferson so that his anxieties must have been known and shared on the mountain tops of Albemarle as well as in Orange County.

Then a letter came to Montpelier addressed in a familiar hand. The three precious pages were read hurriedly, then more slowly, and finally Madison must have managed a smile unlike any his family had seen for years. Dolley took three pages, but she had said YES! A sick foreign visitor took up much of Madison's time, but when a spare hour was available he wrote to Dolley, who had moved from Hanover County to Berkeley County, some 75 miles north of Montpelier, avoiding the roads through Orange County for proper reasons. "I can not express, but hope you will conceive the joy it gave me," Madison told his betrothed. "If the sentiments of my heart can guarantee those of yours," he said, their lives were entering a new era but "the welcome event" would have to wait for a few weeks. His visitor's illness would detain him and the poor man could not be left alone because he was a stranger in "utter ignorance of our language," while Madison was "the only person here who knows a word of his."[17] Ever the gentleman, even to a stranger who knew embarrassing little English and was sick to boot, Madison tarried at Montpelier for several weeks. The news was too good to keep, however, for Dolley Todd's good looks and her recovery from the double tragedy of a year earlier made for good conversation up and down the roads leading to Orange Court House.

Finally the stranger was gone. At last, Madison headed for Harewood, the home of George Steptoe Washington in the Blue Ridge foothills, just beyond the Shenandoah River. Washington was the president's nephew and the husband of Lucy Payne, Dolley Todd's sister. A commodious plantation home, with a fine parlor, heart-of-pine floors, and high ceilings to help keep folks cool in the summer heat—all these enticements added to Madison's joy. But the purpose of his trip was to take a wife, which he did on September 15, 1794, with none of his family present. Before she took her vows, Dolley told her dearest friend "this day I give my Hand to the Man who of all other's I most admire." She was gaining a husband and a protector for her baby. "In this Union I have every thing that is soothing and greatful in prospect—& my little Payne will have a generous & tender protector."[18] After the ceremony was over, after the wedding supper, after her first twenty-four hours together with the friend-turned-husband, the bride penned an extra line on a friendly note: "Dolley Madison! Alass!"

Terribly hurt by his encounter with Kitty Floyd years before, Madison may have been vulnerable to the winning ways of any pleasant young woman. In Dolley Todd, as he must have imagined, Madison had found no ordinary woman. For all her pleasant features and handsome figure, there were other qualities about the lady—Madison had not been her only suitor. Aaron Burr had done him a favor, but nobody needed to help Madison make up his mind. On his own, Madison had won Dolley Todd's hand and heart. Henceforth, the Madisons would be part of the social scene wherever they traveled; and the tentative flirtation matured quickly into a solid marriage that became the greatest blessing of James Madison's private life.

A few days after the ceremony, Madison took his bride on a trip to visit his sister Nelly. They had scarcely had time to refresh themselves when Dolley became ill, so sick that the bridegroom insisted a doctor be summoned from Winchester. The malady was diagnosed as "fever and ague," with a strong dose of quinine bark prescribed. "A decisive administration of the Bark soon expelled the complaint," a relieved Madison reported to his father as he tried to explain that the newlyweds were not coming home to Montpelier but must head northward forthwith.[19] The elder Madison would wait many months before he laid eyes on the daughter-in-law who had captured his son's heart. Jefferson wrote: "Adieu, a thousand respects to mrs. Madison & joys perpetual to both."[20]

As it turned out, the Madisons hurried back to the temporary capital unnecessarily. Congressmen and senators straggled in so casually that by mid-November 1794 there was still no quorum in the Senate, leaving everything official at a standstill. Madison used the enforced leisure to survey the recent congressional elections to determine whether the Hamiltonians would be gaining or losing. In most of the North the Federalists had done well, but the New York delegation was about evenly divided and in Pennsylvania Madison detected signs of a Republican shift. The Maryland delegation was already so bad, Jefferson was told, that any change would be an improvement.

Part of the problem was that pesky Whiskey Rebellion, which broke out after Hamilton's excise taxes goaded distillers in western Pennsylvania beyond endurance. More than tax money was at stake. William Bradford, once Madison's bosom friend at Princeton, was now in Washington's official family, having succeeded Edmund Randolph as attorney general (Randolph took Jefferson's State Department post). How friendly Madison and Bradford now were is problematical, for by 1794 Bradford joined the Federalists in condemning the obstreperous tax-rebels. "I am satisfied there is a formed & regular plan for wrecking & perhaps overthrowing the General Govt.," Bradford told a fellow Federalist. "If the friends of the Union slumber & sleep much longer it is possible the Democratic Societies may give us cause to regret our weakness."

Madison was upset because he believed "the general tendency of insurrections [is] to increase the momentum of power," as the demand for a larger army proved. Hurriedly formed after Washington issued a proclamation ordering "all persons being insurgents" to disperse, an army raised by the Federalist hue and cry headed for western Pennsylvania. Blustering threats from disgusted taxpayers were taken for fact, so that a 13,000-man force under Henry Lee's command spread over the hostile countryside to restore law and order. Washington went out to look things over but came home long ahead of Hamilton, who was now wearing a general's epaulets. Republican newspapers began to ridicule the army, and Hamilton in particular, as all the signs indicated that the expedition's value was questionable. Twenty miserable prisoners were paraded through Philadelphia in an effort to prove how real the threat had been.

The situation was exacerbated when Washington's annual message to Congress hinted that "certain self-created societies" (the Democratic Societies Bradford alluded to) had fomented the Whiskey Rebellion. Everybody knew who belonged to these societies, which were ordinarily called Democratic Republican clubs and met in places where Jefferson and Madison were regularly toasted. Madison was taken aback by Washington's swipe. "The denunciation of the 'Self created Societies' . . . by the President was perhaps the greatest error of his political life," Madison told Monroe.

Madison saw the fine hand of Hamilton involved in writing the speech. The issue surfaced when the House attempted to answer the president and fell into a bitter debate over whether the Republican clubs deserved the reprimand. By narrow votes the effort to censure the clubs first failed but then was revived, and a motion "to limit the censure to the Societies within the scene of insurrection . . . was carried by the casting vote of the Speaker." In that form, Madison told Jefferson, "the whole proposition was abandoned." "It was obvious that a most dangerous game was playing agst. Republicanism," Madison continued. "The insurrection was universally & deservedly odious. The Democratic Societies were presented as in league with it." Federalists hoped to make the whole business a matter of being for or against Washington, a tactic that upset Madison all the more as he pondered the clever use of the great man's name.[21] "If the people of America are so far degenerated already as not to see or to see with indifference, that the Citadel of their liberties is menaced by the precedent before their eyes, they require abler advocates than they now have, to save them from the consequences."

All the camaraderie of 1789 had disappeared in the House as Ames wrote a friend: "Madison and Parker are honorary [club] members. Oh shame! where is thy sting!"[22] Undoubtedly some damage had been done to reputations, for Madison spoke less frequently during the House sessions, a circumstance the Federalists attributed to his declining influence. Gleefully they applauded the Whiskey Rebellion as "the happiest event that ever happened to the United States. It has exhibited Democracy in practice, and even Democrats are frightened with the horrid monster."[23] Representative Fisher Ames delivered a lengthy attack on the Democratic clubs, in which he denounced them as "hateful," "usurping," and "corrupt." Madison finally became fed up with Federalist efforts to show that the club movement was essentially anti-Washington in nature. The club members exercised their rights as citizens to express their opinion on a public issue. Congress had no right to censure the clubs. "Opinions are not the objects of legislation," Madison said, adding: "If we advert to the nature of Republican Government, we shall find that the censorial power is in the people over the Government, and not in the Government over the people." If the societies deserved any kind of punishment, let them "stand or fall by the public opinion; no line can be drawn in this case."[24]

Congressman Zephaniah Swift, no admirer of Madison's, told a friend that the Virginian vainly attempted to answer Ames. "I assure you he is a child in comparison with Ames. A hollow, feeble voice—an awkward, uninteresting manner—a correct stile without energy or copiousness—are his distinguishing traits." The Connecticut member thought Madison was "wholly destitute of vigour of genius, ardour of mind, and brilliancy of imagination." Then, contradicting himself, Swift added: Madison "calculates upon everything with the greatest nicety and precision; he has unquestionably the most personal influence of any man in the house of Representatives. I never knew a man that better understood [how] to husband a character and make the most of his talents; and he is the most artificial, studied character on earth."[25] Madison might have been flattered by such a backhanded compliment, but he was worried about the way things were going in the country's newspapers. He was concerned about the Federalists' ability to score favorably with newspaper reports of their speeches. Ames's attack on the Republican clubs received far more attention than Madison's defense, and with the congressional elections in Virginia delayed until March 1795 Madison feared the impact of the reported debates. The attempt to link Republicans with anti-Washington pronouncements might afford "some new turn in Virga. before the elections in Spring," Madison noted. One report out of Virginia threw fuel on the flames, as Fisher Ames told of an incident "at a meeting of a county in Virginia" where a candidate for the House "gave at a dinner, in a large company, this toast: 'A speedy death to General Washington.'"[26] No wonder Madison's brow was furrowed.

Meanwhile the mission undertaken by John Jay to London became an open secret. Washington turned to the chief justice in desperation, hoping the staid New Yorker could melt some of the British reserve so that boundary questions, Indian war-whoops, and relaxed trade regulations could be wrapped into one diplomatic bundle. "Nothing from Mr. Jay," Madison reported to friends and family in Virginia.[27] As Congress played a waiting game, Federalist Samuel Dexter posed an honest question for Madison, since the New Englander was becoming disillusioned with his party. "My respect, & that of the public, for your talents & Integrity have ever induced me to wish exceedingly for knowledge of the Motives for your present line of politics, when compared with your former Measures," Dexter wrote. Full of courtesy, Madison explained to Dexter he was eager to have an opportunity to remove any impression that there was an inconsistency "between my present & former line of politics."[28]

Madison's rationale is not difficult to discern. In January 1794 he rejected the charge of inconsistency before the full House by claiming that he had been steadfast throughout his public life "in vindicating our national interests, against the policy of Great-Britain towards us: that in all the public stations with which he had been honored since the peace, and on every occasion that had occurred, his conduct had been marked by an adherence to this principle." A year later, he had not changed, but the "monocrats" with their thirst for personal gain and incredible willingness to hand the American market to England on a platter accounted for the perceived difference between the Madison of 1787 and the man who was battling his former comrades in the 1790s.

What made Madison look strange in the eyes of some shrewd political observers was the unexpected economic boom, which was the talk of the country, when the Virginian was still on his honeymoon. Napoleon's armies overwhelmed continental opponents and frightened England into a posture for war, with one result being a greater demand for American products abroad. Warring Europeans needed American wheat and looked to Yankee sailors for their exports of coffee, sugar, and other commodities which were no longer luxuries. Re-exports by American shipping (from West Indian ports to New York or New England and thence to European markets) rose from $1 million in 1792 to nearly $50 million when the decade ended.[29] Madison and most of the Republicans were a bit bewildered by this sudden wave of prosperity. Some of the influx of specie trickled down to the farmers, but fortunes were being made on the pathways to Beacon Hill in Boston and along Chestnut Street in Philadelphia. Thus Republicans suspected that speculation, vast profits, and continued gambling in the public securities was a poor foundation for national well-being; and unless Jay brought home a package that proved them wrong, the Republicans were ready to deny the Federalists any credit for the upswing in crop prices in the spring of 1795.

The postponed congressional elections in Virginia loomed as word from Jay was awaited. Dolley Madison suffered a kind of relapse which was diagnosed as pleurisy, but with the tender care of her bridegroom evident she began to recover. No time was left for a campaign trip to Virginia, so Madison let his brother William relay discreet letters to important men in the key counties—more he could not do. There was a rumor that Madison intended to retire, and that had to be squelched. Jefferson had heard that gossip and dismissed it by saying that Madison's absence from Congress was unthinkable "unless [Madison had plans for moving] to a more splendid & a more efficacious post."[30] In short, if Madison wanted to run for president, he might be allowed to forgo another term in the House. "There I should rejoice to see you," Jefferson said, "I hope I may say I shall rejoice to see you." All Madison needed to indicate, so it seemed, was his availability.

Instead, Madison replied that he harbored no such ambition. "Reasons of *every* kind, and some of the, of the most *insuperable* as well as *obvious* kind, shut my mind against the admission of any ideas such as you seem to glance at," Madison wrote.[31] Madison promised more of an explanation when they were together, but the gist of his remarks was that Jefferson himself was the man most likely to become Washington's successor. "You ought to be preparing yourself to hear truths, which no inflexibility will be able to withstand," he added.

Some consolation came to both Jefferson and Madison as Hamilton made good his threat to resign. Before leaving the cabinet on January 31, 1795, Hamilton issued a report on the national debt that laid out a plan for repayment over a thirty-year period. Predictably, Madison regarded Hamilton's "long Valedictory Rept." as unsatisfactory; and he was more than skeptical when told that Hamilton "is going to N. Y. and does not mean to return into public life at all."[32] In the back of Madison's mind must have been the suspicion that Hamilton was leaving Washington's cabinet to start campaigning to be the great man's successor.

Of idle speculation there was no end. Nothing official on the Jay Treaty came to Congress but there were bits and pieces of rumors that Madison drew together until it was plain to him that the concessions to England were a capitulation unworthy of a sovereign nation. But Dolley was on the mend, which meant he had to think about things like teacups and damask curtains. To James Monroe, now settled in Paris as the American minister, Madison sent a small order for bed and window curtains at whatever price Parisian merchants demanded, plus "1 Tea Sett of China" and one full dinner service. "You will be able to judge of the stile suitable to my faculties & fashions," Madison added, "by the rule you mean to pursue in providing for your own future accomodation." Good husband that he strove to be, Madison went further and asked Monroe "to go beyond the enumerated articles into others which you may know to be acceptable to a young House-Keeper." Monroe got the point and went on a buying spree that eventually cost Madison about £2,500. Madison's consolation was Monroe's assurance that the prices paid were bargains "compared with what is usual in America."[33]

The return of Dolley Madison's good health was welcome news, as was the report from Orange County that Madison had won reelection. "I went to the Courthouse," a kinsman noted, "it being the day for Election of the Representatives for Congress. But few people met, the number who voted did not amount to 30, all for J. Madison." Less reassuring was the continuous flow of rumors concerning the treaty negotiated by Jay, and as more information leaked out Madison saw that much had been surrendered to the British while little was gained. The western fur-trading posts were to be handed over, as had been promised in 1783, but the method of the British turnover left Americans at a disadvantage; and more disturbing was the report about an article prohibiting for a decade the discriminatory tariff Madison believed essential to American prosperity. If true, Madison regarded such a concession "strikingly revolting." But Madison also knew the dangers of jumping to conclusions. "It is wrong however to prejudge," he told Jefferson, "but I suspect that Jay has been betrayed by his anxiety to couple us with England, and to avoid returning with his finger in his mouth."[34] Until the president gave the treaty to the Senate, all was a matter of speculation, yet the signs portended another tiresome party struggle.

Perhaps in anticipation of a fight unlike anything that had taken place since 1789, Madison took up his pen again to write an anonymous pamphlet meant to correct misrepresentations on his conduct and motives. The writing project took more foolscap and time than he intended, so that other business and pleasure were thrust aside. Simply titled *Political Observations*, the pamphlet has been neglected by historians who like to think of Madison as a turncoat nationalist who had converted from earlier beliefs in strong federal action to become a states' rights spokesman. This pamphlet proves that nothing of the sort was in Madison's mind in 1795. Full of frustration at the success Federalists achieved in the Third Congress, Madison made the plea that he was an exponent of constitutional government while the Federalists had taken the road of liberal constructionism. Like miners and sappers, they were preparing the Constitution for some kind of explosive situation that would jeopardize all the gains from 1776 onward. In his listing of the excesses of Federalist power—the Funding Act; the charter for the United States bank, and the refusal to invoke commercial discrimination against England—all these black marks had been given the glow of political approval by the men who wished "to turn the tide of public opinion into a party channel."

Without mentioning Hamilton by name, Madison placed the blame on the men surrounding the Treasury secretary and "the newspapers of a certain stamp." At a time when newspapers were the chief means of reaching the general public, Madison feared that the Federalists' attacks, unless challenged, could make converts at the ballot box. Hamilton's pen moved day and night, causing Jefferson to look on his stream of essays in grudging admiration. "Hamilton is really a colossus to the antirepublican party," he told Madison. "Without numbers, he is an host within himself. . . . In truth, when he comes forward, there is nobody but yourself who can meet him." To counter the Federalists' overbearing influence (they controlled perhaps 80 percent of the country's newspapers), Madison defended Republicans attacked by the Federalist press, claiming that Hamilton's critics had been depicted "in all the deformity which the most industrious calumny could devise."[35]

Partly in anger, partly as a defensive mechanism, Madison began hewing planks for the Republican party platform. Nothing distressed Madison more than the Federalists' repeated attempts to enlarge the size of the army, which the Virginian saw as a means of adding to the Federalists' patronage plums—commissions by the score for the sons and nephews of congressmen and lesser officeholders. Thus to the catalog of Federalist mistakes Madison added the clamors for a large standing army, said to be needed by the threat of war. "The cry of war has . . . been echoed throught the continent, with a loudness proportioned to the emptiness of the pretext." And most of the Federalist misdeeds had been masked with the ruse that "the president wants it." Thus Madison added his pet peeve:

> There are not a few ever ready to invoke the name of Washington; to garnish their heretical doctrines with his virtues, and season their unpalatable measures with his popularity. Those who take this liberty, will not, however, be mistaken; his truest friends will be the last to sport with his influence, above all, for electioneering purposes.

Madison also reserved a few bolts for those who pretended that Republicans really wanted the United States to behave like a French colony. Whoever made such a suggestion, he wrote, ignored the fact that France was "the freest nation in Europe" and failed to perceive the French Revolution "as a blessing to mankind."

Madison probably had no intention of setting any stage for a battle against the Jay treaty with his pamphlet. Rather he wrote in an angry, frustrated mood because he thought the Federalists not only had had their way in Congress but they also had used the newspapers and printing presses in every state to blacken the motives of Republicans. Madison told Jefferson he wrote the screed because of "the entreaties of some friends, just at the close of the Session."[36] He was not particularly proud of the performance, but in its preparation Madison was forced to think about the proper role for an opposition party. He must have concluded that the time had come to use every weapon in his political arsenal to stop the onrush of Federalist policies. Hamilton was only out of sight, not out of mind.

With Jefferson far removed from the battle, Madison knew he had to be the driving force behind any effort to thwart the Federalists. Nothing portrayed the fundamental differences in the battle about to be joined as distinctly as the Jay treaty. Aware that the treaty provisions would invite protests, a Virginia Republican, breaking the senatorial mandate for secrecy, had leaked the treaty to the press. The fury of Republicans is difficult to understand if the temper of the 1790s is not taken into account. Long-festering grievances, such as compensation for slaves released by the British during the Revolution, were ignored; the western forts were to be evacuated, but British fur traders had unlimited access to American territory. One article, allowing American ships into the West Indian market, was so full of restrictions the Senate threw it out. What really stuck in the Republicans' craw was the implied sense that the American negotiator had been outsmarted, overwhelmed, and then told to "take it or leave it."

Madison understood the nature of the challenge at once. All pretense that political parties were not useful or desirable was now dropped. Here was a real issue, and Madison was ready to declare his own private war on the Federalists. Since he was the acknowledged leader of the opposition, Madison took command. Before he finished, a Republican party with a program and clear purpose was in the field.

⚯

Almost a year elapsed before the Jay treaty officially came before the House of Representatives. Until then the struggle went on in the Senate and in the newspapers, with no quarter given on either side. Madison's inner conviction was that no matter how the votes in the Senate went, the people shared his belief that the treaty was a long backward step in America's effort to become a truly sovereign nation. In Madison's view the treaty was the last straw, for the "monocrats" had shed all pretense that they were Americans first-last-and-always by giving up the right to squeeze the British at the customs shed. Jefferson reinforced this idea when he wrote:

> A bolder party-stroke was never struck. For it certainly is an attempt of a party, which finds they have lost their majority in one branch of the legislature, to make a law by the aid of the other branch and of the executive, under color of a treaty, which shall bind up the hands of the adverse branch from ever restraining the commerce of their patron-nation.[37]

The Senate passed the treaty, but only by the scant two-thirds majority required by the Constitution. Madison must have wondered if Washington would sign it, but he no longer was on terms of intimacy with the president.

Despite his anxious moments, Washington was finally nudged toward approving the treaty because of Edmund Randolph's indiscretions. Washington bristled under the continued British seizures of American ships, but Randolph's inopportune borrowings from the French minister became public knowledge. Washington decided he had to sign the treaty or make it seem as if the French had inordinate influence in the new republic.

Washington's signature shifted the battle to new ground, and at the same time left Madison facing a dilemma that was, like all dilemmas, a matter of painful choice. The Federalists and Republican newspaper editors were going at each other hammer and tong. The only avenue left for Madison was through the device of House implementation, since the Senate had the sole power to ratify treaties. Madison's friends made it clear that they expected him to lead the battle. Bishop James Madison in Williamsburg read the treaty and threw up his hands in alarm. "A vast Feild is now opened to you, & I believe all America looks up to yourself and our Friend Mr Jefferson" to stop the Jay treaty cold.[38] But freshman congressman Edward Livingston of New York was afraid Madison was not up to the job of derailing the treaty. "His great fault as a politician appears to me a want of decision and disposition to magnify his adversaries Strength," Livingston confessed to his brother. Livingston, not Madison, introduced a resolution instructing Washington to lay all the documents related to the treaty before the House. Madison thought the reach of the resolution too broad, so he offered an amendment that left to the president any choice of such papers. The House was in no mood to temporize, however, and Madison's proposal lost by ten votes. Instead of vigorously supporting Livingston, Madison paused on the threshold of an all-out fight. "By his hesitancy," Jerald A. Combs wrote, Madison "lost his control of the Republican faction in the House of Representatives. The leadership passed to more decisive and more headstrong men."[39] Livingston's resolution passed, but then Washington refused to submit any papers to the House by claiming executive privilege.

At this juncture, as historian Noble Cunningham has shown, the anti-treaty members of the House held their first caucus to talk about ways of crippling the effects of the Senate vote. They discussed the Jay treaty in terms of the appropriations needed to carry out the provisions, since all spending money from the public treasury had to originate in the House. Through this back door Madison entered, and on April 6, 1796, he widened the wedge created by the constitutional issue. There was more to the business than that, however, for at the heart of the matter was Madison's innate feeling that Great Britain had never accepted the full implications of the 1783 peace treaty. Like it or not, Great Britain's attitude toward her former colony was to regard the United States as a pipsqueak among nations. A great nation does not make concessions to a pipsqueak.

The prevailing notion had been that once the Senate ratified a treaty, the business was finished. Madison attacked this concept by insisting that the House, under the Constitution, had certain delegated powers which included the implementation of treaties. He was emboldened by a substantial majority vote in support of his interpretation, and in the ensuing debates Madison struck at the Federalists' prediction that if the United States rejected the treaty, England would retaliate with a declaration of war. "No man would say that the United States, if an independent people, had not a right to judge their own interests, and to decline any Treaty that did not duly provide from them." A rejection by America was not an act of provocation but of sovereignty.

> But apart from this, was it conceivable that Great Britain, with all the dangers and embarrassments which are thickening upon her, would wantonly make war on a country which was her best market she had in the world for her manufactures, which paid her an annual balance in specie of ten or twelve millions of dollars, and whose supplies were moreover essential to an important part of her dominions?

Such a threat was nothing more than a chimera in the minds of misguided Federalists, for "an unprovoked war with Great Britain, on this country, would argue a degree of madness greater than under any other circumstances that could well be imagined." A few days after he spoke, Madison confided to Jefferson his belief that the Republicans had enough votes to cripple the treaty. "I trust without being sure that the House will be firm," Madison concluded.[40]

Defections in the Republican majority apparently began the moment the votes had been tallied, for a week after Madison spoke with some assurance, he was alarmed by the conduct of lukewarm party men. "The majority has melted, by changes and absence, to 8 or 9 votes," he told Jefferson. "Whether these will continue firm is more than I can decide."[41] A week later, all the guesswork was over. On April 29 the House voted, 50 to 49, "for carrying the Treaty with Great Britain into effect." Thus the opportunity provided by the Jay treaty, which Madison thought would end in a Federalist defeat so decisive "as to fortify the Republican cause," had boomeranged to leave the party "in a very crippled condition."[42]

In the aftermath of defeat it was clear that Madison had miscalculated Republican strength. Madison took the early majority at face value, not calculating upon the pressures exerted by the commercial community that believed its interests were threatened. Before the final vote, Madison took note of the circulating petitions in northern cities meant to influence votes in the House. "Every possible exertion is made as usual on the other side," he noted. "Among other extraordinary manoeuvres, the Insurance Companies here & in New Y[ork] stopt business, in order to reduce prices & alarm the public," the congressman noted as he saw a force exerted in American politics that he did not fully comprehend—the lobbyist. Bankers had spread the word that rejection of the treaty would have dire effects on business, and at "that moment there is a general pinch for money. Under such circumstances, a Bank Director soliciting subscriptions is like a Highwayman with a pistol demanding the purse," Madison observed.[43] By then it was too late—the pressures from the Federalists in banking and commerce swayed all the weak reeds—with results which Madison and Jefferson could only lament, not change.

In the long run, ratification of the Jay treaty was the best thing that could have happened to Madison. The outcome forced him to awaken from his ideological dream and realize that many of the things he had argued in *The Federalist #10* were true—vested interests do have a way of placing pressure in politics and those interests place pocketbook above patriotism in a great many instances. He had now witnessed one such example, and as he told Jefferson: "The progress of this business throughout has been the most worrying & vexatious that I ever encountered; and the more so as the causes lay in the unsteadiness, the follies, the perverseness, & the defections among our friends, more than in the strength or dexterity, or malice of our opponents."[44] The remedy lay in party organization and discipline. Madison paid dearly to learn the lesson, but he had learned it.

Until the final approval of the Jay treaty, the Republicans as a party had been a somewhat sociable group of like-minded politicians without any fixed commitment to a philosophy or a leader. Within twelve months this group gave way to a corps of politicians who knew that the cardinal sin in public life was to lose an election. They set themselves on a course designed to steer them to victory in local contests, statewide balloting, and finally to the presidential election. If it was too late to do much about the presidential election only a few months away, the clear signal to Madison and Jefferson was that they had only four years to set things aright. Allow the pro-British "monocrats" to hold power beyond 1800 and their Republican vision would be blurred beyond recapture. In simple terms, the salvation of the Republic depended on their ability to turn the country around by 1800 at the latest.

Thus the Republican-Democratic party was to rise from the ashes of the Jay treaty defeat. Within the space of the next six months, Jefferson was forced from his mountain retreat and shoved into the vortex of the political whirlpools that formed as Washington jostled homeward for the last time. If Jefferson had wanted to push Madison forward as a presidential candidate, he could have written to friends in New York, Pennsylvania, and Virginia and suggested that a Madison boom was needed to turn aside the pretensions of John Adams. Jefferson did nothing of the kind, possibly in deference to Madison's wishes. Jefferson seemed more interested in mold-board plows and clover fields than in a sustained drive to oust the Federalists. "Jefferson's political foes were largely responsible for the circulation of the idea," Noble Cunningham discerned, "that Jefferson was pulling all the strings from the drawing room at Monticello."

Hamilton's influence undoubtedly was the chief reason that Federalist leaders feared Jefferson, even as they talked of "Madison's party." Madison, a Federalist congressman said, was "the great man of the party." But as with their New York opponents, within the circle of Virginia politicians there was a different view: Madison was the party wheel horse, but Jefferson held the reins. Madison and Beckley worked from a Philadelphia base, accepting this premise. The more Jefferson said he wanted to stay a farmer the rest of his life, the harder his Virginia friends labored to make him president. With his insight into Washington's plans, Madison told Monroe in February 1796 that Adams would probably be the Federalist candidate for president. "The Republicans, knowing that Jefferson alone can be started with hope of success," Madison wrote, "mean to push him." Madison clearly understood that Jefferson was the outstanding man in their party and his fame, as Dumas Malone has noted, was "owing in no small degree to the advertisement his enemies had given him."

In short, Jefferson was loved for the enemies he had made. "It is now generally understood that the President will retire," Madison wrote. "Jefferson is the object on one side Adams apparently on the other."[45] After the treaty issue was settled congressmen relaxed but rumors floated through the corridors in Philadelphia. "Our politics assume a pacific and insipid face," Federalist Fisher Ames reported. "Who shall be President and Vice, are questions that will put an end to the armed neutrality of parties."[46]

Jefferson himself seemed above it all (a posture taken by most presidential candidates until the twentieth century). After Washington finally broke the suspense with his Farewell Address, the political temperature quickly rose to a feverish height. Publication of Washington's valedictory was, a shrewd congressman said, "a signal, like dropping a hat, for the party racers to start."[47] Without making a single public gesture, Jefferson tacitly approved the efforts Madison and Beckley made in Philadelphia to relay the word: choose local electors who will make a firm commitment to vote for Jefferson. Under the constitutional system of the time, each presidential elector voted "for two Persons, of whom one at least shall not be an Inhabitant of the same State with themselves." That provision ruled out any chance for a Jefferson-Madison ticket, making the second choice fall almost by default on New Yorker Aaron Burr. But the party existed more on paper than in fact, and nothing proved this more than the haphazard recommendations made to Republican electors. In effect, they were urged to vote for Jefferson and one other Republican—Burr, Samuel Adams, George Clinton, anybody but John Adams. That suited Madison, for he apparently had discussed retirement with his wife and was eager to escape the halls of Congress. Madison may have talked to Jefferson about what might happen if the voters picked the man from Monticello as their president, but this is uncertain. A sense of propriety that we can scarcely comprehend in this century would, in the eighteenth, have precluded much speculative conversation.

The timing of Washington's Farewell Address kept the 1796 presidential campaign mercifully short. The president released his statement declining reelection on September 19 and it was several weeks before the tidings spread across the Union. Meanwhile elections had been scheduled for early November in most places so that the buttonholing of voters was held to a minimum. There really was no precedent for a rollicking campaign since in the first two presidential elections everybody knew the winner before the race started.

In the changed circumstances of 1796 congressmen played a key role with the lines clearly drawn months in advance between Adams and Jefferson. Some kind of informal Republican caucus among congressmen settled on a helter-skelter strategy but Madison held himself aloof, leaving the paperwork to Beckley in Philadelphia while he rested at Montpelier and made a point of not visiting Jefferson. Few men in politics knew the trends better than Madison, but on this occasion he found it difficult to assess the impact of Washington's late withdrawal and Jefferson's seeming indifference. "I have not seen Jefferson and have thought it best to present him no opportunity of protesting to his friend[s] agnst. being embarked in the contest," Madison told Monroe. "Whether he will get a majority of vote[s] is uncer[tain]—I am by no means sanguine."[48] When a friend living in Tidewater Virginia told Madison in early October that voters in his neighborhood "are generally by profession supporters of Mr Jefferson's election," Madison countered with a curt sentence. "I am . . . but little informed of the present state of electioneering politics, either out of or in Virginia."[49]

How much Madison worked behind the scenes for Jefferson, writing letters to the influential New York and Pennsylvania public men who knew the political leanings in their states, is anybody's guess—for no evidence of such activity has survived. If Madison was the passive supporter, Beckley made up for Madison's discretion by working overtime to see that Pennsylvania was safe for Jefferson. Beckley was ever the optimist and clever enough to see that Aaron Burr was on the campaign trail making a plea on behalf of Jefferson's candidacy that carried a hint of Burr's own presidential aspirations. The indefatigable Beckley became a workhorse, writing to Republican leaders in key states, counting votes until he determined that Pennsylvania was the vital state. "If Pennsylvania do well the Election is safe," he predicted.[50]

With a wife to consider Madison began to worry about a place to stay in Philadelphia when Congress reconvened. Beckley was no help, Dolley Madison's house was leased to a long-term tenant, and although the honeymoon was over Madison had no intention of spending a Pennsylvania winter in a tent. Around Montpelier these were busy times, for Madison's father was ailing as work proceeded on the grist mill which the family was building a few miles north of Orange Court House. Rumors of Madison's plans to retire from Congress circulated beyond his district. Word came from Richmond that Madison could be elected governor of Virginia if only he would say the word. "It is probable that there will be no opposition" in the state legislature, Madison was told, "and it is certain, that if there should be one, it will be unavailing."[51] Flattered but firm in his resolve to become a private citizen, Madison advised friends he was not available. The next session of Congress, scheduled to begin December 5, would be his last.

Good roads and good weather made the journey to Philadelphia half-way pleasant, but the housing problem was exacerbated when Madison's sister Fanny, who was twenty-two and still unwed, decided to join them for the winter. Dolley Madison was a matchmaker of some note, but she found it easier to find a house than a beau for Fanny.

Meanwhile, Madison and fellow Republicans scanned the daily news for election results. In early December, with the vote too close to call, Madison feared the Federalists would pull enough tricks to keep Jefferson at home. A few days before Christmas 1796 the suspense ended when tabulations showed Adams had three more electoral votes than his nearest rival, Jefferson. A disappointed Madison wrote Jefferson: "You must prepare yourself . . . to be summoned to the place Mr. Adams now fills."[52] Before the results were known, Jefferson once again said he thought Madison was the one who should move into the executive branch, but he did not labor the point.

While still worried about the presidential race Madison had to face several urgings that he forgo plans to retire in March. One more term "is all we ask," a friend entreated, for two more years "will not break in on your domestick happiness or wishes." A Richmond merchant assured Madison that even the Virginia Federalists esteemed his "Virtue, & patriotism, they rely on your wisdom & talents—they acquiesce—they love you from the right source. . . . Our critical situation calls on a proof of your love of Country, for one Congress more at least."[53]

By this time, Madison knew how to say "no" firmly, just as he was beseeching Jefferson to say "yes." Jefferson not only told Madison he would take the vice-presidency but he sought his friend's advice on a congratulatory letter he had drafted for the president-elect. Madison was left free to send it on to Adams or not, depending on his judgment as to its tone and style. Madison advised Jefferson to drop the matter, for the tone was a bit too congratulatory. "The tenderness due to the zealous and active promoters of your election makes it doubtful whether their anxiety and exertions ought to be depreciated by anything implying the unreasonableness of them," Madison suggested.[54] Jefferson got the idea: the letter was never sent.

As a lame-duck congressman Madison consoled himself that Jefferson was coming on the scene as he left it. The chief worry the two Virginians shared was that the Federalists were shoving the country toward war with France. In the wake of French depredations on American merchantmen in the Caribbean, Washington recalled Monroe from Paris and Secretary of State Timothy Pickering seemed eager for a fight. "A war with France & an alliance with G. B. enter both into print & conversation," Madison reported.[55] With Washington half out of office and Adams half in, Congress seemed inert. Even a Federalist congressman complained: "I could write a book, without rising from my chair, on the bad tendency of this disposition."[56]

With only a few weeks left in the session, Madison busied himself more with family than with national affairs. If the record of debates in Congress is accurate, Madison spoke hardly at all but managed to send instructions homeward on buying more land and the planting of clover, wheat, and rye on various tracts at Montpelier. He also arranged to purchase a riding horse, set a time for a slave to come to Philadelphia to help in the packing, and figured he could bring sister Fanny and his wife home late in March.[57] Well-meaning friends decided that if Madison would not serve in Congress he might well go the Virginia legislature, and began to sound him out.

Amidst the ordering of crates and the packing of china Madison went to his last session in the House of Representatives on March 3. Too much unfinished business forced the representatives to adjourn for dinner, then return to a candlelit session where Madison's last speech concerned a belated effort to help free Lafayette, who had been imprisoned by the Austrians since 1792. Nothing was done about Lafayette, despite Madison's efforts, and a weary Madison wound his way home through the familiar Philadelphia streets. Little seemed to have changed since he trod over them a decade earlier. In 1787 Madison had wondered if the republic could be saved. Now he speculated on the future of the republic without Washington. Starting on the morrow, America would be without its greatest man.

The moment for Adams's inauguration neared. Jefferson arrived a few days early, spent one night with the Madisons, and while there managed an interview with the president-elect. Jefferson learned that Adams was thinking about sending a three-man mission to France to arbitrate their differences amicably, and Madison was to be one of the three. Jefferson, knowing Madison's aversion to an ocean voyage, told Adams he doubted if Madison would accept the assignment. Still, a rumor leaked to other public men that Madison would soon be on his way to France, carrying an olive leaf. Some leading Federalists, including Hamilton, thought Madison's appointment would be a stroke of statesmanship, for was he not an honorary French citizen? "Were I Mr. Adams, then I believe I should begin my Presidency by naming an extraordinary Commission to the French Republic," Hamilton wrote an admirer (knowing it would go straight to the target). "And I think it would consist of three persons, Mr. Madison Mr. Pinkney & Mr. Cabot. I would pursue this course for several reasons, because I would have a man as influential with the French as Mr. Madison yet I would not trust him alone lest his Gallicism should work amiss."[58] But Madison himself stopped the rumor in its tracks, and left it to Jefferson to relay his refusal to the president-elect.

At high noon on March 4 the people's choices appeared in the Senate chamber of Congress Hall alongside the retiring Washington. Surely the Madisons were among the crowd that saw Jefferson take his oath of office a few hours earlier. Adams's speech was heartening, for the new president spoke warmly of his past association with the French and his hopes for continued friendship with them. Madison was willing to give Adams the benefit of the doubt, but dedicated Francophobes Pickering and Hamilton thought the president's talk disappointing.

In a matter of days, Jefferson headed back for Virginia and the Madisons were not far behind. Jefferson figured his duties as vice-president permitted him to return and look after spring plantings. He carried a letter from Madison to his father explicitly forbidding the use of his son's name in the county election for the legislature.

Madison was beginning to worry more about the planting of clover seed than the rumors of war from Europe. He watched eagerly as a team of horses was hitched to the coach that would carry his party to the Blue Ridge mountains, obviously expecting a kind of second honeymoon in the same neighborhood where he spent the first. For twenty-one years Madison had been in and out of legislatures and congresses. Now all that was ended. Let Jefferson and Beckley and Albert Gallatin manage the Republican party strategy. For the first time in his life, the forty-six-year-old Virginian was going to try and make a living as a planter. Madison returned to Montpelier, suspecting that he would spend the rest of his life there. What an appealing prospect!

CHAPTER SEVEN

APPRENTICESHIP
FOR THE
WHITE HOUSE

"Mr. Madison is to retire," John Adams told his wife when the news spread in Philadelphia. "It Seems the Mode of becoming great is to retire. Madison I Suppose after a Retirement of a few Years is to be President or V.P. . . . It is marvellous how political Plants grow in the Shade."[1] Adams knew Madison better than Madison knew himself. One of Madison's last acts before he left Philadelphia was to take out an insurance policy on the Walnut Street house inherited by his wife, which would be leased for the income it produced—money that might be needed in Virginia. Building was under way at the national capital on the banks of the Potomac by 1800, but Madison made no inquiries concerning a lot in the new federal district. Instead Madison foresaw the gradual assumption of all the duties a plantation master performed during his father's declining years. He looked forward to spending the remainder of his life amongst his kin and the tiny Montpelier community with its main house, slave quarters, and several tenant homes.

Madison's years as a legislator had been rewarding but unprofitable. Keenly scrupulous, he avoided any investment that might have been made from information gained when the Funding Act was debated, with its potential profits too tempting for some colleagues. His purchase of the Mohawk Valley lands with Monroe in 1786 had brought only a modest profit, so that Madison returned to Montpelier with custodianship of his wife's property, his status as an eldest son, and a small cash balance in the bank. The farm lands in his own name adjoined the main Montpelier holdings, and were not extensive. Like most of his landed contemporaries in piedmont Virginia, Madison was "well off" but he was far from wealthy. Moreover, the fact that his father was seventy-four and infirm may have prompted Madison's decision to leave Congress.

Montpelier, encompassing several farms, many pastures, and nearly five thousand acres, made demands on Madison far different from his public life. One change was soon noticeable. No longer was Madison chained to his writing desk. His correspondence shrank to a few letters to merchants, relatives, several political associates, and, of course, the new vice-president. Rotating crops, fertilizing tired fields, and supervising field hands became an absorbing interest for Madison during this hiatus. Dolley Madison seemed to get along well with her mother-in-law. The younger woman had a way of winning over all the Madisons, so that meal times were convivial occasions breaking into the daily routine of horseback rides with overseers, newspaper reading, and keeping accounts with agents in Philadelphia, Fredericksburg, Richmond, and Liverpool.

In his chosen exile from politics Madison was kept informed of events by Jefferson, who frequently stopped at Montpelier on trips to and from Philadelphia. The Fifth Congress convened early in May 1797, owing to President Adams's anxieties concerning the French situation. The personal news Madison heard of the goings-on in Congress must have caused him to sigh with relief that he was no longer a member, for vitriol had replaced courtesy as Federalists and Republicans swapped insults and talk of duels.

After a brief truce, when even Hamilton spoke of a buried hatchet, the ancient animosities revived. "The insolence and scurrility of the british faction here can scarcely be born," a fellow Virginian reported.[2] The bitterness grew when a letter Jefferson had written to Philip Mazzei in Europe appeared in American newspapers. Jefferson wrote Mazzei during the Jay treaty fight, and thinking he was writing a private letter he had mentioned Washington in terms not complimentary. "Men who were Sampsons in the field and Solomons in the council . . . have had their heads shorn by the harlot England," Jefferson wrote. Shocked by the public reaction, Jefferson wrote Madison and Monroe (who had recently returned from France) for advice: should he ignore the letter or try to explain its contents away? Monroe was all for candor, but Madison thought otherwise. Both Washington and Adams had avoided public explanations, Madison said, and Jefferson ought to follow their precedent. "I consider it moreover as a ticklish experiment to say publickly yes or no to the interrogatories of party spirit," Madison counseled.

Jefferson pleaded with Madison to join him at Monticello for a conference on this and other problems already facing their barely weaned party. Madison promised nothing, for he found farming life more demanding than expected. Madison's perspective on politics was far different in Orange County than it had been in Philadelphia. Napoleon's victories in Europe unsettled the Federalists and helped bolster the price of wheat, but Madison must have found he was thinking more about the sale of his grain than Bonaparte's latest success. Jefferson's faithful weekly reports from Philadelphia, telling of Federalist saber-rattling and intrigue, drew only a short retort from Madison and most of that concerned crop or weather conditions. All those worries vexing his friends in Philadelphia seemed far away when Madison heard Dolley Madison's voice down the hall, calling him to dinner.

Not that life at Montpelier was always a bed of roses. There was no period in Madison's life longer than a week or two when he did not complain of some ailment, and during the summer of 1797 when Jefferson wanted to arrange a reunion with the Monroes Madison excused himself from a commitment by saying he had suffered, only two days earlier, from "something like a cholera morbus or bilious cholic, of which, tho' much relieved, I still feel the effects."[3] Before the summer ended, the Madisons managed to visit Monticello for a week. There Jefferson brought his friend up to date on the Adams administration. But they also talked about less weighty matters, and by Christmas the merchant who had imported Italian marble for Monticello was speculating that a similar chimney piece for Montpelier might be delivered in ten months if all went well. The Monroes finally reached Albemarle County and repeated Jefferson's plea for a visit. Monroe offered the invitation after one of his common complaints that he was short of money and could use "a draft for two or three hundred dolrs."[4] Madison found it hard to say no.

An unusually cold early winter in 1797–98 kept the Madisons near the Montpelier fireplaces as the thermometer dipped to 10 degrees, but the new year was ushered in with "a fine spell of open weather with plentiful rains at proper intervals."[5] The good weather left Madison in a buoyant mood, although he admitted the winter wheat crop presented "the most unpromising aspect." He was planting more and more grain at Montpelier to lessen the old dependence upon tobacco. Unlike tobacco, which required constant tending by the slaves, wheat could be sown and left alone until harvest time—a circumstance that had great appeal for Madison. When the good weather persisted into February, Madison sent to Jefferson's nail factory for 50,000 handmade nails and dispatched two bushels of seed potatoes to Monroe, who lived a few miles beyond Monticello and was now trying to make a living as a lawyer in Charlottesville. "Mrs. M. insists on adding for Mrs. Monroe a few pickles & preserves with half a dozen bottles of Gooseberries & a bag of dried cherries," Madison explained.[6]

By words written and spoken Jefferson conveyed to Madison the impression that President Adams had been maneuvered into a belligerent stance against France by the leading Federalists. Franco-American relations were so strained that armed ships flying the stars and stripes answered the salvos of frigates under the French tri-color. Only a report of progress from the three peace negotiators Adams had dispatched to Paris would stop the Federalists from their plans to add strength to the navy and increase army appropriations. Both measures were anathema to Republicans, since shipbuilding and increased armaments spelled higher taxes. Madison took time away from his planter's duties to compare Adams with Washington:

> There never was perhaps a greater contrast between two characters, than between those of the present President & of his predecessor, altho' it is the boast & prop of the present, that he treads in the steps of his predecessor. The one cool considerate & cautious, the other headlong & kindled into flame by every spark that lights on his passions: the one ever scrutinizing into the public opinion, and ready to follow where he could not lead it: the other insulting it by the most adverse sentiments & pursuits: W. a hero in the field, yet overweighing every danger in the Cabinet. A. without a single pretension to the character of a Soldier, a perfect Quixotte as a Statesman: the former cheif Magistrate pursuing peace every where with sincerity, tho' mistaking the means; the latter taking as much pains to get into war, as the former took to keep out of it.

Besides his distress at Adams's apparent eagerness for a war with France, Madison told Jefferson he was also disturbed by the recent disgraceful scene on the floor of the House. Republican Matthew Lyon spat on the face of Federalist Roger Griswold, and the offended Connecticut congressman flayed Lyon with a cane. House members talked endlessly about the incident, but ultimately decided to do nothing. "The affair of Lyon & Griswold is bad eno' [in] every way, but worst of all in becoming a topic of tedious & disgraceful debates in Congress."[7]

Flaring tempers were a sign of far more intense partisan feeling than when Madison sat in n the House. Federalists who expected a war with France were galled by the barrage of criticism leveled at the Adams administration in newspapers with Republican leanings. They were easily infuriated when the Philadelphia *Aurora*, published by Benjamin Franklin Bache (grandson of the celebrated printer-politician), pummeled Adams personally in his columns. "We are now wonderfully popular except with Bache & Co who in his paper calls the President old, querilous, Bald, blind, crip[p]led, Toothless Adams," Abigail Adams complained.[8] Madison read Bache's paper and probably thought the Republican editor was simply giving the Federalists what they deserved; but neither he nor Jefferson fully comprehended the fury building in the breasts of High Federalist congressmen who saw traitors lurking in every Republican alley. To their minds, criticism of the government during times of extreme tension was tantamount to treason.

In the midst of this combustible situation a bomb lit public opinion when Adams sent Congress the "XYZ dispatches," using letters to conceal the names of the three American envoys in France who had been confronted by French demands for a $250,000 bribe and the promise of an American loan. The dispatches were made public after Adams took a report from the three envoys as the basis for a request to Congress for a heavy buildup of armaments in obvious preparation for a war. A furious Jefferson wrote Madison about Adams's "insane message which you will see in the public papers" while admitting the president's message "has had great effect."[9] The Republicans had demanded proof of French duplicity. Now Adams gave it to them, causing their ploy to backfire, for it was patent that Talleyrand and his minions were treating the American representatives with studied contempt.

War with France was all but declared. As Jefferson wrote Madison, "the question of war & peace now depends on a toss of cross and pile."[10] The momentous question could go either way and nobody was prepared to make a prediction with assurance. Madison pondered the situation and told Jefferson that the Constitution "supposes, what the History of all Govts. demonstrates, the Ex. is the branch of power most interested in war, & most prone to it." Adams stood, however, at the precipice without being forced over it. While he played for time, the Federalists in Congress assumed war was only a nudge away and set out on a legislative program that forced Madison back into the trenches of party warfare.

As Madison's successor in the House noted, it would have been a pity had America gone to war on the theory that two wrongs make a right. "I hope we shall not go to war on account of an intemperate speech from the President," John Dawson wrote, "or the dishonest conduct of a minister of foreign relations."[11] Nonetheless, the Federalists smelled blood and moved to squelch all dissent in the country so that if war came the nation would appear to be totally united. As has happened in America several times since 1798, the fear of a foreign threat was used as an excuse to stretch the Bill of Rights far beyond its original shape—and all in the name of public safety. With Jefferson a mere witness and the Republicans in Congress essentially powerless, the Federalists pushed through a series of laws known to history as the Alien and Sedition Acts. Meant to stem the tide of pro-French sentiment in America, the acts were in fact the high tide of reactionary Federalist politics.

While the Federalists worked overtime on their anti-French program, Jefferson decided that Madison could not stand on the sidelines. Albert Gallatin had replaced Madison as the Republican leader in Congress, but there was no writer of Madison's stature when it came to cogent newspaper essays. A series of Federalist attacks by "Marcellus" convinced Jefferson that it was time for Madison to forgo the sweet isolation of retirement and answer the upstart Federalist. As in 1793 and 1795, when

Madison had responded by penning long rebuttals, Jefferson became insistent. "You must, my dear Sir, take up your pen against this champion," who presumably was the archenemy Hamilton himself. "There is no person but yourself who can foil him. For heaven's sake then, take up your pen, and do not desert the public cause altogether."[12] Madison's reply was tactful because he disagreed with Jefferson—one of the few such incidents in their entire friendship–over the need for a retort. The Federalist screeds were not as threatening to Madison, but even if their bad tendency was admitted, he believed there were others better qualified to write an answer. Besides, Madison added, he was so overwhelmed with work at Montpelier that he could not agree to take on the task. Madison concluded his letter with a flurry of bad news about crops and cattle in Orange County, clearly showing that he was more worried about weevils and lost calves than any Federalist machinations 210 miles away.[13] After Madison read the XYZ dispatches he expressed shock at Talleyrand's indiscretion but volunteered no journalistic effort to counteract the damage, and concluded his note by adding that a killing frost had destroyed the peach and cherry buds.[14]

Practical matters forced Madison to push aside political alarms during his Montpelier interlude. The house in Philadelphia needed painting, and the lessee complained that the taxes were so high he would be forced to move out unless Madison paid the levy himself. Construction at Montpelier sites and probably at the grist mill forced Madison to ask a favor of Jefferson. "I break thro' every restraint," he apologized, but the urgency of the matter led him to add "to the trouble of which you have had more than enough."[15] Could he have 190 window panes, six brass locks, and "Brass spiral Hinges for 8 doors" shipped from Philadelphia? Madison wrote and acted like a man who had no further interest in being a party stalwart. Enmeshed in domestic concerns, where a faulty well pulley could cause a major crisis, Madison appears to have passed the leadership of the Republican party on to Jefferson without regret.

However much Madison wanted to forget politics, Jefferson would not allow it. This was not done in an overbearing way—far from it— for Jefferson's relationship with Madison was so intimate that he assumed their minds flowed in the same direction most of the time. Thus when Jefferson discerned a Federalist plot to embarrass the able Gallatin, to deport suspicious French aliens, and to stifle newspapers friendly to the Republican cause Jefferson counted on Madison's aid for a counterattack. "One of the war-party, in a fit of unguarded passion declared sometime ago they would pass a citizen bill, an alien bill, & a sedition bill," Jefferson revealed. The object of the latter was "the suppression of the whig presses. Bache's has been particularly named." The prediction proved all too true, and ultimately Madison was forced to move back into politics more out of duty than because of ardor. The catalyst came with passage of the

Alien and Sedition Acts by the Federalists' congressional majority, which had been strengthened by the XYZ disclosures. Before those measures passed, however, the Federalists enacted laws that authorized the navy to seize French privateers, cut off all commerce with France, and placed a tax on farm land. The wonder is that the Federalists did not insist upon a declaration of war. Madison saw the Federalist program as a means of feeding the English "at the expence of the farmers of this Country," he noted. "Already flour is down. I hear at 4 dollars a barrel."[16]

Planter Madison was upset. It was bad enough to suffer from the shrinking wheat prices, but Madison was also alarmed that the Federalists were unraveling all the good will that had existed between America and France. President Adams went out of his way to do this in an anti-French speech about which Madison heard with horror. "It throws some light on his meaning when he remarked to me, 'that there was not a single principle the same in the American & French Revolutions.' " The plan to throttle Republican newspapers, Madison said, should arouse public opinion until it would "recoil on the wicked authors. No other check of desperate projects seems now to be left." The Alien bill moving through Congress at that moment was "a monster that must for ever disgrace its parents."[17] To political catastrophes Mother Nature added more woes. A severe drought plagued Virginia, with hardly enough rain to measure during a vital thirty-day growing season.

Madison expected public opinion to curb excessive Federalist zeal but the fact was that, for the moment anyway, public sentiment was moving away from the Republicans. Powerful newspapers in the key cities teemed with essays proving that the French had mocked American diplomacy while capturing American ships in the West Indies. No Federalist editor was more belligerent than Benjamin Russell, who looked on the tension with France as a pocketbook issue and thus borrowed from the tactical book of Republicans. Amidst the flurry of petitions and public meetings fostered by the contending parties, Bostonian Russell attacked the Republican disclaimer that Talleyrand was acting out of personal greed. In fact, the *Columbian Centinel* observed, the proof that the French minister acted under orders from the Directory was manifested by French actions in the Caribbean. "If immediate vigorous measures are not taken to rid our seas of the pirates which infest them we shall soon see our commerce totally annihilated, our seamen starving, our mechanicks without employment, and the produce of our soil rotting in our stores."[18]

Illness, absenteeism, and defections in the Republican ranks in Congress gave Federalists an opportunity to close the session with laws meant to punish the opposition by identifying pro-French sentiment with treason. Bache's *Aurora* obtained and printed a conciliatory letter from Talleyrand. Dr. George Logan, a Republican and a Quaker full of good intentions, sailed for France on a one-man peace mission. Federalists ached to squelch Bache and Logan, but nothing in the statute books offered consolation until late June 1798. Rushing to pass a law before adjournment, the Federalists offered a bill that specifically named France as an enemy, provided the death penalty for treason in peacetime, and outlawed any criticism "written, printed, uttered or published" of government officials, congressmen, or the president if "false, scandalous and malicious."[19] The first version proved too strong even for some ardent Federalists, but the bill as passed (44–41 in the House) and signed into law by Adams on July 14 had enough teeth in it to drive the Republicans to the wall. That was its purpose. The several alien acts were aimed at a foreign threat, but the capstone sedition act was pointed toward a domestic enemy. In its most overt form, the bill constituted a legal mechanism for destroying the Republican party. "No acts ever passed by Congress had been so clearly the work of one party; no laws had ever been so unanimously opposed by the other party," Noble Cunningham noted in his history of party formation.[20]

Although they probably understood the risks involved, the Federalists launched a war on two fronts—against France and against the Republicans—with a haughty contempt for both. When Republican newspapers insisted that the First Amendment provisions for freedom of speech and press were patently violated by the new law, the Federalists dismissed these charges as party billingsgate. Jefferson fumed, and when there was rumbling on the Monticello mountain the shock waves went northward about 28 miles to Montpelier. During the next four months (from late June to late October 1798) the co-founders of the Republican party decided on a course of action. Out of their conversations—during the first week in July and again in late autumn—there came an unusual manifesto of party purposes and philosophy that would reverberate well into the nineteenth century.

There is still a slight aura of mystery surrounding the manifesto—the Virginia and Kentucky Resolutions—because Jefferson meant to keep their authorship a private secret.[21] (No doubt the point was to make it appear that the protests originated spontaneously, in the same way that public meetings at courthouses had taken public stands since 1765.) The general idea must have originated with Jefferson both as a means of declaring unconstitutional acts of Congress void (one has to remember that *Madison v. Marbury* was still a few years away) and as a signal statement of Republican principles.

As the vice-president, Jefferson chose to keep his name out of the controversy, but he drafted one set of resolutions to remind citizens that when their rights were in jeopardy they were not powerless. From his conferences with Madison came the collaborative effort, with Jefferson's true role masked for decades. In ordinary circumstances both Jefferson and Madison looked upon the courts as the guardians of civil liberty; but with the likes of Samuel Chase and other High Federalists on the federal bench, the Virginians realized that there was little likelihood of judicial redress. Their strategy was disarmingly simple. They would draft a protest and plan of action, send the document to friends in the state legislatures of neighboring states as well as to Richmond, and urge all the states to join in a general protest of the Alien and Sedition laws on the grounds of their unconstitutionality. The specifics of what came to be called "nullification" were purposely left vague.

While the constitutional issue was paramount in the shaping propaganda battle, Madison agreed with Jefferson that the deeper issue was the survival of the elective process by protecting the rights of opposing parties. The purpose of the sedition act was to squelch political opposition. If the Constitution meant anything, the elective process had to proceed on the assumption that the incumbents must be accountable for their records and defend their actions in a vigorous public debate. Thus Republicans used the term "monocrats" for their opponents because proof was at hand that the Federalists imitated the royal principle of infallibility by passing a law that banned criticism of public officials.

From the facts we can deduce that Jefferson agreed to write a protest and seek a friendly sponsor in the North Carolina legislature, with Madison committed to do the same for a set of resolutions that would go to a member of the Virginia General Assembly that fall. Circumstances led to Jefferson's set going to Kentucky instead of North Carolina, a change in plans that little affected the overall situation, while Madison prepared a protest for his own state legislature. Their plans matured by October and on November 8, 1798, Virginia-born John Breckinridge introduced the first set in the Kentucky legislature. On December 10, John Taylor of Caroline offered Madison's series of resolutions in the Virginia House of Delegates. The resolutions banked heavily on the constitutional theory of delegated powers and the rights of states "to interpose for arresting the progress of evil," since the Constitution itself was created by a compact of the several states. A lamentation that the Federal government had been enlarging its powers "by forced constructions . . . so as to destroy the meaning and effect of the particular enumeration which necessarily explains and limits the general phrases" was followed by the specific charge that the Alien and Sedition Acts subverted both "the general principles of free government" and the Constitution. By arresting "the right of freely examining public characters and measures," the new law acted in direct contradiction to a constitutional amendment meant to ensure "free communication among the people . . . which has ever been justly deemed the only effectual guardian of every other right."[22]

Having made his case for a strict construction of the Constitution and the right of a state to interpose when a federal law violated it, Madison then reminded citizens that Virginia had been in the forefront of states enacting legal protection for freedom of religion and of the press. Any failure at this juncture to resist federal encroachment would betray an "indifference . . . to the palpable violation of one of the rights thus declared and secured." In the closing paragraphs Madison payed homage to the affection Virginians felt for "their brethren of the other States," and asked for a concurrence by the other legislatures in a declaration "that the acts aforesaid are unconstitutional; and that the necessary and proper measures will be taken by each for co-operating with this State" in maintaining the "rights, and liberties reserved to the States respectively, or to the people."

So much has happened since 1798 to give a different coloration to the key points in the Virginia resolutions that it is necessary to recall their contemporary impact as an expression of bedrock Republican party philosophy. All the use of interposition, and its implications, by the nullifiers of the next century would embarrass Madison as an old man, but in 1798 he and Jefferson were searching for a clear issue to distinguish sharply between the Federalists and themselves. That they succeeded is proved by the immediate public reaction, which forced the Federalists on the defensive as a "loose construction" party more interested in power than in public good. Further, the resolutions (along with Jefferson's counterparts) delineated opposing views as to the rights of citizens to speak and write freely or criticize their public officials. How deep a chord Madison's ideas struck is indicated by the allusions, in the presidential campaign of 1836, to the "Resolutions of '98" as all that was needed more than a generation later for the Democratic party platform.

Madison was a bit uncertain in his mind as to whether a state legislature could nullify an unconstitutional law or whether a state convention (as in 1788) was needed, but in general he was satisfied with the way the resolutions moved along at Richmond and were signed by the governor. The Kentucky resolutions, with their more dramatic language and clear statement that the Sedition act was "not a law, but is altogether void," had an electrifying effect in both Federalist and Republican circles. Neither Madison nor Jefferson seemed prepared for the official reaction however, as the resolutions were either ignored by the state legislatures or their purposes rebuffed by the northern assemblies. The attendant public attention, particularly in the Republican newspapers, served notice that the Republicans were intent upon capturing control of the federal government by 1800. Although the general public remained in the dark as to the authorship of the resolutions (Madison's involvement was not revealed until a decade later, by John Taylor in a roundabout way, and Jefferson's authorship was masked until 1819), the message Republicans received was clear enough. Jefferson wanted to be president, and Madison could be coaxed out of retirement.

Without his knowledge or consent, Madison was thrust back into the Virginia political scene by Federalist tacticians who wished to deny Senator Henry Tazewell a second term. John Taylor had introduced Madison's resolutions in the Virginia legislature on December 10, and cynical Federalists nominated Madison on the following day for the Senate seat in an effort to confuse Tazewell's supporters. The ploy failed, for Tazewell's partisans mustered 117 votes against 28 votes for the unauthorized candidacy of Madison.[23] For his part, Madison had no wish to go to the Senate, but when beseeched by leading Republicans early in 1799 to step forward as a candidate for the state legislature Madison's willpower weakened. Madison gave in after six congressmen told him that while they understood his reluctance to go back into public life, "at the same time the Growth & Conduct of the executive Party, since your retirement, have continued more & more to render the Inaction of republican Principles & Talents deplorable & injurious." Perhaps Madison could have ignored this entreaty, but John Taylor followed it with a rumor that Patrick Henry was going back to the legislature partly out of spite. "His apostasy is capable of solution, only by considering it as the issue of personal enmity to Mr. Jefferson and yourself, to gratify which he has sacrificed his principles to a party, determined on your destruction," Taylor warned.[24]

Facing pleadings and warnings, Madison heeded a call to duty. "Consider that Virginia is the hope of republicans throughout the union," Taylor explained, and Henry's popularity might undermine "her resistance to monarchical measures . . . if you will not save yourself or your friends— yet save your country."

Taylor had been the go-between for Madison and now wanted the Orange County citizen to speak out publicly. Besides the resolutions which he offered early in December, Taylor had carried into the House of Delegates a similar set concerned with the anti-French program of the national government. Offered on January 4, 1799, the resolutions (presumably drafted by Madison) rejected the charge that Virginia Republicans were "under the influence of any foreign Power," beheld with alarm the depredations on American commerce as well as the impressment of American seamen, and then insisted that notwithstanding the tense international situation "our militia render a standing army unnecessary." Finally, the resolutions held that only an invasion of American soil justified a declaration of war and therefore the legislators went on record to "deplore and deprecate the evils of war for any other cause."

Out of the conversations, letters, and resolutions that moved back and forth between Montpelier, Monticello, and Richmond between August 1798 and January 1799 six distinctive Republican party principles emerged: low taxes; no navy; a tiny army; no tinkering with a citizen's civil rights; a commitment to eliminate the federal debt (to reduce taxes further); and a pledge to avoid foreign entanglements with a reduced "diplomatic establishment." The Republican party had a platform sturdy enough to hold until the crashing events a half-century later.[25]

Madison must have talked often with Jefferson about this republican philosophy, and as was usually the case, they were in near-perfect agreement. By February 1799 they saw that what needed to be done to counter the Federalist threat was to win congressional elections everywhere (except New England) and arrange for slates of presidential electors who would be sympathetic to the Republican cause. Madison won his spring election to the House of Delegates handily, then placed politics aside to push for completion of the remodeling at Montpelier and other personal affairs. Jefferson reported from Philadelphia that President Adams had thwarted the warhawks by sending a dovelike minister to Paris, to leave the saber-rattlers in the cabinet and Congress frustrated and angry with the chief executive. The mood of the country gave neither Jefferson nor Madison cause for elation, however, as the elections in North Carolina and parts of Virginia increased the slender Federalist majority from the preceding Congress.

With the leadership roles now reversed, Jefferson in Philadelphia discerned the flaw in their national program as an old weakness: the lack of a strong national newspaper (Bache had died of yellow fever, to rob the Republicans of their boldest journalistic warrior). Jefferson attempted to raise money to support a powerful party organ, for he was convinced that only a national newspaper was lacking for a total Republican victory. To Madison and others Jefferson sent the message that one hundred dollars for such a purpose was subscribed in their name. Madison may have offered help but no record is left except that Jefferson finally abandoned the scheme for lack of funds.

Jefferson was no stranger to disappointment, so he decided that if the newspapers would not come to the Republicans, they would go to the newspapers. Not a single state legislature had joined forces with the Virginia-Kentucky axis by commending the 1798 resolutions, a fact Jefferson accepted only as a challenge. Again he asked Madison to visit Monticello for a council of war. "That the principles already advanced by Virginia & Kentuckey are not to be yielded in silence, I presume we all agree," Jefferson wrote. By a provocative thrust at the state legislatures that failed to cooperate, Jefferson explained, the Republicans would rally the people "before it shall be too late." If all else failed, Jefferson added, the Republicans might be prepared "to sever ourselves from that union we so much value, rather than give up the rights of self government which we have reserved, & in which alone we see liberty, safety & happiness."[26] Jefferson's plan envisioned a propaganda device that would remind voters during the winter of 1799–1800 how close they had come to losing their liberties under the Alien and Sedition Acts. Never mind that some of the leading Federalists had admitted the laws were a failure, or that they were designed to be erased from the statute books on March 3, 1801. The point, as Jefferson told Madison, was to make a public protest "against the principle & the precedent" which arose "from these palpable violations of the constitutional compact by the Federal government."[27]

Madison went along with most of Jefferson's plan but was taken aback by the suggestion that if recalcitrant states should again fail to "rally with us round the true principles of our federal compact" it would be better to split the country up like a piece of firewood. This was too strong for Madison. At a hastily called conference at Monticello, Madison persuaded Jefferson to abandon the threatening words in the resolutions planned for the fall legislative sessions. Bowing to Madison's logic, Jefferson agreed to drop the hint of secession "in deference to his judgment," admitting that "we should never think of separation but for repeated and enormous violations."[28] By common agreement, a new set of resolutions reiterating the 1798 principles were readied for the forthcoming Virginia and Kentucky legislative sessions.

Despite Jefferson's pleas for all Republicans to bestir themselves, during the autumn of 1799 Madison played his role as a planter as though it would be a lifetime occupation. The absence of news concerning Dolley Madison's health indicates she was uncommonly well. There was much hammering and sawing around Montpelier as flooring was laid in the new additions, with carpenters moving back and forth between Madison's home and Jefferson's. Jefferson was remodeling, too, and wanted one of the workmen back before he had to set out for Philadelphia. "My floors can only be laid while I am at home," he wrote, "and I cannot get a workman here." In the next breath Jefferson mentioned his "draught of the Kentuckey resolves. I think we should distinctly affirm all the important principles they contain."[29]

Monroe talked Jefferson out of visiting Montpelier on the grounds that such a meeting would be publicized "throughout the continent" and thus set Federalist tongues wagging.[30] To keep matters straight, Jefferson sent Madison an outline of a political program for Republicans to use in 1800:

1. peace even with Gr. Britain. 2. a sincere cultivation of the Union. 3. the disbanding of the army on principles of economy and safety. 4. protestations against violations of the true principles of our constitution . . . but nothing to be said or done which shall look or lead to force, and give any pretext for keeping up the army.

Rumors of internecine fighting in Adams's cabinet prompted Jefferson to add that if the Federalists were split, Republicans should "only [be] arbitrating between them by our votes, but doing nothing which may hoop them together."

Personal affairs took up most of Madison's time, but he could not dam the flow of political information crossing his threshold. By late November 1799 he learned that the presidential election "seems to engage the attention of every person already." Recent balloting in Pennsylvania and north of the Hudson caused elation in Republican ranks, giving rise to a prediction that "every thing depends on Virginia & N. Carolina."[31] Madison understood what Jefferson wanted for the presidential campaign—a well-circulated document that would sharply define the Republican commitment to personal liberty and to freedom of the press. As the October session of the Virginia General Assembly loomed, Madison pondered the task. The most convenient target was the Federalists' sarcastic retorts to the Virginia resolutions, particularly those from the New England legislatures, which attacked Madison's logic. The Massachusetts lawmakers insisted that the right to declare an act of Congress null and void, as the Virginia resolves suggested, was a pernicious doctrine that would reduce the Constitution "to a mere cipher" if accepted by her sister states.[32] Madison decided to focus his report on constitutional issues, defend the 1798 resolutions clause by clause, and teach Americans a few lessons on how to maintain their Constitution.

Forced into a sickbed by "a dysenteric attack" which sapped his strength for a week, Madison thought of the new report Jefferson wanted as "a vindication of the Resolutions of the last Session agst. the replies of the other States." In that spirit Madison drafted the committee report as an answer to the several state legislatures, using his knowledge of events from May 1787 onward to buttress his claim that the states by their sanction had created the Constitution and "there can be no tribunal, above their authority, to decide, in the last resort, whether the compact made by them be violated."

Splitting hairs in a way that must have brought admiration from Republican lawyers, Madison carefully wove into his argument the claim that the states, not the courts, were the ultimate authority on the constitutionality of a measure. But central to Madison's argument that the state legislatures had a duty to speak out against unconstitutional measures was his corollary point: the protests were simply protests, not a call for any kind of overt action. Madison used several extra pages to delineate the nature of self-government as Republicans viewed it, clearly intending his words to form a kind of Republican gospel for the 1800 elections.

Madison's excessive wordage almost buried an important statement on freedom of the press in his polemic. He demolished the idea that the Alien Act was constitutional by showing that it combined legislative and judicial powers in the executive branch—a clear violation of the Constitution. Madison also made a relic of the claim that Congress could base criminal statutes on the common law. Then Madison wrote an extraordinary defense of a free press, prefacing his detailed examination of the Sedition Act by saying that the noxious law "ought to produce universal alarm, because it is levelled against that right of freely examining public characters and measures, and of freely communicating thereon, which has ever been justly deemed the only effectual guardian of every other right." No modern-day libertarian would quarrel with the rest of Madison's charge that the Sedition Act struck at the press, which had an almost unlimited right to criticize officeholders of all ranks.

Ironically, Madison's excursion into the intent behind the First Amendment was too far ahead of its time to have much impact until the twentieth century. Few of Madison's colleagues in Congress would have declared that *all* writings in the press had immunity from prosecution. "Is . . . the Federal Government . . . destitute of every authority for restraining the licentiousness of the press?" Madison asked. Yes, Madison answered, "the answer must be, that the Federal Government is destitute of all such authority." Nearly 150 years would pass before the Supreme Court borrowed Madison's constitutional logic. As historian Leonard W. Levy has shown, Madison's explanation of what constituted a free press came from "an uncommon authority" who held "that a popular, or free, republican government cannot be libeled; that the First Amendment intended to supersede the common law on speech and press; and that the amendment guaranteed an absolute freedom against the federal government, because no authority of the United States could abridge it."[33] By striking at the common-law rule that freedom of the press meant that printers could not be restrained from printing a libel but could be prosecuted for it later, Madison made an enormous stride toward the broadest interpretation of the First Amendment. "It would seem a mockery to say that no laws should be passed preventing publications from being made, but that laws might be passed for punishing them in case they should be made," he argued. In short, a printer or writer could *never* be accused of a libel against a public person or the government. Madison's point, brilliant as it was, was almost ignored by contemporaries.

The reinforcing resolutions from Kentucky were a model of brevity compared to Madison's lumbering, point-by-point justification. But the inclusion of the scare-word "nullification" (as "the rightful remedy" when unconstitutional laws were passed) in the Kentucky resolves gave them a special ring then and again during the 1830s. Both the 1799–1800 Virginia and Kentucky resolutions were widely distributed through newspapers. But in politics, where timing is all-important, an unforeseen event in December 1799 shattered much of the resolutions' impact. After a brief illness, Washington died on December 14, 1799. The newspapers spread the news with black-bordered editions that crowded all other news into insignificant corners, including Madison's *tour de force*. The purpose

of the resolves was to shake public apathy, but instead the American
people were too immersed in mourning Washington to think ahead to
the coming presidential elections.

Unlike the resolves of 1798, these latest resolutions called for no
response, and in New England they seem to have been either ignored
or treated as tedious repetitions. In any event, there was a general "failing
to perceive that there was an important difference between the two sets"
and their impact seems to have been confined to Virginia and perhaps
North Carolina.[34] Within the inner circle, however, Madison's overlong
attack on the Federalist legislation appealed to Republican strategists.
"Your Report . . . cannot be too highly estimated by every real Friend
to free & rational Government," his cousin James Madison wrote. "You
have really swept the Augean Stable . . . you have cleansed the Constitution from that Filth which Ambition Avarice & Ignorance was
heaping up around it."[35]

Forced into a behind-the-scenes role, Jefferson was eager to have
copies of Madison's resolutions sent to Philadelphia for relay to Republican
enclaves. "Nobody here has received mr. Madison's report *as it passed
the house*," he complained, and congressmen from "the different states
are waiting to receive & forward a single copy to their states to be reprinted there."[36] Jefferson's estimate of the propaganda value of the 1799–
1800 resolutions was overblown, as it turned out. What really hurt the
Federalists was their internecine warfare, most notably exhibited in
Hamilton's public letter attacking Adams as unfit for office. If the Sedition
Act had been enforced against Hamilton, as by law it should have, then
he would have been indicted for a blatant attack on the president of the
United States beyond anything in Republican newspapers.

Before the Virginia legislature adjourned, Madison worked for a bill
that would create a statewide ticket for general electors. The point of
the bill was to give Jefferson all of Virginia's twenty-one electoral votes,
but hardheaded Federalists fought back at Richmond. "It passed by a
majority of 5 votes only," Madison reported, adding that "the avowed
object of it is to give Virga. *fair play*."[37] John Beckley and Senator Stevens
Thomson Mason picked up the slack in Madison's correspondence to
urge Republicans everywhere to enforce party discipline during the spring
elections. James Monroe heard ugly stories about how Federalists planned
to squelch the opposition that summer by cracking down on Republicans
through a strict enforcement of the Sedition Act. Some 400 militia were
based close to Richmond and were marching to Harper's Ferry "to sow
cabbage seed." Monroe was saying in effect: just let the Federalists try
to steal this election. Madison, drinking his morning coffee at Montpelier,
was more relaxed. Madison permitted his name be used on the Jefferson
ticket as an elector, but with characteristic reserve he tried to avoid the
appearance that he was an electioneering busybody. Even stories of Fed-

eralist plots to rig the electoral vote in Pennsylvania failed to shake his confidence in a rising Republican tide.

The emerging plan was for Republicans to vote for Jefferson and Burr, with the clear understanding that Burr was to take the vice-presidency. The strategy seemed to be working well when early in May Madison was told by his successor in Congress: "The republic is safe. Our ticket has succeeded in the city of N. York by a majority of about four hundred."[38] So the Burr machine had triumphed, and although there were fretting rumors from Maryland and South Carolina, Madison counseled his fellow electors in Virginia to stick by the Jefferson-Burr ticket to the end. In the interim, Madison asked Jefferson for more nails to finish the remodeling at Montpelier, not too worried by a frantic letter from Charles Pinckney warning that one vote might make all the difference in the forthcoming election.[39]

As it became clear that the North would vote for Adams and Charles Cotesworth Pinckney, and the South was going for Jefferson and Burr, the possibility of an extremely close election loomed larger by early October. "Can we, may we rely on the integrity of the southern States?" asked a New York Republican who had made a head count and was fearful of a single defection in the Virginia or North Carolina ranks. Virginia was sound, but North Carolina Federalists made inroads. And further south there were troublesome signs. "The accts. from S. Carolina are rather ominous," Madison admitted to Jefferson in early November, but there might be defections and the reports from Pennsylvania heartened the Republican chieftains. As for his home district, Madison noted, the Jefferson-Burr ticket won in a landslide, "the votes were 340 odd to 7."[40] (At the time the states voted on different days, from September in Vermont to November in South Carolina.)

Before it was clear that an unexpected wrench had been dropped into the campaign machinery, Jefferson was required to head for the new federal city to preside over the Senate. Rhode Island was safely in Jefferson's camp, Madison knew, because he had letters from Burr and his lieutenant reporting the fact. But did that mean Jefferson had won? On shaking Madison's hand as he departed, some words concerning the likelihood of an early meeting must have been spoken. More than a few "ifs" would have been part of the conversation. To make matters more tense, the elder James Madison was feeling poorly. When Jefferson stretched out at Conrad and McMunn's boardinghouse on the night of November 27, the election outcome was still uncertain.

From day to day the presidential contest dominated the conversation at Montpelier, with the best news coming from Albany. David Gelston assured Madison that New York electors "will unequivocally give 12 votes for our Jefferson" and apologized when he pleaded for Madison's promise that Virginians would not renege on their pledge to back Burr. He did not want to believe the rumor "that a kind of calculation is to be made, that one two or more votes must be taken from Colo. Burr in order to insure Mr. Jeffersons election as Presidt." It was unthinkable, of course, Gelston admitted.

> Integrity and honour we rely upon in Virginia, we shall be faithfull and honest in New York, we know that the honour of the Gentlemen of Virginia and N.Y. was pledged . . . we have our attachments for Colo Burr, we will not however *even think* of taking a vote from Mr. J. . . . We are well aware from good information that three States, two at least, will give Mr. J. 3 or more votes, more than Mr. B will have, but I trust that it never will be said that either Virga. or N Y could be guilty of such a subterfuge.[41]

Madison had to believe the word of one of Burr's trusted aides. He must have gone to sleep that night thinking that Jefferson's election was finally assured.

Days passed with nothing settled, despite the *National Intelligencer* report on December 12 that South Carolina had chosen Republican electors, which meant that "Mr. Jefferson may, therefore, be considered as our future President." The electors would choose a Republican all right, but which Republican?

By the year's end, Jefferson realized that he would be tied with Burr in the Electoral College when the electors' ballots would be opened in February. Sure enough, both Burr and Jefferson receiving seventy-three votes each in the electoral college. All of the South except North Carolina had stayed faithfully with Jefferson and Burr, as the North had held to Adams and Pinckney. But Maryland was evenly split and Rhode Island, instead of falling safely in Jefferson's column, gave Adams four votes and Pinckney three, and wasted one on John Jay. The resulting tie threw the election into the House of Representatives. Burr told a Republican stalwart in Maryland he was stepping aside, but he did not. As his father barely clung to life, Madison perhaps wondered if he had erred in playing the gentleman's role to the hilt. A single vote away from Burr in the Virginia delegation would have changed everything. But to have reneged on a promise was unthinkable. He was a Virginian!

Almost a generation later, Madison looked back on the bizarre happenings of early 1801 with a feeling that he and the Republican party had been double-crossed.[42] Basing their actions on "false assurances" from a supporter of Burr, the Republicans had not foreseen the tie vote or they could have easily arranged for one man to be indisposed or change his vote. The belief that Rhode Island and South Carolina electors would vote for Jefferson but not Burr led to miscalculations, and treated the nation to the spectacle of thirty-six ballots in the House of Representatives before Burr's support melted. While the country held its breath, Madison heard from Jefferson a report of Federalist skulduggery beyond belief. "The

Feds appear determined to prevent an election, & to pass a bill giving the government to mr Jay, appointed Chief Justice, or to Marshall as Secy. of state," the vice-president wrote.[43] Like most of the rumors of the day, the report exaggerated Federalist strength, but Jefferson had worries enough in his own party.

What is remarkable about the whole crisis is that it was a matter of honor. If only one Republican had cracked somewhere down the line, the country would have been tossed into a whirlpool that might have sucked the Constitution itself into the vortex. Even Madison, the un-appointed expert on governmental crises, was so upset by the unexpected turn of events that he suggested that a joint proclamation of Congress might be the only way out. He was ready to fall back on this expedient, he admitted, because he believed "the intentions of the people would undoubtedly be pursued."[44] Madison was so unsure of himself that he sent the letter suggesting this extreme measure to Jefferson unsigned. Madison also brushed aside the suggestion that he ought to come to Washington and make an appearance, possibly to bolster Republican morale. Besides s the ailments afflicting his father, Madison said, he had his own bodily ills to consider. "My health still suffers from several complaints, and I am much afraid that any changes that may take place are not likely to be for the better," he wrote Jefferson.

The House vote called for by the Constitution was scheduled to start on February 11. Congressman John Dawson consoled Madison with a report from the wooded slopes of the new capital. "I think nine States will be found decided for Mr. J. and that the others will give way," Dawson predicted.[45] He came close to calling the final score, but for six days nothing seemed to give. After nineteen ballots on the first day, Jefferson may have been despondent but Madison was spared this ordeal. He was at the bedside of his father, who was failing fast. The Jefferson-Burr deadlock finally snapped on February 17, when crucial votes for Burr were lacking and Jefferson won ten states on the thirty-sixth and final ballot. Ten days later, Madison read the good news as he ordered the black mourning crepe mounted at Montpelier.

Madison had cause to be relieved. The death of his aged father brought a merciful end to much suffering, as did the outcome of the House balloting. Torn between loyalty to his family and to his friend, Madison had promised to be in Washington for Jefferson's inaugural. Fate intervened, giving him time to take the events of the past year in some perspective. Unquestionably, he would serve as Jefferson wished, as the secretary of state. But first there were family matters that needed tending—the burial, inventories for the probate, the will to be read and reread—and his mother needed comforting. Madison told Jefferson he would come to Washington as soon as these circumstances allowed. Then he made an observation on the political ineptness that afflicted their party. Like the good eighteenth-century Republican that he was, Madison took comfort in the way the tie vote had taught a lesson to the nation. What had saved America from a spectacle of bloodshed? In Madison's mind the answer was crystal-clear: the lack of a standing army. He never expected the anti-Jefferson forces to win, he confessed to the newly elected president, for it would have been impossible to oppose the people's will "without any military force to abet usurpation." Ever the optimist, Madison said the whole experience had been beneficial. "And what a lesson to America & the world, is given by the efficacy of the public will when there is no army to be turned agst. it!"[46]

Between the lines there was a silent message. A year earlier, Burr had been the heir-apparent to Jefferson, the rising star who was not far behind the vice-president in party esteem. Then the tie vote in the Electoral College whetted Burr's insatiable ambition. Solemn promises were broken. The New Yorker's postelection conduct and ambiguous expressions made even his supporters squirm and ruined him in the eyes of the Jeffersonians, so that the precedent of vice-presidential promotion set in the case of both Adams and Jefferson suddenly meant nothing. Treachery was on the lips of many congressmen who filed out of the House chambers, and insofar as Madison was concerned, Burr had forfeited any respect earned during their years of friendship that extended back to happier times at Nassau Hall in Princeton. Henceforth, in Republican circles around the president Burr was a social outcast. Politically, he was dead.

Madison met the small crisis at Montpelier with resignation. His father had added codicils to his will, and heirs mentioned in the will had preceded the old man in death. All these vexations had to be sorted out with the help of a lawyer while Dolley Madison talked about what needed to be packed for the journey to the new capital. Somehow the problems were surmounted (Dolley had a wonderful way of making things more cheerful than they really were), and then suddenly Jefferson was on the Montpelier doorstep as part of a quick trip home following the March 4 ceremonies. Naturally they talked about ways and means of undoing some of the Federalist mischief that had been done in the old Congress—such as a bill creating new judgeships that became Federalist patronage plums. Surely they also discussed the need for a constitutional amendment to prevent the recurrence of the crisis they had barely survived. Burr's name was undoubtedly mentioned, too, and Jefferson needed no urging to make plain his feelings about the new vice-president. Burr was a ruined man, and would never be president if Jefferson had anything to say about it.

CHAPTER EIGHT

THE REVOLUTION OF 1800 PROCEEDS

Much of the discussion between Madison and President Jefferson was never recorded during the next eight years. "A short conference saves a long letter," the president himself acknowledged near the end of his second term, and he operated that way from the outset of his administration.[1] Thus Jefferson described his dealings with Madison during his two presidential terms, when daily conferences allowed the two old friends to discuss everything from patronage to foreign policy without leaving any record of their conversation. History is perhaps the poorer for it, but at no time before or since have a president and his secretary of state worked in such close harmony.

Madison's trip to Washington in the spring of 1801 had been unpleasant, to say the least. Heavy rains made the roads resemble quagmires, Madison still felt unwell, and the trip of nearly eighty miles to Fairfax Court House and then into Washington was one mudhole after another. Still the Madisons (with a sister-in-law in tow) arrived in good spirits and for almost a month took quarters in the President's House. By June the Madisons had rented quarters nearby, not far from the pathway to Georgetown, which was a settled seaport community with more amenities and better water than Washington. Dolley Madison soon radiated good will, and with a widower as president it was not long before she was seated next to the president on occasions both formal and relaxed.

When Madison finally took the seals of office on May 2, 1801, he saw the world through the same Republican spectacles that Jefferson wore.

Jefferson termed the events "the Revolution of 1800," and so they were, in the sense that the Republicans set out to undo as much of the Federalist damage as they could accomplish with propriety. Taxes would be cut, the army reduced, the navy cut back, and the first priority would be given to reduction of the national debt. These issues were not campaign promises made from a stump, but had been implicit in the conduct of Republicans in Congress from 1795 onward. If there were some things that could not be undone (such as the Bank of the United States), the number of ministers abroad could be reduced in the name of economy, and the large army contemplated in the last session of Congress was not to be. Madison's and Jefferson's commitment to republicanism was total, for they believed that the young Republic had narrowly escaped the threat of monarchy. When Madison and Jefferson spoke of the Boston "Monocrats" they believed beyond all doubt that moneyed men in the shadow of Beacon Hill really wished to see America living under a monarch who would found on American shores an imitation of the British royal family. During the next eight years, nothing happened to shake this belief.

What made the whole experience so remarkable was the fact that this Revolution of 1800 was bloodless. When Jefferson made his famous "We are all Republicans, we are all Federalists" remark at his inaugural, the lesson was not lost on his audience. "I have this morning witnessed one of the most interesting scenes, a free people can ever witness," Margaret Bayard Smith wrote on March 4. "The changes of administration, which in every government and in every age have most generally been epochs of confusion, villainy and bloodshed, in this our happy country take place without any species of distraction, or disorder."[2] The observant newspaper editor's wife saw to the heart of the matter as clearly as Madison or Jefferson or Hamilton. The Constitution had been tested along with the nation's sense of what was right and proper. Ultimately, although the vote was close and hotheads made threats, a commitment to orderly change and fair play had won out.

Madison was so busy that he probably had little time to philosophize on the long-term implications of Jefferson's election. A constitutional remedy to prevent a repetition of the election crisis was surely on his mind. With immediate access to the President's House, where a succession of young Virginians acting as secretaries kept Jefferson's door ajar, Madison quickly assumed the role of an assistant chief executive. More foreboding to Madison was the social scene, but he was content to leave such matters in his wife's hands. The real challenge for the new secretary of state was the magnitude of the office he assumed.

What was started as an office to handle foreign affairs became, during the 1790s, a catchall for federal responsibilities that Congress pushed onto the executive branch. Each Congress added to the weight of the office in jerry-built fashion. By the time Madison took over, he was the keeper of the Great Seal; head of the Patent Office; official issuer of all passports, copyrights, and federal commissions; director of the printing of public laws; and the official liaison with all the territorial governments. That burden fell on top of the secretary's duties as the cabinet officer charged with conveying official policy to the American ministers abroad as well as over fifty consuls and chargés d'affaires from the Baltic southward to the Cape of Good Hope. Since the attorney general had no cabinet rank or office space, even the paperwork related to federal legal business fell in the State department "in" basket. To cope with this mountain of correspondence Madison relied on a chief clerk, six copying clerks, and a messenger. The annual salaries for this eight-man operation, including Madison's, totaled $11,910.

Arriving two months late, Madison found much catch-up work on his desk. Adams's administration had negotiated a treaty with the French, ending the undeclared war which had brought the two former allies to the brink of a shooting one (in fact, a lot of shots were fired, but not with the official approval of either Congress or the French directorate). The business of implementing the convention, including the matter of spoliation claims, became Madison's responsibility. The Barbary States were causing trouble in the Mediterranean, seizing American ships and imprisoning Yankee seamen for ransom. Something had to be done about that intolerable situation. Rumors came from European capitals that Napoleon had designs on Louisiana, the French had been forced out of Saint-Domingue by a black rebellion, and Spanish Florida was a nettlesome reality to many chauvinistic Americans. Every dispatch ship plowing up the Chesapeake brought more news from distressed ship captains, merchants who owned vessels or cargoes, or seamen captured by British or French privateers or regular naval squadrons. American shipping was invading the world's sealanes, but a price was exacted for this venturesome surge into international commerce. Most of the complaints landed on Madison's desk simply because the nation's experience was so limited, and international law existed more in theory than in practice. Frustrated merchants, ship captains, and relatives of captive seamen knew of only one place to turn.

Daily routine was one thing, a fixed policy regarding foreign relations with the major world powers was another. Madison and Jefferson came into office accused of being pro-French and anti-British, and they interpreted the voting in 1800 as a partial repudiation of the High Federalists' Anglophilism. Madison had fought vainly in Congress, year after year, for some discriminatory tariffs against British goods and high port charges for English vessels. Nothing could be done about this for another five years, thanks to the prohibition on economic sanctions against the British written into the Jay treaty.

France was another quandary, with Napoleon at the helm of state.

Jefferson had been a minister to France and one of the first to applaud the French Revolution in its early stages. These facts were no secret, but now that both Virginians were in the executive branch, their responsibility to the nation demanded that they examine every policy and make decisions on one criterion only: what course of action was dictated by the self-interest of the United States?

Admittedly, they had their prejudices. Since the Franco-British war began in 1793 they had followed the course of Napoleon's triumphant armies, with enthusiasm at first, then with some doubts as to the First Consul's intentions. His use of massed armies with staggering losses heralded an awful and new kind of warfare they hardly comprehended. But their distaste, not to say disillusionment, with the Jay treaty in 1795 had led to the political schism that solidified the Republican party; and a fundamental tenet of their party was that Great Britain had never fully recognized the independence of the United States. At the heart of the matter was the constant effort made by British diplomats to assert their nation's superiority; and few pains were taken to conceal an arrogant assumption that the United States was only a second- or third-rate power. As a future Republican legislator told Madison, the United States needed to shake off the inferiority complex that George III's ministers repeatedly tried to fix on Americans by treating them as mere "Colonists de facto."[3]

A corollary of this attitude, strongly felt in Republican circles, was a perception of America's mission. If the American Revolution meant anything, it signaled the opening of a new era where the "the lost rights of Mankind" would be recovered and revered in a republican setting. As the nation's most articulate spokesman of republicanism, Madison saw only three forms of government possible in modern society. The world had groaned under military despotisms or corrupt oligarchies until the events from 1775 onward pointed in a new direction. The third system of self-government drew "its energy from the will of society" and gained support "by the reason of its measures," Madison observed in 1792. "Such is the government for which philosophy has been searching, and humanity been sighing, from the most remote ages. Such are the republican governments which it is the glory of America to have invented, and her unrivalled happiness to possess."[4] His experience in Congress and scholarly research only reinforced Madison's belief that America was somehow afforded a unique opportunity to demonstrate the unlimited possibilities of self-government. Now they were in office, and Madison and Jefferson shared this pressure to make republicanism work.

Insofar as the State department was vital to the overall success they sought, Madison and Jefferson based many of their actions on the premise that the Atlantic had afforded them a merciful buffer from European institutions. Thus they thought in terms of the classical position of a neutral power, as defined in the works of Vattel, Hugo Grotius, and other writers on international law. In fact, at the outset of his admin-istration Jefferson assured the major powers represented in Washington that he would encourage a friendly relationship with their home gov-ernments. At the same time, Madison and his chief realized that the delicate balance of power in Europe was threatened by Napoleonic bluster. Certainly the ardor of Madison and Jefferson for the French position dampened after Napoleon's *coup d'état* ended the republic. The campaign rhetoric of 1800 contained a good deal of praise for the liberty cap and twists of the British lion's tail, but once in office the Republicans looked at the world more soberly. The fall in London of government bond prices and the London *Times* commentary on the news of Jefferson's election ("The result is certainly unpleasant towards this Country") were a typical overreaction by the British.[5]

Good fortune, brought along by long negotiations, favored the new administration's dealings with both England and France. An old source of friction with the English, the pre-Revolutionary debt mentioned in the Jay treaty, was finally settled when the American cabinet approved an offer of £600,000. The American minister in London, Federalist Rufus King, was kept in his post and worked conscientiously until the British agreed to close the nasty business (which some ungracious Northerners claimed was mostly unpaid Virginians' debts anyway). A similar agreement closed the matter of American claims against the British for sea captures after 1793. King also signed the convention settling the U.S.-Canadian border around Passamaquoddy Bay in the Maine area, where Madison was more anxious to preserve American shipping rights than territorial claims. Knowing the region only from books, Madison wanted fishing rights for Yankee seamen but he was indifferent to the real estate involved, including "the trifling island of Campo Bello" that England occupied.[6] Such negotiations were holdover affairs from the Adams administration, and the main credit owed to Madison is that he tried to interfere as little as possible. Similarly, the Convention of 1800 with France, ending the quasi-war with that nation, also was ratified during Jefferson's first term to the relief of all concerned.

Another good break for the Republicans came as the war clouds hanging over Europe lifted. War-weary England grabbed an olive branch offered by Napoleon in 1801, bringing peace after eight years. Interna-tional markets soon were reopened, affording American commerce new opportunities without the danger of seizures at sea. The one exception, of course, was the profitable ocean lane in the Mediterranean skirting the African coast, and there Republican diplomacy was no more successful than that of Madison's predecessors. Privateers, sailing with blessings from the Muslim rulers in the Barbary States, attacked American ships no longer under a British umbrella and expected an annual tribute (a diplomatic word for "bribe") as an alternative to further depredations.

Without a navy large enough to challenge the Barbary rascals, the American solution had been to give annual presents as a means of preventing greater problems. Almost one-fifth of the American exported foodstuffs went to ports that could be reached only by passing through the Straits of Gibraltar, and although the British allowed American ships to berth there for water and provisions, the high risks involved sent insurance rates soaring. The situation worsened after 1793, when the British shifted the naval power of their Portuguese ally away from the Straits and the Algerian pirates dashed into the Atlantic sealanes previously denied them. Over a hundred American sailors were seized and awaited ransoming. Altogether it was an untenable situation, as Jefferson recognized when he served in Paris and thought the only way to treat the brigands was with superior firepower, not presents of gold watches, cannon, and finely woven textiles. Yet when the Jefferson administration was confronted with the problem, the question remained whether it was easier to pay a tribute than build a naval force large enough to challenge the corsairs. Thus the Republicans, some of whom had boasted of "not one cent in tribute," came to realize they had little different to offer than the Federalists, who in Washington's administration had voted a $642,500 lump sum settlement (plus an annual tribute of about $30,000) on the Barbary powers.

Clearly the *enfant terrible* was the Bashaw of Tripoli, who was jealous of his counterpart in Algiers and rapacious in ways strange to the Western mind. The Bashaw warned in 1800 that unless his demands were met, he would declare war on the United States. On May 14, 1801, he ordered the American flagpole chopped down as the symbol of a formal declaration. Madison did his homework by plowing through the mountain of dispatches from the several Barbary states, realizing that for all the jeremiads in Congress the United States was eating humble pie. Congressmen rattled rhetorical swords, but more jewelry, firearms, lumber, along with cages for "5 Red Birds" and other gifts were dispatched to suit the whims of the Barbary deys, beys, and pashas.

The bills for these gifts came to Madison for his approval, and how much he disdained the whole business is not recorded. The tremendous time lag between consular reports caused much policy on the Mediterranean situation to be formulated like a shot from the hip. Unaware of what had happened in North Africa, Jefferson's cabinet met on the day after the flagpole incident. What should the United States do if the Bashaw carried out his threat? When the cabinet was polled on the recommended course of action, Madison favored sending the ships with "the object openly declared to every nation."[7] The upshot was that a squadron of four American ships was dispatched to the Mediterranean to protect Yankee commerce, without going on the offensive. Some inconclusive exchange of fire with Tripolitan brigands took place, but the matter was far from settled. All the evidence suggests that Madison was as sick of the kowtowing to the Barbary villains as Jefferson, but incapable of seeing an honorable way out.

Madison was more involved in the official negotiations with the government of Toussaint L'Ouverture in Saint-Domingue, but again he was picking up the pieces left behind by the Adams administration. Neither Jefferson nor Madison was anxious to deal with Toussaint, for the French regarded the former slave as a renegade while American slaveholders were disturbed by the implications of a successful slave rebellion in their own backyard.[8] Facing a commercial community that wished to tap the island's market and conscious of the anxieties of southern congressmen, Madison chose to move slowly in the Caribbean. When Napoleon decided to reverse the ideology of the French Revolution by returning the Caribbean blacks to slavery, he set in motion events that would culminate in an American diplomatic triumph in Paris. But at the time, nobody (including Madison) could foresee anything good coming out of the Caribbean trouble-spot. Meanwhile, Madison withheld formal recognition of Toussaint's government but pressed the American agent to hurry along food supplies sorely needed by civilians on the wretched island.

Neither the Barbary rulers nor the status of Saint-Domingue were major sources of irritation when placed in perspective, and with party discipline holding Congress in line and with peace in Europe, the first two years of Madison's tenure as secretary of state were remarkably tranquil. Gradually, tensions with France eased after the Convention of 1800 went into effect, and with America selling wheat, tobacco, and cotton to England in return for a major share of Britain's exports, an era of prosperity settled on the country.

The Supreme Court decision in *Marbury v. Madison* (1803) had major implications for the future, but insofar as the secretary of state was concerned it was simply another skirmish in the ongoing political struggle between ill-humored Federalists and the triumphant Republicans. Madison became the innocent party in the dispute when office-hungry Federalists tried to force the Republicans to honor a raft of eleventh-hour appointments made by the outgoing president. The matter eventually led to the Supreme Court, where a minor incident was used by Chief Justice John Marshall and his Federalist friends to lay down the first instance of a High Court ruling that Congress had passed an unconstitutional law. Madison was named in the writ of mandamus, since the offended appointee had never received his federal commission, but Marshall and his fellow jurists made legal history when they declared that the Supreme Court had the undoubted right to declare acts of Congress invalid. From Madison's standpoint, Marshall was simply trying to embarrass the Jefferson administration by using the remedy of judicial review as the implementing device. Marshall prevailed in the courtroom, but Mr. Marbury never received his commission.

Unraveling Federalists' patronage schemes was one thing, trying to satisfy Republicans was another. Weeks before Madison officially took over, letters came from every corner of the Republic with messages of congratulation often sandwiched between pleas for a government job. Monroe wrote with recommendations for friends, "sound" Republicans all, who needed employment in the new administration.[9] David Gelston, who had engineered Burr's New York election triumph, thought he deserved the lucrative Manhattan customs collector's post (the job paid about $1,500 more than Madison's cabinet position). Every mail pouch carried a few of these requests, some of them pitiful or pleading in tone, and many loaded with advice. "It is well known that Excise officers in Penna. have made use of the powers the office gave them to its full extent, for Electioneering purposes, & in short, trample on Republicans," a Jeffersonian stalwart warned Madison. "If they are not turned out, in due time, it must & will discourage hereafter the exertions of the Republicans—this is human nature. No danger will result from putting down one set and gradually raising the other in their ste[a]d."[10] The administration was almost under siege as hordes of Republicans clamored for openings on the public payroll. "The task of removing, and appointing officers, continues to embarrass the Ex[ecutive] and agitate particular parts of the Union," Madison told an old acquaintance from Virginia.[11]

At the most, Madison had fewer than eighty appointments under his direct surveillance, while the whole number of patronage openings directly controlled by the president reached 316.[12] Most of the pressure on Madison came because he refused to dismiss the chief State department clerk, Jacob Wagner, who was known to be a dyed-in-the-wool Federalist. Sensitive of the remarks made in Washington circles about Wagner's political leanings, Madison chose to ignore the criticism on the grounds that the man's intrinsic merits outweighed his political shortcomings. Wagner was a linguist, an efficient clerk, and he had been in the department long enough to know the filing system inside out. Despite entreaties from past employees, including one accusation that Madison was harboring a wartime Tory, there was never any purge at the State department. The critics were not able to undermine Wagner any more than they could oust the Federalist Daniel Brent, whose personal connections were so good he outlasted the three Republican presidents he served.

Those aware of the closeness between Jefferson and Madison tried to make it appear that Madison was being used, and was himself an innocent dupe of the entrenched Federalists. "You cannot conceive what injury it has done Mr. Madison here [by] his keeping Waggoner, Brent and Forrest in his office," lamented a Republican loyalist in Pennsylvania.[13] Madison's defense of the three Federalists he refused to fire was eventually brought out by Republicans in Congress as proof that Madison was unreliable when it came to dividing the loaves and fishes among steadfast Republicans.

Madison grew to depend on Wagner, particularly during the summer months when Montpelier became a retreat. Beyond his skills as a file clerk and translator, Wagner discerned Madison's concept of his duties and fitted his own work schedule accordingly. When it became obvious that Madison expected to spend most of the summer at Montpelier, Wagner made it a habit to digest the important dispatches of the day and relay their contents to the secretary. At some stage of his tenure, Wagner was asked to define his functions as chief clerk. His main duty, Wagner reported, was to keep from Madison's view all the trivial messages arriving daily and thus "enable him to devote his time to objects of greater magnitude."[14]

Wagner tried to be a buffer, but Madison still suffered from large doses of routine business. Every report demanded by Congress required a search for documents, a careful arrangement of the requested materials, and a covering letter bearing his signature. Anxious to keep the congressmen happy, but aware from his own experience of the capriciousness behind some resolutions, Madison sought a middle ground so that his clerks could tend to their regular duties during a normal ten-hour workday. Far from being a slavedriver, Madison was regarded by his chief clerk as "an amiable, and, considering the temper of the parties, a moderate man."

Madison's moderation and honesty had been questioned during 1791 when a rumor circulated southward that the Virginia congressman was a surreptitious partner in the Yazoo land company reportedly seeking a huge tract "in a dishonest manner."[15] Madison's father warned of an effort to link him to the brazen Yazoo corruption, but there was no truth in the gossip and Madison easily brushed it aside. The incident was still a burning issue in 1802, however, for the northern investors in the fraudulent land titles had hired a good lawyer. Jefferson appointed Madison to a three-man commission charged with settling the outstanding claims. By early 1804 Madison and his fellow commissioners had made their report, urging a compromise settlement that offered 5 million acres to quiet the claimants. Congress started the legislation toward final passage, and it appeared that at long last the Yazoo scandal was about to receive a decent burial.

Then John Randolph, heretofore an administration stalwart in the House, began the first of his many eccentric blows aimed at Jeffersonian programs with a scathing attack on the recommended settlement. Before Randolph finished he had alienated half the Republican party in the House and had tried to tar Madison with the brush of "Yazooism." The controversy dragged on beyond Jefferson's tenure in the White House and signaled a crack in the Republican solidarity so notable prior to 1804.

If all the party men close to Jefferson had been as free of taint as Madison (who never invested a nickel in the shady scheme), the matter probably would have been settled during Jefferson's first term.

Backbiting from his own party's ranks was not all that Madison faced on the home front. From time to time Federalists circulated rumors that Jefferson and Madison were about to part company; though groundless, gossipmongers predicted that an open break was in the offing. During the first year of Jefferson's administration the Federalists repeated stories of Madison's early departure from the cabinet, and when congressmen were about to scatter for their homes in the spring of 1802, Robert Troup told friends that Madison was finished. "Madison is in a deep decline and it is thought will soon quit his office." One of the Federalists' problems was that they spread stories they hoped were true. As Irving Brant noted, the "Federalists could not accept the fact that a man of Madison's honesty, intelligence and mental balance could be a Democrat; or, being one, that he should not be on the point of quitting such a party or being thrown out of it."[16]

Polarized politically, Washington society also was becoming divided along social lines. This proved no handicap to Dolley Madison, for once the Madisons set up their own quarters in a rented house, invitations to the White House were frequent and compelling. Madison's daily routine included breakfast around seven o'clock, followed by a day at the Six Buildings offices of the State department. Around four in the afternoon Madison went home to dine with his wife and their retinue of cousins and in-laws, unless Jefferson or another high-ranking Republican was having a dinner party. Once Jefferson's daughter Martha was on the scene, Dolley Madison abandoned her role as an unofficial hostess for the president; but she was in constant motion as a giver of tea parties or a visitor to houses clustered around the public square north of the president's official residence.

While Dolley Madison captivated the circle of friends who dined together with the president, Madison seems to have been an amiable guest who stood back to allow his wife full attention. A naturally shy man, Madison liked small talk and good wine, as another diner at one of Secretary of War Henry Dearborn's parties bore witness. Postmaster General Gideon Granger downed several glasses of champagne, whereupon Madison observed "that it was a most delightful wine when drunk in moderation, but that more than a few glasses always produced a headache the next day."[17] Granger listened to Madison, then made a sensible suggestion "that this was the very time to try the experiment, as the next day being Sunday would allow time for a recovery from its effects." Whether Madison agreed is not recorded, but another witness noted that several more bottles were uncorked with the only effect being "animated good humour and uninterrupted conversation."

Champagne aside, Madison's palate for good wines was no secret, and he was able to down more than one glass of Madeira on most occasions. During the sixteen years the Madisons lived in Washington, one of the most frequent entries in their account books was for cases of Madeira. The hospitality of the Madisons was noted by a succession of congressmen's wives, foreign diplomats, and Republican well-wishers—which probably means that a disproportionate share of Madison's $5,000 annual salary as secretary of state was spent on table delicacies, tea, coffee, chocolate, sugars, and other imported luxuries.

During these years Madison followed a regimen in dress and decorum that he would keep for the remainder of his life. Augustus John Foster, a British diplomat, regarded Jefferson as "more of a statesman and man of the world than Mr. Madison, who was rather too much the disputatious pleader." On the other hand, the Englishman admitted, Madison "was better informed, and, moreover, was a social, jovial and good-humoured companion full of anecdote and sometimes matter of a loose description relating to old times."[18] Foster provided the following description: "Mr. Madison was a little man, with small features rather wizened when I saw him, but occasionally lit up with a good-natured smile. He wore a black coat, stockings with shoes buckled, and had his hair powdered, with a tail." Almost thirty years later, when the artist George Catlin painted Madison at the Richmond constitutional convention, Madison was wearing the same garb.

Apart from the diplomatic claptrap, there was a great difference between riding around Montpelier to see that all went well and trying to herd masses of paperwork in Washington efficiently. Madison bore his burden well, since working closely with Jefferson was a special tonic. Now the excitement was increased by the fact that the two arch-Republicans were actually in places of power and could implement the ideas they had discussed and written about since Revolutionary days. As long as the honeymoon with Congress lasted, the Republican president and his chief aide pushed for a program of debt reduction and low taxation that augured well for the mid-term congressional elections.

The diplomatic corps in Washington, headed by the British minister Anthony Merry, failed to grasp the direction of the Republican program and instead quibbled about the lack of protocol in the Jefferson administration. Early on, Merry was offended by a gaffe innocently committed by the president and secretary of state as they took other ladies to their seats at a dinner party, leaving the Merrys to scrabble for a place. Nothing would soothe the Englishman's wounded sense of dignity, although Madison never perceived how much Merry was upset by the incident. "A foolish circumstance of etiquette has created some sensibility in Mrs Merry and perhaps in himself," Madison told Monroe, "but they will find so uniform & sincere a disposition in all connected with the Govt to cultivate a cordial society with them . . . that if any unfavorable impression has happened, it must be very transient."[19]

While Merry's dander was roused (permanently, as it turned out) by the crudeness of American manners, Madison was unperturbed because the Jefferson administration was basking in its first and only great diplomatic coup—the Louisiana Purchase. After Napoleon's dreams of an American empire crumbled in the Saint-Domingue fiasco, the wily French leader reached out for new sources of money as he began cranking up his war machine for a renewal of the struggle with England. Rumors were rampant in European diplomatic circles that France had secretly regained title to Louisiana from Spain. Napoleon had promised the Spaniards that he would never give up Louisiana, but that was before he lost an army of 20,000 trying to oust Toussaint. Madison probably shared Jefferson's fear that French possession of New Orleans would force America to look to England as an ally. "The day that France takes possession of New Orleans," Jefferson told Robert R. Livingston, the American minister in France, "we must marry ourselves to the British fleet and nation."[20]

With what must be regarded as lightning speed, considering the plodding communications of that era, American diplomats tested the Napoleonic waters to find that the Frenchman not only was willing to part with New Orleans, he was ready to sell all of Louisiana at a bargain price. Livingston and Monroe (sent as an Envoy Extraordinary) were supposed to talk only about New Orleans and the Floridas, but once begun the conversations in Paris moved to far more real estate than either man had contemplated. To their credit, they knew a bargain when they saw it. The American envoys came to discuss paying 10 million dollars for New Orleans along with East and West Florida, and left Napoleon's company with a firm offer to buy all the French claims west of the Mississippi for $15 million.

In a singular instance of great understatement, Madison wrote the Americans in Paris about their purchase of some 828,000 square miles of territory at what amounted to less than one penny per acre. "With respect to the terms on which the acquisition is made," Madison ventured, "there can be no doubt that the bargain will be regarded as on the whole highly advantageous."[21] When the Spaniards claimed that they had been cheated, Madison instructed the American ministers to remind the envoys of His Catholic Majesty that when the United States inquired earlier about the status of Louisiana, the Spaniards had told the Yankee negotiators to talk to France. We did what you told us to do, Madison said, and now you accuse us of bad faith. The history of the negotiations would "silence forever the cavils of Spain at the titles of France now vested in the United States."[22]

Madison shared Jefferson's first reaction to the business by wondering if the whole transaction was constitutional. As the magnitude of Napoleon's offer sank in, however, their notion that a constitutional amendment might be needed to acquire Louisiana dissolved as the temper of the country, particularly the southwestern region, swelled into a booming accolade for the Louisiana acquisition. Madison hoped the Floridas might somehow be part of the arrangement until Spain reacted in surprise and anger. For the moment, Madison pushed Florida to the back of his mind. The stars and stripes would fly over that territory, he seems to have assumed, from the day Louisiana was acquired.

American money helped Napoleon as he went to war against his ancient English enemy, yet as the pace of the Franco-British war quickened clashes between neutral Yankee ships and vessels from the belligerent powers soon changed the euphoria at the State Department into a mood of anxiety. There was no sudden worsening of Anglo-American relations, although the snobbish attitude of the resident British minister was proof of a bitter English pudding for Anglophobes. Monroe warned Madison early on that the British regarded "a state of neutrality" as being "a state of universal contempt, for such is the fact." For more than eighteen months, English officers had systematically stopped American ships, ostensibly searching for deserters from the Royal Navy. Nothing galled American pride more than the 1,500 Yankee sailors jerked from ships flying the stars and stripes and forced to serve on George III's men-of-war. Now Monroe was sent to London as Rufus King's replacement and the younger Virginian optimistically reported to Jefferson and Madison his belief that "impressment was the only major issue between the two countries." Trying as the impressment issue was, Monroe explained, the problem could be solved by negotiating and he set out to prove his point.[23] Madison tried to soft-pedal differences with the British, too. When an angry congressman offered a bill that denied the use of American ports to the ships of any country known "to have impressed or otherwise insulted those on board our vessels," Madison told Monroe that he should explain in the right circles around London that "the introduction of the Bill may not be misconstrued into an unfriendly disposition towards G. Britain."[24] All we need to do, Madison counseled, is seek "a just accomodation of all differences with G.B."

Madison wrote with some confidence, for the truculent but weak Spanish garrison at New Orleans had turned over the city to the Americans, and the dispatch pouches from Europe contained no reports of outrage. The good times did not last. Napoleon's armies began a relentless crushing of opposition forces on the Continent. England reacted by creating a flotilla designed to encircle and squeeze France into submission. Triumphant on land but frustrated by Nelson's 1805 victory at Trafalgar, Napoleon could not invade England, while the English barely held a foothold in Europe. American problems multiplied apace as the two great powers "turned in a manner hitherto unprecedented to the economic weapons of trade, seizure, and blockade. . . . To a degree unequaled until World War I, this was total war."[25]

Whatever this new kind of all-out warfare might be called, the Jefferson administration was unprepared for the consequences. As the major neutral shipping power, America was sending vessels to world markets in unprecedented numbers. Great Britain benefited from this upsurge, which made the friction with America all the more troubling. Trade with England flourished as the American merchant fleet grew at an annual rate of about 10 percent, with Yankee tobacco, wheat, and cotton moving to British ports to pay for an expanding export business. Anglo-American trade grew so prodigiously that it formed "the largest single component of international trade," as Americans bought about one-third of all goods exported from Great Britain, "roughly $50 million worth every year."[26]

Even as America became England's best customer, the rise of Yankee commerce imposed an unbearable burden in another sense. England, trying to keep the Royal Navy at full strength, reeled at the desertion rate (Lord Nelson set it at 42,000 for the decade ending in 1803) and began to stop ships flying the American flag, questioning the crews, and hauling away suspicious characters. Madison, perplexed by the widespread impressments, urged Monroe to pick up the threads of negotiation his predecessor had left dangling. Monroe confronted the British Foreign Minister with a list of names American seamen whom the English had impressed since 1801. A slight relaxation of the impressments by the British followed, and for a time Monroe took heart. For one thing, American shipping benefited from a favorable ruling in His Majesty's admiralty courts so that the American carrying trade was booming. "The truth is that our commerce never enjoyed in any way, as much freedom, and indeed favor from this govt. as it now does," Monroe told a skeptical Madison.[27]

As Monroe wrote, the British were planning further restrictions that would end the American shipping bonanza. The reexport trade which England allowed, giving American ships the right to carry cargoes from the French West Indies to France, a right not accorded by French policy in peacetime, was dramatically cut off by an 1805 court ruling in London. Yankee ship captains had cleared the French colonial cargoes through an American port (under the earlier *Polly* decision), but now the English decided that the American ship *Essex* was subject to seizure under a 1756 edict ("the prohibition to neutrals in time of war of traffic closed to them in peace"). From the time the Royal Navy began to enforce this doctrine until the spring of 1815 James Madison's world was never in a settled state. One crisis followed another. What seemed to rational men as ridiculous at one time would soon become the actual state of things.

Take the matter of impressment. How could a sovereign nation allow the warships of another power to stop vessels on the high seas, menace the crew with the business end of twenty or so cannon, and allow part of the ship's company to be dragged away on the charge they were either Englishmen, or deserters, or both? Madison repeatedly protested to the British minister, underscoring his point about the offensive tactics of the Royal Navy's impressment gangs. Anthony Merry mentioned Madison's objections to his superiors in London, and England's adamant position was spelled out time and again, most recently when Lord Harrowby told Merry to stick by his guns. "The Pretension advanced by Mr. Madison that the American Flag should protect every Individual sailing under it on board of a Merchant Ship is too extravagant to require any serious Refutation," the British foreign minister observed. [28]

During the spring of 1805, an accumulation of crises at the foreign desk forced long talks with the president regarding difficulties with the British and Spanish. Monroe's London mission was stalled over the impressment issue and, feeling helpless in England, Monroe traveled to Spain to help negotiate borderlines and other differences with His Catholic Majesty's government. As the thermometer in Washington climbed, the Madisons had expected to find relief from a long sojourn at Montpelier, but a growth on Dolley Madison's leg prevented them from traveling. Confined to her bedroom, she tried to make light of her problem, but at the president's Fourth of July celebration she was not the playful, exuberant *grande dame* who ruled Washington society.

After talking to the local doctors, Madison decided that surgery was the only way to restore his wife's health. He made arrangements for a carriage trip to Philadelphia, and sought some method of keeping in touch with Jefferson, who had already departed for Monticello. Madison received advice that the celebrated Dr. Philip Physick could treat Mrs. Madison successfully. "If every thing goes well it is possible that the detention at Philada. may not exceed two or three weeks," Madison wrote Jefferson, adding a promise to head for Virginia the moment his wife was out of harm's way. The 200-mile carriage ride turned into something of an ordeal for Madison himself, as he had an attack of bilious fever before they reached Philadelphia. Once there Dr. Physick decided that applications of a poultice might prevent the dreaded surgery, and within a few days Dolley Madison's morale improved. Daily applications brought some improvement, while a horde of old friends came to renew acquaintances. "Half the city of Philadelphia had called upon me," she wrote her sister. [29] Thinking back on her expulsion from the Society of Friends for marrying out of the fold, Dolley Madison recalled:

When our *Society* used to control me entirely and debar me from so many advantages and pleasures, altho' so utterly out of their power, I really felt my ancient terror of them revive to a disagreeable degree. This crowd, more like the attendance on a new play, has really become tiresome.

Perhaps without realizing it, Dolley Madison had become a Virginian in her tastes and attitudes. Little of the plain garb or special dialogue of her Quaker background remained in Dolley Madison's lifestyle once she became the mistress of Montpelier.

While his wife's leg healed more slowly than the doctor had predicted, a second threat arose when the annual visitation of yellow fever forced Madison to take his household to higher ground beyond the city. The 1805 epidemic never reached the state of the devastating 1793 plague which had killed Dolley Madison's first husband, but it was another burden atop a pile of problems confronting Madison. Forced to carry on from a makeshift office in his parlor, Madison heard discouraging news from Spain, where the American envoys had failed in their mission. Efforts to buy the Floridas for hard cash drew only resentment from His Catholic Majesty's court and a settlement of old claims negotiated a few years earlier was rejected. The American position that the Louisiana purchase reached the Perdido River was a kind of bluff, anyway, but Madison thought that Florida must someday become part of the United States. A little patience was required.

By late October Dolley Madison's leg had almost healed and the call of urgent business meant a hurried trip back to Washington alone. John Armstrong, Jefferson's choice as the American minister in Paris, talked to Talleyrand and reported to Madison. The United States could have the Floridas and most of Texas, Armstrong wrote, but it would cost at least $7 million in bribes.[30] After cabinet discussions placed the territorial appetites in perspective, Jefferson believed it was time to rid the nation of the Spanish nuisance in Florida where smuggling and fugitive slave colonies bedeviled the boundary areas. Jefferson decided to ask Congress for a secret fund to do whatever needed to be done. As Gallatin advised, it was cheaper to acquire territory with cash than to fight a costly war (the canny Swiss-American knew that all wars somehow become terribly costly).

Jefferson sent a secret message to the House, which brought John Randolph calling at the White House. What did the president have in mind? A discretionary fund of $2 million, Jefferson told Randolph. All this came out when Randolph tried to discredit the president and Madison with a series of newspaper essays under the pseudonym "Decius." Randolph told of a meeting with the secretary of state during which Madison had said "that France would not permit Spain to adjust her differences with us; that France wanted money, and that we must give it to her, or have a Spanish and French war."[31] As Henry Adams noted, Randolph used the incident as the pretext "for declaring a public and personal war" on Madison, "which he waged thenceforward in a temper and by means so revolting as in the end to throw the sympathies of every unprejudiced man on the side of his victim."

Randolph's purposes were always difficult to discern, but in this instance he probably wanted to embarrass Jefferson and throw Madison's critics a bone. He also might have hoped to write the swan song for Madison's presidential chances. Whatever his game, Randolph picked a feud with Madison. His confidence in Madison "had never been very high," Randolph said, "but now it was gone forever."

Randolph's open war with Jefferson and Madison failed to derail the Florida purchase plan. Congress passed the appropriation and Madison sent word to Paris that the deal was on. Spain was not dancing to a tune called from Paris, however, so the proposed Florida purchase fell flat. Since the whole arrangement had been worked out in secret session, the general public was unaware of the administration's attempt at cashbox diplomacy. Indeed, it seemed that most of America's diplomatic coups were the result of luck rather than careful planning. The more midnight oil was burned at the State Department, the more things seemed to go awry.

While Madison shuffled notes back and forth from Europe he found time to read the proofs on his answer to a paper broadside fired by an Englishman who sneered at the American idea of neutral rights. During his wife's convalescence in Philadelphia Madison had searched through all the international law authorities for ammunition he needed to demolish the British doctrine on "the Rule of 1756." Disappointed to find "that so much silence has prevailed among the neutral authors on this subject," Madison decided to write a treatise that would settle the question for every thinking man.[32] Then, during the last weeks of 1805, a ship from England carried copies of James Stephen's tract, *War in Disguise; or, The Frauds of Neutral Flags.* For chauvinistic Englishmen, Stephen's pamphlet told them all they wanted to know about American neutrality, which the author labeled a sham device for wartime profiteering. The American device of bringing in French or Spanish products to a home port and "re-exporting" it made no difference—enemy goods were enemy goods! Madison bristled, for his whole policy was built on the concept that "free ships make free goods," and he was ready to do battle—on paper. He believed he had an unassailable answer ready.

When Madison's 204-page pamphlet, *An Examination of the British Doctrine, Which Subjects to Capture a Neutral Trade, Not Open in Time of Peace,* appeared in January 1806, it had all the earmarks of a rebuttal. Copies were placed on the desk of every congressman. The reaction was not what either Madison or Jefferson had expected. Senator William Plumer waded through it, knew at once who its author was, and complained, "I never read a book that fatigued me more than this pamphlet has done."

Jefferson apparently intended to send the anonymous work far and near as a statement of the official American position, but Senator Plumer's judgment that Madison had failed to state "precisely the doctrine he intends to maintain . . . [which] is really a great defect," seems to have been a common one. Fisher Ames criticized the pamphlet as old-fashioned in tone and facts. "A new state of things exists," Ames wrote, "and a new case requires a new application of old principles." After all his labors, the congressional critics' judgment prevailed. The ability to survey historical precedents and reach valid recommendations, which Madison demonstrated with such force in 1786 and 1787, was now lacking. A disappointed Madison wrote Monroe that the pamphlet had been recalled. If copies reached London, Monroe was advised, "be so good as to consider the whole cancelled, and not to appear in your archives."[33] Starting with the premise, "Between the nations not engaged in the war, it is evident that the commerce cannot be affected at all by a war between others," Madison managed to split enough hairs to confound more readers than he convinced. Meant as a salvo fired at a spurious English doctrine, the pamphlet proved instead to be something of a dud. When John Randolph jibed that Madison's work was "a shilling pamphlet hurled against eight hundred ships of war," he was so close to the truth it hurt.[34]

While his pamphlet gathered dust, Madison's ire was roused further by English arrogance on the high seas. England reacted to Napoleon's land victories by stepping up its blockade tactics, which meant that more American ships were searched and more Yankee sailors pushed and shoved into the holds of His Majesty's men-of-war. Madison would not retreat from the impressment issue in 1806 because the British practice was so insulting in both conception and execution. As one scholar has noted, the high-handed practices of the Royal Navy were to be imitated by the Germans in 1917 with their unrestricted submarine warfare. Impressment, historian H.G. Nicholas noted, "flouted the hypersensitive pride of a new nation, and was unlike any other outstanding grievance "for it touched American lives, and lives are more precious than goods."[35]

Monroe had returned from an abortive mission at Madrid and was now joined in London by William Pinkney, a Federalist but an able lawyer whom Madison recommended for the job. Still hopeful of an Anglo-American treaty to which an end to impressment would be the sine qua non, Madison sent the American envoys instructions that resembled a small book. Madison offered the British a tradeoff—leave American seamen alone and the United States would drop its insistence that "free ships make free goods." On the other hand, Madison said, the right to carry on the money-making re-export business, based on the "broken voyage" concept that contravened the English Rule of 1756, had to be pressed hard. Keep "the general principle in its full extent," Madison charged, but "you are left at liberty, if found necessary, to abridge the right in practice."[36] To give the American negotiators an extra bargaining chip, Congress passed a law that forbade the importation of British goods;

but the act had a discretionary clause, so that Jefferson suspended its operation to await news from London.

The word from London, however, was not good. Almost as Madison wrote, an affirming Admiralty court ruling fixed the *Essex* decision in place with a decree that "set aside the Pretensions of the Americans to legalize their cargoes by fictitious landing & reshipping."[37] A second blow came from the British cabinet in the form of an Order in Council on May 16, 1806, which declared the north coast of Europe to be under blockade but which allowed neutral trade in certain circumstances. Conceived as a kind of concession to the Americans, it was regarded in America differently and came on the heels of a shooting incident involving the Royal Navy. Shots fired by the British frigate *Leander* killed a Yankee seaman in American waters, precipitating riots in New York and outraged demands in the press for a declaration of war.

More notes of protest brought nothing satisfactory in Madison's diplomatic mail pouches from Whitehall. Whether the concept of nonimportation was originally a congressman's idea or not, the general plan of falling back on economic retaliation against England was not new to Madison's bag of tricks. He had preached that sermon in Congress a decade earlier, and since his proposals were not tried then Madison considered the approach as valid in 1806 as it had been in 1765 or 1792. Ever committed to the "political economy" concept so dear to public men of the eighteenth century, Madison was firm in his belief that a trading nation such as England could be coerced only by boycotts or bayonets, and he preferred the former. The thought that the British might retaliate with harsher measures never seems to have crossed Madison's mind. As a scholar who assessed Madison's performance during this period as "unimaginative" remarked, in some respects the secretary of state "was largely occupied with applying ideas of the 1790s to the problems of the next decade."[38]

Madison may have urged Jefferson to prefer economic warfare over a shooting conflict simply because his political ideology held war as the worst thing that could befall a Republic. History taught Madison that wars not only created ruinous public debts but also brought a concentration of power that inevitably spelled ruin to the people's liberties. Believing in the truth of the axiom that "the same causes always produce the same results," Madison must have counseled (or perhaps reinforced) Jefferson's belief in the efficacy of economic sanctions. If there is indeed any lesson to be learned from history, it is that economic sanctions are generally worthless as diplomatic instruments for they either provoke a war or make friends run for cover. But neither Jefferson nor Madison were ready to concede that the greatest trading nation in the world could not be humbled by a mild economic squeeze applied through Yankee legislation.

Monroe and Pinkney found that the Nonimportation Act only made their task at the negotiating table more difficult. Monroe may have thought that Madison's list of demands contained built-in assurances of a failure, which would reflect on him (and hence reduce his rivalry for the presidency), but there is no proof whatever that Madison was devious. All the evidence points in the other direction. Madison was convinced that England would prefer American trade and therefore would not insist on continued impressments. Thus negotiations spurted along with the English willing to make only slight concessions and ignoring the main American points. "It is absolutely necessary that America should be taken off the high horse she has lately mounted," Lord Auckland was told, "but in taking a Lady off her horse care must be taken not to offend her delicacy or shew her legs."[39]

As matters turned out, impressment was a sine qua non for the British, too. Their negotiators flirted with the thought of giving up the time-honored manner of keeping the Royal Navy's manpower at full strength, but the cabinet balked. Then Monroe and Pinkney caved in, on the excuse that the British cabinet could not risk public reaction if impressments were abandoned. On the question of re-exporting French or Spanish goods, the British backed off a bit, allowing the trade to continue after a decent interval in an American port.

Before the negotiators signed a draft of the 1806 treaty Napoleon threw a bombshell under their table. On November 21 the Frenchman issued his Berlin Decree, which declared that the British Islands were "in a state of blockade" with all traffic in English merchandise forbidden along with all shipping to or from a British port. The news hit their conference like a thunderclap, causing both sides to reevaluate their positions; but ultimately they all agreed on December 31, 1806, that they had come to an agreement with advantages for both nations.

The latest Anglo-American treaty reached Washington early in 1807 as Congress was about to adjourn. The new British minister, David Erskine, represented an 180-degree turn from his predecessor, but nothing he could say made the document please either Jefferson or Madison. Madison wrote the American envoys at once, indicating that all was not well. Not until May 20 did Madison lay all the complaints on the line, heading his list with the president's objection. "He cannot reconcile it with his duty to our sea faring citizens, or with the sensibility or sovereignty of the nation, to recognize even constructively, a principle that would expose on the high seas, their liberty, their lives, every thing in a word that is dearest to the human heart," to the caprice of foreign officials who ignored the law of nations.[40] Jefferson thought the treaty so inept that he refused to send it to the Senate for ratification. Thus the house of cards carefully constructed in London collapsed.

Whether America and England were headed for war after that

painstakingly built treaty failed to move Jefferson or Madison is only guesswork. Certainly, the British thought they had given up something; but Monroe felt a deep sense of failure and packed his bags. Pinkney stayed on to become America's frustrated minister at the Court of St. James. In terms of expectations and results, Pinkney might as well have joined Monroe on the homeward-bound voyage.

Another six and a half years would go by before actual war was declared, but the failure of the 1806 treaty etched deep marks on Madison's psyche. He felt pressure from all sides as Senator Samuel Smith of Maryland speculated on the effect of a blunt disavowal of the treaty. "Is it not probable that the sending back [of] the treaty may be attributed to hostility against Mr. Munroe?" the poor-spelling senator asked. From western Virginia Madison learned that grassroots Republicans hoped there was truth to the rumor that the American diplomats had sent the treaty without affixing their signatures. "I heartily wish it may prove true," Madison's brother-in-law reported, "as from the Character of the treaty as *rumor* has announced it, I do not think the American Ministers can resist the overwhelming impetuosity of public disapprobation."[41]

Around Washington so many politicians had their eyes trained on the 1808 presidential race that they judged all events in the light of a Madison–Monroe contest. Aside from the vindictive John Randolph, few gave credence to the notion that Madison wanted to see Monroe fail. If Monroe failed then America failed, and Madison was looking for rays of hope, not signs of despair.

As the situation on the high seas worsened, a homemade crisis took precedent over foreign affairs for the next months. This incident, known to history as the "Burr conspiracy," began after the discredited vice-president stepped down in March 1805. There had been no difficulty in Jefferson's reelection in 1804, but Burr was dropped from the ticket and he realized that in Washington he was persona non grata with all faithful Republicans. How much he intrigued with the British minister or General James Wilkinson and others to bring about a western empire under his personal direction is still a murky matter. The certainty, however, is that Jefferson turned his wrath on Burr and came within a whisker of sending the former vice-president to jail. Madison agreed with Jefferson as to Burr's rascality, and as secretary of state he was charged with the administration of the serpentine proceedings that wound to a courtroom in Richmond, where John Marshall scored another anti-Jefferson triumph by releasing Burr on a technicality. The final verdict on the two charges lodged against Burr came on September 15, 1807. The business had dragged on too long, and national attention had shifted dramatically to other matters by then. In retrospect, the whole affair brought no credit to the president, and Madison must have sighed with relief when he learned that Burr had left for Europe.

The Burr incident left a bitter taste all around. Madison's loyalty to Jefferson was beyond question, so much so that Madison must have reassured the president Burr deserved punishment. But Madison never had Jefferson's enthusiasm for the kind of witch-hunt that left a blot on the president's record.

George Clinton from New York, aged and infirm, took Burr's place as the new vice-president. A constitutional amendment had moved along (but was not yet ratified) to prevent a recurrence of the 1800 election drama. Tight party discipline, however, made repetition of that close call unlikely. But Jefferson had not yet taken the presidential oath in 1805 before the rumormongers began speculating on his successor. Dolley Madison could say things which her husband could not, so that when Monroe's name was mentioned as a rival for the presidential nomination the lady lost a bit of her decorum. A Delaware congressman revealed "he had some conversation with Mrs. Madison upon the presidential electioneering now so warmly carried on, in which she spoke very slightly of Mr. Monroe."[42] When Monroe was trying to negotiate in Europe, John Randolph worked overtime to castigate Madison, who stood at the bottom of Randolph's list of presidential candidates (Monroe was his choice). If Madison "be elected to the Presidency (for which he is straining every nerve, supported by all the apostates of our party—the feds and a *few* good, but misguided men)," Randolph wailed, "we are gone, forever!"[43]

Randolph's venom may have reinforced any presidential yearnings Madison harbored, but he also knew the pattern of decorum expected from a candidate. Like a beautiful lady at a fancy dress ball, who presumably disdains all thoughts of actually dancing, the discreet presidential aspirant was expected to act as though the last thing on his mind was a four-year residency in the President's House. Perhaps Madison spoke to Jefferson of the possibilities in 1808, but there is no proof that he did. In all likelihood he never discussed the matter with anyone else, Dolley Madison excepted. This was not only good politics, it was also an economical way to win an election, for like his three predecessors, Madison was prepared to run without being required to spend a penny on the campaign.

Both men had other things to worry about, anyway, for the Royal Navy was up to its old tricks again, and this time there was bloodshed. In late June 1807 the British man-of-war *Leopard* hailed the newly commissioned American frigate *Chesapeake* as it headed for the open seas off the Virginia capes. When the *Leopard* boarding party wanted to search for British deserters, the Yankee skipper denied them permission. Cannons roared, men screamed in pain, and three Americans were killed in the ensuing skirmish. Searching through the dead and eighteen wounded crewmen, the English found four men they believed were deserters and took them off the disabled *Chesapeake*. His mission accomplished, the *Leopard* commander then ordered the British warship back to a rendezvous at Lynnhaven Bay, within sight of the Virginia coast.

The effrontery of the British capped a black day for the American navy. As reports of the incident trickled into Washington, the *National Intelligencer* editor, who was a close friend of the administration, headed the Chesapeake news: "British Outrage." As more details came to hand, the newspaper gave notice that a public meeting had been called to discuss and act upon "the late ATROCIOUS OUTRAGE offered to *the honor and rights of our country*."[44] Public reaction was the same in every village and crossroads where the humiliating encounter was discussed.

Madison was one of the first in Washington to learn the disheartening news. Surely this was the last nail in the coffin of the Anglo-American treaty, for the *Leopard* commander was under orders from the Halifax station of the Royal Navy. The president was still in town, and the cabinet was called to assemble in Washington so that the next step might be determined. Madison wrote Jefferson the agonizing details, including the return to American waters by the *Leopard* following the unprovoked attack. "Having effected her lawless & bloody purpose," Madison told Jefferson, the *Leopard* "returned immediately to anchor with her Squadron within our jurisdiction. Hospitality under such circumstances ceases to be a duty; it becomes a degradation."[45] Madison urged Jefferson to issue a proclamation declaring American waters off limits to British ships, which the president agreed to do at a cabinet meeting on July 2. In public meetings the sentiment was unmistakable. Either the British made full satisfaction and apologized or "there appeared but one opinion—War—in case that satisfaction is not given," the citizens of Baltimore argued.[46]

The temptation to call Congress into special session immediately and deliver a war message was resisted. Jefferson's proclamation was broadcast to show citizens that the administration was not coddling the British navy, and an armed frigate was dispatched to London bearing an urgent report to Monroe, with instructions for him to demand restitution and punishment for the naval commanders who had permitted the *Leopard* to act so recklessly. Obviously, the Anglo-American treaty was doornail-dead.

The last twenty months of Jefferson's second term passed without a shooting war erupting, owing more to American patience than any friendly gestures from England or France. England issued another Order in Council in November 1807 that threw down a blockade of every European port "where the British flag is excluded." Neutral vessels were subject to search by the Royal Navy and goods headed for Europe were subject to taxes collectible in an English port. This edict, perhaps the most direct cause of the coming war with America, was followed in less than a month by a royal proclamation reaffirming the British navy's right to impress Englishmen on board foreign vessels. Napoleon shot back with a counterdecree from Milan which held that any neutral ship observing the rules set forth in the November Order in Council would be treated as an enemy vessel and become a "good and lawful prize."

These orders and decrees infuriated American shippers who enjoyed a healthy business boom as the exporting of produce from foreign countries in Yankee vessels rose from $13,594,072 in 1803 to $59,643,558 in the current year. With the exports of American produce added, the total value of goods carried in Yankee ships in 1807 came to more than $107 million.[47] If it came to a question of money or honor, here were facts that Jefferson and his cabinet had to ponder.

As far as Jefferson and Madison were concerned, the choice was easy. No consideration outweighed their belief that the American experiment in self-government was the one and only issue that was never negotiable. Whatever was necessary to keep the Republic healthy was their first concern. Jefferson's Anglophobism, dormant during the early years of his first term, dominated his thinking and rubbed off on Madison. Not that Madison needed much goading, for he viewed England as the natural enemy of American nationhood. Could the Republic survive if England was determined to make war on the United States in everything but name? Between the resumption of full-scale war in 1803 and the latest round of decrees and orders the British had far outstripped France in seizing American vessels—538 to 190. Probably the American ship captains grew more cautious in the northern seas and more careless around the Mediterranean, for French seizures after 1807 shot up while the British slacked off. Even so, when war came, British seizures for the whole period were almost double the number captured and condemned by Napoleon and his allies.

Weighing the pros and cons of the situation, Madison knew that if Jefferson decided on a declaration of war the country would support him. "The public indignation is universally excited by the repeated destruction of our unoffending seamen," Elbridge Gerry wrote after the *Leopard* incident. "If redress for the present, & prevention for the future, cannot be obtained, will not a state of warfare, be preferable to such a state of national insult & degradation?" Closer to home, Dolley Madison's brother-in-law, John G. Jackson, told of public sentiment in western Virginia:

A tame submission to such outrages will disgrace the Government & its Friends: it will be the signal for every species of insult, until the national Spirit, broken sunk & degraded, will return with loathing & abhorrence from the Republican system we now so fondly cherish & take refuge against such wrongs in a military despotism, where another Buonaparte or Burr will give Law to the Republic.

The choice, Jackson wrote, was between action and insult.[48] Jackson's remarks, coming with a sheaf of similar statements from loyal Republicans, must have caused Madison to realize that a fundamental policy shift was vital.

The dilemma facing Madison and his chieftain was similar to that confronting Woodrow Wilson when he spoke of America being "too proud to fight." From Madison's vantage point the weakness was not in Republican philosophy but in the European misinterpretation of American strength and purposes. As Congressman Jackson had noted, the Republic was not defective but was in fact "the strongest on earth: rivetted by the affection of the People it cannot be turn asunder without rending every ligament that endears Man to his home, his family, & his Country." Madison bowed to no one in his respect for public opinion, which made the difficulty more acute, since policy decisions depended on public support.

After discussing the national mood with his cabinet, Jefferson decided to let the situation cool off. He called Congress back earlier, but not so early that it sounded as though a war message was in the offing. Isolated at Monticello, Jefferson perceived that the nation wanted action. He instructed Madison to gather all the papers related to American negotiations with England and have them ready for delivery to all the members of Congress. "They will thus have time to bring their minds to the same state of things with ours," Jefferson wrote, and when England's answer to the note on the *Leopard* arrives, "we shall all view it from the same position."[49] Apparently, Jefferson had decided to ask Congress to declare war on England unless the *Leopard* incident had caused the cabinet to change its spots. Madison's report of the whole affair to Monroe instructed the envoy to insist on "reparations for the past, and security for the future."[50]

Madison was a good deal more bellicose than Jefferson's other close adviser, Albert Gallatin. As secretary of the treasury, Gallatin worried about speaking too loudly when America had no reinforcing stick; and he was concerned about hundreds of American ships in international waters that would not make a safe port if an Anglo-American war broke out. The news from London did not ease the situation, for Monroe reported that the British attitude over the *Chesapeake* affair was less than promising. A special emissary was being sent to America to iron out the reparations problems, but impressment was not a subject for negotiation. When he wrote his annual message, Jefferson toned down his anti-British stance enough to make room for a compromise with England. Instead of unleashing "the dogs of war," Jefferson decided to follow the example of the turtle. America would call her ships home and keep them there as the only alternative to more impressments and depredations against Yankee commerce. The cabinet met in mid-December and, after weighing the alternatives, agreed that a general embargo was the only alternative to war.

Madison and Jefferson thought that by restricting American shipping to home ports they would strike a blow at both France and England. "Our commerce is so valuable to them," Jefferson believed, "that they will be glad to purchase it when the only price we ask is to do us justice."[51]

After five years of seizures of men and ships, the surprising thing about the Embargo Act of December 1807 was its slapdash characteristics. Twice postponed, the Nonimportation Act passed the previous spring was to become effective in December. Why not go "whole hog" and stop trading with both France and England? Madison appears to have favored a general embargo because he believed it would have a devastating effect on the British West Indies. Gallatin had second thoughts after the cabinet session, but Jefferson was listening to Madison by now. A presidential message went to Congress after Madison changed it slightly, to play down the portion dealing with preparedness, with the emphasis on preventing "the departure of our vessels from the ports of the United States." A Senate committee hurriedly convened and went over a bill already on the table. Disarmingly brief, the draft called for an embargo on all American ships "bound for any foreign port or place," until further notice. The president alone was empowered to make exceptions, and intercoastal voyages would be allowed only when a bond was posted.

Instead of a carefully worded bill that would clamp an airtight lid on overseas trading, the legislation soon needed supplementary clauses that made life busier for lawyers and more complicated for shippers. What made the bill, which the House acted upon almost as speedily as the Senate, more palatable was a report from London that the British were about to issue a new edict prohibiting all commerce with French-controlled Europe. This was the Order in Council of November 11, 1807, which the *National Intelligencer* hinted was ready for the king's signature even as Congress debated the embargo measure.[52] In theory, the new American legislation made the orders in council dead letters insofar as Yankee commerce was concerned, for it was now illegal to send a ship to Europe anyway.

With hindsight the Embargo Act can be seen as among the most unfortunate pieces of legislation in American history. The effect damaged England only slightly while imposing ruinous conditions on the American shipping industry at the moment it was flourishing; and the secondary effects on American agriculture were almost as devastating. The embargo was salutary in only one respect: it tested the fortitude of the majority. The real sufferers were not the English ministers or merchants who were its targets but the American farmers and seamen who tightened their belts as they affirmed a faith in the righteousness of the Jefferson-Madison program.

The embargo was a historic "amber light" which subsequent Congresses ignored (compare the passage of the Prohibition amendment and the Gulf of Tonkin resolution). Lawmakers rushed headlong into a morass of mistaken motives. Nobody was fully satisfied, but the people wanted action, and both Madison and Jefferson thought the Embargo Act would prevent war in spite of anything the British or French might do. "When in doubt, stay out" seems to have been the administration's message to American shippers who had brought so much pressure on congressmen and the cabinet to offer protection for American crews and cargoes plying the world sealanes.

A series of articles lauding the Embargo Act soon appeared in the chief Republican newspapers, and although confirming evidence is lacking, Madison probably was the author. Their chief message was that matters would inevitably become worse so long as France and England disregarded neutral rights. "Thus the ocean presents a field only where no harvest is to be reaped but that of danger, of spoliation and of disgrace." Given time, the articles predicted, the major powers would come to their senses and be forced "to change the system which has driven our commerce from the ocean." Equally important, the embargo violated "the rights of none" and was clearly "the best expedient in its best form." Clearly Madisonian was the prediction that the embargo would discourage the consumption of foreign luxuries and help revive American industries.

Although the embargo thus seemed to be the perfect weapon to humble the British and French, with our perspective we can see flaws that escaped Madison's attention. "If this was Madison, as seems likely," historian Dumas Malone has observed, the cabinet member most wedded to the idea of economic rather than hot-lead warfare "overstated the case for an untried policy, promising too much for it and grossly underestimating its costs."[53]

A corollary of the Embargo Act in the minds of its two chief supporters was that Americans would react to the law by giving it unqualified support. Nothing prepared Jefferson or Madison for the angry reaction from New England, where the economy depended upon commerce and fishing for its well-being. The proximity to Canada, plus a thousand inlets and secret harbors along the Maine coast, soon proved that full enforcement of the law was impossible. Until his last breath, Madison never understood why New England had not cooperated to make the embargo effective; and he never admitted that the law was defective.

Such worries lay in the future during January 1808, however, for the movers and shakers in the Congress were eager to choose Jefferson's successor. Far in advance of the first local elections, Senator Bradley of Vermont (the chairman at earlier caucuses) called a caucus for Republican members of Congress on January 21. The meeting was attended by nearly one hundred senators and congressmen, but no excitement was provided by persistent rumors that James Monroe (recently returned from his failed British mission) was willing to succeed Jefferson. About fifty Republicans chose to avoid the caucus, which meant they were either ill or indifferent or hostile. What mattered was that on Bradley's first roll call, Madison received eighty-three ballots while George Clinton and Monroe had three each. New York delegates ducked the session, but every other state with Republican congressmen was a party to the business. For practical purposes, the presidential campaign of 1808 was already over.

Surely Dolley Madison beamed at the dinner parties that followed, but Madison himself was the epitome of indifferent decorum. Some intrigue by John Randolph, who talked about nominating Monroe despite the caucus, had to be ignored. There is little doubt that Jefferson tried to prevent any friction between Madison and Monroe. With the first hints of a presidential rivalry, Jefferson wrote Monroe as a father might have:

> I see with infinite grief a contest arising between yourself and another, who have been very dear to each other, and equally to me. . . . I have ever viewed Mr. Madison and yourself as two principal pillars of my happiness. Were either to be withdrawn, I should consider it as among the greatest calamities which could assail my future peace of mind.

Monroe needed no picture drawn after this February 18 letter reached him. Barely fifty and seven years Madison's junior, Monroe could read between the lines of Jefferson's fatherly advice. He wrote Jefferson a noncommittal but reassuring reply.

Monroe's feelings had been hurt, however. Going back to Virginia to practice law, Monroe harbored resentment against Madison. Their cordiality of earlier times vanished when Madison sent the Senate all the messages related to the rejected Monroe-Pinkney treaty, but omitted several letters Monroe wanted included. Madison's oversight was the pretext Monroe chose to break off their correspondence during the spring of 1808. Madison was perplexed by Monroe's conduct, and now it was his turn to feel resentment. The so-called Old Republicans, led by Randolph, started a newspaper campaign on Monroe's behalf and went through all the motions of making him a serious candidate against Madison. Randolph's campaign on behalf of Monroe was mainly an exercise in the politics peculiar to Virginia. Late in the desultory campaign, which Monroe's biographer called "curiously unreal," Monroe released Jefferson's letter and his reply in an apparent attempt to show he was still friendly to the president and not one of Randolph's jackals. The final poll in Virginia gave Madison 14,665 votes to Monroe's 3,408, indicating that the contest was really over before it started.[54] It took two years for both Monroe and Madison to recover from their chagrin.

Madison chose to ignore the Monroe boomlet and put up a good front as the heir-presumptive. The British emissary, George H. Rose, arrived in Washington with limited power to settle the *Leopard-Chesapeake* imbroglio, but as the talks proceeded it became clear that Madison could not link the impressment issue with reparations for the British outrage. The difficulty was that Rose believed that he represented a first-class power and was dealing with a second-class one. He talked about deserters from the Royal Navy, while Madison spoke of the naturalization process which made many former Englishmen American citizens. So they met for weeks on end, going nowhere, until Rose finally said he needed to go to London for further instructions. Everything depended upon a mutual desire to preserve peace, Madison tried to say, but Rose grew impatient. At his last meeting with Jefferson and the cabinet, Rose reported, the president spoke little and Madison steered away from the *Chesapeake* matter altogether. Only Gallatin was talking plainly, and he told Rose "that *nothing* of real difficulty remained between the two countries but his Majesty's Orders in Council."[55] The talks broke off with nothing settled.

Within a matter of weeks the embargo began to strangle the shipping trade from Massachusetts southward. Customs receipts fell to nothing, for there were no incoming goods to be taxed; and this was a time when tariff collections provided the main source of income for the federal government. In 1806, when things were humming along, imports valued at over $60 million came into American ports. During 1807 the figure fell only slightly. Then came the crunch of 1808, when imports plummeted to $12,997,414. At least, this much commerce went through legal channels. Perhaps four times that amount was smuggled into the United States by defiant scofflaws.

Sailors and shippers were hurt by the embargo, but so were farmers and planters. The farm price index reached a high of 106 in 1805, then fell to 71 in 1808. Sea-island cotton sold for 51 cents a pound in 1805, but was not easy to peddle at 24 cents in 1808, for the amount exported in those years slipped from 8.8 million pounds to 900,000.[56] Close to home, tobacco sales fell from 83,186 hogsheads in 1806 to 9,576 during the embargo year. "The distress of the people of this country under the embargo, is and will be such," a Virginian wrote Madison, "that every effort ought to be made to convince them not only of the propriety but the necessity of that measure." He begged Madison to write an essay explaining to the people why the embargo was the only proper response to threats from France and England. "Unless you will do it, I do not know who is capable of doing justice to the subject," Wilson Cary Nicholas pleaded.

American shippers willing to take their chances on the Atlantic found the French more avid than the British in seeking out neutral plunder. Napoleon tightened the vise in April 1808 with the Bayonne Decree, which directed the seizure of all American ships coming into port after April 17 "because no vessel of the United States can now navigate the seas, without infracting a law of the said States, and thus furnishing a presumption that they do so on [a] British account, or in British connexion." Henceforth, the French seizures of American ships outnumbered the British. This trend was all the more startling, for in the Congress dissident Federalists implied that the administration was the mere tool of Napoleon in cutting off commerce with England. John Quincy Adams, who had voted for the embargo, visited with a crusty Federalist judge in Boston who insisted that "the people of this country [are corrupted], already in a state of voluntary subjugation to France, and ready to join an army of Buonaparte."[57]

Clearly, Madison believed with Jefferson that the embargo gave America a breathing spell (a costly one, admittedly) while playing for time. An end to the European war would reopen all the oceans to American commerce, and outstanding differences could be settled in the shade of olive branches. So the president and his right-hand man believed, as they continued to talk peacefully enough. Preparedness measures moved slowly in Congress, until Jefferson finally asked for authority to create eight additional regular army regiments over the next five years. Orthodox Republicans were somewhat horrified. "Liberty, Economy, Frugality" seemed to be the Republican motto as they looked beyond the idle ships and restless merchants, hoping against hope for some dramatic change in the course of the European war.

Apart from the gossip unleashed by Monroe's candidacy, the presidential election proved to be a lackluster affair. Amidst the sub-rosa campaigning on Capitol Hill, Madison stayed close to his desk, cut down on his social engagements, and realized that his actions were going to be watched with more scrutiny than ever. From France he heard that Napoleon assumed that the latest British decree had been the last straw. "His Majesty [Napoleon] has no doubt of a declaration of war against her by the United States" since America had been egregiously wronged. "War exists, then, in fact, between England and the United States." In conversations the American envoy was told that if America came into the war against England, France would see that the flag over Florida bore stars and stripes.

Napoleon's haughty tone and the implied Florida bribe, delivered through his foreign minister, angered the usually mild Madison. The American minister in Paris was ordered to tell the Frenchmen forthwith that Americans did not need French advice on what to do when Yankee toes were being stepped on. "Make that government sensible of the offensive tone implied," Madison instructed John Armstrong.[58]

Madison's displeasure was duly delivered, although John Armstrong was becoming disillusioned with the diplomatic pussyfooting at American expense. "We have somewhat over-rated our means of coercing the two great belligerents to a course of justice," Armstrong cautioned. "The embargo is a measure calculated, above any other, to keep us whole and keep us in peace. But beyond this you must not count upon it." In France, Armstrong continued, the impact was not felt at all. "In England, in the midst of more recent and interesting events of the day, it is forgotten." Napoleon, he said, "would prefer to it, a war on our part with Gr. B."[59]

The closest Madison came to making a campaign pitch that spring came when he wrote a confidential statement for a special senate committee inquiring into the *Leopard-Chesapeake* incident. The report explained the background for the embargo, justified the legislation, and expressed the hope that the law would be supported "by all the manly virtue which the good people of the United States have ever discovered on great and patriotic occasions." Although both England and France were scolded, the report was harder on the English. It pointed out that the enforcement of the latest Order in Council meant that Americans trading in most of southern Europe could do so only by "paying tribute to the British treasury!" A hint at future alternatives, including removal of the trade ban for any belligerent that made an exception to its decrees for American commerce, meant that the embargo was not considered a long-term solution to America's problems on the high seas.[60] A copy of the statement found its way to the offices of both the Richmond *Enquirer* and the *National Intelligencer,* and the report was reprinted by other Republican newspapers as a semi-official statement of the embargo's purposes. Madison apparently told the senators he stood by the report—if the embargo had a fair trial it would produce the desired results.

Madison kept the lights burning long into the night at the State Department, but a slow-paced atmosphere prevailed at the White House. Well before it was a certainty that Madison would be the next White House occupant, circumstances caused the incumbent president to taper off his prodigious letter-writing and administrative chores. Often afflicted with migraine headaches, Jefferson was struck by an oppressive spell that spring which almost incapacitated him. Leaning more heavily on Madison and Gallatin, the president gave his approval to Gallatin's request for a tough law that would plug some of the loopholes in the embargo. More experience was needed, but early indications showed that widespread smuggling was taking place along the Canadian and Florida borders. By late April 1808 the first Enforcement Act had cleared all the legislative hurdles. Much of the responsibility for clamping down on smugglers was laid at the president's doorstep. A Massachusetts congressman compared the sweeping legislation to a short-fused bomb. "Should an attempt be seriously made to carry it into effect among our hardy New Englanders" he ventured, "I dread the consequences."[61]

After Congress adjourned in the spring of 1808, Madison and his wife headed for the Virginia piedmont. There was no campaigning to do—whatever needed to be done would be left to the Republican leaders in New York, Pennsylvania, and Virginia. New England was going its own way, but there would be no speeches or the slightest hint of electioneering around Montpelier. As it happened, the Madisons were barely home before Dolley Madison became ill. She was nursed back to health during the summer, but because of her illness their stay at Montpelier was far from restful. Too soon the Madisons took a carriage back to Washington.

In New England, where Madison's name provoked anger, the maple leaves had barely started turning yellow and red when it became apparent that Madison would be elected president. The Federalists made a poor showing, voting for Charles C. Pinckney in most cases but never in sufficient numbers. The abortive campaign for Monroe made no headway with the Federalists of old, who were not interested in John Randolph's spiteful attempt to embarrass the Jefferson–Madison alliance.

As Jefferson prepared his final State of the Union message for Congress, it was clear that Madison would succeed him with 122 electoral votes to 47 for all opponents combined. Madison helped Jefferson write his farewell address, in which the outgoing president admitted that the intensive negotiations surrounding "this candid and liberal experiment" (of going to extreme lengths to avoid war) had failed. The law had pinched some citizens in the pocketbook, but others were saved by the edict, which kept ships in harbors and cargoes safe in American warehouses. The next move, Jefferson said, was up to Congress.

Several days after the speech, the British minister called at the White House. "He was much alarmed at the convers[atio]n out of doors looking like a dec[laratio]n of war with Gr. Br.," Jefferson noted. "I told him that there were but 3 alternatives, 1. war, 2. embargo, 3. submission, and that no American would look a moment at the last."[62] Jefferson said he explained to Erskine "that Mr. Madison (who it was now pretty well seen wd. be my successor, to which he assented) had entertained the same cordial wishes as myself to be on a friendly footing with England." Only slightly less alarmed was Samuel Taggart, the Massachusetts congressman who looked on the embargo with horror. The president's message simply meant that the Republicans' misguided policies would continue, he told a friend. "It appears that we have quite overrated our consequence as it respects European nations. We are rapidly teaching them to do without us, and if our present system continues they will soon do all but forget that there is such a country as the United States on the globe."[63]

Not all Washington residents were gloomy. Dolley Madison's joy as the Electoral College met to declare Madison the official winner in early December of 1808 requires no strain on the imagination. Before the final victory, John Randolph's friends tried to make a scene. "The Virginians are waxing hot in the Contest for President of the U.S.," Senator Samuel L. Mitchill wrote his wife. "The partisans of Madison & Monroe are becoming vehement."[64] Mitchill misread the situation, for nobody from Virginia thought Madison had serious opposition and the personal nastiness that came to the surface was simply another nail in Randolph's political coffin. As the clerk read the Electoral College ballots, Monroe had not one vote. If the circumstances had been otherwise, Monroe would never have become Madison's successor in the White House.

CHAPTER NINE

WAR AND PEACE, AMERICAN STYLE

No caretaker government stood in the shadows as Jefferson's last days in the White House ticked away. The saber-rattling of December faded as Congressmen studied the news from back home. New England was up in arms over the Enforcement Act but could not stop passage of a second, more severe bill meant to plug up the loopholes. Along strict party lines the bill became law at a time when the embargo itself was losing ground.

Congress moved so strangely that at times it must have seemed that the decisions were capricious; nobody seemed to be in charge. Loyal but bewildered southern farmers were scrambling to find enough cash to pay their taxes. A presidential proclamation went to the governors of Vermont and New York, authorizing the use of militia for widely reported evasions of the embargo. Feisty residents of St. Albans, Vermont, shot back a reply. There was no need for using the militia, for there was no uprising, the town fathers insisted. Continued reports of outright, flagrant smuggling along the New England coast frustrated federal officials but drew little cooperation from local authorities. Defiance at a higher level, from the New England statehouses, was averted only by congressional action. The law they had passed so confidently in December 1807 was laid to rest on February 3, 1809. Jefferson himself never lifted a finger to save it, Madison was a silent spectator, and the Embargo Act was sponged from the books as of March 3, the day before Madison's inauguration.

Congress may have intended to hand the incoming president a freer hand in dealing with England and France. While the repeal debate raged, there was talk on both sides of the congressional aisle about alternatives. In an ugly incident at Gloucester, Massachusetts, a mob seized and destroyed a federal vessel dispatched to stop smuggling. The specter of a civil war flashed across some minds.

Madison was perplexed by the defiance manifested in New England as the embargo withered into something worse than a dead letter. The bad situation was compounded for men of Madison's stamp, since the implication was that the Union was really a flimsy cobweb confederation. Some of that angry sectionalism written between the lines in the Virginia and Kentucky Resolutions of 1798 was evident in what New England men now hinted in their discussions of a regional convention. "The impatience under the Embargo, more particularly in Massachusetts is becoming extremely acute," Madison told the American minister in London. "A preference of war within a very limited period is every where gaining ground."

More than a few Republicans thought that a declaration of war, perhaps against both powers, was the only face-saving way out of the impasse. But Congressman Samuel Taggart said all such gossip was humbug, and he preferred John Randolph's assessment of the situation. Administration offers to repeal the embargo if the English and French revoked their decrees and orders, Randolph said, reminded him of the Mother Goose character "Jack in the tale of the tub," who hung himself on a hook. The administration put the country on a hook and asked "both the belligerents to cut us down, and they had refused and had left us to get down the best way we could."[1]

In cutting the embargo knot Congress blustered ever so slightly by substituting for it a Nonintercourse Act that empowered the incoming president to restore trade with either England or France, or both, if the warring powers would stop harassing American commerce. Meanwhile, commerce with other neutral powers was reopened. Since the Royal Navy commanded all the sealanes, the law seemed to give England a better vantage point. Direct commerce with either belligerent was forbidden, and Madison thought any resumption of seizures or impressment by the major powers would lead to war "against the persevering aggressor or aggressors."[2] True to his republican conception of what a president ought to do, Madison was leaving the ultimate decision on war or peace where the Constitution left it—in the hands of congressmen, not in the president's.

Many notes and hasty conferences preceded the end of Madison's tenure in the State Department offices. As Madison tidied up his secretary's desk, the formality of reading the electoral votes before Congress was enacted amidst mixed feelings. Jefferson, who had allowed nearly all executive business to slide, was relieved to know his hours in office were ending. "James the first of America will take possession of the throne on the fourth of March," a Federalist congressman snorted. "I think Friend James will have rather a troublesome reign. Who will succeed him as

Prime Minister is unknown as yet." Certainly Samuel Taggart intended to do all he could to make Madison's presidency a path of thorns. As to Madison's choice for secretary of state, all of Washington was speculating on the president-elect's decision.

A Virginian who could not wait, and who ached to be appointed himself, was Senator William Branch Giles. His name cropped up in most of the gossip, for Giles had been Madison's co-adjutor in Congress a decade earlier and had been a loyal Republican through most of the embargo debates. If any senator was a thick-and-thin Republican, it was Giles. On the other hand, Giles was deeply involved in a hate campaign against the other stalwart in Jefferson's cabinet, Albert Gallatin. In late February Giles fired a couple of warning shots over Madison's bow concerning cabinet appointments before he let loose 'a broadside. Jefferson's last months in office had been a disaster because of the president's ineptness in handling appointments, Giles warned, and to follow Jefferson's mistakes with more of his own would damage Madison's relations with the Senate. Then Giles launched a diatribe against Gallatin, warning of the consequences if Madison nominated him for secretary of state. "His nomination will be the signal for renewed attacks upon the administration by the whole federal party," Giles predicted, "even the most moderate, whilst it will disgust a very great portion of the Republican party, in my opinion the most respectable and upon which alone you can rely for a support."[3]

Apparently Giles and Madison had discussed the appointment, which explains why the Virginia senator was so upset. Give the number two position to a foreigner instead of a loyal Virginian? Giles's blood boiled at the thought. The senator from Virginia spoke to the president-elect as a teacher addresses an errant pupil. He told Madison that even if the Senate confirmed Gallatin, the appointment would be "highly instrumental in the destruction of the Republican party." Influential Republicans would assume that Madison was continuing the choice of eccentric men for high positions with a "favoritism equally unaccountable." Eight pages were filled with Giles's implied message: drop Gallatin, pick me. Madison must have fingered the letter over and over, for it was a warning signal that could not be ignored. Doubtless there was plenty of conversation in the same vein, for Senator Lieb of Pennsylvania loathed Gallatin, too, even though they both came from the Keystone State's Republican ranks. Senator Samuel Smith of Maryland also despised Gallatin.

With hindsight it is easy to discern what Madison should have done when a small band of Republican senators tried to scare the president-elect. At the time, Madison was trying to finish State Department business, listening to visitors who wanted federal posts ranging from lucrative collectorships to menial post office jobs, and hoping to make a smooth transition into the White House. Like Jefferson, Madison hated to hear discordant noises in his own household. If the Republicans wanted to squabble, he preferred that they stay on Capitol Hill and do it. This desire for the appearance of amicability was probably fed by the social position of his wife. Everybody acknowledged Mrs. Madison's leadership in Washington society. How could there be fighting in the kitchen and tranquillity in the parlor?

Thus besieged by menacing Republicans who had some claim to his friendship, Madison set his administration on a course that was almost blind. Complete chaos would be prevented by the appointment of the one man all the obstreperous party men professed to loathe, Gallatin. Able and usually unflappable, Gallatin had to be a part of the cabinet, and Madison knew it. But to avoid the threatened internecine party battle he failed to nominate Gallatin for the State Department post and therein gave a signal to the Liebs and Gileses. Instead, Madison kept Gallatin on as secretary of the treasury. Madison did not back off because of cowardice but in the interests of party harmony. Nonetheless, from almost his first day in the presidency, Madison was on the defensive against pettiness within his own party. In retrospect, it is obvious that Madison's magnanimity and overoptimistic view of Republican virtues proved to be a distinct handicap during his presidency.

On Madison's Inauguration Day all of this was unknown. As far as the insouciant partygoers were concerned partisan politics had been buried with the Federalists' poor showing in the recent campaign. The Madisons rode up to the capital, and the president-elect was ushered in to the House chamber for the inaugural ceremonies. Most eyes were trained on Mrs. Madison as Chief Justice Marshall held the Bible before his fellow Virginian. Marshall and Madison had come a long way since their days in Richmond battling to save the Constitution; and in the mellowness of the ceremonies perhaps Marshall and Madison were charitable toward each other, one reading the oath of office, the other repeating the words he had helped to write. "I do solemnly swear that I will faithfully execute the Office of President of the United States," Marshall said. Madison repeated the words, then made his way to the carriage through scores of well-wishers. Still in their rented quarters (Jefferson had not finished his packing), a reception for friends proceeded under Mrs. Madison's direction. John Quincy Adams took the whole exercise in his stride (noting that Madison's inaugural speech was short and delivered "in a tone of voice so low that he could not be heard"), then hurried back that afternoon to hear arguments at the Supreme Court in the momentous *Fletcher* v. *Peck* case. The busy day ended with a ball at Long's Hotel. "The crowd was excessive—the heat oppressive, and the entertainment bad," Adams recorded. "At midnight the ball broke up."[4]

Another witness reported the occasion with less solemnity. Following the inauguration, Margaret Bayard Smith noted, the street outside the Madisons' rented quarters were clogged with well-wishers "and we had to wait near half an hour, before we could get in." The First Lady "looked extremely beautiful" dressed in "a very long train, plain round the neck without any handkerchief, and beautiful bonnet of purple velvet, and white satin plumes." That night the celebrating continued, but the rooms became stifling hot, so that when the sashes could not be moved the order was given to break the windows to permit fresh air into the over-crowded home. When the small orchestra struck up "Madison's March" (composed for the occasion) Dolley Madison took her place and "looked a queen."[5] Jefferson appeared and seemed to enjoy the scene. "I do believe father never loved son more than he loves Mr. Madison," Mrs. Smith continued, but Madison's fatigue was evident. "Mr. Madison, on the contrary, seemed spiritless and exhausted."

Perhaps Jefferson was feeling better because the burden had been lifted from his shoulders, while Madison felt all the weight that night. Nothing in the field of foreign affairs had really changed, the jealousy within Republican ranks was getting out of hand, and except for the wonderful smile on Dolley Madison's face the president saw little to buoy his spirits. At midnight, a tired president and his lady took their leave of the company and went to bed.

Madison needed all his energy, for busy days lay ahead. Unwilling to challenge the Senate coterie, but aware of Gallatin's claims (and abil-ities), Madison wasted no time in sending a nomination for secretary of state forward. His choice was Robert Smith, who had served as secretary of the navy in Jefferson's cabinet and (perhaps more important) was the brother of Senator Samuel Smith. The appointment was less than bril-liant. Acerbic John Randolph praised Smith backhandedly, saying that "at least he could spell." Presumably, that was the only virtue needed if Madison planned to be his own secretary of state. Since Gallatin was already in the Treasury, he did not need reappointment. For the other cabinet posts (navy and war), Madison opted for geographic spread rather than proved competence. He nominated Paul Hamilton of South Carolina for the navy post, and chose Dr. William Eustis of Massachusetts (a Rev-olutionary War veteran-surgeon and former congressman) for the War Department. After two working days in office, Madison had his cabinet, but as Henry Adams properly adjudged, it "was the least satisfactory that any President had known."[6]

Within a matter of weeks the mettle of Madison's administration would be tested. The change of presidents was looked upon by the British minister in Washington, David Erskine, as an opportunity to make real progress on the stalemated *Leopard-Chesapeake* negotiations. If that sore point could be removed, there was hope for an Anglo-American rap-prochement. Erskine told his superiors in London there would be a change for the better when Jefferson left office, whereupon the British cabinet discussed a policy alteration that might intrigue the new administration. Jefferson was thought to be an Anglophobe beyond redemption; maybe Madison was more tractable. If so, responsible men at Whitehall decided, discussions might point to some sensible way to revive the Anglo-American trade severely damaged by the embargo. On this pocketbook issue, Foreign Minister George Canning instructed Erskine to speak to the Americans about dropping the detested Orders in Council. Citing Erskine's hint "that the beginning of the new Presidency may be favourable to a change of Policy in America," Canning said the British were ready to talk business.[7] Getting down to cases, Canning suggested that if Madison would allow the Royal Navy to resume the use of American Atlantic coast harbors, the British would return three of the four men seized from the *Chesapeake* (one had already been hanged) and make "provision for the Widows and Orphans of the Men killed in the action . . . as an Act of His Majesty's Spontaneous Generosity."

The Orders in Council, Canning continued, would be withdrawn if the United States suspended "all Nonintercourse and Non-Importation Acts so far as respects Great Britain; leaving them in force with respect to France." America would also have to give up the notion that a neutral power might carry on a "Trade with the Enemies Colonies, from which she was excluded during Peace." In other words, the Rule of 1756 was not going to be revoked to allow trade with the French West Indies.

As he read these instructions, Erskine's enthusiasm for an urgent meeting with Madison and his chief advisers quickened. Married to an American and almost the opposite of his predecessor in attitude toward Yankee ministers and manners, Erskine saw the instructions as an honest-to-God olive branch. Inexperienced and too eager, Erskine read on and failed to see the dangers in Canning's last provision: to make sure that no Americans would trade with France, the Royal Navy would be empowered to enforce a ban on Franco-American commerce. Without this security, Canning said, lifting the embargo "nominally, with respect to Great Britain alone, would in fact raise it with respect to all the World." Rather than risk bringing the Americans to the negotiating table only to have them balk at this sticky point, Erskine seems to have played it down.

When Canning's message reached Washington in early April 1809, Erskine lost no time relaying his interpretation of the instructions to the White House. Amidst the clutter caused by his wife's relatives and his secretary, who had moved in when Jefferson vacated the building on March 11, Madison found a niche of the executive mansion where he could talk with Gallatin, Smith, and the young envoy. Erskine brought up the point about the right of the British to board and seize Americans attempting to trade with France, but when Madison rejected the proposition as "insulting," Erskine dropped it. Instead, he chose to emphasize the cancellation of the Orders in Council and reparations for the *Leopard* attack. Gallatin was a bit wary of Erskine's extravagant claims. "On the subject of the orders in council," Gallatin noted, "how can Mr Erskine promise that they will cease to operate next week?"[8]

Like Erskine, Madison was hearing only what he wanted to hear. If Erskine said that the Orders in Council could be dropped as easily as a wilted daisy, Madison wanted to believe him. Gallatin suspected that the British cabinet had already cancelled the Orders, and that Erskine was only playing cat-and-mouse. In such confused circumstances, but with the best of intentions, Madison chose to take Erskine's word and without any qualms he prepared a proclamation ending the quarantine on commerce with England. Allowing a decent interval of time for the word to spread, Madison declared that on June 10 trade with Great Britain would reopen to coincide with the revocation of the Orders in Council. Surely champagne corks or their equivalent popped that night at the White House. To Jefferson, who was now in glorious isolation at Monticello, Madison reported the diplomatic coup and ventured the thought that England was harboring "the hope that it may embroil us with France." But, Madison added, "if France be not bereft of common sense, or be not predetermined on war with us, she will certainly not play into the hand of her Enemy."[9]

Jefferson had the good news within a couple of days (the postal express to Virginia set up in 1801 was continued at taxpayers' expense), and he too exulted. Their policy of economic sanctions seemed thoroughly vindicated: "I rejoice in it as the triumph of our forebearing & yet persevering system. It will lighten your anxieties, take from cabal it's most fertile ground of war, [and] will give us peace during your time." Jefferson was wary of the negotiating that was likely to ensue, and hoped Madison would insist on a settlement of the impressment issue. Otherwise, Jefferson said, the English would be bragging about "their practice of whipping us into a treaty."[10]

Federalists were taken aback by the sudden turn of events. At Boston, the revival of commerce turned caustic Benjamin Russell, publisher of the *Columbian Centinel,* into a man of charity. As dozens of ships loaded flour, grain, and lumber for the English market, his newspaper hailed the contrast with the nadir of embargo times. At the Fourth of July celebration, the *Centinel* recalled that in 1808 "all our shipping were lying rotting at our wharves . . . [but] on the present Anniversary, a Ship moving gallantly" on parade reminded onlookers of "the jubilee of Trade and Commerce restored, as well as Independence." At Gloucester, celebrants toasted "President Madison—May the whole web of his administration equal the pattern."[11]

Even as Republicans and Federalists exulted, a tiny piece of strange news arrived from England. The cabinet had issued a new Order in Council changing the terms of the 1807 edict, so that neutrals would no longer have to call at a British port before proceeding to all of Europe except France, Holland, Italy, and French colonies. The American minister in London, ignorant of the Erskine-Madison accord, was ecstatic. The new order removed "the most disgusting Features of that System of Violence and Monopoly against which our Efforts have been justly directed," William Pinkney reported. The old orders were simply mean-spirited, aimed at forcing the "Trade of the World . . . through British ports and to pay British imposts."[12]

Pinkney might as well have saved his breath, for the shock waves started rippling as soon as rumors reached Washington that something was amiss. Asked for reassurances, Erskine told Madison that nothing was wrong. "The first declarations of Mr. E. seem to have quieted the distrust which was becoming pretty strong," Madison confessed to Jefferson.[13] Assured by Erskine that nothing could possibly go wrong, Madison helped his wife into a carriage as they started on their annual summer retreat to Montpelier. They reached the family plantation on July 20. Four days later, official Washington was abuzz with a report from London that the British cabinet had disavowed Erskine's promises. Within twenty-four hours the worst was out—the Orders in Council were not revoked—and Erskine had been recalled as a kind of reprimand.

The joy of April turned to shock in July as Madison read Gallatin's quick analysis of what the British move implied. Nothing has really changed, and "from the present ministry [in London] we cannot expect a change of system. . . . What course ought we then to pursue?" Robert Smith thought the British cabinet's action made it clear "that no adjustment consistent with our interest or our honor can be made with that infatuated nation."[14] To make matters worse, Erskine was to be replaced by Francis James Jackson, a British diplomat who gained notoriety when he delivered the ultimatum preceding the Royal Navy's bombardment of Copenhagen. What kind of peace gesture was this tasteless decision by George Canning?

Embarrassed and uncertain of the next step, Madison hurried back to Washington. He overcame some cabinet members' doubts that the president could unilaterally undo the April proclamation on his own by signing a cancelling counterorder.[15] Unhampered by a lawyer's mentality, Madison decided he could undo what he had done without treading on the Constitution. In no mood to greet the new British minister, Madison let the haughty Briton dawdle in Washington for weeks before he himself returned to the capital. Jackson had brought a small army of servants and an overbearing German wife, and he expected better treatment than he received. At his first meeting with Madison, Jackson characterized the president as "a plain and rather mean-looking little man"; when he

knew Madison better he added: "Madison is now as obstinate as a mule."
Soon Jackson and Smith exchanged accusations and counteraccusations
concerning Erskine's instructions. Jackson intimated that Madison and
Smith knew that the British would not make a deal unless the Royal
Navy could be allowed to enforce American laws; and thus by implication
the president and secretary had tried to pull a fraud. A tedious correspondence with Jackson, signed by Smith but written by Madison, erupted
into a display of bad temper in November. Madison resolved the matter
by sending Jackson word that no further communications bearing his
signature would be accepted. In short, "Copenhagen" Jackson had become
persona non grata. Sure of his ground, Madison asked for Jackson's recall.
Anglo-American relations seemed strained to the breaking point.

Jackson threw all the blame on Madison and Smith. "That I did
not show an equal facility with Erskine to be duped by them has been
my great crime," he moaned. Jackson made his way homeward at a leisurely pace, stopping at Federalist strongholds where the sweet reason-
ableness of April had turned sour by November. In Massachusetts, the
governor invited Jackson to visit Boston as his guest while the state legislature passed resolutions exonerating Jackson of blame and implying
that Madison and his administrations were the real culprits.[16] For his
consolation, Madison looked southward as scores of county Republican
meetings issued their own resolutions supporting the president. Party
stalwarts at Nashville, Tennessee, branded the British repudiation of Erskine as "base and perfidious and [it] proves that the cabinet of that
country makes her interest alone, their rule of action." In Washington
County, New York, Republicans condemned England for using "decietful
lures to draw us within the Grasp of the most perfidious rapacity." From
the Georgia legislature, Madison learned of a resolution that offset the
New England criticism. "We conceive the conduct of Francis James Jackson . . . to have been highly insulting and censurable, and . . . with
one voice we approve the spirited and decisive manner of the Executive
of the United States in refusing further to negotiate with the British
Government through the medium of that Minister."[17]

Despite their obvious partisanship, these resolutions were music to
Madison's ears. Not a message of condolence for the shattered Erskine
agreement escaped the president's notice. Madison not only saw to it
that the supportive messages were handed to the *National Intelligencer*
editor for reprinting, he also took the trouble to answer them in his
personal handwriting, using painstaking care in shaping his replies. Perhaps Madison saw in the resolutions more than the makers intended.
"The determination evinced by these Resolns. to maintain the national
rights & honor, agst. aggressions from whatever quarter," he answered
Kentucky Republicans, "can not but be acceptable to those to whose
responsibility those essential objects are in a material degree committed."[18]

Like every president before and since, Madison convinced himself that the people were behind his policies despite the scourging criticism leveled by the Federalist newspapers.

❧

While Dolley Madison was firmly in control of Washington society, her husband felt some discomfort as the first year of his White House tenure came to an end. With the embargo dead and the Erskine agreement cancelled, shippers were uncertain of their next move and commercial houses were in a quandary. To alleviate the confusion, Congress tackled the problem with a different approach, masterminded by Albert Gallatin. Working closely with Congressman Thomas Macon, Gallatin, desperately seeking a renewal of the customs collections needed for the depleted national treasury, wrote a bill that would allow the sealanes to open for American shipping provided the owners and crews were willing to risk encounters with the belligerents. Meanwhile, merchantmen and warships from England and France would be denied use of American harbors. First introduced as Macon's Bill No. 1, the proposal passed the House but was emasculated in the Senate. Madison stood aside, allowing the debate to run its course before a compromise measure made its way to his desk. As Macon's Bill No. 2, the legislation pleased few but it had an interesting feature. If either belligerent dropped its punitive decrees on American commerce, the United States would reimpose its nonintercourse restrictions on the other belligerent (unless that power also called off its anti-Yankee edicts).

Madison left Congress guessing as to whether he favored the crazy-quilt legislation or not, but when the bill finally came to the White House he signed it. Analyzing the law for the American minister in England, Madison showed more perception than his critics believed possible. England was in full command of the Atlantic, Madison admitted, so "that she has now a compleat interest in perpetuating the actual state of things." But France might "turn the tables on G. Britain by compelling her either to revoke her orders, or to lose the commerce of this Country." Indeed, Madison reckoned, a realization "that France may take this politic course would be a rational motive with the B. Govt. to get the start of her."[19] There was much wishful thinking in Madison's analysis of what the warring powers might do, of course, but in time Napoleon saw the opportunity exactly as the president had outlined it. When that occurred, England had one final chance to avoid an American war.

Nobody in Washington was sure of what the next move would be. In Congress, the speculation was partisan in tone. The Federalists were torn between hope that Madison would fail so egregiously that his re-election could not be accomplished and wonderment that Republicans still held office with the voters' approbation. When Madison asked for legislation to authorize a twenty-thousand-man army, both sides of the aisle were confused as to the motives for raising such a force. Madison had an eye on Florida, where some land-greedy Americans were willing to over-throw Spanish rule, then make a deal that would bring West Florida into the union, but the president was reluctant to tell Congress everything. The New England delegations thought Madison wanted an army capable of invading Canada and reacted accordingly. "I believe very few of the hardy yeomanry of New England will be willing to volunteer in a wild goose chase to Canada for nine months," an acerbic Federalist observed.[20] John Randolph, who had been sidelined with illness, came back into the congressional fray eager to block any request for a large military bud-get. Randolph dismissed all the war talk as premature and called for a reduction in arms rather than a buildup. "We have been embargoed and non-intercoursed almost into a consumption," Randolph said, "and this is not the time for battle."[21]

All right, Madison said, do it your way. Convinced that his light-handed policy had the voters' approval, Madison was content to have the nation led by Congress, not the executive branch. Now in his fifty-eighth year, Madison was no longer the innovator anxious to guide the nation into a reform mood. While Congress moved toward adjournment, the lack of forceful leadership provoked Federalist Samuel Taggart to blame Madison. Although most congressmen were Republicans, party ties seemed tenuous in both houses so that Madison never knew how the voting might go. "There is I believe this difference between the last and present President," Taggart observed. "Jefferson by a system of in-trigue and low cunning managed the party. M[adiso]n is a mere puppet or a cypher managed by some chiefs of the faction who are behind the curtain." The New England congressman noted with irony that the radical Republicans overlooked French provocations while pointing the finger at England. "Because France burns our ships, confiscates our property, and imprisons our seamen they want to fight Great Britain."[22] Richard Mentor Johnson from Kentucky saw things differently:

> Why have not the people complained of the increase of the Army and Navy under the last years of Mr. Jefferson's Administration? Because they believed one should have been sent to the Canadas, and the other to drive smuggling vessels from our waters; and the only complaint made is, that we have failed to use the physical force of the nation to chastise the aggres-sions of other nations.

But Johnson was more Republican than warhawk, for he confessed that his concern focused more on the nation's treasury than on its arsenal. "I want," he concluded, "neither armies or navies in time of peace."[23]

American shippers greeted Macon's Bill No. 2 with a flurry of activity that cleaned warehouses of stored commodities. The British market was so flooded with Virginia tobacco that Madison's own crop sold for a paltry threepence per pound. The Royal Navy had turned the Atlantic into a British pond, and Napoleon was furious to the point that in late March 1810 he issued another decree from Rambouillet declaring all American ships in French ports subject to seizure even if they had not come from a British port or had never been searched by the king's sailors. Now it was Madison's turn to show real anger. "The late confiscations by Bonaparte," he told Jefferson, "comprize robbery, theft, & breach of trust, and exceed in turpitude any of his enormities, not wasting human blood." Madison hoped that the American minister in Paris could achieve some softening of Napoleon's harsh edict, once Napoleon had a chance to digest the alternative offered by Macon's Bill No. 2. If the French First Consul was really a clever politician, he could undo the damage of the Rambouillet decree with a flick of his wrist. Madison thought the latest Napoleonic edict was a mask for "French robbery," but he could not suppress his Anglophobic feelings of old. "The public attention is beginning to fix itself on the proof it affords that the original sin agst. Neutrals lies with G.B.," he told Jefferson, "and whilst she acknowledges it, she persists in it."[24]

Napoleon seemed to read Madison's mind. Perusing a translation of Macon's Bill No. 2, he perceived the Yankee law as Madison suggested he might, overruled his foreign minister (who wanted official word before considering the next move), and made a quick decision. In a roundabout way Napoleon let it be known that he was, in effect, willing to repeal his punitive decrees and would in return expect Congress "to reestablish its prohibitions on English commerce."[25]

Obviously Madison, despite being burned by the Erskine experience, was still willing to take a diplomatic move at face value (he learned of Napoleon's about-face from the American minister in London, not from an official French document). Without waiting to learn whether Napoleon had in fact called off his campaign of plundering American ships, Madison reacted to the news from Paris with dispatch. Napoleon appeared to have called Congress's bluff, and Madison acknowledged the move by declaring American trade with France to be free. At the same time, the president asked the British to follow Napoleon's lead at once. The alternative, according to the law, was reimposition of the ban on trade with England. That Madison acted hastily is beyond question; and Henry Adams's charge that the president "made himself a party to Napoleon's fraud" has been echoed by other critics who thought that Madison had naively rushed into a French trap.[26]

Meanwhile a problem closer at hand begged for a solution. A small band of West Floridians had caught the spirit of the times (rebellion against Spain was popular in 1810, from Argentina northward) and had attacked the Spanish garrison at Baton Rouge. In short order they killed the commandant, took over the post, declared their independence, and asked the United States to annex their half-baked republic. Madison shared Jefferson's dream to make Florida a part of the United States, but he was bothered by constitutional qualms. After agonizing over his legal right to move troops into the area, Madison decided not to wait for Congress to reassemble and then raise the annexation issue. Instead, he rebuked the freebooters but issued a proclamation on October 27, 1810, ordering an American occupation of West Florida to proceed toward the Perdido River. The Americans moved only to the Pearl River, however, and the Spaniards dug in around the Perdido. The incident provided fodder for Madison's critics, who claimed he had acted without authority to hit "a just and friendly Power" who was already down.

The American occupation of West Florida added no glory to the stars and stripes. Madison overplayed his hand several months later by asking Congress to authorize him to order the occupation of East Florida in case a foreign power tried to occupy it. In a secret session, Congress voted to give Madison his way, but except for a further extension into West Florida, the swamplands and shores of the coveted peninsula remained beyond Madison's grasp. Ultimately the diplomacy of John Quincy Adams acquired the Florida title that somehow evaded both Jefferson and Madison.

While Madison kept his hand in the State Department and apparently left little more for Robert Smith to do than order the president's letters copied for his signature, the president shied away from a domestic quarrel shaping over the move to renew the Bank of the United States charter, set to expire in 1811. Treasury secretary Gallatin needed the bank to serve as a stabilizing financial resource for federal deposits and as a buyer of government bonds, but within Republican circles his old enemies were plotting its demise. Convinced that he would invite criticism if he tried to interfere, Madison left the recharter strategy to Gallatin and Senator William Crawford. The same senators who had thwarted Madison in March 1809 came down hard on the bank, hoping to bring Gallatin crashing down with it. When a tie vote in the Senate left the final decision up to Madison's vice-president, George Clinton went against recharter. Gallatin offered to resign but was persuaded to stay in the cabinet, even though a dismantling of the Bank left the federal treasury vulnerable if war came.

More bad news followed a few weeks later when the Senate rejected Madison's nomination of Alexander Wolcott for the Supreme Court. Dolley Madison felt her husband's disappointment at the obvious slap. "Some very wicked, & silly doings at home," she commented, while

John Randolph chuckled at the president's embarrassment and held that Madison was chief executive "*de jure* only." "Who exercises the office *de facto* I know not."[27]

Madison realized that a faction within his own party was trying to undermine his policies, foreign as well as domestic. The chief culprit, in Madison's mind, was his secretary of state, Robert Smith. Madison saw him as a misfit who was knee-deep in a closet campaign to undermine confidence in Madison's fitness as president. Looking forward to the 1812 presidential campaign, Smith aligned himself with the Republican dissidents who had become Madison's hairshirt. Through a mutual friend Madison sounded out James Monroe as to his availability as Robert Smith's successor, and when Monroe indicated a willingness to join the president's official family, Madison lowered the boom. Confronting Smith with instances of disloyalty and incompetence, Madison told Smith he was through. As a face-saving gesture, he offered Smith a Russian assignment.

At first Smith indicated he would take the St. Petersburg post and leave the cabinet with good grace. But after checking with his brother, Senator Samuel Smith, and a few other friends Smith decided he would resign and throw his case before the public in a newspaper indictment of Madison. Recalling the incident some time later, Madison told his side of the story and noted: "He took his leave with a cold formality, and I did not see him afterward."[28]

What cooked Smith's goose, insofar as Madison's was concerned, was Smith's talk behind the president's back. Madison learned of Smith's criticism of his foreign policy "and had gone so far as to avow a disapprobation of the whole policy of commercial restrictions, from the Embargo throughout." The last straw had been a rumor that Smith had told an English diplomat in Washington that Madison knew the French edicts had not been revoked but that Madison was too much an Anglophobe to treat England fairly. Madison was willing to write the major dispatches for Smith's signature, but he refused to harbor in his cabinet a man who challenged his fundamental approach to foreign affairs. The president reminded Smith that his diplomatic dispatches were "almost always so crude and inadequate, that I was in the more important cases generally obliged to write them anew myself, under the disadvantage, sometimes, of retaining, thro' delicacy, some mixture of his draft."[29]

Smith was out, Monroe was in, but the messy business was not ended. Smith lashed out at Madison in the Philadelphia *Aurora* (published by a crony who shared his distaste for Madison), and then circulated a pamphlet full of accusations. Smith's point seemed to be that he had tried to stand up to Napoleon but was undercut by a sycophantic president willing to dance to the Frenchman's tune.

Madison wrote a painful account of the incidents leading up to Smith's dismissal, but decided it could not be printed. Instead, he de-

pended on friends for a journalistic counterattack while lamenting to
Jefferson Smith's "wicked publication": "It is impossible however that
the whole turpitude of his conduct can be understood without disclosures
to be made by myself alone, and of course, as he knows, not to be made
at all. Without these his infamy is daily fastening itself upon him." Within
a matter of weeks, Smith's ill-tempered pamphlet had backfired, leading
a congressman who was no particular friend of Madison's to observe that
the attempt to smear the president was a capital blunder. Smith's final
ineptitude thus was "one of the rare instances of a man's giving the finishing stroke to his own character, in his eagerness to ruin his enemy."[30]

While Madison's discomfort amused Federalists, a new British minister came to town. His mission was to talk the Americans out of any
foolhardy action in Florida and gain an admission from the president that
he had acted rashly in accepting Napoleon's promise to cancel his punitive
decrees. The ban on imports from England was hurting, but the men in
Whitehall hoped to gain access to American markets again by rattling
a few sabers along Pennsylvania Avenue. With Monroe as his secretary
of state Madison at last felt comfortable in his cabinet meetings and
allowed his fellow Virginian to do the talking when the English diplomat,
Sir Augustus John Foster, came calling. If Napoleon had really called
off his campaign against American commerce, Foster asked, where was
the proof?

Madison retreated once again to Montpelier, where he took a respite
from reports of more seizures and affronts to the American flag on the
high seas by riding through his corn and wheat fields. As he faced the
disappointment of reading dispatches that repeated only what he had
seen for the past eight years, Madison still believed that his republican
instincts were sound. Nourishing the hope that some rays of hope would
come on the next ship from Europe, Madison read a somber note from
his quondam friend, "Light-horse Harry" Lee. "A continuance in the
present state of half war is of all other the most debasing to the national
character & nearly as injurious as war itself to individual prosperity,"
Lee counseled. "It is better to fight our way to future peace, than to drag
on in this state of disputation & irritation, which must lead to war &
perhaps at a period not so favorable to us as the present moment."[31] The
subject was too serious for Madison to smile, and he knew how irrational
Lee could be. With no navy to speak of, a tiny regular army, and the
national treasury in an anemic state, what in heaven's name made the
present moment so favorable?

Madison perceived that Lee said what many congressmen had been
saying for months: America's standing as an independent nation was in
jeopardy. As he rode along the Montpelier roads, perhaps Madison's mind
wandered back to the earlier crises of 1780 and 1786, when the outlook
had been so bleak. Miracles kept the army in the field, and more miracles

led to the Philadelphia convention; so Madison was not willing to concede that the difficulties of 1811 were insurmountable. On the other hand, Madison read the newspapers and he looked between the lines. By the end of the summer, as he headed back to Washington and a special session of Congress, Madison seemed to have new resolve. America must arm, the citizenry must be roused, and if economic sanctions would not force the belligerents to recognize American rights a war might be necessary. But should America fight England, or France?

As a witness and participant in the creation of a republican presidency in 1787 Madison still wanted all the initiative for war to come from Congress. That was the constitutional way to go to war. The young congressmen from the West were more excited than usual when reports from the Indian country told of a battle on Tippecanoe Creek where it was claimed that British agents had fomented trouble with the Shawnee tribesmen. More skirmishes between American vessels and the marauding Royal Navy indicated no relaxation of the British Orders in Council, nor was the news from France comforting. Napoleon had not released American seamen jailed when his officers seized the Yankee ships over a year earlier. In the circumstances, Madison used his State of the Union message to stump for increased appropriations for the army and the authority to expand the militia. Thus America would react to fresh evidence "of hostile inflexibility in trampling on rights which no Independent Nation can relinquish."[32]

Congress caught the president's mood, responding with a series of resolutions aimed at placing the nation in a militant, if not warlike, stance. The resolves called for a hurried expansion of the army, with the three-year enlistment of ten thousand more regular troops for a start, and a go-ahead signal to Madison to accept up to fifty thousand volunteers for training. All naval vessels "not now in service" should be made ready for sea duty, and merchant vessels were to be armed.

Then Madison's archenemies in the Senate unlimbered their plan. Why stop at a ten-thousand man army? Senator Giles, now eager to embarrass Madison, pushed for a bill to enlist twenty-five thousand men. If anything, the bloated army bill was another crude effort to harass Madison: where would the money be found to pay that many troops? The cardboard army was only a bluff, "manufactured [more] for exportation than for home consumption," one of Madison's critics in the House observed, "being destined to go out to Europe in the *Hornet* to flatter France and terrify Britain."[33]

Rarely in American history has so much importance been placed on a ship's peacetime voyage as on the trans-Atlantic winter crossing made by the *Hornet*. She would carry the president's call for American rearmament and his hope that someone with power in Paris or London would sense the urgency. Party politics aside, in Madison's mind the congressional actions came close to being an ultimatum.

Meanwhile, the American minister to England returned home, convinced that further negotiation with the intractable British ministry was useless. Across the channel, Madison replaced the minister in Paris with Jonathan Russell, who was to receive the same runaround his predecessor experienced. If by spring neither France nor England had budged an iota, Madison realized, the country would expect action.

Jefferson thought a rumor about George III's illness was encouraging—maybe the old king was about to die—and Jefferson tied the anti-American bias of the British cabinet to the king's whims. But Madison saw the cabinet policy in London as a fixed plan on England's part to damage France while also keeping the oceans free of American ships. The detested Orders in Council were the "bone in the throat" of Madison's administration, and as the *Hornet* sailed for Europe the president must have thought that without a repeal of those edicts war must come. The British minister in Washington was warned by Henry Clay that the country's patience was at the breaking point:

> He [Clay] assured me that in ten days after the return of the *Hornet* sloop-of-war, if she should bring no accounts of justice having been done by France to the United States, and of [no] money being paid or promised to be paid for the spoliations committed by French cruisers upon the American trade, war would be declared against the French as well as the English."

Senator Crawford told the Englishman that if the *Hornet* came home empty-handed (with no return of the ships or cargoes Napoleon had seized), he would favor a war against France.[34] Foster, the British minister, convinced that this was mostly congressional bluster, assured his superiors in London that a declaration of war was most improbable.

Perhaps the English envoy was deceived by the civility of Washington society, for Madison was not kidding. He placed as much store on the *Hornet's* mission as any man in Washington. If the diplomatic dispatches from London and Paris proved disappointing, after so much publicity about the vessel's voyage and purposes, the Republican party would face growing hostility from voters during a presidential election year. Messages from Republican crossroads rallies as well as from state legislatures reinforced Madison's resolve. Citizens gathered at a public meeting in Windsor, North Carolina, spoke to the crux of the matter by condemning the Orders in Council. "The rigorous execution of those orders," they insisted, afforded proof "of British injustice and [a] determined hostility to the United States that is actual war both in purpose and effect on our lawful commerce." The Virginia legislature passed a series of resolutions expressing approval for Madison's conduct of foreign affairs and urging a militant stance. "However highly we value the blessings of peace, and however we may deprecate the evils of war, the period has now arrived when peace, *as we now have it,* is disgraceful, and war is honorable."[35] Madison, who had said in 1792 that "public opinion sets bounds to every Government, and is the real sovereign in every free one," gained confidence for his next move as the clamor grew louder.

Who was America's real enemy? The president still was not playing favorites. At the White House levee on New Year's Day, 1812, Madison went out of his way to dress down the French minister over the lack of confirmation that France was living up to Napoleon's promises. The French envoy tried to melt into the crowd to escape the president's obvious wrath after Madison said the French seizures "were in his eyes just as definite acts of hostility as were those of England."[36]

The Frenchman soon had balm for his wounded pride, however, when a smooth-talking countryman arrived in Washington loaded with enough evidence (he claimed) to blow Anglo-American relations sky-high. Incredible as it now seems, Madison and Monroe were dupes to the charlatan's claim that he had proof the British had sent a secret agent into New England to foment disunion. The French go-between asked for $75,000 for this information, which presumably named the names of New England men who assisted the spy (a remorseful American citizen, John Henry) in his nefarious plans. Shocked by the price, but eager to hold up evidence that the New England Federalists might be flirting with treason, Madison and Monroe scraped up $50,000—enough to build a good-sized frigate—to purchase the so-called Henry Letters. The bombshell proved to be a dud when the letters between Henry and the Canadian governor revealed no more than a dozen newspaper articles would have told any perceptive observer. As for traitors named, there were none.

Trying to salvage something from the wasted $50,000, Madison sent the letters to Congress with a covering statement that here was evidence the British were plotting intrigues with disaffected men "for the purpose of bringing about resistance to the laws, and, eventually, in concert with a British force, of destroying the Union." Overall, the incident proved an embarrassment and showed Madison at his worst. "This may perhaps serve for one of the blackest chapters of political juggling" America had ever seen, a Federalist congressman charged, ". . . as it is generally believed, 50 thousand dollars [was given] to a villain for the purpose of securing Madison's re-election and keeping down the Federalists."[37]

Indeed, Madison's actions from the outset of the election year revealed a president suffering from hesitation if not confusion. Besides the red faces caused by the Henry Affair there was the court-martial for General James Wilkinson, which that strange character had insisted upon to clear his reputation. Earlier Wilkinson had escaped from charges that he was a Spanish informant (which he was, trading silver dollars for American secrets), and Jefferson had supported him in return for testimony that Burr had been a traitor. Then Wilkinson selected a ruinous militia camp-site in the Louisiana Territory that sent hundreds of recruits to early graves. Congressmen howled until more charges of incompetency were hurled, along with revivals of the "Spanish silver" stories. The wishy-washy court-martial became mired in lengthy testimony and finally left the decision on Wilkinson's future career up to Madison. Instead of forthrightly pushing the controversial old soldier into retirement, Madison accepted the court-martial's recommendation for leniency "with regret."[38] The whitewash of Wilkinson did nothing for army morale and was a foretaste of the president's poor judgment in selecting field commanders when a shooting war came.

Taken together, the Henry Affair and the Wilkinson court-martial might have become a terrible burden for the administration with an election looming, but Madison had more on his mind that running for a second term. The dogwood trees along the Potomac started to bud without a sign of the *Hornet*'s sails. Everybody was a bit jumpy, and America's complaint about British arrogance while supplying foodstuffs for the red-coated army fighting in Spain smacked of hypocrisy. While shipments of American grain were feeding Wellington's Peninsular campaign, the Royal Navy kept up a vigilant patrol of the North Atlantic. Did England's right hand know what the left was doing? Did any important Englishman care? When a ship from England brought news that the British cabinet remained adamant on the Orders in Council, Madison wrote Jefferson that it seemed "that they prefer war with us, to a repeal of their orders in Council. We have nothing left therefore, but to make ready for it. As a step to it an embargo for 60 days was recommended to Congs. on wednesday and agreed to in the H. of Reps. by about 70 to 40." The Senate eventually passed the measure, but it was not to be hurried. As Jefferson told Madison: "The temper of that body is known to be equivocal." The new embargo bill Madison signed placed a ninety-day clamp on all American ships normally calling at foreign ports.

Federalists in New England were furious, for small fortunes were being made from the grain shipments to Portugal and Spain. Loathing for Madison's policy of economic sanctions reached a fever pitch, with a strategy emerging for support of a rival candidate within the Republican party who would be safe on the issue of unfettered foreign commerce. They found their man in DeWitt Clinton, nephew of the vice-president, who was now both mayor of New York and the state lieutenant-governor. Acknowledging the unlikelihood that a Federalist could be elected president, Madison's opponents opted for a divide-and-conquer strategy to gain their goals. "The prospect of a Federal President nominally so is hopeless," a New England congressman conceded. Despite Clinton's notorious ambition the Federalists backed him out of desperation. "He is known to be an enemy to the anti-commercial system and wants nothing but to be put in a situation in which he can act to set it aside."[39] For the frustrated Federalists, that was good enough; the word went out to their party oracles to run candidates for the Electoral College who would stick with Clinton.

Madison professed to be too busy to concern himself with elections, but his silence after the Republican nominating caucus (82 to 0 in favor of Madison) was taken to mean that the president would accept reelection. While uneasy with Clinton, Federalists looked for an alternative fusion candidate such as John Jay or John Marshall, but neither man gave them any encouragement. As a last resort, the ill-shaped plan was to procure all the electoral votes above the Potomac for the New Yorker and send Madison home in retirement.

Events that spring moved to a drumbeat that would not have been militant had communications between America and England been swifter. This was still the age of sails, so that any significant news might not cross the Atlantic for anywhere from four to six weeks. Thus Madison applauded the renewed embargo on American shipping at the same time that English merchants were applying pressure in Parliament to drop the Orders in Council. Late in April 1812 a parade of English ironmongers and merchants came before Parliament to reinforce petitions they had presented asking for a repeal of the Orders in Council. Since February 1811, they told the House of Commons, "the Export trade to America has been subject to very great embarrassments and distresses, almost an-nihilating the profit attending it . . . for the last twelve months there has been no Export trade to America, and the manufacturers are reduced to a state of grievous affliction." Witness after witness told Parliament that Birmingham manufacturers sent about £800,000 of iron goods to America annually. Asked if the losses were caused by American retaliation to the Orders in Council, one witness said that £500,000 in British exports were rusting at the Liverpool docks. "They would be shipped immediately on the repeal of the Orders in Council," the witness promised.[40]

Unaware of the case being made on his behalf, Madison grew weary of waiting for the *Hornet*. A bit of spice was added to his life when newspapers reported that the New York presidential caucus had unani-mously chosen DeWitt Clinton as its candidate, but Madison had his own strategy. Vice-president George Clinton had openly shown his dislike for Madison and had cast the damaging vote to kill the Bank of the United States. Even before Clinton became ill, Madison probably wanted to dump the old obstructionist; but the vice-president's death in April 1812 made everything easier. Madison looked to New England for a vice-presidential candidate to offset the High Federalists' search for a winning strategy, and found his man in Elbridge Gerry. Loyal to the core, Gerry had recently lost his bid for a third term as governor of Massachusetts, after engineering a political redistricting meant to preserve Republicans in office without regard to geographic fairness. Federalist newspapers cried "Foul!" first and "Gerrymander!" next, giving the language a much-needed word for political opportunism. At any rate, Gerry gave the ticket a northern balance that Madison thought vital.

Reports that the *Hornet* was overdue bred rumors that England had brushed aside the latest American retaliatory laws like so many annoying gnats. "Ever since her sailing the cant word has been, the *Hornet*, the *Hornet*—what a sting she will bring on her return!" a Kentucky newspaper editor exulted. Madison's favorite newspaper, the Washington *National Intelligencer*, admitted in mid-April that all eyes were scanning the horizon for a glimpse of the *Hornet*'s sails. "The public attention has been drawn to the approaching arrival of the *Hornet*," the newspaper commented, "as a period when the measures of our government would take a decisive character, or rather their final cast." Now there were rumors of British intransigence matched with reports of French accommodation. If these stories proved true, "where is the motive for longer delay? The final step ought to be taken, and that step is WAR."[41] The editor, Samuel Harrison Smith, was one of Madison's closest friends. No genius was needed to figure out what was behind the editor's commentary.

Finally, on May 22, the *Hornet* dropped anchor in an American port. The diplomatic pouches were rushed to Washington and by May 25 the worst was out. France apparently had rescinded her punitive decrees, but had done so in such a way as to leave England "a pretext for enforcing her O. in C.," Madison told Jefferson. "And in all other respects the grounds of our complaints remain the same." The bad news spread down the corridors of the capitol and across the country. "All the letters and accounts from *Washington* affirm that *immediate* WAR with England is inevitable," a Federalist newspaper in Boston lamented, adding that "Mad men" in Congress were unbridled and "the President stood pen in hand ready to sign the *Death Warrant* of the country's prosperity."[42]

The British foreign minister, somehow out of touch with reality, asked the administration for ironclad proof that Napoleon had called off his decrees, and warned that without such proof the Royal Navy would go on seizing American ships headed for Europe. The British minister tried to talk about more negotiations, but Madison was out of patience. His mind made up, Madison did what he had to do and called for war.

If he had tried any other course, Madison would have been a discredited president and might have been impeached. Republican officeholders saw no other avenue of escape after so much publicity attended the *Hornet* sailing. "The honor of the Nation and that at of the party are bound up together and both will be sacrified if war be not declared," a Pennsylvania Republican confessed even before the *Hornet* had docked.

The old warhorse, Elbridge Gerry, smarting from his defeat, wrote Madison a letter that coincided with the *Hornet's* arrival. "Mortified & vexed by the loss of the gubernatorial election," Gerry insisted, the Republicans only needed a rallying cry. "By war, we should be fortified, as by fire."[43] Reading between the lines, Madison saw what he wanted to see: New England would not kick the traces of Union if war came, and might in fact overpower the Federalists when their pro-British prejudices provided an embarrassment.

Ultimately, Madison the republican theorist lost the argument to Madison the Republican president. In 1792 he had insisted that "war contains so much folly, as well as wickedness, that much is to be hoped from the progress of reason; and if anything is to be hoped, every thing ought to be tried."[44] He had tried everything, and nothing had worked. Thus fortified by a belief that he had exhausted every means of averting war, and convinced that the young republic's honor was at stake, Madison sent the expected war message to Congress on June 1, 1812, singling out England as the guilty nation. After reviewing the long train of incidents involving British decrees, the bullying by the Royal Navy, and the insulting tone of English diplomacy, Madison charged that England really sought a worldwide monopoly of commerce and navigation: "She carries on a war against the lawful commerce of a friend, that she may the better carry on a commerce with an enemy; a commerce polluted by the forgeries and perjuries, which are, for the most part, the only passports by which it can succeed."

To the list of British wrongs, including impressment and the pillaging of neutral commerce, Madison added the innuendo that recent Indian problems on the American frontier were exacerbated by British influence. "We behold, in fine, on the side of Great Britain a state of War against the United States; and on the side of the United States, a state of peace towards Great Britain."[45] As for France, Madison admitted that not much had changed since Napoleon claimed to have revoked his decrees, but he alluded to negotiation under way in Paris and promised to share with Congress the results of those talks.

Madison concluded his war message without emotional pleas.* His role as president called for no dramatics but rather a statement of the facts. The power to declare war, according to the Constitution he had helped write, lay with Congress. The warhawks, for all their bluster, found that the House was divided along more than party lines. North of New Jersey almost half the Republicans sided with the Federalists to

---

*Between Presidents Jefferson and Wilson all messages to Congress were read aloud by the House and Senate clerks, which probably robbed the messages of any dramatic impact. Wilson resumed the "live" appearance precedent of Washington and Adams that Jefferson disliked and broke off.

vote against the war. The tempo was far from fervid, in contrast to the crashing speed Congress adopted in declaring later wars. With no sense of urgency whatever, the debates went on behind closed doors; and the New York congressmen opposing the war must have been supporters of DeWitt Clinton hoping to embarrass Madison.

Not a single Federalist voted for war as the declaration passed the House, 79 to 49. The Senate proved more stubborn, until it was clear that the anti-Madison Republicans risked public opprobrium by further foot-dragging. The nation was totally unaware of what was happening at almost that same moment in England, where Parliament heard of the cabinet decision to repeal the Orders in Council. Had Americans known this, the war declaration would have been tabled. But the news was six weeks away.

Seventeen days after he had asked for war, Madison signed the declaration. The languid pace of Congress in declaring England the official enemy would be matched by American generals and sea captains in their conduct of the actual fighting.

The Senate voting was an open secret, but the British minister pretended to be ignorant of events and called at the White House, where he found the Republican bigwigs "all shaking hands with one another, but the President was white as a sheet."[46] Certainly to Madison the starting of a war was no time for jubilation. After all, the policies he and Jefferson had fostered and believed would keep the peace had failed.

Thus the struggle his opponents labeled "Mr. Madison's War" began on June 18, and for the next thirty-one months, the commander-in-chief struggled for one war aim above all others: to prove that the United States was a sovereign nation, deserving the respect of the world community.

New England reacted as Madison had feared. Federalists insisted that the president vacillated on everything except plans for his own re-election. "Madison is trembling in the palace, and Monroe, Gallatin & Co. are trembling, perhaps not so much on account of the danger of the country as of their [losing] places," a surly congressman observed. Former president John Adams thought it was wise to keep Madison in the White House. "If I had a vote I should give it to Mr. Madison at the next Election," Adams wrote, "because I know of no Man who would be better."[47] But most of the public men in New England thought differently. The Massachusetts legislature passed a resolution on the heels of the war declaration urging citizens to impede the war effort. The Bay State governor issued a proclamation calling for a day of fasting and asking for prayers to protect Americans from the "entangling and fatal alliance" with an undesirable French ally. On August 6 a Boston town meeting condemned the war and by implication urged citizens to discourage enlistments. These actions enraged Adams, who read his newspaper and lamented "the Power of the Tories . . . the British Faction, whose Justice is Machiavellianism and whose tender Mercies are Cruelty, and whose Gratitude is Treachery and Perfidy." A New England congressman of a different stripe said Madison was acting like "an old clucking hen." "The truth is [that] as a President he is but little better than a man of straw and has no independence in anything."

A military history of the ensuing months, leading up to the disgraceful British invasion of Washington in the summer of 1814, can be compressed into a few paragraphs because, as president, Madison was a spectator rather than an active participant. He was the first wartime president who had never heard a shot fired in anger. All his earlier research and reading led Madison to conclude that war was an evil, but he did not agree with Franklin that there had never been a good war or a bad peace. Madison's reading of Grotius and Pufendorf convinced him that in a century crowded with wars there were rules that civilized nations observed. Although he knew of the American Revolution only from dispatches and rumors, Madison realized that that long war had been fought when never more than 18,000 men were under arms at any given time. War in Madison's eyes was a kind of international chess game, with a checkmate possible and the war itself a series of maneuvers by small bodies of troops. The Atlantic moat loomed large in Madison's thinking. Thus to the president war embodied no mass destruction, no burning and looting, no rapine, and little gore. At the moment when Napoleon triumphed at Wagram, at a cost of nearly 80,000 lives, Madison was vacationing at Montpelier and mulling the possibility of a war with France—a war the president presumed would become a series of diplomatic manuevers, with few canonnades and much negotiating.

Thus wedded to an old-fashioned concept of a "gentlemen's war," Madison gradually accustomed himself to the idea of a war with England after 1807. He spoke of "national degradation as the only calamity which is not greater than war" itself, and paid attention to suggestions made in cabinet meetings that war with either France or England was inevitable. And so, after talking and saber-rattling for more than a decade, America went to war led by a president who was ill-prepared to render the firm and fast decisions a war demands.

If Madison was behind the times in his "war-is-a-game" attitude, the country at large was no better prepared for genuine conflict against one of the world's great powers. America's tradition of plunging into war in an unprepared state began with the War of 1812. The United States army was spread over a thousand-mile frontier, the navy was tiny enough not to crowd a single shipyard, and its leadership in the field was (with a few exceptions) uncommonly incompetent. The opening strategy to capture Canada, assumed to be a matter almost of walking into the British possession and intimidating the populace, proved the ineptness of American arms. General William Hull was talked into commanding the western forces in a three-pronged attack on lower Canada, but his July march turned into an August rout at Detroit, and Hull finally surrendered more than 2,000 men without allowing a single musket fired. Madison, hearing the news while heading for Montpelier and his summer vacation, turned around and dashed back to Washington. A court-martial recommended that Hull be shot. Madison, mindful of the old man's conduct during the Revolution, remanded the sentence and searched for a better general.

Despite the humiliation at Detroit, Madison won reelection that fall, but the voting patterns worried him. Clinton won most of the electoral votes above the Hudson River and made inroads into the small coastal states. Vermont, however, went for Madison to prevent a Federalist sweep of New England. In the final balloting Madison had 128 electoral votes to Clinton's 89. Elbridge Gerry, who became the vice-president (giving the ticket national balance), called Madison's reelection "an event of vast magnitude . . . for had it been defeated, G. Britain would have had a well founded prospect of a triumph over our liberty." Had Madison lost, Gerry continued, "all the Powers of Europe, would have considered her [England's] corrupt influence over us, as being paramount to our political Virtue, and to our sense of national honor."

Samuel Taggart, a Federalist of the I-told-you-so school, said he had not expected Clinton to win and claimed Republicans had stolen the Vermont election. The Republicans had labeled the news of Hull's defeat "an electioneering trick," according to Taggart; and had insisted that Hull had in fact won a victory. Beyond that,

> there was an understanding between the Governor of Vermont and the Executive of the United States that the militia which had been detached were not to be called out until after the election, and the report was industriously circulated and credited that they would not be called for. As soon as the election was over I know not but the very next day, they were ordered to march.[48]

With every move he made interpreted as a political calculation, Madison's sense that New England was ripe for a secession movement never lessened.

His reelection secure, Madison renewed his search for a competent general. He never found one. Dearborn, Wilkinson, and the other veteran officers had no conception of discipline, supply, or overall strategy. Madison fired his secretary of war and appointed John Armstrong, the former minister to France, as his replacement. Armstrong was as bad an appointment as Robert Smith, bringing neither luster nor ability to his post. When the British found time to take the war seriously, Armstrong (who had either harassed his field commanders or allowed internecine feuds to rage) was among the first casualties.

Americans prefer to link the War of 1812 to the Great Lakes battles, where the few successes recorded during the entire war were a testimony to American valor. The accomplishments of Oliver Hazard Perry added to the nation's storehouse of patriotic sayings ("We have met the enemy and they are ours"), while on the high seas the ironsided *Constitution* defeated the H.M.S. *Guerriere* to lift sagging American morale early in the war. Indeed, the dilatory Francis James Jackson was still waiting for a ship back to England when the shooting started in earnest, and his comment for English ears and eyes was: "As to the conduct of the naval war against the Americans, it would disgrace the sixth form of Eton or Westminster." Most of the American plans for a land war went awry, however. A peace feeler from England, after the Orders in Council had been repealed, excited Madison's curiosity; and he "upped the ante" by seeking a commitment from England that impressments would cease. That was farther than Robert Castlereagh, the foreign secretary in Britain's cabinet, was willing to go. Meanwhile, Napoleon had started his eastern trek toward Moscow so the pressure at home was eased. The war continued.

Madison's chief asset proved to be Albert Gallatin, who probed for ways and means to finance the war. The unremitting hatred of the Federalists in Boston closed the Beacon Hill ranks, which meant that no money could be borrowed from that financial bastion. With revenue sources from customs down to a trickle, Gallatin negotiated loans where he could find them and gave up (at least temporarily) any effort to prevent a huge buildup of the national debt. When Czar Alexander of Russia dropped a hint that he would be glad to negotiate a settlement of the war, Madison snapped at the chance offered and sent Gallatin as the head of a diplomatic mission to Europe. There the American diplomats were to seek an end to impressment and an acknowledgment of neutral rights on the high seas. A temporary improvement in the American campaign—a Canadian invasion went right and the Yankees celebrated by burning York (Toronto)—put the Americans in a better bargaining position in the summer of 1813. But the victory laurels soon withered, and by June of 1814 Madison confronted his cabinet with some basic facts. The treasury was depleted, the army was a huge disappointment, and the British army was pushing Napoleon around. Was this a time to demand an end to impressment, or leave the negotiating table if the British balked? No, said the cabinet. Should the peace treaty be "silent on the subject of Impressment"? No again, the cabinet said half-heartedly. A few days later, the cabinet dropped its insistence on a British renunciation of impressments, and told the American diplomats (now strengthened by Madison's addition of Henry Clay to their number) to drop the subject and seek the best terms possible on neutral rights.[49] A dispatch ship was sent to Ghent, where the negotiators had been meeting, to deliver the latest instructions, and Madison settled back, hoping that a respite from official duties would allow him to retreat to Montpelier.

Soon, Madison and all of official Washington retreated not out of choice but to escape the invading British force lying in Chesapeake Bay. Madison's generals had been so busy working up a Canadian invasion that they had forgotten to watch the back door. Secretary of War Armstrong's incompetence finally forced Madison to turn elsewhere for guidance, but he chose another military misfit, General William Winder, to defend the capital. Wild rumors flew through the city, causing Dolley Madison to wonder what might happen next. She confessed to Gallatin's wife, safe in Philadelphia, that the British presence "within 20 miles of the City" and the disaffected citizens made "incessant difficulties for the Government." "They say if Mr. M. attempts to move from *this House*, in case of an attack, they will *stop him*, & that he shall *fall with it*," she lamented. "I am not the least alarmed at these things, but entirely disgusted, & determined to stay with him."[50]

In a matter of days four thousand British troops landed almost without opposition a few miles below the national capital. Events of the ensuing week added much to the nation's folklore but did little for the nation's wounded pride. After routing the Americans, on August 24 the British burned the White House, the capitol, and any other government building they had marked on their maps in retaliation (it was said) for the burning of York. Madison was on horseback most of the time during the hectic skirmishing, while Dolley Madison made her niche in history by delaying her departure until the last moment, gathering up precious possessions including the gigantic painting of Washington. Uncertain of her husband's whereabouts, she stayed at a Virginia plantation house that first night when the skies were aglow from the fiery buildings. A rainstorm and tornado dampened the looters' enthusiasm, and then a powder magazine blew up, killing nearly a hundred redcoats. After these unexpected setbacks the British general regrouped his army, and by August 30 the invaders were back on Royal Navy decks to await developments. Madison finally caught up with his wife at a crossroads tavern, and after the British withdrawal was confirmed, they returned to view the White House ruins.

Madison's stamina (he was sixty-three, and had been in the saddle for most of four days and nights) amazed his cabinet as well as the citizens who came out of hiding. The president called a cabinet meeting, held in a makeshift post office building, where the discussion centered on possible next moves. Everybody was sour on Armstrong, and within hours the secretary of war knew he was through, although Madison showed no vindictiveness and allowed the disgruntled New Yorker to resign. With the British navy still anchored a few miles down the Potomac, Madison turned to Monroe and asked his fellow Virginian to wear two hats, as secretary of both war and state. For a temporary home, the Madisons stayed with brother-in-law Richard Cutts until better quarters were available. Two weeks after they found the White House in ashes, the Madisons accepted Colonel John Tayloe's invitation to use his Octagon House (a stone's throw from the White House grounds) as their residence while the presidential mansion was rebuilt. By November 2 the imperturbable Dolley Madison had resumed her weekly presidential levees.[51]

The heroic defense of Baltimore salvaged a sliver of American pride and gave the country "The Star-Spangled Banner." An unusual American victory at Plattsburg, along with a spectacular feat of seamanship by the Americans on Lake Champlain, took some of the steam out of British plans to make Americans weary of more war. By the onset of winter, a stalemate prevailed everywhere except in the vicinity of New Orleans.

Madison's opponents in New England had not been idle. Convinced that America could not win the war, and bitter over the stagnation of commerce that accompanied the war, the Federalists induced the Massachusetts legislature to call neighboring states to a convention in December 1814 to discuss and adopt means of thwarting the Republican war effort. Secession was not their goal, but the secret meetings at Hartford were aimed at blocking a conscription bill, keeping tax money at home, controlling defenses in the area, and prohibiting lengthy embargoes. The obstreperous Federalists had no confidence in the American negotiators at Ghent, and three emissaries were appointed to carry their demands to Washington. A hint of the perfect solution to their problem came from one of the delegates, who informed a Connecticut newspaper that if Madison really wanted national harmony he might take the first step—by resigning.

Madison's stock, to use a Wall Street analogy, hit rock bottom in August. Then his courageous actions following the failed defense of the capital won back some public esteem. When he sent his sixth State of the Union report to Congress less than a month after the British invasion, Madison reviewed recent disasters and victories with straightforward rhetoric. "It is not to be disguised that the situation of our country calls for its greatest efforts," he wrote. England was a powerful adversary posed to deal "a deadly blow at our growing prosperity, perhaps at our national existence." There was more talk of sacrifice in terms of dollars, even of blood; but Madison concluded with a promise that the United States sought only "peace and friendship on honorable terms."[52]

Madison needed a miracle to keep the Republic from tottering, and the train of events following New Year's Day, 1815, seemed heaven-sent. First, news reached Washington that General Andrew Jackson's men had decimated the British invaders at New Orleans. Over 2,600 British troops were killed, wounded, or captured; Jackson's rag-tag army had thirteen killed and less than sixty wounded. Ten days later, while the euphoria from that report still lingered, a dispatch from Ghent told of the signed peace treaty. The war was over!

The Federalists from Hartford, who had arrived a day earlier with their pseudo-ultimatum for the president, were taken aback. Dolley Madison ordered all the Octagon House windows lighted with candles as part of a victory celebration. Well-wishers pressed through the Octagon House doors as shouting crowds bore torchlights along Pennsylvania Avenue. This was no place for the Hartford dissenters, whose timing was a classic blunder. Lead by former congressman Harrison Gray Otis, who was offended because he had no official invitation to visit the president, the delegates were embarrassed by the celebration and the cause for it. Otis seemed sorry that the war was over, for he had expected to confront Madison with their demands. Even so, Otis told his wife "the little pigmy shook in his shoes at our approach."[53]

Peace struck the country like a thunderbolt. The Treaty of Ghent allowed the warhawks to claim victory, even though the document itself called for no territorial changes or reparations. Impressment was passed over in silence. Everything remained as it was, but in terms of a renovated national pride, the change was enormous. "Peace finds us covered with glory, elevated in the scale of nations, enlightened by experience," the Richmond *Enquirer* exulted. "The native stamina of a young and free people will now shoot forth with greater luxuriance. . . . The sun never shone upon a people whose destinies promised to be grander."[54]

Between August 1814 and February 1815 Washington was transformed from a hell into a heaven. The blackened ruins were the only reminder of bad times as Madison sent a special message to Congress accompanying the treaty from Ghent. "The late war, although reluctantly declared by Congress," he said, "had become a necessary resort to assert the rights and independence of the nation." Glossing over the military blunders, Madison asked Congress to prevent a complete demobilization of the army by providing for "an adequate regular force" and the means "for cultivating the military art in its essential branches." The president also charged Congress with protecting and encouraging the industries that sprang into existence when war disrupted the flow of imported goods. Madison closed his eulogy with a call for unceasing "fidelity to the Union, as constituting the palladium of the National independence and prosperity."[55] Madison's main mission, during the remainder of his life, was to preach the gospel of Union throughout the land.

Madison's message showed no hint of vindictiveness toward the New England states that had dragged their feet during the war. His pleasure must have been evident, however, when Madison read a letter sent from Republican citizens who attended a mass meeting in Boston. The message contained a public apology for the misconduct of their region and thanked

Madison for his part "in defending our commercial rights from foreign Aggressions, & maintaining the honor of the American Flag against those who had arrogantly assumed the Sovereignty of the Ocean." The internal dissension fomented in New England raised the specter of "a Jealousy between the Northern & Southern states, which might eventually lead to a dissolution of the government & involve this Country in all the dreaded consequences of a Civil War."[56] Happily, the steadfastness Madison displayed had dispelled this fear, and now all good citizens "will commemorate your Name in the American Annals with lasting honor & Applause."

The mail pouches delivered to Madison's office were filled with similar messages from citizens tasting what they believed to be the cup of victory. No letter was more treasured that the one bearing a Monticello dateline. "I sincerely congratulate you on the peace; and more especially on the éclat with which the war closed," Jefferson wrote.[57] The return of peace gave the president an opportunity to push hard for a return to Republican principles, and nowhere was this more needed than in foreign affairs. Jefferson warned Madison against entering into treaties with European powers as a means of stimulating trade: "Indeed we are infinitely better without such treaties with any nation. . . . We cannot too distinctly detach ourselves from the European system, which is essentially belligerent, nor too sedulously cultivate an American system, essentially pacific." Jefferson reinforced the advice Washington gave in his farewell address, concluding that instead of signing treaties the United States ought to tell the world it was a friendly but unattached power, "leaving every thing else to the usages & courtesies of civilized nations."

The Madisons were in a holiday mood as they packed in March for an early vacation at Montpelier. The president left instructions with his cabinet officers, set up a mail express to keep him informed of important matters, and took to his carriage through the mudholes that accompanied April rains. Smiling citizens waved as the carriage moved through the Virginia countryside, past fields pungent with the smell of freshly plowed earth. Up and down the land, a self-assessment took place with none more perceptive than that of Madison's cabinet pillar, Albert Gallatin. "The war has been productive of evil and good," he observed, "but I think the good preponderates." The loss of lives aside, the war benefited the nation because it forced Republicans to give up their aversion to "permanent taxes and military establishments" and accept political and fiscal reality. Moreover, Gallatin said,

> The war has renewed and reinstated the national feelings and character which the Revolution had given, and which were daily lessened. The people have now more general objects of attachment with which their pride and political opinions are connected. They are more Americans; they feel and

act more as a nation; and I hope the permanency of the Union is thereby better secured. [58]

Nobody summarized the national mood better than Gallatin, thus closing the book on those who raised questions about whether the war produced anything but widow's weeds and a large national debt.

America was now a nation. Further negotiations with England would be necessary to settle unmarked boundary lines, but British diplomats treated their American cousins far differently after the Battle of New Orleans. The humiliating tribute paid to the Dey of Algiers came to an explosive end when the American navy pounded the Barbary coast so thoroughly that the once-arrogant ruler sued for peace. America had no direct interest in the Congress of Vienna that met in 1815, but the accords reached there prevented another outbreak like the Napoleonic wars and postponed for a century further quarrels over the American claim that "free ships make free goods." Then another Princeton graduate in the White House would revive Madison's main argument for neutral rights.

CHAPTER 10

HAIL TO THE
CHIEF—IN RETIREMENT

Madison's final two years in the White House were a tea party compared to the first six. With Napoleon safely on St. Helena, England relaxed its many trade restrictions, the impressed seamen were sent home, and for a brief period America flourished in unexcelled grandeur. Planter Madison, who found it hard to save money on his $25,000 salary, was pleased to learn that his tobacco, which sold for as little as three cents a pound in 1812, climbed to eight cents in the first year of peace and reached an all-time high of fourteen cents in 1816.[1] Farmers generally were excited by the blessings of peace as exports of sea-island cotton jumped from two and a half cents a pound in 1814 to nearly ten cents in 1816. Imports climbed, restoring a healthy glow to the federal treasury, while the harbors at Boston, New York, and Charleston were clogged with ships hoisting the flags of every trading nation in the world. From $45,000,000 in 1815, exports of American products shot up to $65,000,000 a year later, and exceeded $68,000,000 in 1817. The national debt had soared to $120,000,000, but the 6 percent U.S. treasury bonds rose from 85 in July 1816 to 105 toward the end of Madison's tenure.[2]

The rising prosperity was somewhat offset by declining land prices. With the unholy trio of Giles, Lieb, and Smith gone from the Senate, a bill rechartering the Bank of the United States passed in 1816. His wartime experience with staggering financial problems matured Madison's judgment concerning banks and, indeed, the whole question of government finance. Straining the Republican philosophy to its limit, Madison was more flexible when questions arose concerning the proper use of

235

federal funds. The nation that emerged from the war was in a confident mood, which the president reflected in his willingness to bend with the temper of the times. Madison had vetoed a rechartering bill in 1815 on the grounds that the legislation was constitutionally flawed, but must have recalled the problems of wartime finance when he signed the 1816 measure. The new bank reopened its doors in the fading days of Madison's administration.

Madison and his wife, always easy host and hostess, threw wide the doors of both their temporary White House and Montpelier. They entertained lavishly and a proportionately high cost in the president's budget for wining and dining went for a superb Madeira imported by the caseload. The Madisons' domestic happiness was marred only by Dolley Madison's son, Payne Todd, who refused to settle down. A handsome, high-spirited lad, he grew into manhood without any of the compensatory charms of young southern gentlemen. He drank excessively, visited the brothels of whatever city he happened to be visiting, and still managed to convince his mother that he was only inches away from becoming a responsible adult. In time, young Todd's extravagances forced Madison to cover up the bad debts, and in his old age Madison reckoned he has spent close to $40,000 trying to keep Dolley Madison from worrying excessively about the ne'er-do-well son she adored.

Perhaps in reaction to his stepson's wasted youth, Madison increasingly turned his attention toward a means of improving higher education in the Republic. (Once, John Adams had suggested to Jefferson that Madison might be bored in retirement since he had no grandchildren to frolick with. Jefferson assured the second president that his university scheme was afoot, and if it succeeded Madison would "raise up children" enough "to employ his attention through life."[3]

While still president Madison became a patron of the United States Military Academy at West Point, recommended its enlargement, and favored the establishment of offshoot training centers in other parts of the Union. In his 1815 annual message to Congress, Madison renewed Washington's recommendation for "a national seminary of learning within the District of Columbia." Not at all concerned that the Constitution was silent on the subject, Madison told Congress: "Such an institution claims the patronage of Congress as a monument of their solicitude for the advancement of knowledge, without which the blessings of liberty can not be fully enjoyed or long preserved." With his friend Jefferson busy trying to start a university in Virginia, Madison expected Congress to appropriate money for a national college in Washington. Congress balked, and Madison had to be content with the progress Jefferson made in wheedling the parsimonious Virginia legislature into voting funds for establishing a state university almost within the shadow of Monticello.

Although Henry Adams claimed that Madison's final months in

office ended in "political stagnation," there is much evidence that contemporary Americans viewed matters differently. The outcry over the
effort members of Congress made to raise their own salaries indicates
something far from lassitude. Congressional heads rolled, but Madison
stayed above the din, concerning himself more with the maze of federal
finances than petty politics. When Congress caucused to pick a Republican nominee for the presidency, Madison must have been consulted by
the managers, but the White House maintained a discreet silence as the
candidacy of James Monroe gathered momentum. Articles in Madison's
favorite newspaper, the National Intelligencer, were slanted to give Monroe
the edge over the only other prominent Republican challenger, William
H. Crawford.[4] The caucus vote was probably closer than Madison wished,
for Monroe defeated Crawford by only eleven votes. More of a consolation
to Madison was the fact that the presidential race was over before it
began—the Federalist barely mounted token opposition, and much of
that in a mean-spirited display of animosity that a *fourth* Virginian was
to lead the nation!

With his successor chosen and the Federalist party in a state of di-
shevelment, Madison relaxed during his last year in office. The Madisons
returned to Montpelier in the spring, stayed there through the summer,
and returned to Washington with no dread of party battles or brickbats
from the newspapers. Henry Adams conceded that Madison "seemed to
enjoy popularity never before granted to any President at the expiration
of his term." Adams might have understood the situation better if he
had read his own great-grandfather's assessment of Madison's two terms.
Writing to Jefferson, John Adams said: "Notwithstanding a thousand
Faults and blunders," Madison's administration "has acquired more glory,
and established more union; than all his three predecessors . . . put together."[5]

In his last State of the Union message, Madison must have had a
sense of *déjà vu* as he reported that the British were still denying American
ships entry into their colonial harbors in the West Indies; and as he had
been preaching for more than twenty-five years, once again he asked
Congress to retaliate against British trade. With relish Madison pointed
to the reduced national debt, and announced that federal expenditures
"for the maintenance of all its institutions, civil, military, and naval"
would come to less than $20,000,000 in the coming year.[6] The president
acknowledged that his public career was coming to a close when "the
American people have reached in safety and success their fortieth year
as an independent nation." An entire generation had grown to manhood
under the Constitution, a document that reconciled "public strength with
individual liberty." He closed by foreseeing an America flourishing under
"a Government pursuing the public good as its sole object . . . a Government, in a word, whose conduct within and without may bespeak the

most noble of all ambitions—that of promoting peace on Earth, and good will to man."

During the last months of the winding-down process, the Madisons received invitations and accolades from former colleagues and old friends. Congress, embarrassed by the public outcry against its salary-raising bill, repealed the measure but kept the money it had already pocketed. Madison told Jefferson of the lawmakers' about-face "which has finally taken the most exceptionable of all turns." More important was the House action on a bill close to his heart, "a navigation Act, reciprocating the great principle of the British Act, which if passed by the Senate, will be felt deeply in G. B. in its example." In a sense this bill, which Madison signed on March 1, 1817, was Madison's going-away present from Congress. Imposing the same restrictions on foreign ships as their home country imposed on American vessels, the law fulfilled the recommendations Madison first made in 1790.

From Monticello, Madison learned that Jefferson was proceeding with plans to start a state university at Charlottesville; but they would delay their first board of visitors meeting until Madison's attendance was a certainty.[7] The lifelong dreams of the two old Virginians were coming to pass.

Madison's final official act was his veto of the so-called Bonus Bill. Madison's vetoes were rare but notable. In 1811 Madison had vetoed a bill incorporating a church in the District of Columbia on the grounds that it infringed on the prohibition against religious establishments. A short time later Madison vetoed a bill granting public lands incorrectly surveyed to a small Baptist church in Mississippi, asserting that such a gift was in violation of the First Amendment. In 1817 the issues were not so clear-cut but they were of considerable magnitude, since the measure was the brainchild of John Calhoun and others who looked on profits from the Bank of the United States with a covetous eye. Their bill allocated a $1,500,000 bonus paid by the Bank, along with future dividends on its stock, for a canal and road-building scheme—"internal improvements" in the language of the day. The Constitution-maker became the interpreter, as Madison held that the power to regulate commerce had been stretched too far by Congress. There was no specific power in the Constitution to allow the use of federal money in the way thus planned, and, Madison went on, neither the "necessary and proper" nor the "general welfare" clause could be cited with propriety. Reluctant to allow "an inadmissible latitude of construction" in the Constitution, Madison half-apologized for his veto.[8] The president's strict constructionism took Congress by surprise and touched off a long debate over where and how and why Congress could dispense federal money.

Monroe's inauguration ceremony saw an old friend watching a new president take office, a repetition of another March 4 when Jefferson left the White House. With Monroe, there was no White House ready to receive the new president, the repairs for the British burning having fallen behind while the funds required grew larger. These problems Madison gladly turned over to his successor as Dolley ordered the servants to pack up the possessions that were not government property for shipment to Montpelier. Then the Madisons waited for a break in the miserable early-March weather to permit a leisurely trip. This time the Madisons left Washington in a steamboat that sailed down the Potomac, past Mount Vernon to Aquia Creek landing, where his carriage awaited. An eyewitness reported: "If ever man rejoiced sincerely in being freed from the cares of Public Life it was him. During the voyage he was as playful as a child; talked and jested with every body on board, & reminded me of a school Boy on a long vacation."[9] Madison's exuberant mood lasted as they worked their way to Orange Court House. Less than an hour later, the outlines of Montpelier were visible on a distant hillside. Mr. and Mrs. Madison were "at home."

❦

In the last months of Madison's presidency the movement to find an African colony for the resettlement of freed American blacks finally took form. The American Colonization Society was seeking funds to purchase a vast area in Africa where manumitted and free-born Negroes could be transported to begin a new life. As a Southerner long embarrassed by the fact of slavery, but also the son of a planter who owned close to one hundred field hands, Madison looked to the Society as the best solution for a problem he sensed was becoming more acute. Like the best minds of his generation in Virginia public life—Mason, Washington, Jefferson—Madison knew slavery was a curse but he never expected miracles. When he prepared to leave the Continental Congress in 1783 he faced the prospect of forcing Billey, a slave he had inherited from his grandmother, to return to Virginia (presumably against the black man's will). Several years among the black community in Philadelphia had worked a change in Billey's mind, making him "too thoroughly tainted to be a fit companion for fellow slaves in Virga.," Madison told his father. Under Pennsylvania law, Billey might be sold but would be a freeman after seven years.

> I do not expect to get near the worth of him; but cannot think of punishing him by transportation merely for coveting that liberty for which we have paid the price of so much blood, and have proclaimed so often to be right, & worthy the pursuit, of every human being.[10]

Obviously the hypocrisy of slaveholders spouting about liberty and human rights was not lost on Madison. While still in the Continental Congress,

Madison had suggested that a Virginia bill offering slaves as a recruiting bounty might be altered. "Would it not be as well to liberate and make soldiers at once of the blacks as to make them instruments for enlisting White soldiers?" Madison asked. "It wd. certainly be more consonant to the principles of liberty which ought never to be lost sight of in a contest for liberty."[11]

Although he never committed to paper his expectations concerning the 1808 ban on slave importations in the Constitution, surely Madison believed that another twenty years would see the dreadful business in its dying stages. That he discussed ways of eliminating slavery with such friends as Jefferson and the capitol's architect, William Thornton, is beyond doubt. The idea of a western refuge for free slaves in the public domain appealed to him, as it did to other public men before the speed of western settlement made such a dream became a chimera.

While serving in the First Congress, Madison's thoughts had turned to the proposal for an African colony that would be established for freedmen by the great nations of the world. Thornton, a fellow boarder, became involved in the abolitionist movement and doubtless their discussions lay behind a memorandum the Virginian wrote in furtherance of the colonizing plan. "A Settlement of freed blacks on the Coast of Africa," Madison wrote, might encourage manumission among southern slaveholders "and even afford the best hope yet presented of putting an end to the slavery in which not less than 600,000 unhappy negroes are now involved."[12] A haven for former slaves on the African coast, Madison added, "might induce the humanity of Masters, and by degrees both the humanity & policy of the Governments, to forward the abolition of slavery in America." Admittedly, Madison made no effort to rush things along. He was sympathetic to Quaker petitions forwarded to Congress protesting the slave trade, but he had to ponder the reaction at home. "The Senate have met with great Applause for not taking Notice of the Quakers Memorial," a Virginian wrote Madison, "and people find great fault with your House for wasting so much time and Expence, in a frivolous manner."

The upshot of the Quaker petitions was that the constitutional ambiguities concerning slavery were debated in the House during March 1790. At the heart of the matter was a doubt as to whether the Constitution conferred on Congress any power to regulate domestic slavery. The Quaker theory was that the "general welfare" clause carried such an implied power, an idea that sent the South Carolina delegation into a fury. After the extremists filibustered against a set of resolutions staking a claim for Congress to regulate "the peculiar institution," Madison took the initiative by offering a substitute motion that appealed to the antislavery Quakers in the House gallery. Madison's motion, which the House accepted, denied Congress any power either to emancipate slaves or to concern itself with slaves' treatment, "it remaining with the several States alone to provide any regulations therein, which humanity and true policy may require." Another motion Madison made limited Congress to interdicting the foreign slave trade.[13] Perhaps Madison's motive was to defuse an explosive issue that fell in the midst of the Funding Bill debates. None of his maneuvers riled southern slaveholders unduly, for his motions left control over slavery in local hands where it had been and where they wanted it to remain. Had the Quakers understood the long-range implications of Madison's substitutes, they might have realized that the slavery time-bomb was still ticking away.

Madison never spoke or wrote as explicitly on slaves as Jefferson did in his *Notes on Virginia,* so no case can be made that Madison believed with his friend in the innate inferiority of blacks. Madison did, however, share Jefferson's view that blacks and whites could not flourish together harmoniously.

After retiring to Montpelier, Madison was besieged by correspondents from every corner of the Union who wished the elder statesman's advice or views on public questions. Slavery was foremost in the minds of many, and Madison shared his views to those who seemed well-motivated. In 1819 Madison reported his belief that the condition of slaves was much improved since the Revolution, owing in part to "the sensibility to human rights, and sympathy with human sufferings" that grew out of the Revolution.[14] Pressed on the subject of abolition a few months later, Madison said that "general emancipation ought to be 1. Gradual. 2. Equitable, and satisfactory to the individual immediately concerned. 3. Consistent with the existing and durable prejudices of the nation."[15] By this time, Madison firmly believed that free Negroes "ought to be permanently removed beyond the region occupied by, or allotted to, a white population." Mixing of the races was an "insuperable" problem which the proposed African colonization plan would solve, Madison added, and thus the experiment "merits encouragement from all who regard slavery as an evil, who wish to see it diminished and abolished by peaceable and just means, and who have themselves no better mode to propose."

These views on slavery came, of course, as the nation was embroiled in the Missouri question which made a shambles of Madison's 1790 resolution and caused Jefferson to recoil in horror from the implications of a divided nation, half-slave, half-free. Madison made no similar statement, but we can assume that the public uproar also struck Montpelier "like a fire-bell in the night." The requirements for a government-funded emancipation program, Madison estimated, would exceed $600,000,000, a sum so staggering that a nation fighting through the Panic of 1819 could not consider the cost as reasonable. Time, Madison believed, was on the side of those who wished to see slavery ended; and he longed for leadership that would use the vast public domain as a resource for paying the bills for gradual emancipation.[16]

By 1833, when land prices in Virginia fell to rock bottom, Madison argued with the racist-oriented Thomas Dew that the depression in the Old Dominion was caused by a market for fertile lands "in the West and S. W." that sold for $1.25 an acre, which caused Virginia prices to slump by 50 percent. Hard-pressed planters felt the economic exigencies of the situation and had only their slaves as a last financial resource.

It was foolhardy to talk about gradual emancipation in such circumstances. Even so, Madison toyed with the idea, and in 1819 fell back on the old chimera of paying off slaveowners with sales of public lands. "On the whole the aggregate sum needed may be stated at about 600 Mil[lion]s of dollars," Madison noted, which only required the sale of 200 million acres of public lands "at 2 doll[a]rs per Acre a quantity which tho' great in itself, is perhaps not a third part of the disposable territory belonging to the U. S. And to what object so good so great & so glorious, could that peculiar fund of wealth be appropriated?"[17]

Eventually, the slavery issue became entwined with the greater question of Union. When disturbing reports from South Carolina reached Montpelier, telling of brash legislators who counseled secession if the North attempted any constitutional change in the status of slaves, Madison's blood boiled. Northern interests had compelling reasons to work for a preservation of the Union, he wrote Henry Clay. "On the other hand, what *madness* in the South to look for greater safety in disunion. It would be worse than jumping out of the frying-pan into the fire; it would be jumping into the fire for fear of the frying-pan." Madison was alarmed that the proposed Southern Conventions might become sounding boards for disunion sentiment and work against a time-tested method of adjusting North–South differences: legislative compromise.[18]

The din of public debate, however, was never heard at Montpelier after Madison returned to his father's home to spend his retirement years as a farmer. What a difference between 1817, when a barrel of Virginia flour sold for as much as 15 dollars, and the pitiful price in 1827 when the bottom dropped out of the market, and a bushel of wheat brought 38 cents if a buyer could be found. Following Jefferson's example, Madison experimented with crop rotation and various kinds of moldboard plows, and sought through a diversified crop system to escape the vagaries of an inefficient marketing system. Still dependent on four-footed transportation, Madison and his generation of planters gradually sank deeper into debt as they competed with growers closer to cheaper transportation for the major markets. Perhaps Madison was, as Jefferson insisted, "the best farmer in the world," but his bank balance never proved it.

Jefferson's hand was probably behind the invitation to Madison from the Albemarle Agricultural Society when it called upon the Orange County planter to serve as its president. Madison accepted the honor and in May 1818 delivered a speech that filled thirty-one printed pages when it was later broadcast to other agricultural groups. Sprinkled with Malthusian ideas on population and food supply, the address was also a warning for southern farmers to end wasteful practices that fostered soil erosion. Madison showed he had read the latest works on plow construction and deep-furrow plowing, and he spoke with authority when he asked Virginia farmers to imitate the New England yeomen in their economy by ending "the excessive destruction of timber and fire wood."[19] Reprinted in the *American Farmer*, Madison's remarks were read wherever horses were shod or corn was shucked. Hardly a letter ever passed between Montpelier and Monticello without some reference to crop conditions, rainfall, or some innovation in planting and plowing.

Farming is a sedentary life, which was what Madison wanted when he took his last backward look at Washington. Once in Orange County, Madison felt no need to travel further than a kinsman's plantation for a social visit, or for a board of visitors meeting at Jefferson's new university. Madison always found it hard to say no to Jefferson. In August 1818 he was one of the commissioners appointed to choose a university site who met at Rockfish Gap in the Blue Ridge Mountains.[20] Nobody in Richmond was too surprised that the commissioners, headed by Jefferson, finally settled on Charlottesville. When the University of Virginia board met for the first time in 1819 Madison was present and helped elect Jefferson as the first rector. The annual appropriation for the state institution was fixed at $15,000, which meant that land acquisitions cut deeply into the funds available for buildings. Nonetheless, the visitors had a priceless asset in the architectural genius of the rector, who donated his services as he drafted plans, then made constant site visits to supervise bricklayers, carpenters, and joiners. Between times, Jefferson reported on the proposed curriculum, asked Madison for a list of books on religion that could be safely offered to the students, and discussed the pros and cons of hiring professors from abroad.

If Madison resented the time spent helping his old friend shape the physical side of the University of Virginia as he molded a philosophy of education, we know nothing of it. Both men believed that an educated citizenry was vital for the American experiment in self-government to succeed. While Jefferson labored to finish his academic dream village, Madison was asked for advice on a general education plan for Kentucky. After thinking about the magnitude of starting, almost from scratch, a tax-supported public system of education, Madison praised Kentuckians for approaching the problem carefully. "Learned Institutions ought to be favorite objects with every free people," Madison observed. "They throw that light over the public mind which is the best security against crafty & dangerous encroachments on the public liberty." He reminded the Kentuckians of Jefferson's 1779 statute "for the more general diffusion of knowledge," which placed a premium on merit and talent so that the rich and poor "should be carried forward at the public expence."[21] Kentucky, Madison said, could influence other states if her educational plan deserved "salutary emulation." And what was the point of it?

The point was that Americans had to work at being good citizens. Public education was the surest, safest means of creating a vigilant citizenry. "It is universally admitted," Madison said in 1822, "that a well-instructed people alone can be a permanently free people."

> The American people owe it to themselves, and to the cause of free Government to prove by their establishments for the advancement and diffusion of knowledge, that their political Institutions which are attracting observation from every quarter, and are respected as Models, by the newborn States in our own Hemisphere, are as favorable to the intellectual and moral improvement of man, as they are conformable to his individual & social Rights. What spectacle can be more edifying or more seasonable, than that of Liberty & Learning, each leaning on the other for their mutual and surest support?

Free inquiry in American classrooms would demonstrate to the world "the principles and the blessings of Representative Government." This was Madison's educational philosophy.

Being part of Jefferson's educational establishment had its ups and downs, Madison learned. In 1824 he was invited to the University when Lafayette, making his triumphant tour of America, visited Charlottesville. The French hero, Jefferson, and Madison rode in a landau to the recently completed Rotunda and from its steps greeted well-wishers. The next year, the university already experienced a student riot (protesting "foreign professors"). Jefferson, flanked by Madison and Monroe (who had also joined the board) confronted the rebellious students but was so disheartened by the situation that tears filled his eyes and he sank into his chair. Nobody present ever forgot that scene.[22]

For eleven years running, Madison attended every annual meeting of the board of visitors. As their fifty-year friendship approached its end, Jefferson asked Madison to carry on his work at the University when he was gone. "It is a comfort to leave that institution under your care, and an assurance that it will not be wanting." Jefferson took solace from the fact that they had worked together to pass on to posterity "in all their purity, the blessings of self-government."

> If ever the earth has beheld a system of administration, conducted with a single and steadfast eye to the general interest and happiness of those committed to it . . . it is that to which our lives have been devoted. To myself you have been a pillar of support thro' life. Take care of me when dead, and be assured that I shall leave with you my last affection.

Jefferson struggled to his last board of visitors meeting, then died on July 4, 1826. Informed at once, Madison wrote to the family assembled at Monticello. His encomium was short, for they all knew Jefferson's virtues as a patriot, advocate of liberty, and benefactor of mankind: "In these characters I have known him . . . for a period of fifty years, during which there was not an interruption or diminution of mutual confidence and cordial friendship for a single moment in a single instance."[23] Madison never traveled the road up to Monticello again, but he honored his promise to serve as rector at the university until his health forced a respite. After missing three meetings "in consequence of the feeble state of his health," Madison resigned as rector in 1834.[24]

During his last years Jefferson talked to Madison about their accumulation of papers, and particularly the notes Madison had made at the Federal Convention of 1787. Only one copy of those notes had ever been made, and that was for Jefferson's personal use. Madison realized, particularly as most other delegates had died, that the notes had taken on enormous historical significance. "It has always been my intention that they should, some day or other, see the light," he told a friend.[25] "In general I have leaned to the expediency of letting the publication be a posthumous one." Madison was not going to be "smoked out" by the publication in 1821 of the notes kept by New York delegate Robert Yates, but Madison reviewed his manuscript against the Yates text and later made over fifty alterations in his own.[26]

From 1821 until his death in 1836 Madison went over his correspondence and the notes, making such changes as he believed were justified in the name of historical accuracy or to avoid offense to the living (he changed a letter written about Lafayette, deleting a remark about the Frenchman's "vanity"). The fuss made over the Declaration of Independence in 1826 may have influenced Madison, too, for engravings of the original document and numerous reproductions flooded the market. Madison began to perceive that his notes were probably the most valuable asset he possessed; unlike Montpelier and his other property, his convention notes were free and clear of all encumbrances. They were his, to do with as he wished. Thus he spoke to Dolley Madison about the notes as a piece of property—a family heirloom that should be sold after his death—and preferably to the nation.

The scholarly bent of his mind also told Madison that something in the air would make a clear understanding of the Constitutional Convention important in the nation's future. The author of *The Federalist* #10 needed no reminding that America was a nation full of tensions, both sectional and racial. In his own state there was mounting distress within the slaveless western areas, which resented the power of tidewater slaveholders in state government. Years of complaint led in 1829 to the calling of a state constitutional revising convention in Richmond, and the smell of battle was too strong for Madison to resist. When his neighbors in Orange County chose Madison as a delegate, he agreed to go because the 1776 constitution was so manifestly outmoded. The western reformers wanted suffrage for all white males without regard to property holdings, a restriction fast giving way in northern states. Remembering the compromises of 1787, Madison took off for Richmond.

Never before had Richmond seen such a collection of celebrities huddled under one roof. Madison was joined by Monroe, and the two former presidents rubbed elbows with future president John Tyler, Chief Justice John Marshall, former senator William Branch Giles, and that relic from the Revolution of 1800, John Randolph of Roanoke. As the only survivor of the 1776 convention, Madison occupied a central role in the early debates, so that when a committee was appointed to tackle the key issue of proportional representation he was named chairman. The southern euphemism for slavery, "the peculiar institution," crept into Madison's speech when he discussed the gravest issue the convention faced. "The essence of Government is power," he said, and the great trick in a republic was to see that the powerful majority never oppressed minority rights. Madison minced few words. They were at odds, Madison said, because of "that peculiar feature of our community which calls for a peculiar division in the basis of our Government, I mean the coloured part of our population."[27] The eastern slaveowning citizens were fearful of a majority that held no slaves and thus might "by excessive taxation" work an unjust hardship on them. Slaves were property, Madison said, but they were also human beings.

Dressed in his black smallclothes, with his white hair brushed forward, Madison spoke in a low voice. He was fighting the old fight before a new audience, and unlike 1776, most of the delegates were not attuned to Madison's plea for justice and fairness. If only Negroes were not black, he seemed to say, for the main problem boiled down to one of skin coloration. "If they were of our own complexion, much of the difficulty would be removed," he argued, "but the mere circumstances of complexion cannot deprive them of the character of men." So why not compromise, as they had in 1787, by adopting a three-fifths ratio "in forming a basis for representation, by its simplicity, its certainty, its stability, and its permanency."

Eloquent though he was, Madison fought a losing fight. Most Virginians were loath to admit that slavery and republicanism were the strangest of bedfellows. Madison was chairman of a committee that offered some concessions to the western Virginians on suffrage, and some to the easterners with regard to slaves. "I am offering a *scheme* for compromise," Madison said, "a scheme which I humbly think, requires only to be understood, in order to be embraced." Ultimately, Madison was overruled as the final draft left the vortex of power with the slaveholding easterners. In his report to Lafayette on the convention, Madison played down the conflicts (Lafayette had asked if emancipation of slaves could be discussed). "The Convention was composed of the Elite of the Community," Madison wrote, and "an allusion in the Convention to the subject you have so much at heart, would have been a spark to a mass of Gunpowder. . . . The Colonization Societies are becoming more and more one of its agents. Outlets for the freed blacks are alone wanted for a rapid erasure of that blot from our Republican character."[28] The man who was for overt action in 1787 favored patience in 1830. When the American Colonization Society called Madison to its presidential chair in 1833, he accepted the honor in full knowledge that many Southerners would not approve. Moreover, instead of flourishing, the Society was broke. Madison signed a circular appeal for funds, and pinched though he was for cash, enclosed a check for fifty dollars.[29]

Madison's return trip from Richmond was the last long ride he made. Madison's mother, cheerful and conversant to the last, had died in 1829 at the age of ninety-seven. The Montpelier routine changed little afterward except that the master of the plantation had given up his daily rides to the various farms. Instead, he would take a chair onto the western portico, overlooking the Blue Ridge mountains, and while guests smoked cigars or sipped coffee he would relate anecdotes of public characters. "He was a man of wit, relished wit in others, & his small bright blue eyes would twinkle wickedly," a guest recalled, "when lighted up by some whimsical composition or exposition."[30]

Visitors were the lifeblood of Virginia society, so the Madisons never knew how many to expect for dinner or how many beds would be occupied before morning. Mrs. Samuel Harrison Smith visited the Madisons in 1828 and was charmed by the house and the host. In the drawing room overlooking the east portico the walls were covered with paintings, including "six or eight by Stewart [Gilbert Stuart]." Like Jefferson, Madison filled his parlor with busts and figurines, giving the room a museumlike appearance. Dinner was served at four in the afternoon and took two hours, and then the company adjourned to hear Madison's absorbing stories. "His conversation was a stream of history" as the host touched on the Convention of 1787, told anecdotes about Franklin and Washington with complete frankness, and spared no detail that would make the stories more compelling. "It was living History!" the enraptured lady from Georgetown recalled.[31] "Some of Mr. M.'s anecdotes were very droll, and we often laughed heartily. . . . Mrs. M. says he is as fond of a frolic and of romping with the girls as ever."

Although his eyesight was fading, Madison read the Richmond and Washington newspapers to keep abreast of national affairs. After returning from the Richmond convention Madison found his name turning up in strange, irritating places. The great debate over tariffs raging in the Senate had brought recollections of the Virginia and Kentucky resolutions of 1798 as some Southerners, upset with what they considered a discriminatory tariff, blithely talked of nullification as though the doctrine was first introduced by Jefferson and Madison. Even such former friends as William Branch Giles cited the 1798 resolutions to support the doctrine of nullification as a crisis loomed. His ire aroused, Madison disavowed the right of a state to nullify a national law. To Southerners supporting the excitable South Carolinians who claimed otherwise, Madison reminded them that "the *Virga.* doctrine of 98–99" came within the context of a *"Constitutional Union"* where questions ultimately were decided by the Supreme Court.[32]

Bad as the slavery controversy was, Madison thought that the hotheads who were glibly talking secession were a greater menace to the United States. Madison's pen moved day and night as he denounced "anti-union" heresies in essays carefully reasoned and copied for transmittal to friendly newspaper editors. The *North American Review,* a magazine widely circulated above the Potomac, printed Madison's letter to Congressman Edward Everett in which he clarified the constitutional origins of power over the states and made the point that once the states entered a compact, they were bound to follow the Constitution to the letter. "What the fate of the Constitution of the U. S. would be if a small proportion of States could expunge parts of it particularly valued by a large majority, can have but one answer."

After four decades of public service, much of it spent in the spotlight, Madison was being forced to eat his own words. The process was painful. In 1788 he insisted that the proposed Constitution was "derived from the superior power of the people," not from states acting collectively; but in the Virginia Resolution of 1798 and the 1800 *Report* Madison spoke of the Constitution "as the compact to which the states are parties." Hence the states were "in duty bound to interpose" when a federal act of questionable constitutionality denied states their rights. "It follows of necessity that there can be no tribunal above their authority to decide." Then, confronted with Calhoun's logic in defense of states' rights, Madison recanted. State efforts to nullify federal laws, he finally pleaded, were simply protests only worth whatever sympathy they could arouse in the court of public opinion.[33]

To discredit Madison, his critics raised the cry of inconsistency. He opposed the Bank of the United States in the 1790s, then signed the recharter bill as president. He spoke of states' rights in 1798 and was now pontificating on the indivisibility of the Union. Hearing these noises, Madison took the trouble to explain the facts of long service in public life. "Whatever my political errors may have been," he wrote, "I was as little chargeable with inconsistencies, as any of my fellow laborers thro'

so long a period of political life."[34] Political science classes are still de-
lineating "the two James Madisons: the Nationalist of 1787 and the State
Sovereignty man of 1798," which is all right as far as an academic exercise
goes. But historian Harold S. Schultz placed the matter in perspective
when he wrote that practical politicians of Madison's day were far more
inclined to give the Virginian high marks than most historians writing
on his public career after 1800. Schultz suggested that "their judgments
differed from the historians because they knew more intimately the political intricacies of his administration and unduly sympathized with a
fellow practioner of their own vocation."

In his day, Madison had been adept at hairsplitting over such matters
as impressment and neutral rights on the high seas. When rabid slavery
supporters in his home state joined hands with the South Carolinians to
seek Madison's endorsement of their attacks on President Jackson, Madison rebuked their efforts. Angered by Jackson's stern warning to the
nullifiers, Virginians pressed Madison to chastise Jackson for his high-
handed orders to withdraw federal deposits from the Bank of the United
States. Perceiving the link between nullification and secession, Madison
gave Jackson's critics little comfort. Jackson might have abused his power
as president in the bank withdrawals, Madison said, but the nullifiers
were playing with real fire. "Nullification has the effect of putting powder
under the Constitution and Union, and a match in the hand of every
party to blow them up at pleasure."[35] Disgusted Southerners who were
enthralled by John C. Calhoun's rhetoric dismissed Madison's remarks
as "trash."

Far less sensitive now that he was a retired planter, Madison answered
his critics as best he could, writing with his arthritic scribble that diminished to tiny scratchmarks. Madison revised his drafts, wrote dockets
on hundreds of old letters, and apparently continued to assure Dolley
Madison that his notes on the Federal Convention would provide a financial cushion for her declining years. A flow of the famous and not-
so-famous continued to filter through Montpelier. When the English
feminist Harriet Martineau visited Madison in 1835 she found him complaining of deafness and rheumatism. "He seemed not to have lost any
teeth, and the form of the face was therefore preserved," she noted,
"without any striking marks of age. It was an uncommonly pleasant
countenance."

What struck the Englishwoman most forceably was Madison's faith
in self-government.

> His inexhaustible faith . . . [held] that a well-founded commonwealth may,
> as our motto declares, be immortal; not only because the people, its con-
> stituency, never die, but because the principles of justice in which such a
> commonwealth originates never die out of the people's heart and mind.

Mrs. Martineau admitted that if Madison had one weakness, it was his continued faith in colonizing societies as an answer to slavery. [36] Madison confessed that he had been "in despair" regarding slavery "till the institution of the Colonization Society." Mrs. Martineau thought Madison's faith more than naive, since "the facts were before him that in eighteen years the Colonization Society had removed only between two and three thousand persons, while the annual increase of the slave population in the United States was upward of sixty thousand." What shocked Mrs. Martineau the most was Madison's revelation that to feed his blacks properly, he "had yet been obliged to sell a dozen of his slaves the preceding week."

The truth was that Madison was becoming land and slave poor. He tried to keep his slaves together, but with a third of them under five years of age the drain on his resources was beyond Madison's means. Like every slaveholder, Madison also rationalized his own embarrassment away by explaining that he sold his slaves because they had a "horror of going to Liberia, a horror which he admitted prevailed among the blacks, and which," said Mrs. Martineau, "appears to me decisive as to the unnaturalness of the scheme."

There was nothing more to be said on the subject. Whatever his humanitarian instincts were, Madison submerged them when he faced the declining revenue from his land holdings. Jefferson died owing debts of over $100,000; and Monroe also suffered from acute financial distress in his final years. Madison was determined to leave Dolley Madison in comfortable circumstances.

Madison had higher priorities, however, than his wife's well-being. Madison had an unshakable faith in the ability of men to work out their problems provided their minds were unshackled. In his last years he returned to the notion that liberty and union were America's greatest attributes, worth maintaining at any sacrifice. All the rights in his First Amendment were precious, but that which promised a complete separation of church and state loomed larger as the years went by. While president, Madison had twice vetoed measures he believed in violation of that hallowed principle, and now he saw dangers lurking in "silent accumulations & encroachments by Ecclesiastical Bodies."

In a curious document that included impressions of Franklin and Washington along with commentaries on banks and monopolies, Madison boldly struck at what he discerned as a trend in the United States toward breaches in the wall separating church and state. He made no specific charges, but pleaded for insurmountable barriers to protect religious freedom. Anything less would "leave crevices at least, thro' which bigotry may introduce persecution; a monster, that feeding & thriving on its own venom, gradually swells to a size & strength overwhelming all laws divine & human. [37] So complete was Madison's commitment that he came to regret his own presidential proclamations of thanksgiving, the chaplains paid to serve in Congress, and the tax exemptions states extended to church property. Laxity in allowing churches to acquire vast holdings of property seemed a trifling worry, Madison inferred, yet "the people of the U. S. owe their Independence & their liberty, to the wisdom of descrying in the minute tax of 3 pence on tea, the magnitude of the evil comprized in the precedent. Let them exert the same wisdom, in watching agst. every evil lurking under plausible disguises." As to the impropriety of a president signing a religious proclamation for thanksgiving or related services, Madison cited the salutary example of President Jefferson. "During the administration of Mr. Jefferson no religious proclamation was issued."

Apart from his worries over breaches in the wall separating church and state Madison developed a Malthusian concern for the America he envisioned a century hence. Calculating that the America of 1929 would number 192 million souls, Madison pondered a Republic where farmers would be outnumbered and outvoted, surrounded by teeming cities filled with day-laborers. Could the Republic survive? Madison was too much Jefferson's disciple to give way to pensive pessimism. All political problems could be subsumed under one general heading: Preserve the Union.

Madison never tired of pointing out the blessings of a collected but diverse population, where strengths could be magnified and weaknesses overcome through a joint commitment to free elections and individual liberty. Sometime in 1834 he took pains to see that his last testimonial was written down, as a final gift to his beloved country. "The advice nearest to my heart and deepest in my convictions is that the Union of the States be cherished and perpetuated."[38]

As the spring of 1836 faded, Madison began to sink rapidly. Weak though he was, Madison tried to be a fitting companion as his eyesight dimmed and he could raise his hands only with pain. There is a story, perhaps apocryphal, that a well-meaning friend came to Madison in late June and suggested that he might take some medication to prolong life until the sixtieth anniversary of the Fourth of July. After all, John Adams, Thomas Jefferson, and James Monroe had all died on that sacred day. He was the last survivor of the Virginia Convention of 1776 and the Federal Convention of 1787. What could be more fitting? Madison is said to have ridiculed the notion. A man died when his time had come. James Madison's came on June 28, 1836. He was buried in the family cemetery on the following day. Funeral bells tolled, the slaves at Montpelier wept, and Dolley Madison fought back the tears.

After the Boston mayor and council urged him to deliver Madison's eulogy John Quincy Adams took his assignment with dead seriousness. Adams studied Madison's career and read over Jefferson's correspondence during the critical years when Madison was Jefferson's lieutenant, aide-de-camp, and prime minister; and the experience revived in Adams's mind memories that led him to an unflattering conclusion about Jefferson. Allowing for the prejudice of an Adams against a Jefferson, the sixth president's assessment is worth remembering. Jefferson's attachment "to those of his friends whom he could make useful to himself was thorough-going and exemplary. Madison moderated some of his excesses and refrained from following others. He was in truth a greater and a far more estimable man."[39]

Through the vale of history we have come to identify eras with presidents, so that Lincoln is tied forever with the war years of 1861–65, Wilson is the leader of 1917–19, and the Great Depression of 1929–39 became Franklin D. Roosevelt's passport to greatness. The War of 1812 conjures the burning of Washington, and defenders of Madison's reputation are forced to recall the events of 1787–88 as his greatest stake for fame. Henry Adams severely damaged Madison's reputation with his multivolumed history that has transfixed recent generations of historians. They have accepted Adams's interpretation of the fourth president as an inept, confused, and bungling man. Madison "would have been much more at home as president of the University of Virginia," a scholar adjudged in 1951, "than he was as President of the United States."[40] Perhaps it is unfair to blend history with a sense of failure, for there are many avenues to the truth and the judgment of historians and biographers can never be final.

Robert Frost may have been closer to the truth than anybody has ever come in assessing Madison's career. Late in life, Frost read *The Federalist* with care, and its rediscovery had a great impact on his thinking about America, its goals, and its leadership. Frost was taken by the dream of the Founding Fathers which, as he saw it, was "a vision to occupy the land with character."

> And lately I've decided the best dreamer of it was Madison. . . . I think I know . . . what Madison's dream was. It was just a dream of a new land to fulfill with people in self control.[41]

Perhaps it was Frost's influence that prompted John F. Kennedy to surmise that Madison was "our most under-rated president."

But poets cannot have the last word, either. The Union so cherished by Madison has outlived his prediction that by in the twentieth century the United States might no longer be the sanctuary of liberty and self-government. Madison never foresaw the carnage of the Civil War; nor could he have predicted that the most important constitutional decision in our nation's history was made by bayonets, not black-robed Justices of the Supreme Court. Who cherished the Union more, Madison or Lincoln?

Madison suffered from the same blind spot as most politicians—he was poor at predicting the future. History must look at the whole man, and in that light, Madison stands on a pedestal reserved for only a handful Americans. From 1786 onward he was the principal character in the reform movement that created the Constitution. His political career probably reached a peak in 1791, when he was majority leader in the House of Representatives and forced the Bill of Rights upon a reluctant Congress. Even as co-founder of the Democratic-Republican party, he was never again the consummate political figure. As secretary of state, Madison worked with his chief to shape a peaceful policy in a world at war. He failed in that mission and was not a forceful figure in the White House, owing to his convictions on the role of the executive branch in a republic. But luck was on his side in 1814–15, and he left the presidency far stronger than the office had been in Jefferson's last year. Madison's bumpy eight years made the way smooth for James Monroe, whose republicanism was close to Madison's and vital to the era of good feeling that soon descended on the land.

Thus by criteria based on accomplishment, Madison's place in history is both high and secure. By the criteria of his own time, James Madison was our last great republican. By the criteria of our own, Madison was *the* Founding Father.

NOTES

The abbreviations and symbols used below pertain to printed sources or manuscript collections in depositories listed in the *National Union Catalogue*. JM stands for James Madison. The principal sources of citations are:

PJM	*The Papers of James Madison*, edited by William T. Hutchinson et al., 16 volumes to date. Chicago and Charlottesville, Va., 1962-
Farrand, *Records*	*The Records of the Federal Convention*, edited by Max Farrand, 4 vols. New Haven, Conn., 1966 reprint.
"Autobiography"	"James Madison's Autobiography," edited by Douglass Adair. *William & Mary Quarterly*, 3rd series, volume 2 (1945).
Hunt, *Writings*	*The Writings of James Madison*, edited by Gaillard Hunt, 9 vols. New York, 1900–1910.
Brant, *Madison*	*James Madison*, by Irving Brant, 6 vols. Indianapolis and New York, 1941–1961.
DLC	The Library of Congress, Manuscript Division.
DNA	The National Archives, Washington, D.C.
ViU	University of Virginia, Alderman Library.

CHAPTER ONE

1. Washington to JM, 5 Nov. 1786. *PJM*, 9:161.
2. JM to Edmund Randolph, 26 July 1785. Ibid., 8:328.
3. William Bradford to JM, 13 Oct. 1772. Ibid., 1:72.
4. "Autobiography," p. 197.
5. JM to William Bradford, 24 June 1774. *PJM*, 1:106.
6. H. D. Parish, ed., *Journal and Letters of Philip Vickers Fithian* (Williamsburg, Va., 1943), pp. 167–68.

7. Robert S. Alley, ed., *James Madison and Religious Liberty* (Buffalo, N.Y., 1985), p. 52.
8. JM to Jefferson, 12 May 1786. *PJM*, 9:53. JM to Jefferson, 8 Dec. 1784. *PJM*, 8:178.
9. "Vices of the Political System of the United States," April 1787. Ibid., p. 355.
10. "Autobiography," p. 199; JM to John G. Jackson, 28 Dec. 1821. ViU.
11. JM never claimed that the Virginia Plan was his exclusive brainchild, but compare the text to JM's letter to Jefferson, 19 Mar. 1787, or to Randolph, 8 April 1787, or to Washington, 16 April 1787. *PJM*, 9:317–22, 368–71, 382–87.
12. One exception was Hamilton's long speech of 18 June, which took a whole day to deliver. The other was "the sketch furnish'd by Mr. Randolph of his speech on the introduction of his propositions."
13. JM to Jared Sparks, 6 April 1831. Hunt, *Writings*, 9:447–51.
14. Debate of 30 June, 1787. *PJM*, 10:90. Clinton Rossiter, *1787: The Grand Convention* (New York, 1966), p. 150; Brant, *Madison*, 3:155–56; Harold S. Schultz, *James Madison* (New York, 1970), p. 77.
15. Farrand, *Records*, 3:94–95.
16. Ibid., 3:237.
17. JM to Jefferson, 6 Sept. 1787. *PJM*, 10:163–64.
18. JM to Jefferson, 24 Oct. 1787. Ibid., 10:172.
19. Ibid., 10:213.
20. Jefferson to JM 20 Dec. 1787. *PJM*, 10:336–37.

CHAPTER TWO

1. Edward Carrington to JM, 23 Sept. 1787. *PJM*, 10:172.
2. R. H. Lee to George Mason, 1 Oct. 1787. Robert A. Rutland, ed., *The Papers of George Mason*, 3 vols. (Chapel Hill, 1970), 3:996.
3. JM to Jefferson, 24 Oct. 1787. *PJM*, 10:217.
4. Quoted in Robert A. Rutland, *The Ordeal of the Constitution* (Norman, Okla., 1966), p. 18.
5. JM to Jefferson, 6 Sept. 1787. *PJM*, 10:164.
6. JM to Washington, 30 Sept. 1787. *PJM*, 10:181.
7. Washington to JM, 10 Oct. 1787. Ibid., 10:189.
8. Mason to Elbridge Gerry, 20 Oct. 1787. Rutland, *Mason Papers*, 3:1006.
9. JM to Washington, 30 Sept. 1787. *PJM*, 10:181.
10. Farrand, *Records*, 2:631.
11. Jefferson to JM, 11 Aug. 1793. *PJM*, 15:57.
12. Edmund Randolph to JM., c. 29 Oct. 1787. Ibid., 10:230.
13. Gouverneur Morris to Washington, 30 Oct. 1787. *Documentary History of the Constitution*, 5 vols. (Washington, D.C.: 1894–1905), 4:357–58.
14. JM to Washington, 18 Nov. 1787. *PJM*, 10:55n., 254.
15. "Autobiography," p. 202. The words within brackets are conjectural additions.
16. Farrand, *Records*, 1:288.

17. Robert Dahl, A *Preface to Democratic Theory* (Chicago, 1956), p. 5.
18. Rufus King to JM, 20 Jan. 1788; same to same, 6 Feb. 1788, *PJM*, 10:400, 475.
19. JM to Washington, 3 March 1788. Ibid., 10:555.
20. Edmund Randolph to JM, 29 Feb. 1788. Ibid., 10:542.
21. Edward Carrington to JM, 18 Jan. 1788. Ibid., 10:383.
22. *The Federalist #37*. Ibid., 10:360.
23. *The Federalist #39*. Ibid., 10:379–80.
24. From James Gordon Jr., 17 Feb. 1788. Ibid., 10:516.
25. JM to Washington, 20 Feb. 1788. Ibid., 10:526–27.
26. Farrand, *Records*, 4:56–57.
27. Joseph Spencer to JM, *PJM*, 10:540–41.
28. JM to Eliza Trist, 25 March 1788. *PJM*, 11:5–6.
29. JM to John Brown, 9 April 1788. *PJM*, 11:16–17.
30. JM to George Nicholas, 8 April 1788. *PJM*, 11:14; John Brown to JM, 12 May 1788. *PJM*, 11:42.
31. Speech of 24 June 1788. *PJM*, 11:174.
32. Monroe to Jefferson, 12 July 1788. Julian Boyd et al. eds., *Papers of Thomas Jefferson*, 21 vols. to date (Princeton, N.J., 1950–   ).
33. William C. Rives, *History of the Life and Times of James Madison*, 2 vols. (New York, 1859–68), 2:612n.
34. Washington to JM, 23 June 1788. *PJM*, 11:170.
35. JM to Edmund Randolph, 16 July 1788. *PJM*, 11:188.
36. JM to A. Hamilton [20] July 1788. *PJM*, 11:188.
37. Rutland, *Ordeal of the Constitution*, pp. 262–66.
38. Tench Coxe to JM, 23 July 1788. *PJM*, 11:194–95.
39. JM to Jefferson, 10 Aug. 1788. *PJM*, 11:226.
40. JM to Washington, 11 Aug. 1788. *PJM*, 11:230.
41. JM to Edmund Pendleton, 20 Oct. 1788. *Doc. Hist. of Constitution*, 5:94.
42. JM to Washington, 11 Aug. 1788. *PJM*, 11:230.
43. JM to Edmund Randolph, 17 Oct. 1788. *PJM*, 11:305.
44. George Turberville to JM, 24 Oct. 1788. *PJM*, 11:316.
45. JM to George Turberville, 2 Nov. 1788. *PJM*, 11:331–32 and n. 1.
46. JM to George Turberville, 27 Oct., 10 Nov., 1788. *PJM*, 11:319, 347.
47. JM from Edward Carrington, 9 Nov., 1788; JM from George Turberville, 16 Nov. 1788. *PJM*, 11:336, 347.
48. JM from George Turberville, 10 Nov. 1788. *PJM*, 11:346.
49. JM from Edward Carrington, 9 Nov. 1788. *PJM*, 11:336–37.
50. JM from George Turberville, 13 Nov. 1788. *PJM*, 11:344.
51. JM from Edmund Randolph, 2 Nov. 1788. *PJM*, 11:329. JM from Richard Bland Lee, 17 Nov. 1788. *PJM*, 11:348.
52. JM from Edward Carrington, 14 Nov. 1788. *PJM*, 11:345–46.
53. JM from Francis Corbin, 12 Nov. 1788. Ibid., 11:342; JM from Edward Carrington, 14 Nov. 1788. Ibid., 11:346.
54. Rev. James Madison to JM, 22 Nov. 1788. *PJM*, 11:360.
55. Edward Carrington to JM, 18 Nov. 1788. *PJM*, 11:352.
56. Henry Lee to JM, 19 Nov. 1788. *PJM*, 11:356.
57. Edward P. Smith, "The Movement Towards a Second Convention in 1788,"

in J. Franklin Jameson, ed., *Essays in the Constitutional History of the U.S.* (Boston, 1889; 1970 reprint), p. 110.
58. Jonathan Trumbull to Washington, quoted in ibid., pp. 109–110.
59. G. Sterling to G. Nicol, 14 Dec. 1788, quoted in Louise I. Trenholme, *The Ratification of the Federal Constitution in North Carolina* (New York, 1932), p. 202.
60. JM to Jefferson, 8 Dec. 1788. *PJM*, 11:382–83.
61. Burgess Ball to JM, 8 Dec. 1788. *PJM*, 11:385.
62. Joseph James to JM, 14 Dec. 1788. *PJM*, 11:394.
63. Andrew Shepherd to JM, 14 Dec. 1788. *PJM*, 11:396.
64. Hardin Burnley to JM, 16 Dec. 1788. *PJM*, 11:398.
65. JM to George Eve, 2 Jan. 1789. *PJM*, 11:404–405.
66. Washington to JM, 16 Feb. 1789. *PJM*, 11:446–47n.
67. JM to Thomas Mann Randolph, 13 Jan. 1789. *PJM*, 11:416–17.
68. JM to Washington, 14 Jan. 1789. *PJM*, 11:418.

CHAPTER THREE

1. Miles King to JM, 3 Mar. 1789. *PJM*, 12:1.
2. Robert Ballard to JM, 7 Mar. 1789; John Beckley to JM, 13 Mar. 1789. Ibid., 12:4, 11.
3. JM to Jefferson, 29 Mar. 1789. Ibid., 12:37–38.
4. Speech on Import Duties, 8 April 1789. Ibid., 12:65.
5. Ibid., 12:70. See Drew R. McCoy, "Republicanism and American Foreign Policy: James Madison and the Political Economy of Commercial Discrimination, 1789–1794," *William and Mary Quarterly*, 3d. ser., 31(1981): 633–46.
6. Ibid., 12:71, 73.
7. Fisher Ames to George Minot, 29 May 1789. Seth Ames, ed., *The Works of Fisher Ames*, 2 vols. (Boston, 1854), 1:49.
8. George W. Corner, ed., *The Autobiography of Benjamin Rush* (Princeton, N.J., 1948), 181.
9. Address to the President, 5 May 1789. *PJM*, 12:132.
10. Reply to the President, 8 May 1789. Ibid., 12:141–42.
11. JM to Jefferson, 30 June 1789. Ibid., 12:268–70.
12. Edward Dumbauld, *The Bill of Rights and What It Means Today* (Norman, Okla., 1957), pp. 28–30.
13. JM to Jefferson, 23 May 1789. *PJM*, 12:182–83.
14. JM to Jefferson, 27 May 1789. Ibid., 12:186.
15. *Annals of Congress*, 1st Cong., 1st Sess., p. 442.
16. Ibid., p. 447.
17. Speech, 8 June 1789. *PJM*, 12:193.
18. Speech on Amendments to Constitution, 8 June 1789. Ibid., 12:196–97.
19. Ibid., 12:204–205.
20. Ibid., 12:202, 206.
21. Ibid., 12:207.

22. Ames to Thomas Dwight, 11 June 1789, Ames, *Works of Fisher Ames*, 1:53; Tench Coxe to JM, 18 June 1789. *PJM*, 12:239.
23. Quoted in Robert A. Rutland, *The Birth of the Bill of Rights 1776–1791* (revised ed.; Boston, 1983), 204–205.
24. Edmund Randolph to JM, 30 June 1789. *PJM*, 12:273.
25. JM to James Madison, Sr., 5 July 1789. Ibid., 12:278.
26. Jefferson to JM, 29 July 1789. Ibid., 12:315.
27. *The Journal of William Maclay . . . 1789–91* (New York, 1927), pp. 94–95.
28. JM to Jefferson, 11 Aug. 1783; Jefferson to JM, 13 Aug. 1783. *PJM*, 7:268, 298.
29. *Journal of William Maclay*, p. 363.
30. Speech on Location of the Capital, 4 Sept. 1789. *PJM*, 12:381.
31. *Journal of William Maclay*, pp. 142–43.
32. Farrand, *Records*, 1:476.
33. Ibid., 1:486.
34. Memorandum on African colony, c. 20 Oct. 1789. *PJM*, 12:438.
35. Ibid., 12:437.
36. Speech on Duty on Slaves, 13 May 1789. Ibid., 12:162.
37. JM to Jefferson, 8 Oct. 1789. Ibid., 12:433.

CHAPTER FOUR

1. George Nicholas to JM, 2 Nov. 1789. *PJM*, 12:445.
2. JM to Henry Lee, 4 Oct. 1789. Ibid., 12:426.
3. Ibid., 12:426–27, n. 3.
4. Grayson to JM, 7 Oct. 1789. Ibid., 12:431–32.
5. Hamilton to JM, 19 Oct. 1789. Ibid., 12:436.
6. JM to Hamilton, 19 Nov. 1789. Ibid., 12:449–50.
7. Ibid., 12:450–51.
8. JM to Washington, 4 Jan. 1790. Ibid., 12:467.
9. "Conversation with George Beckwith," Oct. 1789. Harold C. Syrett and Jacob E. Cooke, eds., *The Papers of Alexander Hamilton*, 27 vols. (New York, 1961–81), 5:488.
10. JM to James Madison, Sr., 21 Jan. 1790. *PJM*, 13:1.
11. Syrett and Cooke, *Hamilton Papers*, 6:77.
12. JM to Jefferson, 24 Jan. 1790. *PJM*, 13:4.
13. "Report on Public Credit," 9 Jan. 1790. Syrett and Cooke, *Hamilton Papers*, 6:69.
14. *Journal of William Maclay*, p. 189.
15. Speech on Holders of Public Debt, 11 Feb. 1790. *PJM*, 13:34–35.
16. Elizabeth Fleet, "James Madison's Detached Memorandum," *William and Mary Quarterly*, 3rd ser., vol. 3 (1946):204–205.
17. *Journal of William Maclay*, p. 195.
18. "Foreigner" to JM, 17 Feb. 1790. *PJM*, 13:44.
19. Sharp Delany to Hamilton, 23 Feb. 1790. Syrett and Cooke, *Hamilton Papers*, 6:276.

20. Hamilton to Edward Carrington, 26 May 1792. Ibid., 11:428–29.
21. Winfred E. Bernhard, *Fisher Ames: Federalist and Statesman* (Chapel Hill, N.C., 1965), p. 132.
22. Speech on Original Holders of Public Debt, 18 Feb. 1790. *PJM*, 13:54.
23. Speech on Obligation of Contracts, 17 June 1790. Rutland, *Mason Papers*, 3:1089.
24. JM to JM, Sr., 27 Feb. 1790. *PJM*, 13:66.
25. *Journal of William Maclay*, pp. 174, 321.
26. Speech on Assumption of State Debts, 24 Feb. 1790. *PJM*, 13:61.
27. Rush to JM, 27 Feb. 1790. Ibid., 13:68.
28. Speech on Assumption of State Debts, 3 Mar. 1790. Ibid., 13:85.
29. Ames to William Tudor, 3 Mar. 1790. Mass. His. Society *Collections*, 2nd ser. 8(1819):322.
30. Speech on Public Debt, 11 Mar. 1790. *PJM*, 13:101.
31. JM to Edward Carrington, 14 Mar. 1790. Ibid., 13:104–105.
32. Edward Carrington to JM, 27 Mar. 1790. Ibid., 13:127.
33. *Journal of William Maclay*, pp. 202–203.
34. Quoted in Berhard, *Fisher Ames*, pp. 144–45.
35. *Journal of William Maclay*, p. 231.
36. JM to Henry Lee, 13 April 1790. *PJM*, 13:147–49.
37. JM to Monroe, 17 April 1790. Ibid., 13:151.
38. Speech on Assumption of State Debts, 20 April 1790. Ibid., 13:153.
39. Ibid., 13:166.
40. Speech on Public Credit, 26 April 1790. Ibid., 13:177.
41. JM to JM, Sr., 2 May 1790. Ibid., 13:183–84.
42. JM to Edmund Randolph, 6 May 1790. Ibid., 13:189.
43. JM to the Governor of Virginia, 25 May 1790. Ibid., 13:227.
44. JM to Monroe, 1 June 1790. Ibid., 13:234.
45. JM to JM, Sr., 13 June 1790. Ibid., 13:242.
46. Versions of the compromise abound, but none are more believable than the discussion in Noble Cunningham, *The Jeffersonian Republicans: The Formation of a Party Organization* (Chapel Hill, 1957), pp. 4–5, and Dumas Malone, *Jefferson and His Times*, 6 vols. (Boston, 1948–81), 2:300–301. See also Malone's "Long Note on . . . the Residence-Assumption Bargain," ibid., 2:507.
47. Jefferson to George Gilmer, 25 July 1790. *PJM*, 13:28n; Boyd, *Papers of Jefferson*, 17:269.
48. Memorandum on the Residence Act, c. 29 Aug. 1790.
49. JM to Washington, 17 Sept. 1790. Ibid., 13:297.
50. Instructions for the Montpelier Overseer, 8 Nov. 1790. Ibid., 13:303.
51. Memorandum (Folio 3124), DLC: William Thornton Papers.
52. *Gazette of the United States*, 2 May 1789.
53. Moustier delighted in sending gossip about Madison to Jefferson, as his letter to Jefferson of 29 Dec. 1788 proved. Boyd, *Papers of Jefferson*, 14:399.
54. Mary Coxe to Tench Coxe, Jan. 1789. Tench Coxe Papers, Historical Society of Pennsylvania, Philadelphia.
55. Henry Lee to JM. 19 Oct. 1786. *PJM*, 9:144.
56. JM to Edmund Pendleton, 2 Jan. 1791. Ibid., 13:344.

57. Jefferson to JM, 12 Jan. 1791. Ibid., 13:344.
58. Speech on the Bank Bill, 2 Feb. 1791. Ibid., 13:373–81.
59. Memorandum for Roger Sherman, 4 Feb. 1791. Ibid., 13:382.
60. Draft Veto of the Bank Bill, 21 Feb. 1791. Ibid., 13:395.

CHAPTER FIVE

1. Jefferson to Francis Hopkinson, 13 Mar. 1789, Boyd, *Papers of Jefferson*, 14:650; *Federalist #37, PJM*, 10:364.
2. Merrill Peterson, *James Madison: A Biography in His Own Words*, 2 vols. (New York, 1973), 1:182.
3. Hamilton to Edward Carrington, 26 May 1792, Syrett and Cooke, *Hamilton Papers*, 11:427–44.
4. JM, Sr., to JM, 11 May 1791, *PJM*, 14:21.
5. Malone, *Jefferson and His Times*, 2:358–59; Paul L. Ford, ed., *The Writings of Thomas Jefferson*, 10 vols. (New York, 1892–99), 5:351.
6. Robert Troup to Hamilton, 15 June 1791, Syrett and Cooke, *Hamilton Papers*, 8:478.
7. Notes on the Lake Country Tour, 31 May–7 June 1791. *PJM*, 14:25–29.
8. Jefferson to Monroe, 10 July 1791. Ford, *Writings*, 5:351.
9. JM to Jefferson, 10 July 1791. *PJM*, 14:43.
10. JM to Jefferson, 8 Aug. 1791. Ibid., 14:69.
11. JM to Jefferson, 10 July 1791. Ibid., 14:43.
12. Ibid.
13. Daniel Carroll to JM, 22 Nov. 1791. *PJM*, 14:122–23.
14. Ames to George R. Minot, 17 Feb. 1791; Ames, *Works of Fisher Ames*, 1:96.
15. E. P. Oberholtzer, *Robert Morris, Patriot and Financier* (New York, 1903), p. 308.
16. Ames to George R. Minot, 17 Feb. 1791, Ames, *Works of Fisher Ames*, 1:95.
17. Ames to William Tudor, 24 Nov. 1791, Mass. His. Society *Collections*, 2nd ser., 8:325.
18. JM to JM, Sr., 13 Nov. 1791. *PJM*, 14:106.
19. "Public Opinion," c. 19 Dec. 1791. Ibid., 14:170.
20. William Madison to JM, 3 Dec. 1791. Ibid., 14:137–49.
21. Quoted in Cunningham, *The Jeffersonian Republicans*, p. 20.
22. Hamilton to Edward Carrington, 26 May 1792. Syrett and Cooke, *Hamilton Papers*, 11:431.
23. "Spirit of Governments," 18 Feb. 1792, *PJM*, 14:234.
24. "Brutus No. 1," *National Gazette*, 15 Mar. 1792.
25. Hamilton to Edward Carrington, 26 May 1792. Syrett and Cooke, *Hamilton Papers*, 11:434–44.
26. JM to Henry Lee, 15 April 1792. *PJM*, 14:288.
27. JM to Edmund Pendleton, 25 March 1792. Ibid., 14:262.
28. Ibid.
29. Memorandum on President's Retirement, 5 May 1792; George Washington to JM, 20 May 1792. *PJM*, 14:302, 310–12.

30. JM to Jefferson, 12 June 1792; Jefferson to JM, c. 18 May 1792. Ibid., 14:309–10, 318.
31. "T.L. No. 1," 25 July 1792. Syrett and Cooke, *Hamilton Papers*, 12:107.
32. JM to Edmund Randolph, 13 Sept. 1792. *PJM*, 14:365.
33. "A Candid State of Parties," 22 Sept. 1792. *PJM*, 14:370–72.
34. Letter to *Dunlap's American Daily Advertiser*, 20 Oct. 1792. Ibid., 14:387–92.
35. "Who Are the Best Keepers of the Peoples' Liberties?" 20 Dec. 1792. Ibid., 14:426.
36. Joseph Jones to JM, 24 Dec. 1792. Ibid., 14:429.
37. JM to Edmund Pendleton, 23 Feb. 1793. Ibid. 14:452.
38. Resolutions Censuring the Secretary of the Treasury, 1 Mar. 1793. Ibid., 14:466, 468 and n.1.
39. JM to George Nicholas, 15 Mar. 1793, Ibid., 14:472.
40. Minister of the Interior to JM, 10 Oct. 1792. Ibid., 14:381.
41. Malone, *Jefferson and His Time*, 2:484.
42. JM to the Minister of the Interior, April 1793, *PJM*, 15:4.
43. Jefferson to JM, 25 Mar. 1793; JM to Jefferson, 12 April 1793. Ibid., 15:1–7.
44. Hamilton and Knox to Washington, 2 May 1793 (enclosure). Syrett and Cooke, *Hamilton Papers*, 14:383.
45. JM to Jefferson, 8 May 1793. *PJM*, 15:13.
46. "Pacificus No. III," 6 July 1793. Syrett and Cooke, *Hamilton Papers*, 15:68–69.
47. Jefferson to JM, 7 July 1793. *PJM*, 15:43.
48. Jefferson to JM, 8 Sept. 1793. Ibid., 15:103.
49. Jefferson to JM, 19 May 1793. Ibid., 15:19.
50. Jefferson to JM, 3 Aug. 1793. Ibid., 15:50.
51. JM to James Monroe, 15 Sept. 1793. Ibid., 15:110–11.
52. Jefferson to JM, 8 Sept. 1793. Ibid., 15:104.

CHAPTER SIX

1. J. H. Powell, *Bring Out Your Dead: The Great Plague of Yellow Fever in Philadelphia in 1793.* (Philadelphia, 1949), p. 234. John Beckley to JM, 20 Nov. 1793. *PJM*, 15:14.
2. Malone, *Jefferson and His Time*, 3:154–60.
3. Boston *Columbian Centinel*, 19 Feb. 1795.
4. William Lyon to Samuel Henshaw, 17 Jan. 1794. Independence National Historical Park, Philadelphia.
5. Smith to Otho Holland Williams, 20 Mar. 1794. Maryland Historical Society: Williams Papers.
6. JM to Jefferson, 2 Mar. 1794. *PJM*, 15:269.
7. JM to Jefferson, 12 Mar. 1794. Ibid., 15:278.
8. Horatio Gates to JM, 13 Mar. 1794. Ibid., 15:283.
9. Walter Jones to JM, 25 Mar. 1794. Ibid., 15:293–94.
10. JM to Jefferson, 26 Mar. 1794. Ibid., 15:295.

11. Jefferson to JM, 3 April 1794. Ibid., 15:301.
12. Speech on Nonintercourse Resolution, 18 April 1794. Ibid., 15:312–13.
13. Speech on the Excise Bill, 2 May 1794. Ibid., 15:321.
14. JM to Jefferson, 11 May 1794. Ibid., 15:327.
15. JM to Jefferson, 1 June 1794. Ibid., 15:340.
16. Catharine Coles to Dolley Payne Todd, 1 June 1794. Ibid., 15:342.
17. JM to Dolley Payne Todd, 18 Aug. 1794. Ibid., 15:351.
18. Dolley Payne Todd to Eliza Collins Lee, 16 Sept. 1794. Ibid. 15:357.
19. JM to JM, Sr., 5 Oct. 1794. Ibid., 15:361.
20. Jefferson to JM, 30 Oct. 1794. Ibid., 15:366.
21. JM to Jefferson, 30 Nov. 1794. Ibid., 15:397–98. R. A. Harrison, *Princetonians 1769–1775: A Biographical Directory* (Princeton, N.J., 1980), p. 189; JM to Monroe, 4 Dec. 1794. *PJM*, 15:406.
22. Ames to Thomas Dwight, 29 Nov. 1794. Ames, *Works of Fisher Ames*, 1:153–54.
23. Zephaniah Swift t to David Daggett, 11 Nov. 1794, American Antiquarian Society *Proceedings*, 4(1885–87):373.
24. *Annals of Congress*, 3rd Congress, 1st Sess., 934.
25. Zephaniah Swift to David Daggett, 13 Dec. 1794. American Antiquarian Society *Proceedings*, 4(1885–87):374.
26. Ames, *Works of Fisher Ames*, 1:161.
27. James Madison (cousin) to JM, 26 Jan. 1795. *PJM*, 15:456.
28. Samuel Dexter, Jr., to JM, 3 Feb. and 5 Feb. 1795, *PJM*, 15:463, 466.
29. Drew R. McCoy, *The Elusive Republic: Political Economy in Jeffersonian America* (Chapel Hill, N.C., 1980), p. 66. Speech on Commercial Discrimination, 30 Jan. 1794. *PJM*, 15:220.
30. Jefferson to JM, 28 Dec. 1794, *PJM*, 15:428.
31. JM to Jefferson, 23 Mar. 1795, *PJM*, 15:493.
32. JM to Jefferson, 26 Jan. 1795, *PJM*, 15:455.
33. Monroe to JM, 23 Oct. 1795. DLC: Madison Papers.
34. Francis Taylor Diaries, vol. 9, 16 Mar. 1795. Virginia Historical Society.
35. "Political Observations," 20 April 1795. *PJM*, 15:511.
36. JM to Jefferson, 14 June 1795. DLC: Madison Papers.
37. Malone, *Jefferson and His Times*, 3:247.
38. Bishop James Madison to JM, 25 July 1795. DLC: Madison Papers.
39. Edward Livingston to Robert R. Livingston, 1 Feb. 1796. New York Historical Society: Robert R. Livingston Papers; Jerald A. Combs, *The Jay Treaty* (Berkeley, Calif., 1970), pp. 15–76.
40. *Annals of Congress*, 4th Congress, 1st Sess., 986–87; JM to Jefferson, 18 April 1796. DLC: Madison Papers.
41. JM to Jefferson, 23 April 1796. DLC: Madison Papers.
42. JM to Jefferson, 22 May 1796. Ibid.
43. JM to Jefferson, 23 April 1796. Ibid.
44. JM to Jefferson, 1 May 1796. Ibid.
45. JM to Monroe, 14 May 1796. Ibid. JM to Monroe, 26 Feb. 1796. DLC.
46. Ames to Thomas Dwight, 19 May 1796. Ames, *Works of Ames*, 1:193.
47. Quoted in Cunningham, *The Jeffersonian Republicans*. p. 93.
48. JM to Monroe (partly in code), 29 Sept. 1796. DLC: Madison Papers.

49. Henry Tazewell to JM, 18 Oct. 1796. Manuscript Collection, National Historical Park, Morristown, N.J.
50. John Beckley to JM, 15 Oct. 1796. New York Public Library. Cunningham, *The Jeffersonian Republicans,* p. 103.
51. John Taylor to JM, 16 Nov. 1796. DLC: Rives Collection, Madison Papers.
52. Jefferson to JM, 17 Dec. 1796. DLC: Madison Papers.
53. Lawrence Taliaferro to JM, 4 Jan. 1797; Robert Gamble to JM, 21 Jan. 1797. DLC: Madison Papers.
54. JM to Jefferson, 15 Jan. 1797. DLC: Madison Papers.
55. JM to Jefferson, 29 Jan. 1797. DLC: Madison Papers.
56. Ames to Timothy Dwight, 5 Jan. 1797. Ames, *Works of Ames,* 1:213.
57. JM to JM, Sr., 5 Feb. and 13 Feb., 1797. DLC: Madison Papers.
58. Hamilton to Theodore Sedgwick, 26 Feb. 1797. Syrett and Cooke, *Hamilton Papers,* 20:522.

CHAPTER SEVEN

1. John Adams to Abigail Adams, 14 Jan. 1797. Mass. His. Society: Adams Family Papers (reel 383).
2. Henry Tazewell to JM, 11 June 1797. DLC: Rives Collection, Madison Papers.
3. JM to Jefferson, 5 Aug. 1797. DLC: Madison Papers.
4. Monroe to JM, 10 Dec. 1797. DLC: Rives Collection, Madison Papers.
5. JM to Jefferson, 21 Jan. 1798. DLC: Madison Papers.
6. JM to Monroe, 5 Feb. 1798. DLC: Madison Papers.
7. JM to Jefferson, c. 18 Feb. 1798. DLC: Madison Papers.
8. Abigail Adams to Mary Cranch, 28 April 1798. Quoted in James M. Smith, *Freedom's Fetters: The Alien and Sedition Laws & American Civil Liberties* (Ithaca, N.Y., 1956), p. 9.
9. Jefferson to JM, 21 Mar. 1798. DLC: Madison Papers.
10. Jefferson to JM, 29 Mar. 1798. DLC: Madison Papers.
11. John Dawson to JM, 5 April 1798. DLC: Madison Papers.
12. Jefferson to JM, 5 April 1798. DLC: Madison Papers.
13. JM to Jefferson, 15 April 1798. DLC: Madison Papers.
14. JM to Jefferson, 22 April 1798. DLC: Madison Papers.
15. JM to Jefferson, 29 April 1798. DLC: Madison Papers.
16. Jefferson to JM, 26 April 1798; JM to Jefferson, 10 June 1798. DLC: Madison Papers.
17. JM to Jefferson, 5 May and 20 May 1798. DLC: Madison Papers.
18. Boston *Columbian Centinel,* 26 May 1798.
19. U.S. Statutes-at-Large, 2:596-97. See also Smith, *Freedom's Fetters,* 94–111.
20. Cunningham, *The Jeffersonian Republicans,* 126.
21. Adrienne Koch and Harry Ammon, "The Virginia and Kentucky Resolutions: An Episode in Jefferson's and Madison's Defense of Civil Liberties," *William & Mary Quarterly,* 3rd ser., 5(1948):154–55.
22. The Virginia Resolutions, 4 Jan. 1799. Hunt, *Writings,* 6:326–31.

23. Norman Risjord, *Chesapeake Politics, 1781–1800* (New York, 1978), pp. 535–36.
24. Walter Jones and others to JM, 7 Feb. 1799; John Taylor to JM, 4 Mar. 1799. DLC: Madison Papers.
25. Jefferson spelled out this party program in his 26 Jan. 1799 letter to Elbridge Gerry, quoted in Cunningham, *The Jeffersonian Republicans*, pp. 211–12.
26. Jefferson to JM, 23 Aug. 1799. DLC: Rives Collection, Madison Papers.
27. Ibid.
28. Jefferson to Wilson Cary Nicholas, 5 Sept. 1799. Ford, *Writings*, 7:391.
29. Jefferson to JM, 17 Nov. 1799. DLC: Rives Collection, Madison Papers.
30. Monroe to JM, 22 Nov. 1799. DLC: Madison Papers.
31. John Dawson to JM, 28 Nov. 1799. DLC: Madison Papers.
32. Jonathan Elliot, ed., *Debates in the Several State Conventions in the Adoption of the Constitution (and Other Papers)*, 5 vols. (Philadelphia, 1861), 5:534.
33. Virginia Report of 1800, January 1800. Hunt, *Writings*, 6:371–72. See also Leonard W. Levy, *The Emergence of a Free Press* (New York, 1985), pp. 315–16.
34. Frank M. Anderson, "Contemporary Opinion of the Virginia and Kentucky Resolutions," *American Historical Review*, 5 (1899–1900):243–44.
35. Bishop James Madison to JM, 9 Jan. 1800. DLC: Madison Papers.
36. Jefferson to Monroe, 6 Feb. 1800. Ford, *Writings*, 7:424.
37. JM to Jefferson, 18 Jan. 1800. DLC: Madison Papers.
38. John Dawson to JM, 4 May 1800. DLC: Madison Papers.
39. Charles Pinckney to JM, 30 Sept. 1799. DLC: Madison Papers.
40. David Gelston to JM, 8 Oct. 1800; JM to Jefferson, c. 11 Nov. 1800. DLC: Madison Papers.
41. David Gelston to JM, 21 Nov. 1800. DLC: Rives Collection, Madison Papers.
42. JM to Jefferson, 14 Jan. 1824. DLC: Madison Papers.
43. Jefferson to JM, 26 Dec. 1800. DLC: Jefferson Papers.
44. JM to Jefferson, 10 Jan. 1801. DLC: Madison Papers.
45. John Dawson to JM, 29 Jan. 1801. DLC: Madison Papers.
46. JM to Jefferson, 28 Feb. 1801. DLC: Madison Papers.

CHAPTER EIGHT

1. Jefferson to JM, 1 Sept. 1807. DLC: Madison Papers.
2. Margaret Bayard Smith, *The First Forty Years of Washington Society*, ed. Gaillard Hunt (New York, 1906), p. 25.
3. Walter Jones to JM, 25 May 1794. *PJM*, 15:294.
4. "Spirit of Governments," 18 Feb. 1792. *PJM*, 14:233–34.
5. Daniel G. Lang, *Foreign Policy in the Early Republic* (Baton Rogue, La.: 1985), 142–45; Bradford Perkins, *The First Rapprochement: England and the United States 1795–1805* (Berkeley, Calif., 1967), p. 130.
6. JM to Rufus King, 8 June 1802. National Historical Park, Morristown, N.J.
7. Cabinet notes, 15 May 1801. Ford, *Writings*, 1:294.
8. Malone, *Jefferson and His Time*, 4:251–52.

9. Monroe to JM, 12 May 1801. Princeton University Library, Princeton, N.J.
10. William Irvine to JM, 23 Mar. 1801. DNA: State Dept. Records, Miscellaneous Letters.
11. JM to Wilson Cary Nicholas, 10 July 1801. Mass. His. Society, Boston.
12. Noble Cunningham, *The Process of Government under Jefferson* (Princeton, N.J., 1978), 172.
13. Quoted in ibid., 178.
14. Quoted in ibid., 94.
15. JM, Sr., to JM, 11 May 1791. *PJM*, 14:21, 22 n.5.
16. Irving Brant, *Madison*, 4:86.
17. Smith, *The First Forty Years in Washington*, pp. 35–36.
18. Augustus John Foster, *Jeffersonian America: Notes on the United States of America*, ed. Richard B. Davis, (Westport, Conn., 1980), 155.
19. Hunt, *Writings*, 7:76.
20. Jefferson to Robert R. Livingston, 18 April 1802. Merrill Peterson, ed., *The Portable Thomas Jefferson* (New York, 1975), 486. See also Lang, *Foreign Policy in the Early Republic*, 142–43.
21. JM to Monroe and Robert R. Livingston, 29 July 1803. Hunt, *Writings*, 7:63.
22. JM to Robert R. Livingston, 6 Oct. 1803. Ibid., 7:69.
23. Monroe to JM, 23 Oct. 1803. DLC: Rives Collection, Madison Papers; Perkins, *The First Rapprochment*, 173.
24. JM to Monroe, 26 Dec. 1803. Hunt, *Writings*, 7:78n.
25. Herbert G. Nicholas, *The United States & Britain* (Chicago, 1975), pp. 14–15.
26. Bradford Perkins, *Prologue to War: England and the United States, 1805–1812* (Berkeley, Calif., 1968), pp. 24, 26.
27. Monroe to JM, 1 July 1804. DLC: Madison Papers.
28. Bernard Mayo, ed., "Instructions to the British Ministers to the United States, 1791–1812," American Historical Assn. *Annual Report* (Washington, 1936), 209.
29. JM to Jefferson, 24 July 1805. DLC: Jefferson Papers; Dolley Madison to Anna Cutts, 1 Aug. 1805. Mass. His. Society, Boston.
30. John Armstrong to JM, 10 Sept. 1805. DNA: Diplomatic Dispatches, France.
31. Quoted in Henry Adams, *History of the United States During the Administration of Jefferson and Madison*, 9 vols. (New York, 1889–91), 2:134.
32. JM to Monroe, 24 Sept. 1805. DNA: Madison Papers.
33. JM to Monroe, 13 Jan. 1806. DLC: Madison Papers. Everett S. Brown, ed., *William Plumer's Memorandum of Proceedings in the United States Senate 1803–1807* (New York, 1923), pp. 388–89: Ames, *Works of Ames*, 1:356.
34. Quoted in Peterson, *James Madison*, 2:255.
35. Nicholas, *The U.S. and Britain*, p. 12.
36. JM to Monroe, 13 Jan. 1806. DLC: Madison Papers.
37. Perkins, *Prologue to War*, p. 84.
38. Schultz, *Madison*, p. 139; McCoy, *The Elusive Republic*, pp. 140–43.
39. Quoted in Perkins, *Prologue to War*, p. 123.

40. JM to Monroe and Pinkney, 20 May 1807. DNA: House of Representatives Records.
41. Samuel Smith to JM, 14 May 1807. DLC: Rives Collection, Madison Papers; John G. Jackson to JM, 26 March 1807. V:U.
42. John Quincy Adams, *Memoirs*, ed. Charles F. Adams, 12 vols. (Philadelphia, 1874–77), 1:428.
43. Burton Spivak, *Jefferson's English Crisis, 1803–04: Commerce, Embargo & the Republican Revolution* (Charlottesville, Va., 1979), p. 43n.
44. *National Intelligencer*, 27 June, 1 July 1807.
45. JM to Jefferson, 29 June 1807. DLC: Jefferson Papers.
46. Quoted in Malone, *Jefferson and His Time*, 5:425.
47. Charles E. Hill, "James Madison," in *The American Secretaries of State*, ed. Samuel Flagg Bemis, 10 vols. (New York, 1958 reprint), 3:130.
48. Elbridge Gerry to JM, 5 July 1807; and John G. Jackson to JM, 5 July 1807. DLC: Madison Papers.
49. Jefferson to JM, 26 Aug. 1807. DLC: Madison Papers.
50. JM to Monroe, 6 July 1807. DLC: Rives Collection, Madison Papers.
51. Quoted in Norman Graebner et al., *A History of the United States*, 2 vols. (New York, 1970), 1:362–63.
52. *National Intelligencer*, 18 Dec. 1807.
53. Malone, *Jefferson and His Time*, 5:489.
54. Ford, *Writings*, 9:177–178; Harry Ammon, *James Monroe* (New York, 1971), pp. 276–77.
55. Hunt, *Writings*, 8:1–11; Adams, *History of the U.S.*, 4:197.
56. L. C. Gray, *History of Agriculture in the Southern United States to 1860*, 2 vols. (Washington, 1933), 2:1031–32. Wilson Cary Nicholas to JM, 11 April 1808. DLC: Rives Collection, Madison Papers.
57. John Quincy Adams, *Diary*, ed. Allan Nevins (New York, 1929), p. 56.
58. *American State Papers, Foreign Relations*, 3:249–252.
59. John Armstrong to JM, 30 Aug. 1808. DLC: Madison Papers.
60. *American State Papers, Foreign Relations*, 3:219–20.
61. "Letters of Samuel Taggart," *Amer. Antiq. Society Proceedings*, n.s., 33(1923):331.
62. "Anas," 9 Nov. 1808. Ford, *Writings*, 1:335–38.
63. "Letters of Samuel Taggart," *Amer. Antiq. Society Proceedings*, n.s., 33(1923):318–19.
64. Samuel Mitchill to his wife, 15 Dec. 1808. Museum of the City of New York: Mitchill Papers.

CHAPTER NINE

1. JM to Pinkney, 3 Jan. 1809. DNA: "Letters of Samuel Taggart," *Amer. Antiq. Society Proceedings*, n.s., 33(1923):321.
2. JM to Pinkney, 10 Feb. 1809. DNA: Diplomatic Instructions, Great Britain.
3. "Letters of Samuel Taggart," *Amer. Antiq. Society Proceedings*, n.s.,

33(1923):331–32; William B. Giles to JM, 27 Feb. 1809. DLC: Rives Collection, Madison Papers.

4. Adams, *Diary*, p. 58.
5. Smith, *The First Forty Years*, pp. 61–62.
6. Adams, *History of the U.S.*, 5:9.
7. Mayo, "Instructions to British Ministers," AHA *Annual Report* (1936), pp. 261–66.
8. Albert Gallatin to Robert Smith, 14 April 1809 (enclosure). *PJM-Presidential Series* (hereafter cited as *PJM-PS*), 1:118.
9. JM to Jefferson, 24 April 1809. *PJM-PS*), 1:135.
10. Jefferson to JM, 27 April 1809. *PJM-PS*, 1:134.
11. Boston *Columbian Centinel*, 5 July, 8 July, 1809.
12. Pinkney to JM, 3 May 1809. *PJM-PS*, 1:161.
13. JM to Jefferson, 20 June 1809. Ibid., 1:261–62.
14. Gallatin to JM, 24 July 1809. Ibid., 1:299–300; Robert Smith to JM, 24 July 1809. Ibid., 1:303.
15. From the Litchfield Republican Meeting, 13 Mar. 1809; to the Hancock County Republican Society, 15 Mar. 1809. *PJM-PS*, 1:40, 53.
16. Lady Jackson, ed., *The Bath Archives—the Diaries and Letters of Sir George Jackson*, 2 vols. (London, 1873), 1:20, 28, 45, 83–84.
17. From the Republican Meeting of Nashville, Tenn., c. 11 Sept. 1809. *PJM-PS*, 1:372–73. From the Republican Meeting of Washington County, N.Y., 14 Sept. 1809. Ibid., 1:376–77. Resolutions of the Georgia Legislature, 12 Dec. 1809. DLC.
18. To the Chairman of the Republican Meeting of Washington County, Ky., 27 Sept. 1809. *PJM-PS*, 1:391–92.
19. JM to Pinkney, 23 May 1810. DLC: Rives Collection, Madison Papers.
20. "Letters of Samuel Taggart," Amer. Antiq. Society *Proceedings*, n.s., 33(1923):346. Isaac J. Cox, *The West Florida Controversy, 1798–1813* (Baltimore, 1918), pp. 329–30.
21. Quoted in Adams, *History of the U.S.*, 5:199.
22. "Letters of Samuel Taggart," Amer. Antiq. Society *Proceedings*, n.s., 33(1923) 3:347–48.
23. *Annals of Congress*, 11th Cong., 2d sess., 1867.
24. JM to Jefferson, 22 June 1810. DLC: Madison Papers.
25. Quoted in Perkins, *Prologue to War*, p. 246.
26. Adams, *History of the U.S.*, 5:297–304.
27. Dolley P. Madison to James Taylor, 13 March 1811. DLC: Madison Papers; quoted in Henry Adams, *Life of Albert Gallatin* (Philadelphia, 1879), 430.
28. William C. Rives and Philip R. Fendall, eds., *Letters and Other Writings of James Madison*, 4 vols. (Philadelphia, 1865), 2:506.
29. Ibid., 2:501.
30. JM to Jefferson, 8 July 1811; quoted in Perkins, *Prologue to War*, p. 269.
31. Henry Lee to JM, 29 Aug. 1811. DLC: Madison Papers.
32. Message to Congress, 5 Nov. 1811. DNA: House of Representative Records.
33. *National Intelligencer*, 30 Nov. 1811; *Annals of Congress*, 12th Cong., 1st sess., pp. 39–41; "Letters of Samuel Taggart:, Amer. Antiq. Society *Proceedings* 33(1923):365.

34. Foster, *Jeffersonian America*, pp. 96–97.
35. Citizens of Windsor, N.C., to JM, 26 Nov. 1811. DNA: State Dept., Misc. Letters; Va. House of Delegates Journal (Oct. 1811 session):73.
36. Quoted in Perkins, *Prologue to War*, p. 368.
37. Samuel Eliot Morison, *By Land and Sea* (New York, 1953), pp. 265–86; *American State Papers, Foreign Relations*, 3:545; "Letters of Samuel Taggart," Amer. Antiq. Society *Proceedings*, n.s., 33(1923):371.
38. Thomas R. Hay and M. R. Werner, *The Admirable Trumpeter: A Biography of General James Wilkinson* (Garden City, N.Y., 1941), pp. 303–307.
39. "Letters of Samuel Taggart," Amer. Antiq. Society *Proceedings*, n.s., 33(1923):371.
40. Public Record Office, London, *Parliamentary Sessional Papers*, 1812 (microfilm), 3:3, 6, 16, 17. ("Examination by the Committee of the Whole House.")
41. Lexington, Ky., *Reporter*, 21 March 1812; *National Intelligencer*, 14 April 1812.
42. JM to Jefferson, 25 May 1812. DLC: Madison Papers. *Columbian Centinel*, 6 June 1812.
43. John Burns to J. Roberts, 5 May 1812, quoted in Sanford W. Higginbotham, *The Keystone in the Democratic Arch: Pennsylvania Politics, 1800–1816* (Harrisburg, Pa., 1952), p. 253. Elbridge Gerry to JM, 19 May 1812. DLC: Gerry Papers.
44. "Universal Peace," *National Gazette*, 31 Jan. 1792. *PJM*, 14:207.
45. Message to Congress, 1 June 1812. Forbes Magazine Manuscript Collection, New York.
46. Foster, *Jeffersonian America*, 100.
47. Adams to B. Waterhouse, 11 Mar. 1812, W. C. Ford, ed. *Statesman and Friend: Correspondence of John Adams with Benjamin Waterhouse* (Boston, 1927), p. 77.
48. "Letters of Samuel Taggart," Amer. Antiq. Society *Proceedings*, n.s., 33(1923):414–15; ibid., 354, 370–71; Paul A. Varg, *New England and Foreign Policy, 1789–1850* (Hanover, N.H., 1983), p. 63; Gerry to Mercy Warren, 28 Feb. 1812, Mass. His. Society *Collections* (1917), 73:374.
49. Cabinet notes, 23, 24, 27 June 1814. DLC: Madison Papers.
50. Dolley Madison to Mrs. Albert Gallatin, 23 July 1814. New York Historical Society: Gallatin Papers. For the Washington campaign of 1814, see J. C. A. Stagg, *Mr. Madison's War* (Princeton, N.J., 1983), 409–18.
51. Conover Hunt-Jones, *Dolley and the Great Little Madison* (Washington, 1977), pp. 50–51.
52. Sixth Annual Message. Hunt, *Writings*, 7:309–12.
53. Samuel Eliot Morison, *Harrison Gray Otis, 1765–1848: The Urbane Federalist* (Boston, 1769), 391.
54. Richmond, Va., *Enquirer*, 18 Feb. 1815.
55. Special Message, 18 Feb. 1815. DNA: House of Representatives Records.
56. "Address of the Republican Meeting in Boston," 23 Feb. 1815. DLC: Madison Papers.
57. Jefferson to JM, 23 Mar. 1815. DLC: Madison Papers.
58. Gallatin to Matthew Lyon, 7 May 1816, quoted in Henry Adams, ed., *The*

Writings of Albert Gallatin, 3 vols. (New York, 1960 reprint), 1:700. See also Steven Watts, "The Republic Reborn: The War of 1812 and the Making of Liberal America," Univ. of Missouri Ph.D. dissertation, 1984.

CHAPTER TEN

1. Gray, *History of Agriculture*, 2:1039.
2. *American State Papers, Commerce & Navigation*, 1:929; Adams, *History of the U.S.*, 9:127–28.
3. Adams to Jefferson, 2 Feb. 1817, Lester Cappon, *The Adams–Jefferson Letters*, 2 vols. (Chapel Hill, N.C., 1959), 2:507–508; Jefferson to Adams, 5 May 1817. Ibid., 2:512.
4. Ammon, *James Monroe*, pp. 354–55.
5. Cappon, *Adams–Jefferson Letters*, 2:508.
6. Annual Message to Congress, 3 Dec. 1816. DNA: House of Representatives Records.
7. JM to Jefferson, 15 Feb. 1817. DLC: Madison Papers; Jefferson to JM, 8 Feb. 1817. Ibid.; Jefferson to JM, 10 March 1817. ViU.
8. Hunt, *Writings*, 8:386–88; Irving Brant, "Madison's 'On The Separation of Church and State,'" *William & Mary Quarterly*, 3d ser., 8(1951):18.
9. James K. Paulding, "An Unpublished Sketch of James Madison," Ralph Ketcham, ed., manuscript, ViU.
10. JM to JM, Sr., 8 Sept. 1783. *PJM*, 7:304.
11. JM to Joseph Jones, 28 Nov. 1780. Ibid., 2:209.
12. Memorandum on an African Colony, c. 20 Oct. 1789. Ibid., 12:437–38.
13. Adam Stephens to JM, 25 April 1790. Ibid., 13:176. Howard A. Ohline, "Slavery, Economics, and Congressional Politics, 1790," *Journal of Southern History*, 46(1980):351–53. See also "James Madison's Attitude Toward the Negro," *Journal of Negro History*, 6(1921):74–102; Alfred H. Kelly, W. A. Harbison, and Herman Belz, *The American Constitution*, 6th ed. (New York, 1983), p. 251.
14. JM to Robert Walsh, 2 March 1819. DLC: Madison Papers.
15. JM to Robert Evan, 15 June 1819. Ibid.
16. JM to R. R. Gurley, 28 Dec. 1831. Ibid.
17. JM to Thomas R. Dew, 23 Feb. 1833. Ibid.; JM to Robert Walsh, 27 Nov. 1819, Hunt, *Writings*, 8:443.
18. JM to Henry Clay, June 1833. Ibid.
19. "Address Delivered Before the Agricultural Society of Albemarle," 12 March 1818. New York Public Library, Ford Collection.
20. Philip A. Bruce, *The History of the University of Virginia 1819–1919*, 5 vols. (New York, 1920), 1:211.
21. JM to W. T. Barry, 4 August 1822. DLC: Madison Papers.
22. Bruce, *History*, 2:299–330.
23. Jefferson to JM, 17 Feb. 1826. DLC: Jefferson Papers; JM to Nathaniel P. Trist, 6 July 1826. DLC: Trist Papers. The Jefferson-Madison friendship is treated with scholarly empathy in Adrienne Koch, *Jefferson & Madison: The Great Collaboration* (New York, 1970).

24. Board of Visitors Minute Book, Vol. 2. ViU; "Dr. Robley Dunglison's Memoirs," Amer. Philosophical Society *Transactions*, 53:55–56; Nicholas Biddle to JM, 26 April 1825. DLC.
25. JM to John G. Jackson, 27 Dec. 1821. DLC: Madison Papers.
26. Farrand, *Records*, 1:xviii.
27. *Proceedings and Debate of the Virginia State Convention of 1829–30* (Richmond, 1830), pp. 537–41.
28. JM to Lafayette, 1 Feb. 1830. Pierpont Morgan Library, New York.
29. JM to Philip R. Fendall, 12 June 1833. DLC: American Colonization Society Papers.
30. Paulding, "Unpublished Sketch." ViU.
31. Smith, *The First Forty Years*, pp. 233–36.
32. JM to Joseph C. Cabell, 7 Sept. 1829. Hunt, *Writings*, 9:347–51.
33. JM to Edward Everett, 28 Aug. 1830. Ibid., 9:400–401. See Edward S. Corwin, "James Madison: Layman, Publicist, and Exegete," in Richard Loos, ed., *Corwin on the Constitution* (Ithaca, N.Y., 1981), esp. pp. 222–24.
34. JM to Joseph C. Cabell, 27 Dec. 1832. Hunt, *Writings*, 9:494.
35. Schultz, *Madison*, 188; Brant, *Madison*, 6:512–14.
36. Harriet Martineau, *Retrospect of Western Travels*, 2 vols. (London, 1838), 1:190–91.
37. "Detached Memorandum," *William & Mary Quarterly*, 3d rev., 3(1946):536–68.
38. Rives and Fendall, *Letters and Other Writings of Madison*, 4:29; "Advice to My County" (undated). DLC: Madison Papers.
39. John Quincy Adams, *Diary*, 468.
40. Leonard D. White, *The Jeffersonians* (New York, 1951), p. 36.
41. Robert Frost, "A Talk for Students," *Fund for the Republic Publications* (New York, 1956). For a contrary view, see Richard K. Matthews, *The Radical Politics of Thomas Jefferson* (Lawrence, Kansas, 1984), pp. 116–17.

MADISON CHRONOLOGY

March 5 (old style), 1751	Born at Port Conway, Virginia
August 1769–April 1772	Studies at College of New Jersey, Princeton
December 1774	Elected to Orange County, Virginia, Committee of Safety
May–December 1776	Attends Virginia Convention in Williamsburg as Orange County delegate and then serves in General Assembly
November 1777	Chosen by General Assembly to serve on Virginia Council of State
January 1778–December 1779	Serves on Council of State under Governors Patrick Henry and Thomas Jefferson
December 14, 1779	Elected to Virginia delegation in Continental Congress
March 6, 1780	Departs from Montpelier for Continental Congress
November 2, 1783	Term in Continental Congress expires
December 5, 1783	Returns to Montpelier after forty-month absence
May–July 1784	Serves in Virginia House of Delegates
November 1784	Resumes seat in Virginia General Assembly
c. June 20, 1785	Writes "Memorial & Remonstrance" on behalf of religious freedom
October 1785	Returns to House of Delegates; works for passage of Jefferson's Statute for Religious Freedom
January 1786	Religious Freedom Statute becomes law
September 11–14, 1786	Attends Annapolis Convention as Virginia delegate
October 1786	Returns to Virginia General Assembly and is elected delegate to Continental Congress
February 1787	Arrives in New York; takes seat in Continental Congress and promotes call for a Federal Convention to revise Articles of Confederation
May 1787–September 1787	Serves on Virginia delegation at the Federal Convention; helps prepare Virginia Plan; keeps shorthand notes of proceedings for personal use

September 17, 1787	Signs completed draft of Constitution
September 24, 1787	Returns to New York; resumes seat in Continental Congress
October 1787–March 1788	Directs campaign for ratification of proposed Constitution; assists Alexander Hamilton in writing *The Federalist* essays
June 1788	Serves in Richmond Convention; leads debate for Federalists, who succeed in ratifying Constitution
February 1789	Elected from his Virginia district to serve in First Federal Congress
March 1789–March 1797	Serves in House of Representatives; opposes Funding and Assumption bills central to Hamilton's financial program; assists Jefferson in formation of national Republican party
September 1794	Marries Philadelphia widow Dolley Payne Todd
April 1797	Returns to Montpelier
September–October 1798	Prepares resolutions for Virginia legislature as protest against Alien and Sedition Acts
October 1799	Returns to Virginia House of Delegates; introduces "Report of 1800" which justifies the Virginia Resolutions of 1798
November 1800	Serves as presidential elector for Jefferson
May 1801–March 1809	Serves as secretary of state in Jefferson's cabinet; helps devise the embargo law as means of avoiding war with France or England
December 1808	After his nomination by congressional causus, elected by majority of voters to serve as president
March 4, 1809–March 3, 1817	Serves two terms as president
June 12, 1812	Delivers his war message to Congress
August 1814	Flees from Washington when British invade the capital
February 1815	Receives news that Treaty of Ghent is signed; learns of American victory at New Orleans
April 1817–June 1836	Retires to Montpelier; acts as senior statesman and opposes Nullification doctrine; as last survivor of the Federal Convention, prepares his convention notes for posthumous publication
June 28, 1836	Dies at Montpelier

INDEX

INDEX

For brevity's sake, the following symbols have been used in this index: JM (James Madison); AH (Alexander Hamilton); TJ (Thomas Jefferson); GW (George Washington).

Crawford, William: as senator, 215, 219; as presidential candidate, 237
Culpeper County, Va., 118; crucial for JM's election, 46, 48, 90
Cutts, Richard, 230
Clymer, George, 86, 87

Dawson, John: succeeds JM as congressman, 153, 167
Dearborn, Henry: in TJ's cabinet, 178; in War of 1812, 227
Declaration of Independence: celebrated in 1826, 245
Delaware River: capital site discussed, 89
Democratic-Republican societies: denounced by Federalists, 134–35
Dexter, Samuel, 136
Dickinson, John, 5
District of Columbia: early land sales disappointing, 106; hostile feelings toward move, 107; early surveys, 109; as site for national university, 236; church incorporation vetoed, 238
Duer, William, 2, 113

Embargo Act (1807): passage and effect, 194–95, 197, 199; repealed in 1809, 203, (see also New England)
Enforcement Act (1808), 199; stronger version passed, 203
Enquirer (Richmond), 199, 231
Erskine, David: as British diplomat, 188, 200; seeks accord with U.S., 207–10; disavowed by Canning, 210
Essex (ship); admiralty decision, 182, 187
Eustis, William: in JM's cabinet, 207
Eve, George, 47, 48
Everett, Edward, 248

Fauchet, Jean-Antoine-Joseph: appointed minister to U.S., 131
Fauquier County, Va., 44, 90
Federal Gazette (Philadelphia), 111
Federalist ("Publius" papers), 2–3, 26, 30–31; #10 in modern context, 31
Federal Convention of 1787: called by Congress, 14; proceedings, 15–19; approves public debt provision, 58; JM

keeps notes of debates, 16, 65, 245, 249; rejected charter powers, 96
Federal District: see District of Columbia
Federalist party: favors Constitution, 28; fights second-convention scheme, 44–46; as political party after 1788, 87, 101, 105–106; pro-British attitude, 127, 128, 140, 226; favors Alien and Sedition laws, 153, 155–56; TJ calls "war party," 154; role in 1800 election scored, 166–67; removed from office, 174–75; oppose war declaration in 1812, 224–25; control New England, 227; support Hartford Convention, 230–31; token opposition in 1816, 237
Florida, 217; occupied by Spain, 171; U.S. seeks by purchase, 180–81, 184–85; as French bribe-bait, 198; annexation desired by JM, 213, 215; filibusterers seize W. Fla., 214–15; JM orders occupation, 215
Floyd, Catherine ("Kitty"), 67, 94, 133
Forrest, Richard, 176
Foster, Augustus John: as British diplomat, 179; returns to capital, 217; reports Clay's prediction, 219; rules out war, 219; claims French duplicity, 223
France: difficulties under Louis XVI, 12–13; beginning of French revolution, 101, 102; names JM honorary citizen, 119, 120; treaty with U.S. suspended, 121; seeks repayment of war loans to U.S., 131; navy attacks U.S. ships, 147, 152, 155, 171, 192, 197; U.S. convention of 1800 negotiated, 171, 173, 175; offers Louisiana to U.S., 180–81, 184
Franklin, Benjamin, 67, 250
Freneau, Philip, 110, 123; attends Princeton, 8, 9; urged to edit newspaper, 105–107; edits National Gazette, 108, 111; attacked by AH, 115–16
Frost, Robert, 252

Gallatin, Albert: as party leader, 148, 153; Federalist enmity toward, 154; in TJ's cabinet, 184, 193, 197, 199; disliked by Republican faction, 205; in

Massachusetts *(continued)*
opposes war, 225; calls regional convention, 230
Mazzei, Philip, 150
Merry, Anthony, 179–80, 183
Mississippi river: American navigation rights on, 44, 73
Mitchill, Samuel L., 201
Montesquieu, Charles Louis de Secondat, Baron de: theory refuted by JM, 20, 30–31, 110
Monroe, James, 144, 145, 161, 164, 176, 179, 186, 244; assesses GW's influence, 37; opposes JM in election, 44, 46, 48, 49; practices law in Virginia, 86; JM's partner in land speculation, 92, 149; coauthor of defense of TJ, 117; assists JM in petition movement, 122; moves to Albemarle County, 123; Paris purchases for JM, 137–38; recalled by GW, 147; advice sought, 150; as U.S. envoy in Europe, 180, 181, 183, 186, 188, 189, 190, 191; as JM's rival, 196, 200, 201; JM's friendship restored, 216; in JM's cabinet, 217, 220, 230; picked by caucus, 237; financial troubles, 250; death, 251
Montpelier (Madison family estate), 92; described, 150, 151; JM's involvement in management, 154, 242; construction, 154, 160–161; furnishings and routine, 247
Morris, Gouverneur: declines role in "Publius" essays, 2; analyzes voting for constitution, 29
Morris. Robert: attends Federal convention, 5; as supt. of finance, 53; as land speculator, 92, 107, 113
Moustier, Eleonor-François-Elie, Marquis de: gossips about JM, 93

Napoleon I, 151; orders troops to Caribbean, 171; waning of U.S. support, 172–73; sells Louisiana to U.S., 180–81; frustrated by royal navy, 181; issues Berlin decree, 188; issues Milan decree, 192; issues Bayonne decree,

197–98; desires U.S. as ally, 199; defeated by British, 228
National Gazette (Philadelphia), 106, 115, 116; as party organ, 106–109, 111; prints JM's essays, 108, 110–11, 116–17, 118; attacks AH, 119; fails in 1793, 123
National Intelligencer (Washington, D.C.): friendly to Republican party, 191, 194, 199, 211, 223; supports Monroe, 237
Neutrality: *see* impressment; Rule of 1756; United States
New England: opposes rum tax, 58; benefits from AH's program, 91; rejects Virginia-Kentucky resolutions, 162; hostile to embargo, 195, 200; opposes enforcement act, 203; attitudes upset JM, 203–204; powerful local interests, 41, 86, 89, 221; pro-British stance, 54; position on national capital, 69; treasonous activities claimed, 220; loyalty tested, 224; opposes war, 225; secession movement feared, 227; promotes Hartford convention, 230–31
New Hampshire: in economic straits, 7; holds ratifying convention, 32, 37
New Jersey, College of: *see* Princeton University
New Orleans, La.: site of 1815 victory, 230–31, 233
New York (city): as capital in 1789, 51; JM opposes as permanent capital site, 68; anti-British mass meeting, 127; carried by Republicans, 165, 166
New York (state): Antifederalist stronghold, 2–3; ratifies constitution, 39; promotes second-convention call, 44
Nicholas, George: as leader in Kentucky, 73
Nicholas, Wilson Cary, 197
Nicholson, John, 92
Nonintercourse Act (1809): as stop-gap measure, 204; suspension sought, 208
North Carolina, 157, 160, 162, 165; delayed ratification, 39, 45, 62; congressmen oppose assumption bill, 85–86; congressmen defect to AH, 131; supports J. Adams in 1800, 166

ABOUT THE AUTHOR

Robert Allen Rutland is author or editor of numerous books, including *The Democrats: From Jefferson to
Clinton*, *The Republicans: From Lincoln to Bush* (both
available from the University of Missouri Press), *The
Presidency of James Madison*, and *James Madison and
the American Nation*. He was the Editor-in-Chief of
The Papers of James Madison from 1971 to 1987 and is
Professor Emeritus of American History at the University of Virginia.